THE ROMAN ANTIQUITIES

OF

DIONYSIUS OF HALICARNASSUS

VI

THE ROMAN ANTIQUITIES

OF

DIONYSIUS OF HALICARNASSUS

WITH AN ENGLISH TRANSLATION BY
EARNEST CARY, Ph.D.

ON THE BASIS OF THE VERSION OF
EDWARD SPELMAN

IN SEVEN VOLUMES

VI

CAMBRIDGE, MASSACHUSETTS
HARVARD UNIVERSITY PRESS
LONDON
WILLIAM HEINEMANN LTD
MCMXLVII

Printed in Great Britain

CONTENTS

THE ROMAN ANTIQUITIES

OF

DIONYSIUS OF HALICARNASSUS

ΔΙΟΝΥΣΙΟΥ

ΑΛΙΚΑΡΝΑΣΕΩΣ

ΡΩΜΑΙΚΗΣ ΑΡΧΑΙΟΛΟΓΙΑΣ

ΛΟΓΟΣ ΕΝΑΤΟΣ

XXV. Τῷ δ' ἑξῆς ἔτει περὶ τὰς θερινὰς μάλιστα
τροπὰς Σεξτιλίου μηνὸς παραλαμβάνουσι τὴν ὑπατείαν ἄνδρες ἔμπειροι πολέμων Σερούιός[1] τε Σερ-
ούίλιος καὶ Αὖλος Οὐεργίνιος, οἷς ὁ πρὸς τοὺς
Τυρρηνοὺς πόλεμος καίτοι μέγας καὶ χαλεπὸς ὢν
χρυσὸς[2] ἐφαίνετο παρὰ τὸν ἐντὸς τείχους ἐξεταζό-
μενος. ἀσπόρου γὰρ τῆς χώρας ἐν τῷ παρελθόντι
χειμῶνι διὰ τὸν ἐπιτειχισμὸν τοῦ πλησίον ὄρους
καὶ τὰς συνεχεῖς καταδρομὰς γενομένης, καὶ οὐδὲ
τῶν ἐμπόρων ἔτι τὰς ἔξωθεν ἐπεισαγόντων ἀγοράς,
σπάνις ἰσχυρὰ σίτου τὴν Ῥώμην κατέσχε μεστὴν
οὖσαν ὄχλου τοῦ τε κατοικιδίου καὶ τοῦ συνερρυη-
2 κότος ἐκ τῶν ἀγρῶν. τῶν μὲν γὰρ ἐν ἥβῃ πολιτῶν

---

[1] Σπόριος Gelenius.   [2] χρυσὸς Ba : χρηστὸς R.

---

[1] For chaps. 25 f. cf. Livy ii. 51, 4–52, 1.
[2] See note on i. 32, 5.
[3] The MSS. all give the praenomen as Servius both here

2

THE ROMAN ANTIQUITIES

OF

DIONYSIUS OF HALICARNASSUS

BOOK IX

XXV. The following year,[1] about the summer solstice,[2] in the month of August, Servius[3] Servilius and Aulus Verginius succeeded to the consulship, both being men of experience in warfare. To them the Tyrrhenian war, though great and difficult, seemed pure gold[4] in comparison with the conflict inside the city walls. For since the land had gone unsown the preceding winter because the enemy had fortified the adjacent hill[5] against them and had kept up incessant raids, and since not even the merchants any longer imported the usual provisions from outside, Rome suffered from a great scarcity of corn, as the city was then crowded not only with its permanent population, but also with a multitude that had flocked thither from the country. For of adult

and in chap. 28; but we should probably read Spurius, the form found in Livy, Cassiodorus and Diodorus. A Spurius Servilius Priscus was censor a century later.

[4] See note on i. 57, 2.

[5] The Janiculum; see ix. 24.

DIONYSIUS OF HALICARNASSUS

ὑπὲρ τὰς ἔνδεκα μυριάδας ἦσαν, ὡς ἐκ τῆς ἔγγιστα
τιμήσεως εὑρέθη, γυναικῶν δὲ καὶ παίδων καὶ τῆς
οἰκετικῆς θεραπείας ἐμπόρων τε καὶ τῶν[1] ἐργαζο-
μένων τὰς βαναύσους τέχνας μετοίκων (οὐδενὶ γὰρ
ἐξῆν Ῥωμαίων οὔτε κάπηλον οὔτε χειροτέχνην
βίον ἔχειν) οὐκ ἔλαττον ἢ τριπλάσιον τοῦ πολιτικοῦ
πλήθους· οὓς οὐκ ἦν παραμυθήσασθαι ῥᾴδιον ἀγα-
νακτοῦντας ἐπὶ τῷ πάθει καὶ συντρέχοντας εἰς τὴν
ἀγορὰν καὶ καταβοῶντας τῶν ἐν τοῖς τέλεσιν ἐπί
τε τὰς οἰκίας τῶν πλουσίων κατὰ πλῆθος ὠθουμένους καὶ διαρπάζειν ἐπιχειροῦντας ἄτερ ὠνῆς
3 τὰς ἀποκειμένας αὐτοῖς[2] τροφάς. οἱ δὲ δήμαρχοι
συνάγοντες αὐτοὺς εἰς ἐκκλησίαν καὶ κατηγοροῦντες
τῶν πατρικίων ὡς αἰεί τι κακὸν ἐπὶ τοῖς πένησι
μηχανωμένων καὶ πάνθ' ὅσα πώποτε δεινὰ συνέβη[3]
κατὰ τὴν ἀτέκμαρτόν τε καὶ ἀφύλακτον ἀνθρώποις
τύχην ἐκείνων ἔργα λέγοντες, ὑβριστὰς εἶναι πι-
4 κροὺς ἐξειργάσαντο. τοιούτοις συνεχόμενοι κακοῖς
οἱ ὕπατοι πέμπουσι[4] τοὺς συνωνησομένους σῖτον ἐκ
τῶν σύνεγγυς τόπων μετὰ πολλῶν χρημάτων, καὶ
τὸν ἐν ταῖς οἰκίαις ἔταξαν εἰς τὸ δημόσιον ἀναφέρειν τοὺς εἰς τὸν ἑαυτῶν βίον πλείονα τοῦ με-
τρίου παραθεμένους, τιμὴν ὁρίσαντες ἀποχρῶσαν.
ταῦτα δὴ καὶ ἄλλα πολλὰ μηχανώμενοι τοιαῦτα
ἐπέσχον τῶν πενήτων τὰς παρανομίας καὶ ἀναστροφὴν ἔλαβον τῆς εἰς τὸν πόλεμον παρασκευῆς.
XXVI. Ἐπεὶ δ' αἱ μὲν ἔξωθεν ἐβράδυνον ἀγοραί,
τὰ δ' ἐντὸς τείχους τροφῆς ἐχόμενα πάντα κατ-
ανάλωτο, ἀποστροφὴ δὲ τῶν κακῶν οὐδεμία ἦν

---

[1] τῶν R : om. B, Jacoby.   [2] αὐτοῖς A : ἐν αὐτοῖς B.
[3] συνέβη C, by correction : om. R.
[4] πέμπουσι ACmg : ὥστε BC.

4

citizens there were more than 110,000, as appeared by the latest census ; and the number of the women, children, domestics, foreign traders and artisans who plied the menial trades—for no Roman citizen was permitted to earn a livelihood as a tradesman or artisan—was not less than treble the number of the citizens. This multitude was not easy to placate ; for they were exasperated at their misfortune, and gathering together in the Forum, clamoured against the magistrates, rushed in a body to the houses of the rich and endeavoured to seize without payment the provisions that were stored up by them. In the meantime the tribunes assembled the people, and by accusing the patricians of always contriving some mischief against the poor, and calling them the authors of all the evils which had ever happened at the caprice of Fortune, whose whims men can neither foresee nor guard against, they inspired them with insolence and bitter resentment. The consuls, beset by these evils, sent men with large sums of money to the neighbouring districts to purchase corn, and ordered all those who had stored up more than a moderate amount of corn for their own subsistence to turn it over to the state ; and they fixed a reasonable price for it. By these and many other like expedients they put a stop to the lawless actions of the poor and thus got respite for their preparations for war.

XXVI. But when the provisions from outside were slow in coming and all the food supplies in the city had been consumed and there was no other means of averting the evils but to choose one of two courses

5

ἑτέρα, ἀλλὰ δυεῖν θάτερον ἐχρῆν, ἢ τοὺς πολεμίους
ἐκβαλεῖν ἐκ τῆς χώρας ἁπάσῃ δυνάμει παρακινδυ-
νεύσαντας ἢ τειχήρεις μένοντας ὑπὸ λιμοῦ τε καὶ
στάσεως διαφθαρῆναι, τὸ κουφότερον αἱρούμενοι
τῶν κακῶν ἔγνωσαν ὁμόσε χωρεῖν τοῖς ἐκ τῶν
2 πολεμίων δεινοῖς. προαγαγόντες δὲ τὰς δυνάμεις
ἐκ τῆς πόλεως περὶ μέσας νύκτας διέβησαν τὸν
ποταμὸν ἐπὶ σχεδίαις καὶ πρὶν ἡμέραν λαμπρὰν
γενέσθαι πλησίον τῶν πολεμίων κατεστρατοπέδευσαν. τῇ δ' ἑξῆς ἡμέρᾳ προελθόντες ἔταξαν ὡς[1]
εἰς μάχην τὸν στρατόν. εἶχε δὲ τὸ μὲν δεξιὸν τῶν
κεράτων Οὐεργίνιος, τὸ δ' εὐώνυμον Σερουΐλιος.
3 ἰδόντες δ' αὐτοὺς εὐτρεπεῖς ὄντας οἱ Τυρρηνοὶ πρὸς
τὸν ἀγῶνα σφόδρα ἐχάρησαν, ὡς ἑνὶ τῷ τότε
κινδύνῳ κατὰ νοῦν χωρήσαντι τὴν Ῥωμαίων καθ-
ελοῦντες ἀρχήν, εἰδότες ὅτι πᾶν ὅσον ἦν κράτιστον
στρατιωτικὸν αὐτῶν εἰς τὸν ἀγῶνα ἐκεῖνον ὥρμητο,
καὶ δι' ἐλπίδος ἔχοντες, ἐν ᾗ πολὺ τὸ κοῦφον ἦν,
ῥᾳδίως αὐτῶν κρατήσειν, ἐπειδὴ τὴν μετὰ Μενηνίου
δύναμιν ἐν δυσχωρίαις παραταξαμένην σφίσιν ἐνίκη-
σαν. γενομένης δ' ἰσχυρᾶς καὶ πολυχρονίου μάχης,
πολλοὺς μὲν ἀποκτείναντες Ῥωμαίων πολλῷ δ'
ἔτι πλείονας τῶν σφετέρων ἀποβαλόντες, ἀνεχώ-
4 ρουν βάδην[2] ἐπὶ τὸν χάρακα. ὁ μὲν οὖν Οὐεργίνιος
τὸ δεξιὸν κέρας ἔχων οὐκ εἴα διώκειν τοὺς σφετέρους, ἀλλ' ἐπὶ τῷ κατορθώματι μένειν, ὁ δὲ Σερουΐλιος ὁ τεταγμένος ἐπὶ θατέρου κέρως ἐδίωκε
τοὺς καθ' ἑαυτὸν ἑπόμενος ἄχρι πολλοῦ. ὡς δ' ἐν
τοῖς μετεώροις ἐγένετο, ὑποστρέψαντες οἱ Τυρρηνοί,
καὶ τῶν ἐκ τοῦ χάρακος ἐπιβοηθησάντων, ἐνσείου-
σιν αὐτοῖς. οἱ δ' ὀλίγον τινὰ δεξάμενοι χρόνον

[1] ὡς Β : om. R.   [2] βάδην Β : om. R.

—either to hazard an engagement with all their forces, in order to drive the enemy out of the country, or by remaining shut up within their walls to perish both by famine and by sedition—they chose the lesser of these evils and resolved to go forth to meet the perils from the enemy. Marching out of the city, therefore, with their forces, they crossed the river about midnight on rafts, and before it was broad daylight encamped near the enemy. The next day they came out of their camp and drew up their army for battle, Verginius commanding the right wing and Servilius the left. The Tyrrhenians, seeing them ready for the contest, rejoiced greatly, believing that by this single battle, if it turned out according to their wish, they would overthrow the empire of the Romans ; for they knew that all their foe's best soldiery was entered in this contest, and they entertained the hope, which was very ill founded, of defeating them with ease, since they had conquered the troops of Menenius when these had been arrayed against them in a disadvantageous position. But after a sharp and protracted battle, in which they killed many of the Romans but lost many more of their own men, they began to retreat gradually toward their camp. Verginius, who commanded the right wing, would not permit his men to pursue the enemy, but urged them to rest content with the advantage they had gained ; Servilius, however, who was posted on the other wing, pursued the foes who had faced him, following them for a long distance. But when he reached the heights, the Tyrrhenians faced about and, those in the camp coming to their aid, they fell upon the Romans. These, after receiving their attack for a short time, turned their backs

7

ἐγκλίνουσι τὰ νῶτα καὶ κατὰ τοῦ λόφου διωκό-
5 μενοι σποράδες ἀπώλλυντο. μαθὼν δὲ Οὐεργίνιος
ἐν οἵαις ἦν τύχαις ἡ τὸ ἀριστερὸν κέρας κατέχουσα
στρατιά, πᾶσαν ἔχων τὴν δύναμιν ἐν τάξει πλαγίαν
ἦγε διὰ τοῦ ὄρους ὁδόν. γενόμενος δὲ κατὰ νώτου
τῶν διωκόντων τοὺς σφετέρους, μέρος μέν τι ταύτῃ
καταλείπει τῆς στρατιᾶς κωλύσεως ἕνεκεν τῶν ἐκ
τοῦ χάρακος ἐπιβοηθησόντων, τὸ δὲ λοιπὸν αὐτὸς
ἄγων ἐπεφέρετο τοῖς πολεμίοις. ἐν δὲ τούτῳ καὶ
οἱ μετὰ τοῦ Σερουϊλίου θαρσήσαντες τῇ παρουσίᾳ
τῶν σφετέρων ὑποστρέφουσί τε καὶ καταστάντες
ἐμάχοντο. κυκλωθέντες δ' ὑπ' ἀμφοῖν οἱ Τυρρηνοὶ
καὶ οὔτε πρόσω διεκπορευθῆναι δυνάμενοι διὰ τοὺς
ὁμόσε χωροῦντας οὔτ' ὀπίσω φεύγειν ἐπὶ τὸν
χάρακα διὰ τοὺς κατόπιν ἐπιόντας, οὐκ ἀνάνδρως,
6 ἀτυχῶς δ' οἱ πλείους κατεκόπησαν. γενομένης δ'
οἰκτρᾶς νίκης περὶ τοὺς Ῥωμαίους καὶ οὐ παντά-
πασιν εὐτυχὲς τέλος εἰληφότος τοῦ ἀγῶνος, οἱ μὲν
ὕπατοι πρὸ τῶν νεκρῶν καταστρατοπεδευσάμενοι
τὴν ἐπιοῦσαν νύκτα ηὐλίσαντο.

Οἱ δὲ κατέχοντες τὸ Ἰάνικλον Τυρρηνοί, ἐπειδὴ
οὐδεμία παρὰ τῶν οἴκοθεν ἤρχετο ἐπικουρία, καταλιπεῖν ἔκριναν τὸ φρούριον, καὶ ἀναστρατοπεδεύ-
σαντες νυκτὸς ἀπῆραν εἰς τὴν Οὐιεντανῶν πόλιν
ἐγγυτάτω σφίσι τῶν Τυρρηνίδων πόλεων κειμένην.
7 τοῦ δὲ χάρακος αὐτῶν οἱ Ῥωμαῖοι κρατήσαντες
τά τε χρήματα διαρπάζουσιν ὅσα ὑπελείποντο
ἀδύνατα ὄντα ἐν φυγῇ φέρεσθαι, καὶ τραυματίας
λαμβάνουσι πολλούς, τοὺς μὲν ἐν ταῖς σκηναῖς ἀπο-
λειφθέντας, τοὺς δ' ἀνὰ τὴν ὁδὸν ἅπασαν ἐστρωμέ-
8 νους. ἀντείχοντο γάρ τινες γλιχόμενοι τῆς οἴκαδε

8

and, being pursued down hill, were slain as they
became scattered. When Verginius was informed
of the plight of the left wing of the army, he led his
entire force in battle array by a transverse road that
passed over the hill. Then, finding himself in the
rear of those who were pursuing his troops, he left
a part of his army there to block any who should be
sent from the camp to the relief of their comrades,
and he himself with the rest attacked the enemy.
In the meantime the troops also under Servilius,
encouraged by the arrival of their comrades, faced
about and, standing their ground, engaged. The
Tyrrhenians, being thus surrounded by both forces
and being unable either to break through in front,
by reason of those who engaged them, or to flee back
to their camp, by reason of those who attacked them
in the rear, fought bravely but unsuccessfully, and
were almost all destroyed. The Romans having thus
gained a melancholy victory and the outcome of the
battle being not altogether fortunate, the consuls
encamped before the bodies of the slain and there
spent the following night under the open sky.

The Tyrrhenians who were occupying the Janiculum, when no reinforcements came to them from
home, decided to abandon the fortress ; and breaking
camp in the night, they withdrew to Veii, which
lay nearest to them of the Tyrrhenian cities. The
Romans, having possessed themselves of their camp,
plundered all the effects which the enemy had left
behind as being impossible to carry away in their
flight, and also seized many of their wounded, part
of whom had been left in the tents, while others lay
scattered all along the road. For some, eager to be
on their way home, were holding out and with hearts

9

DIONYSIUS OF HALICARNASSUS

ὁδοῦ καὶ διεκαρτέρουν παρὰ δύναμιν ἀκολουθοῦν-
τες, εἶτα βαρυνομένων αὐτοῖς τῶν μελῶν ἡμιθνῆτες
κατέρρεον ἐπὶ τὴν γῆν· οὓς οἱ τῶν Ῥωμαίων
ἱππεῖς ἐπὶ πολὺ τῆς ὁδοῦ προελθόντες ἀνείλοντο·
καὶ ἐπειδὴ οὐδὲν ἔτι πολέμιον ἦν, καθελόντες τὸ
φρούριον καὶ τὰ λάφυρα ἄγοντες ἧκον εἰς τὴν
πόλιν, τὰ σώματα τῶν ἐν τῇ μάχῃ τελευτησάν-
των κομίσαντες, οἰκτρὰν ὄψιν ἅπασι τοῖς πολίταις διὰ πλῆθός τε καὶ ἀρετὴν τῶν ἀπολομένων.
9 ὥστε ὁ μὲν δῆμος οὔτε ἑορτάζειν ὡς καλὸν ἀγῶνα
κατορθώσας ἠξίου, οὔτε πενθεῖν ὡς ἐπὶ μεγάλῃ καὶ
ἀνηκέστῳ συμφορᾷ· ἡ δὲ βουλὴ τοῖς μὲν θεοῖς τὰς
ἀναγκαίους ἐψηφίσατο θυσίας, τὴν δ' ἐπινίκιον τοῦ
θριάμβου πομπὴν οὐκ ἐπέτρεψε ποιήσασθαι τοῖς
ὑπάτοις. μετ' οὐ πολλὰς δ' ἡμέρας ἀγορᾶς ἐπλή-
σθη παντοδαπῆς ἡ πόλις τῶν τε δημοσίᾳ πεμφ-
θέντων καὶ τῶν εἰωθότων ἐμπορεύεσθαι πολὺν
εἰσαγαγόντων σῖτον, ὥστ' ἐν τῇ προτέρᾳ πάντας
εὐετηρίᾳ γενέσθαι.

XXVII. Καταλυθέντων δὲ τῶν ὑπαιθρίων πολέμων ἡ πολιτικὴ στάσις αὖθις ἀνεκαίετο τῶν δημάρχων πάλιν ταραττόντων τὸ πλῆθος, καὶ τὰ μὲν
ἄλλα πολιτεύματα διεσκέδασαν αὐτῶν ἀντιταττό-
μενοι πρὸς ἕκαστον οἱ πατρίκιοι, τὴν δὲ κατὰ
Μενηνίου δίκην τοῦ νεωστὶ ὑπατεύσαντος καίτοι
πολλὰ πραγματευθέντες ἀδύνατοι ἐγένοντο διαλῦ-
2 σαι· ἀλλ' ὑπαχθεὶς ὁ ἀνὴρ εἰς δίκην ὑπὸ δυεῖν[1]
δημάρχων Κοΐντου Κωνσιδίου[2] καὶ Τίτου Γενυκίου,
καὶ λόγον ἀπαιτούμενος τῆς στρατηγίας τοῦ πολέ-

---

[1] δυεῖν B : τῶν δυεῖν R.
[2] Κωνσιδίου Sigonius : καὶ κοιντιλίου AC, κοιντίνου R.

stout beyond their strength were persisting in following their comrades; then, when their limbs grew heavy, they collapsed half dead to the ground. These the Roman horsemen slew as they advanced a good distance along the road. And when there was no longer any sign of the enemy, the army razed the fortress and returned to the city with the spoils, carrying with them the bodies of those who had been slain in the battle—a piteous sight to all the citizens by reason both of the number and of the valour of those who had perished. Accordingly, the people did not think it fitting either to hold festival as for a glorious victory or to mourn as for a great and irreparable calamity; and the senate, while ordering the required sacrifices to be offered to the gods, did not permit the consuls to conduct the triumphal procession in token of a victory. A few days later the city was filled with all sorts of provisions, as not only the men who had been sent out by the commonwealth but also those who were accustomed to carry on this trade had brought in much corn; consequently, everybody enjoyed the same abundance as aforetime.

XXVII. The foreign wars [1] being now ended, the civil dissension began to flare up again as the tribunes once more stirred up the populace. And though all their other measures were defeated by the patricians as the result of marshalling their forces against every proposal, yet they were unable to suppress the accusation against Menenius, the late consul, in spite of all their efforts, but he was brought to trial by Quintus Considius and Titus Genucius, two of the tribunes. And being called upon to give an accounting of his

---

[1] *Cf.* Livy, ii. 52, 2-5.

μου τέλος οὔτ᾽ εὐτυχὲς οὔτ᾽ εὐπρεπὲς λαβόντος,[1]
μάλιστα δὲ διαβαλλόμενος ἐπὶ τῷ Φαβίων ὀλέθρῳ
καὶ τῇ Κρεμέρας ἁλώσει, δικάζοντος τοῦ δημοτικοῦ ὄχλου κατὰ φυλάς, οὐ παρ᾽ ὀλίγας ψήφους
ὦφλεν, υἱὸς ὢν Ἀγρίππα Μενηνίου τοῦ καταγα-
γόντος ἐκ τῆς φυγῆς τὸν δῆμον καὶ διαλλάξαντος
πρὸς τοὺς πατρικίους, ὃν ἀποθανόντα ἡ βουλὴ ἐκ
τῶν δημοσίων χρημάτων λαμπροτάταις ἐκόσμησε
ταφαῖς, αἱ δὲ γυναῖκες αἱ Ῥωμαίων ἐνιαύσιον
ἐπένθησαν χρόνον πορφύραν καὶ χρυσὸν ἀποθέμεναι.
3 οὐ μέντοι θανάτου γε αὐτὸν[2] οἱ καταδικασάμενοι
ἐτίμησαν, ἀλλ᾽ ἐκτίσματος ὃ πρὸς μὲν τοὺς νῦν
ἐξεταζόμενον βίους γέλωτος ἂν ἄξιον φανείη, τοῖς
δὲ τότε ἀνθρώποις αὐτουργοῖς οὖσι καὶ πρὸς αὐτὰ
τὰ ἀναγκαῖα ζῶσι, μάλιστα δ᾽ ἐκείνῳ τῷ ἀνδρὶ
πενίαν κληρονομήσαντι παρὰ τοῦ πατρός, ὑπερφυὲς[3] ἦν καὶ βαρύ, δισχιλίων ἀριθμὸς ἀσσαρίων.
ἦν δ᾽ ἀσσάριον τότε χάλκεον νόμισμα βάρος λι-
τριαῖον, ὥστε τὸ σύμπαν ὄφλημα ταλάντων ἑκ-
4 καίδεκα εἰς ὁλκὴν χαλκοῦ γενέσθαι. καὶ τοῦτο
ἐπίφθονον ἐφάνη τοῖς τότε ἀνθρώποις, καὶ ἐπανορθώσασθαι βουλόμενοι αὐτὸ τὰς μὲν χρηματι-
κὰς ἔπαυσαν ζημίας, μετήνεγκαν δ᾽ εἰς προβάτων
ἐκτίσματα καὶ βοῶν, τάξαντες καὶ τούτων ἀριθμὸν
ταῖς ὕστερον ἐσομέναις ὑπὸ τῶν ἀρχόντων τοῖς
ἰδιώταις ἐπιβολαῖς.[4] ἐκ δὲ τῆς Μενηνίου κατα-
δίκης ἀφορμὴν αὖθις εἰλήφεσαν οἱ πατρίκιοι τῆς
πρὸς τὸ δημοτικὸν ὀργῆς καὶ οὔτε τὴν κληρουχίαν

---

[1] Reiske : λαβούσης O, Jacoby.
[2] αὐτὸν B : αὐτῷ R.
[3] ὑπερφυὲς Casaubon, ἀφειδὲς Jacoby, ἐπαχθὲς Capps,
ἀπηνὲς Post : ἀφ᾽ ἧς O.
[4] ἐπιβολαῖς Ab : ἐπιβουλαῖς AaBC.

conduct of the war, the outcome of which had been
neither fortunate nor honourable, and being blamed
particularly for the destruction of the Fabii and the
capture of Cremera, he was condemned by no small
majority of the votes when the plebeians passed
judgement upon him by tribes—even though he was
the son of Agrippa Menenius who had brought the
populace home after their secession and reconciled
them with the patricians, the son of a man whom the
senate after his death had honoured with a most
magnificent funeral at the public expense and for
whom the Roman matrons had mourned a whole year,
laying aside their purple and gold. However, those
who convicted him did not impose death as the
penalty, but rather a fine—one which if compared
with the fortunes of to-day would appear ridiculous,
but to the men of that age, who worked their own
farms and aimed at no more than the necessaries of
life, and particularly to Menenius, who had inherited
poverty from his father, was excessive [1] and oppress-
ive, amounting to 2000 *asses*. The *as* was at that
time a copper coin weighing a pound, so that the
whole fine amounted to sixteen talents of copper in
weight. And this appeared invidious to the men of
those days, who, in order to redress it, abolished all
pecuniary fines, changing them to payments in sheep
and oxen, and limiting the number even of these in
the case of all fines to be imposed thereafter by the
magistrates upon private persons. From this condemnation of Menenius the patricians took fresh
occasion for resentment against the plebeians and
would neither permit them to carry out the allot-

[1] The first of these two adjectives has been corrupted in
the MSS. and the correct word must remain in doubt.

ἐπέτρεπον ἔτι αὐτῷ ποιεῖσθαι οὔτ' ἄλλο ἐβούλοντο
5 ἐνδιδόναι μαλακὸν οὐδέν. μετ' οὐ πολὺ δὲ καὶ
τῷ δήμῳ μετέμελε τῶν δεδικασμένων, ἐπειδὴ τὴν
τελευτὴν τοῦ ἀνδρὸς ἐπύθετο· οὐδὲ γὰρ εἰς ἀνθρώπων ἔτι συνῆλθεν ὁμιλίας οὐδ' ἐν δημοσίῳ τινὶ
πρὸς οὐδενὸς ὤφθη τόπῳ, ἐξόν τε αὐτῷ τὴν ζημίαν
ἐκτίσαντι μηδενὸς ἀπελαύνεσθαι τῶν κοινῶν (ἕτοιμοι γὰρ ἦσαν οὐκ ὀλίγοι τῶν ἐπιτηδείων αὐτοῦ τὴν
καταδίκην ἀπαριθμεῖν) οὐκ ἠξίωσεν, ἀλλὰ θανάτου
τὴν συμφορὰν τιμησάμενος, οἴκοι μένων καὶ οὐδένα
προσιέμενος ὑπό τ' ἀθυμίας καὶ σίτων ἀποχῆς[1]
μαρανθεὶς ἀπέστη τοῦ βίου. καὶ τὰ μὲν ἐν τούτῳ
πραχθέντα τῷ ἐνιαυτῷ τοιάδε ἦν.

XXVIII. Ποπλίου δὲ Οὐαλερίου Ποπλικόλα καὶ
Γαΐου Ναυτίου παραλαβόντων τὴν ἀρχὴν ἕτερος
ἀνὴρ πάλιν τῶν πατρικίων Σερούιος Σερουίλιος, ὁ
τῷ παρελθόντι ὑπατεύσας ἔτει, μετ' οὐ πολὺν ἢ
τὴν ἀρχὴν ἀποθέσθαι χρόνον εἰς τὸν ὑπὲρ τῆς
ψυχῆς ἀγῶνα ἤχθη. οἱ δὲ προθέντες αὐτῷ τὴν ἐν
τῷ δήμῳ δίκην δύο τῶν δημάρχων ἦσαν, Λεύκιος
Καιδίκιος καὶ Τίτος Στάτιος, οὐκ ἀδικήματος,
ἀλλὰ τύχης ἀπαιτοῦντες λόγον, ὅτι κατὰ τὴν πρὸς
Τυρρηνοὺς μάχην ὠσάμενος ἐπὶ τὸν χάρακα τῶν
πολεμίων ὁ ἀνὴρ θρασύτερον μᾶλλον ἢ φρονιμώ-
τερον, ἐδιώχθη τε ὑπὸ τῶν ἔνδον ἀθρόων ἐπεξ-
ελθόντων καὶ τὴν κρατίστην νεότητα ἀπέβαλεν.
2 οὗτος ὁ ἀγὼν ἁπάντων ἐφάνη τοῖς πατρικίοις
ἀγώνων[2] βαρύτατος, ἠγανάκτουν τε συνιόντες πρὸς
ἀλλήλους καὶ δεινὸν ἐποιοῦντο, εἰ τὰς εὐτολμίας
τῶν στρατηγῶν καὶ τὸ μηδένα κίνδυνον ὀκνεῖν, ἐὰν

---

[1] Sylburg : ἐποχῆς O.
[2] ἀγώνων O : deleted by Jacoby.

ment of lands nor make any other concession in their favour. And not long afterwards even the populace repented of having condemned him, when they learned of his death. For from that time he no longer entered into any intercourse with his fellow men nor was seen by anyone in any public place ; and though it was his privilege by paying his fine not to be excluded from any public doings—for not a few of his friends were ready to pay the fine—he would not accept their offer, but rating his misfortune as a capital sentence and remaining at home and admitting no one, wasted away through dejection and abstinence from food, and so perished. These were the events of that year.

XXVIII. When Publius Valerius Publicola and Gaius Nautius had succeeded to the consulship,[1] another of the patricians, Servius [2] Servilius, who had been consul the preceding year, was put on trial for his life not long after laying down his magistracy. Those who cited him to trial before the populace were Lucius Caedicius and Titus Statius, two of the tribunes, who demanded an accounting, not for any crime, but for his bad luck, inasmuch as in the battle against the Tyrrhenians he had pressed forward to the enemy's camp with greater daring than prudence, and being pursued by the garrison, who rushed out in a body, had lost the flower of the youth. This trial was regarded by the patricians as the most grievous of all ; and meeting together, they expressed their resentment and indignation if boldness on the part of generals and their refusal to shirk any danger were going to be made a ground for

[1] For chaps. 28-33 cf. Livy ii. 52, 6-8.
[2] See note on chap. 25, 1.

ἐναντιωθῇ ταῖς ἐπιβολαῖς αὐτῶν τὸ δαιμόνιον, εἰς
κατηγορίαν ἄξουσιν οἱ μὴ στάντες παρὰ τὰ δεινά·
δειλίας τε καὶ ὄκνου καὶ τοῦ μηδὲν ἔτι καινουργεῖν
τοὺς ἡγεμόνας, ὑφ' ὧν[1] ἐλευθερία τε ἀπόλλυται
καὶ ἡγεμονία καταλύεται, τοὺς τοιούτους ἀγῶνας
3 αἰτίους ἔσεσθαι κατὰ τὸ εἰκὸς ἐλογίζοντο. παρακλήσει τε πολλῇ ἐχρῶντο τῶν δημοτικῶν μὴ
καταγνῶναι τοῦ ἀνδρὸς τὴν δίκην, διδάσκοντες ὡς
μεγάλα βλάψουσι τὴν πόλιν ἐπὶ ταῖς ἀτυχίαις τοὺς
4 στρατηγοὺς ζημιοῦντες. ἐπεὶ δ' ὁ τοῦ ἀγῶνος
ἐνέστη χρόνος, παρελθὼν εἷς τῶν δημάρχων κατ-
ηγόρησε τοῦ ἀνδρός, Λεύκιος Καιδίκιος, ὅτι δι'
ἀφροσύνην τε καὶ τοῦ στρατηγεῖν ἀπειρίαν εἰς πρόδηλον ἄγων ὄλεθρον τὰς δυνάμεις ἀπώλεσε τῆς
πόλεως τὴν κρατίστην ἀκμήν, καὶ εἰ μὴ ταχεῖα
τοῦ κακοῦ γνῶσις ἐγένετο τῷ συνυπάτῳ, καὶ κατὰ
σπουδὴν ἄγων τὰς δυνάμεις τούς τε πολεμίους
ἀνέστειλε καὶ τοὺς σφετέρους ἔσωσε, μηδὲν ἂν
γενέσθαι τὸ κωλῦσον ἅπασαν ἀπολωλέναι τὴν
ἑτέραν δύναμιν καὶ τὸ λοιπὸν ἡμίσειαν ἀντὶ διπλα-
5 σίας εἶναι τὴν πόλιν. τοιαῦτ' εἰπὼν μάρτυρας
ἐπηγάγετο λοχαγούς τε, ὅσοι περιῆσαν, καὶ τῶν
ἄλλων στρατιωτῶν τινας, οἳ τὸ ἑαυτῶν αἰσχρὸν
ἐπὶ τῇ τότε ἥττῃ τε καὶ φυγῇ ζητοῦντες ἀπο-
λύσασθαι τὸν στρατηγὸν ᾐτιῶντο τῆς περὶ τὸν
ἀγῶνα δυσποτμίας. ἔπειτα οἶκτον ἐπὶ τῇ συμφορᾷ τῶν τότε τεθνηκότων καταχεάμενος πολὺν
καὶ τὸ δεινὸν αὐξήσας, τά τε ἄλλα ὅσα εἰς
φθόνον κοινῇ κατὰ τῶν πατρικίων λεγόμενα τοὺς
μέλλοντας ὑπὲρ τοῦ ἀνδρὸς δεήσεσθαι ἀνείρξειν

---

[1] ὑφ' ὧν Reiske : σφῶν O.

accusations, in case Heaven opposed their plans, on
the part of those who had not faced the dangers ;
and they reasoned that such trials would in all probability be the cause of cowardice, shirking and the
lack of any further initiative on the part of commanders—the very weaknesses through which liberty
is lost and supremacy undermined. They earnestly
implored the plebeians not to condemn the man,
pointing out that they would do great harm to the
commonwealth if they punished their generals for
being unfortunate. When the time for the trial was
at hand, Lucius Caedicius, one of the tribunes, came
forward and accused Servilius of having through his
folly and inexperience in the duties of a general led
his forces to manifest destruction and lost the finest
manhood of the army ; and he declared that if his
colleague had not been informed promptly of the
disaster and had not by bringing up his forces in all
haste repulsed the enemy and saved their own men,
nothing could have prevented the other army from
being utterly destroyed and the state from being
reduced henceforth to one-half its former numbers.
After he had thus spoken, he produced as witnesses
all the centurions who had survived and some of the
rank and file, who in the effort to wipe out their own
disgrace arising from that defeat and flight were
ready to blame the general for the ill success of
the engagement. Then, having poured out many
words of commiseration for the fate of those who
had lost their lives upon that occasion, exaggerated
the disaster, and with great contempt of the patricians dwelt at length upon everything else which
by exposing their whole order to hatred was sure
to discourage all who were intending to inter-

17

ἔμελλεν ἐκ πολλῆς ὑπεροψίας διελθών, παρέδωκε
τὸν λόγον.

XXIX. Παραλαβὼν δὲ τὴν ἀπολογίαν ὁ Σερουΐλιος εἶπεν· "Εἰ μὲν ἐπὶ δίκην με κεκλήκατε, ὦ
πολῖται, καὶ λόγον ἀπαιτεῖτε τῆς στρατηγίας,
ἕτοιμός εἰμι ἀπολογήσασθαι· εἰ δ' ἐπὶ τιμωρίαν
κατεγνωσμένην, καὶ οὐδὲν ἔσται μοι πλέον ἀπο-
δείξαντι ὡς οὐδὲν ὑμᾶς ἀδικῶ, λαβόντες τὸ σῶμα
2 ὅ τι πάλαι βούλεσθε χρῆσθε. ἐμοί τε γὰρ κρεῖττον
ἀκρίτῳ¹ ἀποθανεῖν μᾶλλον ἢ λόγου τυχόντι καὶ μὴ
πείσαντι ὑμᾶς (δόξαιμι γὰρ ἂν² σὺν δίκῃ πάσχειν
ὅ τι ἄν μου καταγνῶτε), ὑμεῖς τ' ἐν ἐλάττονι αἰτίᾳ
ἔσεσθε ἀφελόμενοί μου τὸν λόγον καί, ἐν ᾧ καὶ³
εἴ τι ἀδικῶ ὑμᾶς ἄδηλόν ἐστιν ἔτι, ταῖς ὀργαῖς
χαρισάμενοι. ἔσται δέ μοι ἡ διάνοια ὑμῶν ἐκ
τῆς ἀκροάσεως καταφανής, θορύβῳ τε καὶ ἡσυχίᾳ
εἰκάζοντι πότερον ἐπὶ τιμωρίαν ἢ ἐπὶ δίκην κεκλή-
3 κατέ με." ταῦτ' εἰπὼν ἐπέσχε· σιγῆς δὲ γενομένης καὶ τῶν πλείστων ἐμβοησάντων θαρρεῖν τε
καὶ ὅσα βούλεται λέγειν, παραλαβὼν τὸν λόγον
πάλιν ἔλεξεν· "Ἀλλ' εἴ τοι⁴ δικασταῖς ὑμῖν, ὦ
πολῖται, καὶ μὴ ἐχθροῖς χρήσομαι, ῥαδίως πείσειν
ὑμᾶς οἴομαι ὅτι οὐδὲν ἀδικῶ. ποιήσομαι δὲ τὴν
ἀρχὴν τῶν λόγων ἐξ ὧν ἅπαντες ἴστε. ἐγὼ κατ-
έστην ἐπὶ τὴν ἀρχὴν σὺν τῷ κρατίστῳ Οὐεργινίῳ
καθ' ὃν χρόνον ἐπιτειχίσαντες ὑμῖν οἱ Τυρρηνοὶ τὸν
ὑπὲρ τῆς πόλεως λόφον πάσης ἐκράτουν τῆς ὑπ-

---

¹ ἀκρίτῳ B : om. R.
² ἂν Reiske : om. O.
³ καὶ O : deleted by Cobet, Jacoby.
⁴ τοι B : om. R.

cede for the man, he gave him an opportunity of speaking.

XXIX. Taking up his defence, Servilius said : " If it is to a trial, citizens, that you have summoned me, and you desire an accounting of my generalship, I am ready to make my defence ; but if it is to a punishment already determined, and no advantage is to accrue to me for showing that I have not wronged you in any way, take my person and deal with it as you have long desired to do. Indeed, for me it is better to die without a trial than after getting a chance to plead my cause and then failing to convince you—since I should in that case seem to suffer deservedly whatever you determined against me— and you on your part will be less blameworthy for depriving me of the right to plead my cause and for indulging your angry passions while it is still uncertain even whether I have done you any wrong. And your intention will be evident to me by the manner in which you give me a hearing : by your clamour and by your silence I shall judge whether it is to vengeance or to judgement that you have summoned me." Having said this, he stopped. And when silence followed and then the majority cried out to him to be of good courage and say all that he wished, he resumed his plea and said : " Well then, citizens, if you are to be my judges and not my enemies, I believe I shall easily convince you that I am guilty of no crime. I shall begin my defence with facts with which you are all familiar. I was chosen consul together with that most excellent man, Verginius, at the time when the Tyrrhenians, having fortified against you the hill that commands the city, were masters of all the open country and

DIONYSIUS OF HALICARNASSUS

αἴθρου[1] καὶ ἐν ἐλπίδι ἦσαν τοῦ καταλύσειν[2] ἡμῶν
τὴν ἀρχὴν ἐν τάχει. λιμὸς δὲ πολὺς ἐν τῇ πόλει καὶ
4 στάσις καὶ τοῦ τί χρὴ πράττειν ἀμηχανία. τοιούτοις δὴ καιροῖς ἐπιστὰς οὕτω ταραχώδεσι καὶ
φοβεροῖς τοὺς μὲν πολεμίους ἅμα τῷ συνάρχοντι
ἐνίκησα διτταῖς μάχαις καὶ ἠνάγκασα καταλιπόντας
τὸ φρούριον ἀπελθεῖν· τὸν δὲ λιμὸν οὐκ εἰς μακρὰν
ἔπαυσα τροφῆς ἀφθόνου πληρώσας τὰς ἀγοράς, καὶ
τοῖς μετ᾽ ἐμὲ[3] ὑπάτοις τήν τε χώραν παρέδωκα
ὅπλων πολεμίων ἐλευθέραν, καὶ τὴν πόλιν ὑγιῆ
πάσης νόσου πολιτικῆς, εἰς ἃς κατέβαλον αὐτὴν οἱ
δημαγωγοῦντες. τίνος οὖν ἀδικήματος ὑπεύθυνός
5 εἰμι ὑμῖν; εἰ μὴ τὸ νικᾶν τοὺς πολεμίους ἐστὶν
ὑμᾶς ἀδικεῖν. εἰ δ᾽ ἀποθανεῖν τισι τῶν στρατιωτῶν
κατὰ τὴν μάχην[4] εὐτυχῶς[5] ἀγωνιζομένοις συν-
έπεσε, τί Σερουΐλιος τὸν δῆμον ἀδικεῖ; οὐ γὰρ δὴ
θεῶν τις ἐγγυητὴς τοῖς στρατηγοῖς τῆς ἁπάντων
ψυχῆς τῶν ἀγωνιουμένων γίνεται, οὐδ᾽ ἐπὶ διακει-
μένοις καὶ ῥητοῖς τὰς ἡγεμονίας παραλαμβάνομεν,
ὥσθ᾽ ἁπάντων κρατῆσαι τῶν πολεμίων καὶ μηδένα
τῶν ἰδίων ἀποβαλεῖν. τίς γὰρ ἂν ὑπομείνειεν
ἄνθρωπος ὢν ἅπαντα καὶ τὰ τῆς γνώμης καὶ τὰ
τῆς τύχης εἰς ἑαυτὸν ἀναλαβεῖν; ἀλλὰ τὰ μεγάλα
ἔργα μεγάλων ἀεὶ κινδύνων ὠνούμεθα.

XXX. " Καὶ οὐκ ἐμοὶ ταῦτα πρώτῳ πολεμίοις
ὁμόσε χωρήσαντι συνέβη παθεῖν, ἅπασι δ᾽ ὡς
εἰπεῖν ὅσοι μάχας παρακεκινδυνευμένας σὺν ἐλάτ-
τοσι ταῖς σφετέραις δυνάμεσι πρὸς μείζονας τὰς

---

[1] ἀρχῆς after ὑπαίθρου deleted by Reiske.
[2] καταλύσειν C : καταλύειν R.
[3] ἐμὲ Cmg : αὐτὸν O, ἐμαυτὸν Hertlein.
[4] κατὰ τὴν μάχην B : om. R.   [5] εὐψύχως Kiessling.

entertained hopes of speedily overthrowing our empire. There was a great famine in the city, and sedition, and perplexity as to what should be done. Having been brought face to face with so turbulent and so formidable a crisis, I together with my colleague overcame the enemy in two engagements and obliged them to abandon the fort and leave the country, while I soon put an end to the famine by supplying the markets with abundant provisions ; and I handed over to my successors not only our territory freed from hostile arms but also our city cured of every political distemper with which the demagogues had infected it. For what wrongdoing, then, am I accountable to you—unless to conquer your enemies is to wrong you ? And if some of the soldiers happened to lose their lives in the battle while fighting successfully,[1] in what way has Servilius wronged the people ? For naturally no god offers himself as surety to generals for the lives of all who are going into battle ; nor do we receive the command of armies upon stated terms and conditions, namely that we are to overcome all our enemies and lose none of our own men. For who that is a mere mortal would consent to take upon himself all the consequences both of his judgement and of his luck ? No man, I say ; but our great successes we always buy at the cost of great hazards.

XXX. " Moreover, I am not the first to whom it has fallen to suffer this fate when engaging the enemy, but it has happened to practically all who have risked desperate battles against enemy forces

---

[1] Or " courageously," following Kiessling.

DIONYSIUS OF HALICARNASSUS

τῶν ἐχθρῶν ἐποιήσαντο. ἐδίωξαν γὰρ ἤδη τινὲς
ἐχθροὺς καὶ αὐτοὶ ἔφυγον καὶ ἀπέκτεινάν τε τῶν
ἐναντίων πολλοὺς καὶ ἀπώλεσαν ἔτι πλείους τῶν
2 σφετέρων. ἐῶ γὰρ λέγειν[1] ὅτι πολλοὶ καὶ τὸ
παράπαν ἡττηθέντες σὺν αἰσχύνῃ τε καὶ βλάβῃ
μεγάλῃ ἀνέστρεψαν, ὧν οὐδεὶς τῆς τύχης δέδωκε
δίκας· ἱκανὴ γὰρ ἡ συμφορά, καὶ τὸ μηδενὸς ἐπ-
αίνου τυχεῖν, ὡς δεῖ,[2] εἰ καὶ[3] μηδὲν ἄλλο, μεγάλη
τοῖς ἡγεμόσι καὶ χαλεπὴ ζημία. οὐ μὴν ἀλλ'
ἔγωγε τοσούτου δέω λέγειν, ὃ πάντες οἱ μέτριοι
δίκαιον εἶναι φήσουσιν, ὡς οὐ δεῖ με τύχης εὐθύνας
ὑπέχειν, ὥστ' εἰ καὶ μηδεὶς ἄλλος τοιόνδε ἀγῶνα
ὑπέμεινεν εἰσελθεῖν, ἐγὼ μόνος οὐ παραιτοῦμαι,
ἀλλὰ συγχωρῶ τὴν τύχην ἐξετάζεσθαι τὴν ἐμὴν
3 οὐχ ἧττον τῆς γνώμης, ἐκεῖνο προειπών· ἐγὼ τὰς
ἀνθρωπίνας πράξεις τάς τε δυστυχεῖς καὶ τὰς
εὐτυχεῖς οὐκ ἐκ τῶν κατὰ μέρος ἔργων πολλῶν
ὄντων καὶ ποικίλων ὁρῶ κρινομένας, ἀλλ' ἐκ τοῦ
τέλους· καὶ ὅταν μὲν τοῦτο χωρήσῃ κατὰ νοῦν, κἂν
τὰ μεταξὺ πολλὰ ὄντα μὴ καθ' ἡδονὰς γένηται,
οὐδὲν ἧττον ἐπαινουμένας ὑπὸ πάντων ἀκούω καὶ
ζηλουμένας καὶ τῆς ἀγαθῆς νομιζομένας τύχης·
ὅταν δὲ πονηρὰς λάβωσι τελευτάς, καὶ ἐὰν ἅπαντα
τὰ πρὸ τοῦ τέλους ἐκ τοῦ ῥάστου[4] γένηται, οὐ τῇ

[1] λέγειν A : om. R.

[2] ὡς δεῖ A : ὡς δ' B, ὧν δεῖ Kayser, om. Kiessling. It is
easy to believe that not only ὡς δεῖ (or ὡς δ') but also εἰ καὶ
μηδὲν ἄλλο is spurious. The striking similarity of these two
phrases, quite unneeded in this sentence, to ὥστ' εἰ καὶ μηδεὶς
ἄλλος, four lines below, where the words are required by the
context, suggests that their presence here is due to a simple
scribal error; it will be noted that in each case the words
follow an infinitive ending in -χεῖν.

[3] εἰ καὶ B : κἂν A.

more numerous than their own. For there have been
instances where generals after chasing their foes have
themselves been put to flight, and while slaying many
of their opponents have lost still more of their own
men. I shall not add that many even after meeting
utter defeat have returned home with ignominy and
great loss, yet not one of them has been punished for
his bad luck. For the calamity itself is a sufficient
punishment, and to receive no praise, as is inevitable,
even without anything else,[1] is a great and grievous
penalty for a general. Nevertheless, I for my part
am so far from maintaining—what all reasonable men
will allow to be just—that I do not have to render
an accounting of my luck, that, even though no one
else was ever willing to submit to such a trial, I alone
do not decline to do so, but consent that my luck be
inquired into as well as my judgement—after I have
first made this one statement : I observe that men's
undertakings, both unsuccessful and successful, are
judged, not by the several operations in detail, which
are many and various, but by the final outcome.
When this turns out according to their hopes, even
though the intermediate operations, which are many,
may not be to their liking, I nevertheless hear the
undertakings praised and admired by all and regarded as the consequences of good luck ; but when
these measures lead to bad results, even though
every measure before the final outcome is carried out
with the greatest ease,[2] they are ascribed, not to the

---

[1] See the critical note.
[2] Or, following the emendation of Kiessling or that of
Kayser, " in the best possible manner."

---

[4] ἐκ τοῦ ἀρίστου Kiessling, ἀπὸ τοῦ κρατίστου Kayser.

σπουδαίᾳ τύχῃ τῶν πραξάντων ἀποδιδομένας, ἀλλὰ
4 τῇ κακῇ. τοῦτον δὴ τὸν σκοπὸν προθέντες[1] αὐτοὶ[2]
ἐξετάζετε καὶ τὴν ἐμὴν τύχην ᾗ παρὰ τοὺς πολέμους κέχρημαι. καὶ ἐὰν μὲν εὕρητε ἡττημένον με
ὑπὸ τῶν πολεμίων, πονηρὰν καλεῖτέ μου τὴν τύχην,
ἐὰν δὲ κεκρατηκότα τῶν ἐχθρῶν, ἀγαθήν. περὶ μὲν
οὖν τῆς τύχης, οὐκ ἀγνοῶν ὅτι φορτικοὶ πάντες
εἰσὶν οἱ περὶ αὐτῆς λέγοντες, ἔχων ἔτι πλείω
λέγειν, παύσομαι.

XXXI. '' Επειδὴ δὲ καὶ τῆς γνώμης κατηγο-
ροῦσί μου, προδοσίαν μὲν οὐ τολμῶντες ἐπικαλεῖν
οὐδ' ἀνανδρίαν, ἐφ' οἷς αἱ κατὰ τῶν ἄλλων στρατηγῶν γίνονται κρίσεις, ἀπειρίαν δὲ τοῦ στρατηγεῖν
καὶ ἀφροσύνην, ὅτι κίνδυνον ὑπέμεινα οὐκ ἀναγκαῖον ἐπὶ τὸν χάρακα τῶν πολεμίων ὠσάμενος,
βούλομαι καὶ περὶ τούτου λόγον ὑποσχεῖν ὑμῖν,
προχειρότατον μὲν τοῦτ' ἔχων εἰπεῖν, ὅτι τὸ μὲν
ἐπιτιμᾶν τοῖς γενομένοις πάνυ ῥᾴδιον καὶ παντὸς
ἀνθρώπου, τὸ δὲ παραβάλλεσθαι πράγμασι καλοῖς
χαλεπὸν καὶ ὀλίγων· καὶ ὅτι οὐχ ὥσπερ τὰ γεγονότα φαίνεται ὁποῖά ἐστιν, οὕτω καὶ τὰ μέλλοντα
ὁποῖα ἔσται· ἀλλ' ἐκεῖνα μὲν αἰσθήσει[3] καὶ πάθεσι
καταλαμβανόμεθα, ταῦτα δὲ μαντείαις καὶ δόξαις
εἰκάζομεν, ἐν αἷς πολὺ τὸ ἀπατηλόν· καὶ ὅτι ῥᾷστον
ἁπάντων ἐστὶ λόγῳ στρατηγεῖν πολέμους ἔξω τοῦ
δεινοῦ βεβηκότας, ὃ ποιοῦσιν οἱ κατηγοροῦντες
2 ἐμοῦ. ἀλλ' ἵνα ταῦτ' ἀφῶ, φέρε πρὸς θεῶν εἴπατέ
μοι, μόνος ἢ πρῶτος ὑμῖν[4] ἐγὼ φαίνομαι βιάσασθαι
φρούριον ἐπιβαλόμενος καὶ πρὸς ὑψηλὰ χωρία τὰς
δυνάμεις ἀγαγών; ἢ πολλῶν μετ' ἄλλων ὑμε-

---

[1] προθέντες Cobet, προϊδόντες Jacoby : προελόντες O.
[2] αὐτοὶ A : ἑαυτοῖς B.

good, but to the bad luck of their authors. So, taking this point of view, do you yourselves consider what has been my luck in the various wars ; and if you find that I was vanquished by the enemy, call my luck bad, but if I was victorious over them, call it good. On the subject of luck, now, I could say still more ; however, as I am not unaware that all who discuss it are tiresome, I will desist.

XXXI. "But since they censure my judgement also, not daring, indeed, to accuse me of treachery or cowardice, the charges on which other generals are tried, but accuse me of inexperience in the duties of a general and imprudence, in that I undertook an unnecessary risk in pressing forward to the enemy's camp, I wish to render to you an accounting on that point too, since I can make the very obvious retort that it is very easy and lies in the power of any man to censure past actions, whereas to venture upon glorious exploits is difficult and within the power of but few ; also that it is not so apparent what future events will be as what past events are, but, on the contrary, we apprehend the latter by perception and our experiences, while we conjecture the others by divination and opinions, in which there is much that is deceptive; and again, that it is the easiest thing in the world for people to conduct wars by talk when they stand far from the danger, which is what my accusers do. But, to waive all this, tell me, in the name of the gods, do you regard me as the first or the only man who ever attempted to capture a stronghold by force and led his men against lofty positions ? Or have not many

---

³ αἰσθήσει B : αἰσθήσεσι R.
⁴ ὑμῖν B : om. R.

25

τέρων στρατηγῶν, ἐξ ὧν οἱ μὲν κατώρθωσαν, τοῖς
δ' οὐκ ἐχώρησεν ἡ πεῖρα κατὰ νοῦν; τί δήποτ'
οὖν τοὺς ἄλλους ἀφέντες ἐμὲ κρίνετε, εἰ ταῦτα
ἀστρατηγησίας καὶ ἀφροσύνης ἔργα νομίζετε;
πόσα δ' ἄλλα τούτου τολμηρότερα τοῖς ἡγεμόσιν
ἔπεισι[1] πράττειν ὅταν τὸ ἀσφαλὲς καὶ λελογισ-
3 μένον ἥκιστα οἱ καιροὶ δέχωνται; οἱ μέν γε τὰς
σημείας ἁρπάσαντες τῶν σφετέρων ἔρριψαν εἰς
τοὺς πολεμίους, ἵνα τοῖς βλακεύουσι καὶ ἀπο-
δειλιῶσιν ἐκ τοῦ ἀναγκαίου παραστῇ τὸ εὔψυχον,
ἐπισταμένοις ὅτι τοὺς μὴ ἀνασώσαντας τὰ σημεῖα
ὑπὸ τῶν στρατηγῶν δεῖ σὺν αἰσχύνῃ ἀποθανεῖν· οἱ
δ' εἰς τὴν τῶν πολεμίων χώραν ἐμβαλόντες ἔλυσαν
τὰ ζεύγματα τῶν ποταμῶν οὓς διέβησαν, ἵνα τοῖς
φεύγειν διανοουμένοις ἄπορος ἡ τοῦ σωθῆναι ἐλπὶς
φανεῖσα θάρσος παραστήσῃ καὶ μένος ἐν ταῖς
μάχαις· οἱ δὲ τὰς σκηνὰς καὶ τὰ σκευοφόρα κατακαύσαντες ἀνάγκην ἐπέθηκαν τοῖς σφετέροις ἐκ
4 τῆς πολεμίας ὅσων δέονται λαμβάνειν. ἐῶ τἆλλα
μυρία ὄντα λέγειν καὶ ὅσα τολμηρὰ ἔργα καὶ
ἐνθυμήματα ἕτερα στρατηγῶν ἱστορίᾳ τε καὶ πείρᾳ
παραλαβόντες ἔχομεν, ἐφ' οἷς οὐδεὶς πώποτε τῶν
ψευσθέντων τῆς ἐλπίδος ὑπέσχε δίκας. εἰ μὴ ἄρα
ἔχει τις ὑμῶν αἰτιάσασθαί με ὅτι προβαλὼν τοὺς
ἄλλους εἰς προὖπτον ὄλεθρον αὐτὸς ἔξω τοῦ κινδύνου τὸ σῶμα εἶχον. εἰ δὲ μετὰ πάντων τε
ἐξηταζόμην καὶ τελευταῖος ἀπηλλαττόμην καὶ τῆς

---

[1] ἔπεισι B : ἦλθεν ἐπὶ νοῦν A.

---

[1] This passage makes it clear that Dionysius could use
σκευοφόρα in the sense of the simple σκεύη, and that it should
be so rendered in iv. 47, 2.

others of your generals done the same, some of whom
have succeeded, while the attempt of others has not
turned out as they wished? Why in the world,
then, did you let the others off but now try me, if you
consider these actions to be marks of incapacity and
imprudence in a general? How many other undertakings more daring than this does it occur to your
generals to attempt when times of crisis admit of
anything but the safe and well-considered course?
Some indeed have snatched the standards from their
own men and hurled them among the enemy, in
order that the indolent and cowardly might perforce
gain courage, since they knew that those who failed
to recover their standards must be put to death
ignominiously by their generals. Others, after invading the enemy's country, have destroyed the
bridges over the rivers which they had crossed, in
order that any who entertained thoughts of saving
themselves by flight might find their hope vain and
so be inspired with boldness and resolution in the
battles. Still others by burning their tents and
baggage [1] have imposed on their men the necessity
of supplying themselves out of the enemy's country
with everything they needed. I omit mentioning all
the other instances of the kind, which are countless,
and the many other daring actions and expedients of
generals that we know of from both history and our
own experience, for which no general was ever
punished when disappointed in his hopes. Unless,
indeed, someone among you can bring the charge
against me that when I exposed the others to manifest destruction I kept myself out of danger. But if
I took my place in the line with all the rest, was last
to withdraw and shared the same fortune with the

27

αὐτῆς τοῖς ἄλλοις μετεῖχον τύχης, τί ἀδικῶ; καὶ
περὶ μὲν ἐμοῦ ταῦθ' ἱκανὰ εἰρήσθω.

XXXII. " Περὶ δὲ τῆς βουλῆς καὶ τῶν πατρικίων, ἐπειδὴ τὸ κοινὸν ὑμῶν μῖσος, ὃ διὰ τὴν
κωλυθεῖσαν κληρουχίαν ἔχετε, καὶ ἐμὲ λυπεῖ, καὶ
οὐδὲ ὁ κατήγορος αὐτὸ ἀπεκρύψατο, ἀλλὰ μέρος
οὐκ ἐλάχιστον ἐποιήσατο τῆς ἐμῆς κατηγορίας,
2 βούλομαι βραχέα εἰπεῖν πρὸς ὑμᾶς. ἔσται δὲ μετὰ
παρρησίας ὁ λόγος· ἄλλως γὰρ οὔτ' ἂν ἐγὼ δυ-
ναίμην λέγειν οὔθ' ὑμῖν ἀκούειν συμφέροι.[1] οὐ
δίκαια ποιεῖτε οὐδ' ὅσια, ὦ δημόται, τῶν μὲν
εὐεργεσιῶν ἃς εὕρεσθε παρὰ τῆς βουλῆς, πολλῶν
οὐσῶν καὶ μεγάλων, οὐκ εἰδότες αὐτῇ χάριν, εἰ
δέ τι δεομένοις ὑμῖν ἐξ οὗ συγχωρηθέντος μεγάλα
βλάπτοιτ' ἂν τὸ κοινόν, οὐ φθονοῦσα ὑμῖν, ἀλλὰ τὸ
συμφέρον τῆς πόλεως ὁρῶσα, ἠναντιώθη, τοῦτο δι'
3 ὀργῆς λαμβάνοντες. ἔδει δ' ὑμᾶς μάλιστα μὲν ὡς
ἀπὸ τοῦ κρατίστου τὰ βουλεύματα αὐτῆς γενόμενα
καὶ ἐπὶ τῷ πάντων ἀγαθῷ δεχομένους ἀποστῆναι
τῆς σπουδῆς· εἰ δ' ἀδύνατοι ἦτε κατασχεῖν ἀσύμφορον ἐπιθυμίαν λογισμῷ σώφρονι, μετὰ τοῦ
πείθειν τῶν αὐτῶν ἀξιοῦν τυγχάνειν, ἀλλὰ μὴ μετὰ
4 τοῦ βιάζεσθαι. αἱ γὰρ ἑκούσιοι δωρεαὶ τοῖς τε
προϊεμένοις[2] ἡδίους τῶν ἠναγκασμένων εἰσί, καὶ
τοῖς λαμβάνουσι βεβαιότεραι τῶν μὴ τοιούτων. ὃ
μὰ τοὺς θεοὺς οὐ λογίζεσθε ὑμεῖς, ἀλλ' ὑπὸ τῶν
δημαγωγῶν, ὥσπερ θάλαττα ὑπ' ἀνέμων ἄλλων ἐπ'

---

[1] Steph. : συμφέρει ABC, Jacoby.
[2] Cobet : προεμένοις O, Jacoby.

others, of what crime am I guilty ? Concerning myself, then, let this suffice.

XXXII. " But concerning the senate and the patricians I wish to say a few words to you, since the general hatred you plebeians bear toward them because they prevented the allotment of land hurts me also, and since my accuser too did not conceal this hatred, but made it no small part of his accusation against me. And I shall speak with frankness ; for I could not speak in any other fashion, nor would it be to your interest to hear me if I did. You are not doing right in the eyes of men or the gods, plebeians, if, on the one hand, you show no gratitude for the many great benefits you have received from the senate, but, on the other hand, because, when you demanded a measure the concession of which would bring great harm to the public, the senate, not in any spirit of animosity toward you, but having in view the welfare of the commonwealth, opposed it, you angrily resent its action. But what you ought to have done was, preferably, to accept the senate's decisions as having been made with the best of motives and for the good of all and then to have desisted from your selfish striving ; but if you were unable to restrain your inexpedient desire by means of sober reason, you should have sought to obtain these same ends by persuasion and not by violence. For voluntary gifts are not only more pleasing to those who grant them than such as are extorted by force, but are also more lasting to those who receive them than those which are not freely given. Of this truth you, however, as Heaven is my witness, take no account, but you are continually stirred up by your demagogues and roused to fury

ἄλλοις ἐπανισταμένων, ἀνακινούμενοί τε καὶ ἀγρι-
αινόμενοι οὐδὲ τὸν ἐλάχιστον χρόνον ἐν ἡσυχίᾳ
καὶ γαλήνῃ διακεῖσθαι τὴν πόλιν ἐᾶτε. τοιγάρτοι
περίεστιν[1] ἡμῖν[2] κρείττονα ἡγεῖσθαι τῆς εἰρήνης τὸν
πόλεμον· ὅταν μέν γε πολεμῶμεν, τοὺς ἐχθροὺς
κακῶς ποιοῦμεν, ὅταν δ' εἰρήνην ἄγωμεν, τοὺς
5 φίλους. καίτοι, ὦ δημόται, εἰ μὲν ἅπαντα τὰ
βουλεύματα τοῦ συνεδρίου καλὰ καὶ συμφέροντα
ἡγεῖσθ' εἶναι, ὥσπερ ἐστί, τί οὐχὶ καὶ τοῦτο ἓν ἐξ
αὐτῶν ὑπολαμβάνετ' εἶναι; εἰ δὲ μηδὲν ἁπλῶς
τὴν βουλὴν τῶν δεόντων οἴεσθε φρονεῖν, ἀλλ'
αἰσχρῶς καὶ κακῶς τὴν πόλιν ἐπιτροπεύειν, τί δή
ποτε οὐχὶ μεταστησάμενοι αὐτὴν ἀθρόαν, αὐτοὶ
ἄρχετε καὶ βουλεύετε καὶ τοὺς ὑπὲρ τῆς ἡγεμονίας
πολέμους ἐκφέρετε, ἀλλὰ περικνίζετε αὐτὴν καὶ
κατὰ μικρὰ διαλύετε τοὺς ἐπιφανεστάτους ἀναρπά-
ζοντες ἐν ταῖς δίκαις; ἄμεινον γὰρ ἦν[3] ἅπασιν
ἡμῖν κοινῇ πολεμεῖσθαι ἢ καθ' ἕνα ἕκαστον ἰδίᾳ
6 συκοφαντεῖσθαι. ἀλλὰ γὰρ οὐχ ὑμεῖς αἴτιοι τούτων, ὥσπερ ἔφην, ἀλλ' οἱ συνταράττοντες ὑμᾶς
δημαγωγοὶ οὔτε ἄρχεσθαι ὑπομένοντες οὔτε ἄρχειν
εἰδότες. καὶ ὅσον μὲν ἐπὶ τῇ τούτων ἀφροσύνῃ τε
καὶ ἀπειρίᾳ πολλάκις ἂν ὑμῖν τόδε τὸ σκάφος
ἀνετράπη, νῦν δ' ἡ[4] τὰ τούτων σφάλματα ἐπανορ-
θοῦσα καὶ ἐν ὀρθῇ παρέχουσα ὑμῖν τῇ πόλει πλεῖν,[5]
ἡ πλεῖστα δεινὰ ὑπ' αὐτῶν ἀκούουσά ἐστι βουλή.
7 ταῦτα εἴτε ἡδέα ἐστὶν ὑμῖν ἀκούειν εἴτε ἀνιαρά,
μετὰ πάσης ἀληθείας εἴρηταί μοι καὶ τετόλμηται·

---

[1] Kiessling : πάρεστιν O, παρέστη Sintenis, Jacoby, παρ-
έστηκεν Post.   [2] ἡμῖν R (?) : ὑμῖν ABb.
[3] ἦν om. B.   [4] δ' ἡ Reiske : δὴ Ba, δὲ ABb.
[5] πλεῖν added here by Jacoby, after ὀρθῇ by Reiske.

even as is the sea by winds that spring up one after another, and you do not permit the commonwealth to remain calm and serene for even the briefest space of time. The result, therefore, is that we prefer war to peace ; at any rate, when we Romans are at war, we hurt our enemies, but when at peace, our friends. And yet, plebeians, if you regard all the resolutions of the senate as excellent and advantageous, as they really are, why do you not assume this also to be one of them ? If, however, you believe that the senate takes no thought at all for the things it should, but governs the commonwealth dishonourably and basely, why in the world do you not abolish it bag and baggage and yourselves govern and deliberate and wage wars in defence of our empire, rather than pare it down and destroy it by degrees by making away with its most important members in your trials ? For it would be better for all of us to be attacked together in war than for each one separately to be the victim of false accusations. However, it is not you, as I said, who are the authors of these disorders, but rather the demagogues, who keep you stirred up and who are neither willing to be ruled nor capable of ruling. Indeed, so far as their imprudence and inexperience could accomplish it, this ship of yours would have foundered many times over ; but as it is, the power which corrects their errors and enables your common-wealth to sail on an even keel is the senate, so greatly maligned by them. These remarks, whether they are pleasant for you to hear or vexatious, have been uttered and hazarded by me in all sincerity ; and I

31

καὶ μᾶλλον αἱροίμην ἂν παρρησίᾳ συμφερούσῃ τῷ
κοινῷ χρώμενος ἀποθανεῖν ἢ τὰ πρὸς ἡδονὴν ὑμῖν
λέγων σεσῶσθαι.''

XXXIII. Τοιούτους εἰπὼν λόγους καὶ οὔτε πρὸς
ὀλοφυρμοὺς καὶ ἀνακλαύσεις τῆς συμφορᾶς τραπό-
μενος οὔτε ἐν δεήσεσι καὶ προκυλισμοῖς ἀσχήμο-
σι ταπεινὸς φανεὶς οὔτ' ἄλλην ἀγεννῆ διάθεσιν
ἀποδειξάμενος οὐδεμίαν παρέδωκε τὸν λόγον τοῖς
συναγορεύειν ἢ μαρτυρεῖν βουλομένοις. πολλοὶ μὲν
οὖν καὶ ἄλλοι παριόντες ἀπέλυον αὐτὸν τῆς αἰτίας,
μάλιστα δὲ Οὐεργίνιος ὁ κατὰ τὸν αὐτὸν ὑπατεύσας
χρόνον καὶ τῆς νίκης αἴτιος εἶναι δοκῶν· ὃς οὐ
μόνον ἀναίτιον αὐτὸν ἀπέφαινεν, ἀλλὰ καὶ ὡς
κράτιστον ἀνδρῶν τὰ πολέμια καὶ στρατηγῶν
φρονιμώτατον ἐπαινεῖσθαί τε καὶ τιμᾶσθαι ὑπὸ
2 πάντων ἠξίου. ἔφη δὲ δεῖν, εἰ μὲν ἀγαθὸν οἴονται
τέλος εἰληφέναι τὸν πόλεμον, ἀμφοτέροις σφίσι
τὴν χάριν εἰδέναι, εἰ δὲ πονηρόν, ἀμφοτέρους ζη-
μιοῦν· κοινὰ γὰρ αὐτοῖς καὶ τὰ βουλεύματα καὶ
τὰ ἔργα καὶ τὰς ἐκ τοῦ δαιμονίου τύχας γεγονέναι.
ἦν δ' οὐ μόνον ὁ λόγος τοῦ ἀνδρὸς ἀλλὰ καὶ ὁ
βίος πείθων, ἐν ἅπασιν ἐξητασμένος ἔργοις ἀγα-
3 θοῖς. προσῆν δὲ τούτοις, ὃ πλεῖστον ἐκίνησεν
οἶκτον, ὄψεως σχῆμα συμπαθές, οἷον περὶ αὐτοὺς
τοὺς πεπονθότας ἢ μέλλοντας πάσχειν τὰ δεινὰ
γίνεσθαι φιλεῖ. ὥστε καὶ τοὺς προσήκοντας τοῖς
ἀπολωλόσι καὶ δοκοῦντας ἀδιαλλάκτως ἔχειν πρὸς
τὸν αἴτιον σφίσι τῆς συμφορᾶς μαλακωτέρους γενέσθαι καὶ ἀποθέσθαι τὴν ὀργήν, ὡς ἐδήλωσαν.

had rather lose my life by using a freedom of speech that is advantageous for the commonwealth than save it by flattering you."

XXXIII. Having spoken in this manner and without either resorting to lamentations and wailings over his misfortune or abasing himself by entreaties and unseemly grovelling at the feet of anyone, and without displaying any other mark of an ignoble nature, he yielded the floor to those who desired to speak or bear witness in his favour. Many came forward and sought to clear him of the charge, and particularly Verginius, who had been consul at the same time with him and was regarded as having been the cause of the victory. He not only declared Servilius to be innocent, but argued that, as the bravest of men in war and the most prudent of generals, he deserved to be praised and honoured by all. He said that if they thought the war had ended favourably, they ought to feel grateful to both commanders, but if unfavourably, they ought to punish them both ; for not only their plans, but also their actions and the fortunes meted out to them by Heaven had belonged to them both alike. Not only were the man's words convincing, but his whole life as well, which had been tested in all manner of good deeds. He had moreover—and this it was that stirred the greatest compassion—a look of fellow-suffering, such a look as one is apt to see on the faces of those who themselves have suffered calamities or are about to suffer them. Hence even the relations of the men who had lost their lives in the battle and seemed irreconcilable to the author of their misfortune became softened and laid aside their resentment, as they presently made evident. For

ἀναδοθεισῶν γὰρ τῶν ψήφων οὐδεμία φυλὴ τοῦ
ἀνδρὸς κατεψηφίσατο. ὁ μὲν οὖν τὸν Σερουΐλιον
καταλαβὼν κίνδυνος τοιούτου τέλους ἔτυχεν.

XXXIV. Οὐ πολλῷ δ᾽ ὕστερον χρόνῳ στρατιὰ
Ῥωμαίων ἐξῆλθεν ἐπὶ Τυρρηνοὺς ἄγοντος θατέρου
τῶν ὑπάτων Ποπλίου Οὐαλερίου. συνέστη γὰρ
αὖθις ἡ Οὐιεντανῶν δύναμις προσθεμένων αὐτοῖς
Σαβίνων, οἳ τέως ὀκνοῦντες αὐτοῖς συνάρασθαι τοῦ
πολέμου ὡς ἀδυνάτων ἐφιεμένοις, τότε, ἐπειδὴ τήν
τε Μενηνίου φυγὴν ἔγνωσαν καὶ τὸν ἐπιτειχισμὸν
τοῦ πλησίον τῆς Ῥώμης ὄρους, τεταπεινῶσθαι
νομίσαντες τάς τε[1] δυνάμεις τὰς[2] Ῥωμαίων καὶ
τὸ φρόνημα τῆς πόλεως ἡττῆσθαι, συνελάμβανον
2 τοῖς Τυρρηνοῖς πολλὴν ἀποστείλαντες δύναμιν. οἱ
δὲ Οὐιεντανοὶ τῇ τε σφετέρᾳ δυνάμει πεποιθότες
καὶ τῇ Σαβίνων νεωστὶ ἡκούσῃ καὶ[3] τὰς παρὰ τῶν
ἄλλων Τυρρηνῶν ἐπικουρίας περιμένοντες προθυμίαν μὲν εἶχον ἐπὶ τὴν Ῥώμην ἐλαύνειν τῇ πλείονι
τῆς σφετέρας στρατιᾶς, ὡς οὐδενὸς αὐτοῖς ὁμόσε
χωρήσοντος, ἀλλὰ δυεῖν θάτερον, ἢ ἐκ τειχομαχίας
αἱρήσοντες τὴν πόλιν ἢ λιμῷ κατεργασόμενοι.[4]
3 ἔφθασε δὲ τὴν ἐπιχείρησιν αὐτῶν ὁ Οὐαλέριος, ἐν
ᾧ ἔτι ἔμελλον ἐκεῖνοι καὶ τοὺς ὑστερίζοντας συμμάχους ἀνέμενον, αὐτὸς ἀγαγὼν Ῥωμαίων τὴν
κρατίστην ἀκμὴν καὶ τὸ παρὰ τῶν συμμάχων ἐπι-
κουρικόν, οὐκ ἐκ τοῦ φανεροῦ ποιησάμενος τὴν
ἔξοδον, ἀλλ᾽ ὡς μάλιστα λήσεσθαι αὐτοὺς ἔμελλε.
προελθὼν γὰρ ἐκ τῆς Ῥώμης περὶ δείλην ὀψίαν
καὶ διαβὰς τὸν Τέβεριν, οὐ μακρὰν ἀποσχὼν τῆς
πόλεως κατεστρατοπέδευσεν· ἔπειτ᾽ ἀναστήσας τὴν

---

[1] τε deleted by Reiske.   [2] τὰς B : om. R.
[3] καὶ Cmg : om. R.

when the votes had been taken, not a single tribe condemned him. Such was the outcome of the jeopardy in which Servilius had been placed.

XXXIV. Not long afterwards [1] an army of the Romans marched out against the Tyrrhenians under the command of Publius Valerius, one of the consuls. For the forces of the Veientes had again assembled and had been joined by the Sabines. The latter had hitherto hesitated to assist them in the war, fearing that they were aiming at the impossible ; but now, when they learned both of the flight of Menenius and of the fortifying of the hill close to the city, concluding that the forces of the Romans had been humbled and that the spirit of the commonwealth had been broken, they proceeded to aid the Tyrrhenians, sending them a large body of troops. The Veientes, relying both on their own forces and on those of the Sabines which had just come to them, and expecting reinforcements from the rest of the Tyrrhenians, were eager to march on Rome with the greater part of their army, in the belief that none would oppose them, but that they should either take the city by storm or reduce it by famine. But Valerius forestalled their plan, while they were still delaying and waiting for the allies who tarried, by setting out himself with the flower of the Roman youth and with the auxiliary force from the allies, not openly, but in such a manner as would conceal his march from the enemy so far as possible. For, advancing from Rome in the late afternoon and crossing the Tiber, he encamped at a short distance from the city ; then, rousing the army about mid-

---

[1] For chaps. 34 f. *cf.* Livy ii. 53.

⁴ κατεργασόμενοι C : κατεργασάμενοι AB.

στρατιὰν περὶ μέσας νύκτας ἦγεν ἐν τάχει,[1] καὶ
πρὶν ἡμέραν γενέσθαι θατέρῳ χάρακι τῶν πολε-
4 μίων ἐπέβαλε. δύο γὰρ ἦν στρατόπεδα, χωρὶς μὲν
τὸ Τυρρηνῶν, ἑτέρωθι δὲ τὸ Σαβίνων, οὐ διὰ
μακροῦ ἀλλήλων ἀπέχοντα. πρώτη δὲ προσαγα-
γὼν τὴν δύναμιν τῇ Σαβίνων στρατοπεδείᾳ, καθ-
υπνωμένων ἔτι τῶν πλείστων καὶ οὐδεμιᾶς οὔσης
ἀξιολόγου φυλακῆς, οἷα ἐν φιλίᾳ τε γῇ καὶ κατὰ
πολλὴν ὑπεροψίαν τῶν πολεμίων οὐδαμῇ ἀγγελ-
λομένων, ἐξ ἐφόδου γίνεται ταύτης ἐγκρατής.
τῶν δ᾽ ἀνθρώπων οἱ μὲν ἐν ταῖς κοίταις ἔτι ὄντες
κατεσφάγησαν, οἱ δ᾽ ἀνιστάμενοι ἀρτίως καὶ τὰ
ὅπλα ἐνδυόμενοι, οἱ δ᾽ ὡπλισμένοι μέν, σποράδες
δὲ καὶ οὐκ ἐν τάξει ἀμυνόμενοι, οἱ δὲ πλεῖστοι
φεύγοντες ἐπὶ τὸν ἕτερον χάρακα ὑπὸ τῶν ἱππέων
καταλαμβανόμενοι διεφθάρησαν.

XXXV. Τοῦτον δὲ τὸν τρόπον ἁλόντος τοῦ τῶν
Σαβίνων χάρακος ἦγε τὴν δύναμιν ὁ Οὐαλέριος
ἐπὶ τὸν ἕτερον, ἔνθα ἦσαν οἱ Οὐιεντανοὶ χωρίον οὐ
πάνυ ἐχυρὸν κατειληφότες. λαθεῖν μὲν οὖν οὐκέτι
ἐνεδέχετο τοὺς προσιόντας τῷ χάρακι· ἡμέρα τε
γὰρ ἦν ἤδη λαμπρά, καὶ τῶν Σαβίνων οἱ φεύγοντες[2] ἀπήγγειλαν τοῖς Τυρρηνοῖς τήν τε αὑτῶν συμφορὰν καὶ τὴν ἐπ᾽ ἐκείνους ἔλασιν· ἀναγκαῖον δ᾽
ἦν ἐκ τοῦ καρτεροῦ[3] τοῖς πολεμίοις συμφέρεσθαι.
2 γίνεται δὴ μετὰ τοῦτο πάσῃ προθυμίᾳ τῶν Τυρρηνῶν ἀγωνιζομένων πρὸ τῆς παρεμβολῆς ὀξεῖα
μάχη καὶ φόνος ἀμφοτέρων πολύς, ἰσόρροπός τε
καὶ μέχρι πολλοῦ ταλαντευομένη τῇδε καὶ τῇδε ἡ
κρίσις τοῦ πολέμου. ἔπειτα ἐνέδοσαν οἱ Τυρρηνοὶ

---

[1] ἐν τάχει Kiessling : ἐν τάξει O.
[2] φυγόντες Sintenis, Jacoby.

night, he marched in haste[1] and, before it was day, attacked one of the enemy's camps. For there were two camps, separate but at no great distance from one another, one of the Tyrrhenians and the other of the Sabines. The first camp he attacked was that of the Sabines, where most of the men were still asleep and there was no guard worth mentioning, inasmuch as they were in friendly territory and felt great contempt for the enemy, whose presence had not been reported from any quarter ; and he took it by storm. Some of the Sabines were slain in their beds, others just as they were getting up and arming themselves, and still others, who, though armed, were dispersed and fighting in disorder ; but the larger part of them were intercepted and destroyed by the Roman horse while they were endeavouring to escape to the other camp.

XXXV. The camp of the Sabines having thus been taken, Valerius led his forces to the other camp, where the Veientes lay, having occupied a position that was not very strong. Here it was not possible for the attackers to approach the camp without being seen, since it was now broad daylight and the fleeing Sabines had informed the Tyrrhenians both of their own disaster and of the advance of the Romans against the others ; hence it was necessary to attack the enemy with might and main. Then, as the Tyrrhenians fought before their camp with all possible vigour, a sharp action ensued, with great slaughter on both sides ; and the decision of the battle was equally balanced, shifting to and fro for a long time. At last

[1] " In haste " is Kiessling's emendation for " in battle array," the reading of the MSS.

---

[3] κατὰ τὸ καρτερὸν Cobet.

ὑπὸ τῆς Ῥωμαϊκῆς ἐξωσθέντες ἵππου καὶ ἀπ-
εχώρησαν εἰς τὸν χάρακα, ὁ δ' ὕπατος ἠκολούθει,
καὶ ἐπειδὴ πλησίον ἐγένετο τῶν ἐρυμάτων (ἦν δὲ
φαύλως κατεσκευασμένα καὶ τὸ χωρίον, ὥσπερ
ἔφην, οὐ πάνυ ἀσφαλές) προσέβαλε κατὰ πολλὰ
μέρη τό τε λοιπὸν ἐκείνης τῆς ἡμέρας μέρος
ἐπιταλαιπωρῶν καὶ οὐδὲ τὴν ἐπιοῦσαν νύκτα ἀνα-
3 παυσάμενος. οἱ δὲ Τυρρηνοὶ ταῖς συνεχέσι κακο-
παθείαις ἀπειρηκότες ἐκλείπουσι τὸν χάρακα περὶ
τὸν ὄρθρον καὶ οἱ μὲν εἰς τὴν πόλιν ἔφυγον,[1] οἱ δ'
εἰς τὰς πλησίον ὕλας ἐσκεδάσθησαν. γενόμενος δὲ
καὶ τούτου τοῦ χάρακος ἐγκρατὴς ἐκείνην μὲν τὴν
ἡμέραν ἀνέπαυσε τὴν στρατιάν, τῇ δ' ἑξῆς τά τε
λάφυρα ὅσα ἐξ ἀμφοτέρων εἰλήφει τῶν στρατο-
πέδων διένειμε τοῖς ἀγωνισαμένοις πολλὰ ὄντα, καὶ
τοὺς ἀριστεύσαντας ἐν ταῖς μάχαις τοῖς εἰωθόσιν
4 ἐκόσμει στεφάνοις. ἦν δ' ὁ κράτιστα πάντων
ἀγωνίσασθαι δόξας καὶ τρεψάμενος τὴν Οὐιεντανῶν δύναμιν Σερουΐλιος ὁ τῷ προτέρῳ ὑπατεύσας
ἔτει καὶ τὴν ἐπὶ τοῦ δήμου δίκην ἀποφυγών,
πρεσβευτὴς τότε τῷ Οὐαλερίῳ συμπεμφθείς, καὶ
ἐπὶ τῇ ἀριστείᾳ τῇδε τὰς νομιζομένας εἶναι μεγί-
στας παρὰ Ῥωμαίοις δωρεὰς οὗτος ἦν ὁ πρῶτος
ἐξενεγκάμενος. μετὰ ταῦτα τούς τε τῶν πολεμίων
σκυλεύσας νεκροὺς ὁ ὕπατος καὶ τῶν ἰδίων ταφὰς
ποιησάμενος ἀπῆγε[2] τὴν στρατιὰν καὶ πλησίον τῆς
Οὐιεντανῶν πόλεως[3] καταστήσας προὐκαλεῖτο τοὺς
5 ἔνδον. ὡς δ' οὐδεὶς ἐξῄει μαχησόμενος ἄπορον ὁρῶν
χρῆμα ἐκ τειχομαχίας αὐτοὺς ἑλεῖν ἐχυρὰν σφόδρα
ἔχοντας πόλιν, τῆς γῆς αὐτῶν πολλὴν καταδραμὼν

---

[1] Sylburg : ἔφευγον O.   [2] Sintenis : ἐξῆγε O.
[3] πόλεως Sylburg : χώρας O.

the Tyrrhenians, forced back by the Roman horse, gave way and retired to their camp. The consul followed, and when he came near their ramparts— these had been poorly constructed and the place, as I said, was not very secure—he attacked them in many places at once, continuing his exhausting efforts all the rest of that day and not even resting the following night. The Tyrrhenians, exhausted by their continual hardships, left their camp at break of day, some fleeing to their city and others dispersing themselves in the neighbouring woods. The consul, having made himself master of this camp also, rested his army that day; then, on the next day he distributed to the men who had shared in the fighting the spoils, great in quantity, which he had taken in both camps, and honoured with the customary crowns those who had distinguished themselves in the battles. The man who was regarded as having fought with the greatest bravery of all and put the troops of the Veientes to flight was Servilius, the consul of the preceding year, who had been acquitted in his trial before the populace and now had been sent along as legate to Valerius; and in consideration of the superior valour he showed upon this occasion he was the first to receive the rewards which among the Romans are the most esteemed. After that the consul, having stripped the enemy's dead and buried his own, marched away with his army, and encamping near the city of the Veientes, challenged those inside to give battle. But when none ventured out to fight and he saw that it would be a difficult matter to capture them by assault, occupying as they did a city that was exceedingly strong, he overran a great part of their country and then invaded that of the

εἰς τὴν Σαβίνων ἐνέβαλε. λεηλατήσας δὲ κἀκείνην
ἔτι ἀκέραιον οὖσαν ἐπὶ πολλὰς ἡμέρας καὶ βαρεῖαν
ἤδη τὴν ἀποσκευὴν ἔχων ταῖς ὠφελείαις ἀπῆγεν
ἐπ᾽ οἴκου τὴν δύναμιν· καὶ αὐτῷ ὁ μὲν δῆμος πρὸ
πολλοῦ τῆς πόλεως ὄντι ἐστεφανωμένος ὑπήντα
λιβανωτοῖς τε θυμιῶν τὴν πάροδον καὶ κρατῆρσι
μελικράτου κεκραμένοις ὑποδεχόμενος τὴν στρα-
τιάν· ἡ δὲ βουλὴ τὴν τοῦ θριάμβου πομπὴν ἐψηφίσατο.

6 Ὁ δ᾽ ἕτερος τῶν ὑπάτων Γάιος Ναύτιος, ᾧ
προσέκειτο κατὰ κλῆρον ἡ τῶν συμμάχων Λατίνων
τε καὶ Ἑρνίκων φυλακή, βραδυτέραν ἐποιήσατο
τὴν ἔξοδον, οὔτε ἀπορίᾳ οὔτε ὄκνῳ τοῦ κινδύνου
κρατηθείς, τὴν δ᾽ ἀδηλότητα τοῦ πρὸς Οὐιεντανοὺς
πολέμου καραδοκῶν, ἵν᾽ ἐάν τι συμβῇ πταῖσμα
περὶ τὴν ἐκεῖ στρατιὰν ἐν ἑτοίμῳ τις ὑπάρχῃ τῇ
πόλει συνεστῶσα δύναμις ἢ κωλύσει τοὺς πολεμίους εἰς τὴν χώραν ἐμβαλεῖν, ἐὰν ὥσπερ[1] οἱ πρότερον ἐλάσαντες ἐπὶ τὴν Ῥώμην ἐπιτειχίζειν τινὰ
7 κατὰ τῆς πόλεως χωρία ἐπιβάλωνται. ἐν δὲ τῷ
μεταξὺ τούτου χρόνῳ καὶ ὁ κατὰ τῶν Λατίνων
πόλεμος, ὃν ἐπῆγον αὐτοῖς Αἰκανοί τε καὶ Οὐολοῦσκοι, τέλος εὐτυχὲς ἔσχε· καὶ παρῆσάν τινες
ἀγγέλλοντες μάχῃ νικηθέντας ἀπεληλυθέναι τοὺς
πολεμίους ἐκ τῆς χώρας αὐτῶν, καὶ μηδεμιᾶς τοῖς
συμμάχοις ἔτι δεῖν βοηθείας κατὰ τὸ παρόν· ὁ
μέντοι Ναύτιος οὐδὲν ἧττον, ἐπειδὴ τὰ ἐν τῇ Τυρ-
ρηνίᾳ πράγματα καλῶς σφίσιν ἐχώρησεν, ἐξῆγε τὴν
8 στρατιάν. ἐμβαλὼν δ᾽ εἰς τὴν Οὐολούσκων χώραν
καὶ πολλὴν αὐτῆς διεξελθὼν ἔρημον ἀφειμένην,
ἀνδραπόδων μὲν καὶ βοσκημάτων ὀλίγων πάνυ[2]

_____
[1] ὥσπερ Steph. : ὅπερ ABC.

Sabines. For many days he plundered their territory too, which was still untouched, and then, since his baggage train was now heavily laden with booty, he led his troops homeward. While he was yet a long way from the city he was met by the people, who, crowned with garlands, perfumed the route with frankincense as he entered and received the army with bowls of honeyed wine. And the senate decreed to him the celebration of a triumph.

The other consul, Gaius Nautius, to whom the defence of their allies the Latins and the Hernicans had fallen by lot, had delayed taking the field, not because he was swayed by any irresolution or fear of danger, but because he was awaiting the uncertain outcome of the war with the Veientes, to the end that, if any misfortune should befall the army employed against them the commonwealth might have another force assembled in readiness to hinder the enemy from making an irruption into the country, in case this foe, like those who had earlier marched against Rome, should attempt to fortify any places as a threat to the city. In the meantime the war brought upon the Latins by the Aequians and the Volscians had been happily concluded and messengers had arrived announcing that the enemy, defeated in battle, had left the territory of the Latins and that these allies no longer stood in any need of assistance for the present. Nevertheless, Nautius, after affairs in Tyrrhenia had taken a happy turn for the Romans, marched out with his army. Then, having invaded the country of the Volscians and overrun a great part of it which they had left deserted, he possessed

---

² πόνυ B : om. R.

ἐκράτησεν, ἀρούρας δ' αὐτῶν ἐν ἀκμῇ τοῦ σίτου
ὄντος ἐμπρήσας καὶ ἄλλα οὐκ ὀλίγα τῶν ἐν τοῖς
ἀγροῖς λωβησάμενος οὐδενὸς ὁμόσε χωροῦντος
ἀπῆγε τὴν στρατιάν· ταῦτα μὲν ἐπὶ τούτων τῶν
ἀνδρῶν ἐπράχθη.

XXXVI. Οἱ δὲ διαδεξάμενοι τούτους ὕπατοι
Αὖλος Μάλλιος καὶ Λεύκιος Φούριος, ψηφισαμένης
τῆς βουλῆς τὸν ἕτερον αὐτῶν στρατιὰν ἐπὶ Οὐιεντανοὺς ἄγειν, ἐκληρώσαντο περὶ τῆς ἐξόδου, καθάπερ αὐτοῖς ἔθος ἦν. καὶ λαχὼν Μάλλιος ἐξῆγε τὰς
δυνάμεις διὰ ταχέων καὶ πλησίον τῶν πολεμίων
κατεστρατοπέδευσεν. οἱ δὲ Οὐιεντανοὶ τειχήρεις
γενόμενοι τέως μὲν ἀντεῖχον καὶ διεπρεσβεύοντο
πρός τε τὰς ἄλλας τὰς ἐν Τυρρηνοῖς πόλεις καὶ
πρὸς τοὺς νεωστὶ συμμαχήσαντας αὐτοῖς Σαβίνους,
βοήθειαν ἀξιοῦντες ἀποστεῖλαι σφίσι διὰ ταχέων.
2 ὡς δ' ἁπάντων ἀπετύγχανον καὶ τὰς τροφὰς ἀπ-
αναλώκεσαν, ὑπὸ τῆς ἀνάγκης[1] βιασθέντες ἐξῆλθον
ὡς τὸν ὕπατον, ἱκετηρίας φέροντες οἱ πρεσβύτατοί
τ' αὐτῶν καὶ τιμιώτατοι, περὶ καταλύσεως δεόμενοι
τοῦ πολέμου. τοῦ δὲ Μαλλίου κελεύσαντος αὐτοῖς
ἀργύριόν τε εἰς ὀψωνιασμὸν ἐνιαυτοῦ τῇ στρατιᾷ
καὶ διμήνου τροφὰς ἀποφέρειν, ὅταν δὲ ταῦτα ποιή-
σωσιν, εἰς Ῥώμην ἀποστέλλειν τοὺς διαλεξομένους
τῇ βουλῇ περὶ τῶν διαλύσεων, ἐπαινέσαντες ταῦτα
καὶ διὰ ταχέων τό τε ὀψώνιον τῇ στρατιᾷ καὶ τὸ
ἀντὶ τοῦ σίτου συγχωρηθὲν ὑπὸ τοῦ Μαλλίου κατ-
ενέγκαντες[2] ἀργύριον ἧκον εἰς τὴν Ῥώμην· καὶ
καταστάντες ἐπὶ τὴν βουλὴν συγγνώμης ἐπὶ τοῖς
γεγονόσι τυχεῖν ἠξίουν καὶ εἰς τὸν λοιπὸν χρόνον

[1] τοῦ λιμοῦ after ἀνάγκης deleted by Kiessling.
[2] Jacoby : κατενεγκόντες O.

himself of a very few slaves and cattle, and having set fire to their fields, the corn being then ripe, and done not a little other damage to their farmsteads, as none came to oppose him, he led his army home. These were the things accomplished in the consulship of those men.

XXXVI. Their successors in the consulship,[1] Aulus Manlius and Lucius Furius, after the senate had voted that one of them should march against the Veientes, drew lots, according to their custom, to determine which should command the expedition. And the lot falling to Manlius, he speedily led out the troops and encamped near the enemy. The Veientes, being shut up within their walls, defended themselves for some time ; and sending ambassadors both to the other cities of Tyrrhenia and to the Sabines who had lately assisted them, they asked them to send them aid promptly. But when they failed of everything they asked for and had consumed all their provisions, the oldest and most honoured among them, compelled by necessity, came out of the city to the consul with the tokens of suppliants, begging for an end to the war. Manlius ordered them to bring money for a year's pay for the army and provisions for two months and after doing this to send envoys to Rome to treat with the senate for peace. And they, having approved these conditions and speedily brought the pay for the army, together with the money which the consul permitted them to pay in lieu of the corn, came to Rome ; and being introduced into the senate, they sought to obtain forgiveness for the past and for

[1] *Cf.* Livy ii. 54, 1 f.

3 ἀπαλλαγῆς τοῦ πολέμου. πολλῶν δὲ λεχθέντων εἰς
ἀμφότερα τὰ μέρη λόγων ἐνίκησεν ἡ σπένδεσθαι
παραινοῦσα τὸν πρὸς αὐτοὺς πόλεμον γνώμη,
γίνονταί τ᾽ ἀνοχαὶ τοῦ πολέμου πρὸς αὐτοὺς
τεσσαρακονταετεῖς. καὶ οἱ μὲν ἀπῇεσαν πολλὰς
τῇ πόλει τῆς εἰρήνης χάριτας εἰδότες, ὁ δὲ Μάλλιος ἀφικόμενος εἰς τὴν πόλιν, ἐπὶ τῇ καταλύσει
τοῦ πολέμου τὸν πεζὸν θρίαμβον αἰτησάμενος,
ἔλαβεν. ἐγένετο δὲ καὶ τίμησις ἐπὶ τῆς τούτων
ἀρχῆς, καὶ ἦσαν οἱ τιμησάμενοι πολῖται σφᾶς τε
αὐτοὺς καὶ χρήματα καὶ τοὺς ἐν ἥβῃ παῖδας
ὀλίγῳ πλείους τρισχιλίων τε καὶ δέκα[1] μυριάδων.

XXXVII. Οἱ δὲ μετὰ τούτους παραλαβόντες
τὴν ὕπατον ἀρχήν, Λεύκιος Αἰμίλιος Μάμερκος τὸ
τρίτον, καὶ Οὐοπίσκος Ἰούλιος, ἐπὶ τῆς ἑβδόμης
καὶ ἑβδομηκοστῆς ὀλυμπιάδος, ἣν ἐνίκα στάδιον
Δάνδης[2] Ἀργεῖος, Ἀθήνησι δ᾽ ἄρχοντος Χάρητος,
ἐπίπονον σφόδρα καὶ ταραχώδη τὴν ἀρχὴν διετέλεσαν, εἰρήνην μὲν ἄγοντες ἀπὸ τῶν ἔξωθεν πολέμων (ἐν ἡσυχίᾳ γὰρ ἦν πάντα τὰ διάφορα), ὑπὸ δὲ
τῶν ἐν τῇ πόλει στάσεων αὐτοί τε εἰς κινδύνους
ἀχθέντες καὶ τὴν πόλιν ὀλίγου δεήσαντες ἀπολέσαι.
ὡς γὰρ ἀνεπαύσατο τῶν στρατειῶν τὸ πλῆθος, ἐπὶ
τὴν διανομὴν εὐθὺς ὥρμησε τῶν δημοσίων ἀγρῶν.

2 ἦν γάρ τις ἐν τοῖς δημάρχοις θρασὺς καὶ λέγειν οὐκ
ἀδύνατος ἀνήρ, Γναῖος Γενύκιος, ὁ παραθήγων τὰς
ὀργὰς τῶν πενήτων. οὗτος ἐκκλησίας συνάγων
ἑκάστοτε καὶ ἐκδημαγωγῶν τοὺς ἀπόρους προσ-

---

[1] καὶ τρισκαίδεκα B.
[2] Rutgers (cf. Diod. xi. 53, 1) : δάτις A, δάντιος Ba, δάν-
τις Bb.

---

[1] Literally, " the triumph on foot " ; see v. 47, 2 f.

the future to be freed from the war. After many
arguments on both sides, the motion prevailed to put
an end to the war by a treaty, and a truce was granted
to them for forty years. Then the envoys departed,
feeling very grateful to the commonwealth for the
peace. And Manlius, coming to the city, requested
and received an ovation [1] for having put an end to
the war. There was also a census in this consulship ; the number of the citizens who registered
their own names, their wealth, and the names of
their sons who had reached manhood was a little
over 103,000. [2]

XXXVII. These consuls [3] were succeeded by
Lucius Aemilius Mamercus (elected for the third
time) and Vopiscus Julius, in the seventy-seventh
Olympiad [4] (the one at which Dandes of Argos won
the foot-race), when Chares was archon at Athens.
The administration of the new consuls was very difficult and turbulent ; they enjoyed peace, it is true,
from foreign wars—for all their quarrels were in a
state of quiet—but through the dissensions at home
they were not only themselves exposed to dangers,
but came near destroying the commonwealth as well.
For as soon as the populace had a respite from military expeditions, they at once became eager for a
distribution of the public lands. It seems there was
among the tribunes a certain bold man, not wanting
in eloquence, Gnaeus Genucius, who whetted the
passions of the poor. This man, by assembling the
populace on every occasion and cajoling the needy,

---

[2] One of our best MSS. (B) gives 133,000 ; but this is
probably a scribal error.

[3] For chaps. 37-39 *cf.* Livy ii. 54, 2–55, 11.

[4] 471 B.C.

ἠνάγκαζε τοὺς ὑπάτους τὰ ὑπὸ τῆς βουλῆς ψηφισ-
θέντα περὶ τῆς κληρουχίας συντελεῖν. οἱ δ' οὐχ
ὑπήκουον, οὐ τῇ ἑαυτῶν ἀρχῇ λέγοντες ἐπιτετάχθαι
τὸ ἔργον ὑπὸ τῆς βουλῆς, ἀλλὰ τοῖς μετὰ Κάσσιον
καὶ Οὐεργίνιον ὑπάτοις, πρὸς οὓς τὸ[1] προβούλευμα
ἐγράφη· καὶ ἅμα οὐδ' εἶναι νόμους εἰς ἀεὶ κυρίους
ἃ ψηφίζεται τὸ συνέδριον, ἀλλὰ πολιτεύματα και-
3 ρῶν[2] ἐνιαύσιον ἔχοντα ἰσχύν. ταύτας προβαλλο-
μένων τῶν ὑπάτων τὰς αἰτίας ἀδύνατος ὢν ὁ
Γενύκιος αὐτοὺς ἀναγκάσαι μείζονα ἐξουσίαν ἔχοντας ἰταμὴν ὁδὸν ἐτράπετο. τοῖς γὰρ ὑπατεύσασι
τὸ ἔμπροσθεν ἔτος Μαλλίῳ τε καὶ Λευκίῳ δίκην
ἐπήνεγκε δημοσίαν, καὶ προεῖπεν ἥκειν ἐπὶ τὸν
δῆμον ἀπολογησομένους, ὁρίσας ἄντικρυς τὴν αἰτίαν τῆς δίκης, ὅτι τὸν δῆμον ἀδικοῦσιν οὐκ ἀποδείξαντες τοὺς δέκα ἄνδρας οὓς ἐψηφίσατο ἡ βουλή,
4 τοὺς ποιησομένους τὴν τῶν κλήρων διανομήν. τοῦ
δὲ μὴ τῶν ἄλλων τινὰς ὑπάτων ἄγειν ἐπὶ τὴν δίκην,
δώδεκα γενομένων τῶν μεταξὺ ἀρχείων ἀφ' οὗ τὸ
προβούλευμα ἐγράφη, τούτους δὲ προβαλέσθαι τοὺς
ἄνδρας μόνους τῆς ψευσθείσης ὑποσχέσεως, ἐπιεικεῖς ἔφερεν αἰτίας· καὶ τελευτῶν ἔφη μόνως ἂν
οὕτως ἀναγκασθῆναι τοὺς ἐν ἀρχῇ τότε ὄντας
ὑπάτους κληρουχῆσαι τὴν γῆν, ἐὰν ἑτέρους τινὰς
ἴδωσι δίκην τῷ δήμῳ διδόντας, ἐνθυμηθέντας ὅτι
καὶ σφίσιν αὐτοῖς συμβήσεται τὸ αὐτὸ παθεῖν.

XXXVIII. Ταῦτ' εἰπὼν καὶ παρακαλέσας ἅπαν-

[1] τὸ ABa : καὶ τὸ Bb, Jacoby.
[2] καιρῶν B : καιρὸν R ; πολιτεύματα ἕνεκα καιρῶν or π. κατὰ
καιρὸν Capps.

---

[1] Cf. viii. 76, 2.
[2] The decree was passed late in the year 484 (viii. 76, 2) ;

was endeavouring to force the consuls to carry out the decree of the senate concerning the allotment of lands. But the consuls kept refusing to do so, alleging that this duty had been assigned by the senate, not to them, but to the consuls who immediately followed Cassius and Verginius, with reference to whom the preliminary decree had been drawn up.[1] At the same time they pointed out that decrees of the senate were not laws continuing in force forever, but measures designed to meet temporary needs and having validity for one year only. When the consuls put forward these excuses, Genucius, finding himself unable to employ compulsion against them, since they were invested with a superior authority, took a bold course. He brought a public suit against Manlius and Lucius, the consuls of the preceding year, and summoned them to appear before the populace and make their defence, specifying openly the ground for the action, which was that they had wronged the populace in not appointing the decemvirs directed by the senate to distribute the allotments of land. And he advanced plausible reasons for not bringing to trial some of the other consuls, though there had been twelve consulships in the interval since the senate had drawn up this decree,[2] and for accusing only these men of violating the promise. He ended by saying that the only way the present consuls could be compelled to allot the land would be for them to see some others punished by the populace and thus be reminded that it would be their fate to meet with the same treatment.

XXXVIII. After he had said this and exhorted

Genucius was tribune in 471. (Both dates according to Dionysius' chronology.)

τὰς ἥκειν[1] ἐπὶ τὴν δίκην, καθ' ἱερῶν τε ὀμόσας ἦ
μὴν ἐμμενεῖν τοῖς ἐγνωσμένοις καὶ πάσῃ προθυμίᾳ
τῶν ἀνδρῶν κατηγορήσειν,[2] ἡμέραν προεῖπεν ἐν ᾗ
τὴν δίκην ἔμελλεν ἐπιτελέσειν. τοὺς δὲ πατρικίους,
ὡς ἔμαθον ταῦτα, πολὺ δέος εἰσέρχεται καὶ φροντίς,
ὅτῳ χρὴ τρόπῳ τούς τε ἄνδρας ἐκλύσασθαι τῆς
αἰτίας καὶ τοῦ δημαγωγοῦ τὸ θράσος ἐπισχεῖν.
καὶ δὴ ἐδέδοκτο αὐτοῖς, εἴ τι ψηφίσαιτο κατὰ τῆς
ἀρχῆς τῶν ὑπάτων ὁ δῆμος, μὴ ἐπιτρέπειν αὐτῷ
κατὰ τὸ καρτερὸν ἐνισταμένους καὶ εἰ δέοι καὶ εἰς
2 ὅπλα χωροῦντας. οὐ μὴν ἐδέησέ γε τῶν βιαίων
οὐδενὸς αὐτοῖς ταχεῖαν λαβόντος τοῦ κινδύνου καὶ
παράδοξον τὴν λύσιν· μιᾶς γὰρ ἡμέρας οὔσης ἔτι
λοιπῆς τῇ δίκῃ[3] νεκρὸς Γενύκιος ἐπὶ τῆς ἑαυτοῦ
κοίτης εὑρέθη, σημεῖον οὐδὲν ἔχων οὔτε σφαγῆς
οὔτε ἀγχόνης οὔτε φαρμάκου οὔτ' ἄλλου τῶν ἐξ
ἐπιβουλῆς θανάτων οὐδενός. ὡς δ' ἐγνώσθη τὸ
πάθος καὶ προηνέχθη τὸ σῶμα εἰς τὴν ἀγοράν,
δαιμόνιόν τι κωλύσεως συγκύρημα ἔδοξεν εἶναι,
3 καὶ αὐτίκα ἡ δίκη διελέλυτο. τῶν γὰρ ἄλλων
οὐδεὶς ἐτόλμα δημάρχων ἀνακαλεῖν τὴν στάσιν,
ἀλλὰ καὶ τοῦ Γενυκίου κατεγίνωσκον πολλὴν
μανίαν. εἰ μὲν οὖν μηδὲν ἔτι πολυπραγμονοῦντες
οἱ ὕπατοι διετέλεσαν ἀλλ' ἀφῆκαν ὡς ὁ δαίμων
ἐκοίμησε τὴν στάσιν, οὐδεὶς ἂν αὐτοὺς ἔτι κατέλαβε
κίνδυνος, νῦν δ' εἰς αὐθάδειαν καὶ καταφρόνησιν
τοῦ δημοτικοῦ τραπόμενοι καὶ τὸ τῆς ἀρχῆς κράτος
ὅσον ἐστὶν ἐπιδεῖξαι βουλόμενοι, κακὰ ἐξειργάσαντο
μεγάλα. προθέντες γὰρ στρατολογίαν καὶ τοὺς οὐχ

---

[1] ἥκειν Sylburg : ἦγεν O.
[2] ἐμμενεῖν . . . κατηγορήσειν Kiessling ; ἐμμένειν . . . κατηγορεῖν O, Jacoby.

48

them all to be present at the trial and had solemnly
sworn over the victims that he would persist in his
resolution and prosecute the men with all possible
vigour, he appointed a day for holding the trial. The
patricians, upon learning of this, felt great fear and
concern, wondering what course they ought to take
to secure the men's acquittal of the charge and also
to put a stop to the boldness of the demagogue. And
they resolved, in case the populace should pass any
vote to the prejudice of the consular power, to prevent
them from carrying it out, by opposing them with
all their power and even resorting to arms if that
should be necessary. But they had no need to use
any violent means, as the danger was dispelled in
a sudden and unexpected manner. For when only
one day remained till the trial, Genucius was found
dead on his bed without the least sign of stabbing,
strangling, poisoning, or any of the other means of
killing as the result of a plot. As soon as this unhappy occurrence was known and the body had been
brought into the Forum, the event was looked upon
as a kind of providential obstacle to the trial, which
was straightway dismissed. For none of the other
tribunes dared to revive the sedition, but they even
looked upon Genucius as having been guilty of great
madness. Now if the consuls had not committed any
further act of officiousness, but had let the dissension,
as Heaven had put it to sleep, remain so, no further
danger would have beset them ; but as it was, by
turning to arrogance and contempt for the plebeians
and by desiring to display the extent of their power,
they brought about great mischiefs. For, having
appointed a day for levying troops and endeavouring

---

[3] τῇ δίκῃ Kiessling, πρὸ τῆς δίκης Reiske : τῆς δίκης O.

ὑπακούοντας ταῖς τε ἄλλαις ζημίαις καὶ πληγαῖς
ῥάβδων προσαναγκάζοντες εἰς ἀπόνοιαν ἐποίησαν
τραπέσθαι τοῦ δημοτικοῦ τὸ πλέον, ἀπὸ τοιαύτης
μάλιστ᾽ αἰτίας.

XXXIX. Ἀνήρ τις ἐκ τῶν δημοτικῶν τὰ πολέμια λαμπρός, Βολέρων Πόπλιος, ἡγεμονίαν ἐσχη-
κὼς λόχων ἐν ταῖς προτέραις στρατείαις, τότ᾽ ἀντὶ
λοχαγοῦ στρατιώτης πρὸς αὐτῶν κατεγράφετο.
ὡς δ᾽ ἠναντιοῦτο καὶ οὐκ ἠξίου χώραν ἀτιμοτέραν
λαβεῖν οὐδὲν ἡμαρτηκὼς ἐν ταῖς προτέραις στρατείαις, δυσανασχετοῦντες οἱ ὕπατοι τὴν παρρησίαν
αὐτοῦ τοῖς ῥαβδούχοις ἐκέλευσαν τὴν ἐσθῆτά τε
περικαταρρῆξαι καὶ ταῖς ῥάβδοις τὸ σῶμα ξαίνειν.
2 ὁ δὲ νεανίας τούς τε δημάρχους ἐπεκαλεῖτο, καί, εἴ
τι ἀδικεῖ, κρίσιν ἐπὶ τῶν δημοτῶν ὑπέχειν ἠξίου.
ὡς δ᾽ οὐ προσεῖχον αὐτῷ τὸν νοῦν οἱ ὕπατοι, ἀλλὰ
τοῖς ῥαβδούχοις ἄγειν καὶ τύπτειν ἐπεκελεύοντο,
οὐκ ἀνασχετὸν ἡγησάμενος εἶναι τὴν ὕβριν αὐτὸς
3 ἑαυτῷ ταμίας τῆς δίκης[1] γίνεται. τόν τε γὰρ πρῶτον προσελθόντα τῶν ῥαβδούχων παίων εἰς τὸ πρόσ-
ωπον ἐναντίαις πυγμαῖς νεανίας καὶ ἐρρωμένος ὢν[2]
ἀνὴρ ἀνατρέπει καὶ τὸν ἐπὶ τούτῳ. ἀγανακτησάν-
των δὲ τῶν ὑπάτων καὶ πᾶσιν ἅμα τοῖς ὑπηρέταις
προσελθεῖν κελευσάντων δεινόν τι[3] τοῖς παροῦσι
τῶν δημοτικῶν ἐφάνη· καὶ αὐτίκα συστραφέντες
ἀθρόοι καὶ ἀναβοήσαντες τὸ παρακλητικὸν τῆς
ἀλλήλων ὀργῆς τόν τε νεανίσκον ἐξήρπασαν καὶ
τοὺς ῥαβδούχους ἀπέστησαν παίοντες καὶ τελευτῶντες ἐπὶ τοὺς ὑπάτους ὥρμησαν, καὶ εἰ μὴ καταλιπόντες ἐκεῖνοι τὴν ἀγορὰν ἔφυγον, ἀνήκεστον ἄν

[1] τῆς δίκης B : om. R.
[2] ὢν Capps : om. O, Jacoby.   [3] τι B : om. R.

to coerce the disobedient by various punishments, including even scourging with rods, they drove the greater part of the plebeians to desperation. This was caused particularly by the incident I shall now relate.

XXXIX. A certain man of the plebeians, famous for his exploits in war, Volero Publius,[1] who had commanded centuries in the late campaigns, was now listed by the consuls as a common soldier instead of a centurion. Upon his objecting to this and refusing to take a lower rank when he had been guilty of no misconduct in the former campaigns, the consuls, offended at his frankness, ordered the lictors to strip him and lash his body with their rods. The young man called upon the tribunes for assistance, and asked, if he were guilty of any crime, to stand trial before the plebeians. When the consuls paid no heed to him but repeated their orders to the lictors to take him away and flog him, he regarded the insult as intolerable and took justice into his own hands. The first lictor who approached him he struck squarely in the face with his fists, and being a young man and vigorous, he knocked him down ; and the next one likewise. When the consuls in their anger ordered all their attendants to approach him at the same time, the plebeians who were present thought it an outrageous thing. And immediately gathering together in a body and shouting the cry used to incite one another's resentment, they snatched the young man away and repulsed the lictors with blows, and at last made a rush against the consuls ; and if those magistrates had not left the Forum and fled, the mob

[1] The correct form of the name is Volero Publilius (Livy ii. 55, 4).

4 τι κακὸν ἐξειργάσαντο. ἐκ δὲ τούτου διειστήκει
πᾶσα ἡ πόλις, καὶ οἱ τέως ἡσυχάζοντες δήμαρχοι
τότε ἠγριοῦντο καὶ τῶν ὑπάτων κατηγόρουν. περι-
ειστήκει τε ἡ περὶ τῆς κληρουχίας στάσις[1] εἰς
ἑτέραν[2] μείζονα διὰ τὸν[3] ὑπὲρ τοῦ κόσμου τῆς
πολιτείας ἀγῶνα. οἱ μέν γε πατρίκιοι τοῖς ὑπάτοις
ὡς καταλυομένης αὐτῶν τῆς ἐξουσίας συναγαν-
ακτοῦντες τὸν χεῖρας[4] ἐπιβαλεῖν τοῖς ὑπηρέταις
5 τολμήσαντα κατὰ κρημνοῦ βαλεῖν ἠξίουν· οἱ δὲ
δημοτικοὶ συστρέψαντες αὑτοὺς κατεβόων τε καὶ
παρεκελεύοντο μὴ προδιδόναι σφῶν τὴν ἐλευθερίαν,
ἀλλ' ἐπὶ τὴν βουλὴν τὸ πρᾶγμα ἄγειν καὶ τῶν
ὑπάτων κατηγορεῖν καὶ δίκης τινὸς παρ' αὐτῶν
ἠξίουν τυχεῖν ὅτι τὸν ἐπικαλεσάμενον τὴν ἐκ τῶν
δημάρχων βοήθειαν καὶ ἐν τῷ δήμῳ κρίσιν ὑπέχειν,
εἴ τι πλημμελεῖ, βουλόμενον, οὐδετέρου τυχεῖν
εἴασαν τῶν δικαίων, ἀλλ' ἐν ἀνδραπόδου μοίρᾳ τὸν
ἐλεύθερον καὶ πολίτην ἔθεντο παίειν ἐπικελευό-
6 μενοι. ἀντιτεταγμένων δὴ τούτων καὶ οὐδετέρων
εἶξαι βουλομένων τοῖς ἑτέροις, ἅπας ὁ λοιπὸς τῆς
ὑπατείας ἐκείνης ἐδαπανήθη χρόνος οὔτε πολεμι-
καῖς πράξεσι κοσμηθεὶς καλαῖς οὔτε πολιτικαῖς
λόγου ἀξίαις.

XL. Ἐπιστάντων δὲ τῶν ἀρχαιρεσίων ὕπατοι
μὲν ἀπεδείχθησαν Λεύκιος Πινάριος καὶ Πόπλιος
Φούριος. ἐν ἀρχῇ δὲ τοῦ ἔτους εὐθὺς ὀττείας τινὸς

---

[1] στάσις Cmg, Sylburg : om. R.
[2] Kiessling : ἕτερον O, Jacoby.
[3] διὰ τὸν om. Cobet, Jacoby.
[4] χεῖρας added here by Cobet, τὰς χεῖρας after ἐπιβαλεῖν
by Reiske.

would have done some irreparable mischief. As a result of this incident the whole city was divided, and those tribunes who till then had remained quiet grew wild with rage and inveighed against the consuls. Thus the dissension over the land-allotment had turned into another quarrel of greater consequence because of the contest concerning the form of government. On the one hand the patricians, believing that the power of the consuls was being destroyed, shared their indignation and demanded that the man who had dared to lay hands on their attendants should be hurled down from the precipice.[1] On the other hand the plebeians, assembling together, raised a loud clamour and exhorted one another not to betray their liberty, but to carry the matter before the senate, to accuse the consuls and to endeavour to obtain some justice from them because they had refused to permit a man who had invoked the assistance of the tribunes and asked to be tried before the populace, in case he were guilty of any wrongdoing, to obtain either of these rights, but had treated him like a slave, though he was free born and a citizen, when they ordered him to be beaten. The two parties being thus arrayed against one another and neither being willing to yield to the other, all the remaining time of this consulship was consumed without being marked either by any glorious exploits in war or by any achievements at home worthy of mention.

XL. The election of magistrates being at hand,[2] Lucius Pinarius and Publius Furius were chosen consuls. At the very beginning of this year the city

---

[1] The Tarpeian Rock.
[2] For chaps. 40-42 cf. Livy ii. 56, 1-5.

ἡ πόλις ἐπληρώθη καὶ φόβου δαιμονίου τεράτων τε
καὶ σημείων πολλῶν γινομένων. καὶ οἵ τε μάντεις
ἅπαντες καὶ οἱ τῶν ἱερῶν ἐξηγηταὶ χόλου δαιμόνων
μηνύματα εἶναι τὰ γινόμενα ἀπέφαινον, ἱερῶν τινων
2 οὐχ ὁσίως οὐδὲ καθαρῶς ἐπιτελουμένων. καὶ μετ᾽
οὐ πολὺ[1] νόσος ἐνέσκηψεν εἰς τὰς γυναῖκας ἡ[2]
καλουμένη λοιμικὴ καὶ θάνατος ὅσος οὔπω πρότερον, μάλιστα δ᾽[3] εἰς τὰς ἐγκύμονας. ὠμοτοκοῦ-
σαί τε γὰρ καὶ νεκρὰ τίκτουσαι συναπέθνησκον
τοῖς βρέφεσι, καὶ οὔτε λιτανεῖαι πρὸς ἕδεσι καὶ
βωμοῖς γινόμεναι θεῶν οὔτε καθαρτήριοι θυσίαι
περί τε πόλεως καὶ οἴκων ἰδίων ἐπιτελούμεναι
3 παῦλαν αὐταῖς[4] ἔφερον τῶν κακῶν. ἐν τοιαύτῃ δὲ
συμφορᾷ τῆς πόλεως οὔσης τοῖς ἐξηγηταῖς τῶν
ἱερῶν γίνεται μήνυσις ὑπὸ δούλου τινὸς ὅτι μία
τῶν ἱεροποιῶν παρθένων τῶν φυλαττουσῶν τὸ
ἀθάνατον πῦρ, Ὀρβινία, τὴν παρθενίαν ἀπολώλεκε
καὶ τὰ ἱερὰ θύει τὰ τῆς πόλεως οὐκ οὖσα καθαρά.
κἀκεῖνοι μεταστήσαντες αὐτὴν ἀπὸ τῶν ἱερῶν καὶ
προθέντες δίκην, ἐπειδὴ καταφανὴς ἐγένετο ἐλεγχ-
θεῖσα, ῥάβδοις τε ἐμαστίγωσαν καὶ πομπεύσαντες
4 διὰ τῆς πόλεως ζῶσαν κατώρυξαν. τῶν δὲ διαπρα-
ξαμένων τὴν ἀνοσίαν φθορὰν ὁ μὲν ἕτερος ἑαυτὸν
διεχρήσατο, τὸν δ᾽ ἕτερον οἱ τῶν ἱερῶν ἐπίσκοποι
συλλαβόντες ἐν ἀγορᾷ μάστιξιν αἰκισάμενοι καθάπερ ἀνδράποδον ἀπέκτειναν. ἡ μὲν οὖν νόσος ἡ
κατασκήψασα εἰς τὰς γυναῖκας καὶ ὁ πολὺς αὐτῶν
φθόρος μετὰ τοῦτο τὸ ἔργον εὐθὺς ἐπαύσατο.

XLI. Ἡ δ᾽ ἐκ πολλοῦ χρόνου διαμένουσα ἐν τῇ

---

[1] μετ᾽ οὐ πολὺ Jacoby : οὐ μετὰ πολὺ O.
[2] ἡ added by Reiske. [3] δ᾽ added by Reiske.
[4] αὐταῖς R : αὐτοῖς B.

was filled with a kind of religious awe and fear of the gods owing to the occurrence of many prodigies and omens. All the augurs and the pontiffs[1] declared that these occurrences were indications of divine anger, aroused because some rites were not being performed in a pure and holy manner. And not long afterwards the disease known as the pestilence attacked the women, particularly such as were with child, and more of them died than ever before ; for as they miscarried and brought forth dead children, they died together with their infants. And neither supplications made at the statues and altars of the gods nor expiatory sacrifices performed on behalf of the state and of private households gave the women any respite from their ills. While the commonwealth was suffering from such a calamity, information was given to the pontiffs by a slave that one of the Vestal virgins who have the care of the perpetual fire, Urbinia by name, had lost her virginity and, though unchaste, was performing the public sacrifices. The pontiffs removed her from her sacred offices, brought her to trial, and after her guilt had been clearly established, they ordered her to be scourged with rods, to be carried through the city in solemn procession and then to be buried alive. One of the two men who had perpetrated the impious defilement killed himself ; the other was seized by the pontiffs, who ordered him to be scourged in the Forum like a slave and then put to death. After this action the pestilence which had attacked the women and caused so great a mortality among them promptly ceased.

XLI. But the sedition raised by the plebeians

---

[1] Literally, " interpreters of religious matters (or rites)."
Cf. ii. 73, 3.

πόλει στάσις, ἣν οἱ δημόται πρὸς τοὺς πατρικίους
ἐστασίαζον, ἀνίστατο πάλιν. ὁ δ' ἐξεγείρων αὐτὴν
δήμαρχος ἦν Πόπλιος Βολέρων, ὁ τῷ πρόσθεν
ἐνιαυτῷ τοῖς περὶ Αἰμίλιόν τε καὶ Ἰούλιον ὑπάτοις
ἀπειθήσας, ὅτ'[1] αὐτὸν ἀντὶ λοχαγοῦ στρατιώτην
κατέγραφον, οὐ δι' ἄλλο τι μᾶλλον ἀποδειχθεὶς ὑπὸ
τῶν πενήτων τοῦ δήμου[2] προστάτης (γένος τε γὰρ
ἐκ τῶν ἐπιτυχόντων ἦν καὶ τεθραμμένος ἐν πολλῇ
ταπεινότητι καὶ ἀπορίᾳ), ἀλλ' ὅτι τὴν ἀρχὴν τῶν
ὑπάτων βασιλικὸν ἔχουσαν ἀξίωμα τέως πρῶτος
ἔδοξεν ἰδιώτης ἀνὴρ ἀπειθείᾳ ταπεινῶσαι, καὶ ἔτι
μᾶλλον διὰ τὰς ὑποσχέσεις ἃς ἐποιεῖτο μετιὼν
τὴν ἀρχὴν κατὰ τῶν πατρικίων, ὡς ἀφαιρησόμενος
2 αὐτῶν τὴν ἰσχύν. ὃς ἐπειδὴ τάχιστα ἐξεγένετο
αὐτῷ λωφήσαντος τοῦ δαιμονίου χόλου τὰ πολιτικὰ πράττειν, συναγαγὼν τὸν δῆμον εἰς ἐκκλησίαν
νόμον εἰσφέρει περὶ τῶν δημαρχικῶν ἀρχαιρεσίων,
μετάγων αὐτὰ ἐκ τῆς φρατριακῆς ψηφοφορίας, ἣν
οἱ Ῥωμαῖοι κουριᾶτιν[3] καλοῦσιν,[4] ἐπὶ τὴν φυλετι-
κήν. τίς δὲ τούτων διαφορὰ τῶν ἀρχαιρεσίων,
3 ἐγὼ σημανῶ. τὰς μὲν φρατριακὰς ψηφοφορίας
ἔδει προβουλευσαμένης τῆς βουλῆς καὶ τοῦ πλήθους κατὰ φράτρας τὰς ψήφους ἐπενέγκαντος, καὶ

---

[1] ὅτε Sylburg : ὅτι O.

[2] τῶν πενήτων τοῦ δήμου Sylburg : τοῦ τῶν πενήτων δήμου O.

[3] κουριᾶτιν (cf. 46, 4) Cobet : κυράτιν AB.

[4] κυράτιν καλοῦσιν A : καλοῦσι κυράτιν B, καλοῦσιν κουριᾶτιν Jacoby.

---

[1] Cf. ii. 7, 2 f.

[2] Dionysius has no special phrase for the *concilium plebis*,
but uses the same terms as for the assemblies of the whole
people. What he thus ambiguously relates here was probably a change from the *concilium plebis curiatim* to the
concilium plebis tributim. By comparing together the two

against the patricians, which had long continued in
the city, was starting up again. The person who
stirred it up was Volero Publius, one of the tribunes,
the same man who the year before had disobeyed the
consuls Aemilius and Julius when they would have
listed him as a common soldier instead of a centurion.
He was chosen by the poor as leader of the populace,
not so much for any other reason—for he was not
only of common birth, but had been brought up in
great obscurity and want—but because he was regarded as the first person in private life who by his
disobedience had humbled the consular power, which
till then had been invested with the royal dignity,
and still more by reason of the promises he had made,
when he stood candidate for the tribunate against
the patricians, to deprive them of their power. This
man, as soon as it was possible for him to attend to
public business, now that the divine anger had abated,
called an assembly of the populace and proposed a
law concerning the tribunician elections, transferring
them from the assembly of the clans,[1] called by the
Romans the curiate assembly, to the tribal assembly.[2]
What the difference was between these assemblies I
will now point out. In order that the voting in the
curiate assembly might be valid it was necessary
that the senate should pass a preliminary decree and
that the plebeians should vote on it by *curiae*, and that

passages (vi. 87, 3 and 89, 1) in which the establishment of
the tribunate is described, we see that the first tribunes were
elected by a *concilium plebis*, meeting by *curiae*. It is to be
noted that in the second of these passages, as in so many
other places, Dionysius uses the word δῆμος, which can mean
either the plebs alone or the whole people; his distinctive
term for plebeians is δημοτικοί, for plebs δημοτικόν or πλῆθος
(sometimes both together).

μετ' ἀμφότερα ταῦτα τῶν παρὰ τοῦ δαιμονίου
σημείων τε καὶ οἰωνῶν μηδὲν ἐναντιωθέντων, τότε
κυρίας εἶναι· τὰς δὲ φυλετικὰς μήτε προβουλεύματος γενομένου μήτε τῶν ἱερέων[1] τε καὶ οἰωνοσκόπων ἐπιθεσπισάντων, ἐν ἡμέρᾳ μιᾷ τελεσθείσας
ὑπὸ τῶν φυλετῶν τέλος ἔχειν. καὶ ἦσαν ἐκ τῶν
λοιπῶν τεττάρων δημάρχων οἱ συνεισφέροντες
αὐτῷ δύο δήμαρχοι τὸν νόμον· οὓς προσεταιρισά-
μενος ἐλαττόνων ὄντων τῶν μὴ ταῦτα[2] βουλομένων
4 περιῆν. οἱ δ' ὕπατοι καὶ ἡ βουλὴ καὶ πάντες οἱ
πατρίκιοι κωλύειν ἐπεχείρουν τὸν νόμον· ἀφικόμενοί τε κατὰ πλῆθος εἰς τὴν ἀγορὰν ἐν ᾗ προεῖπον
οἱ δήμαρχοι κυρώσειν τὸν νόμον ἡμέρᾳ, παντοδαποὺς διῆλθον λόγους, τῶν θ' ὑπάτων καὶ τῶν
πρεσβυτάτων ἐκ τῆς βουλῆς καὶ ἄλλου παντὸς ὅτῳ
βουλομένῳ ἦν τὰς ἐνούσας ἐν τῷ νόμῳ διεξιόντος
ἀτοπίας. ἀντιλεξάντων δὲ τῶν δημάρχων καὶ
αὖθις τῶν ὑπάτων, καὶ μέχρι πολλοῦ τῆς ἀψιμαχίας
τῶν λόγων ἐκμηκυνθείσης, ἐκείνην μὲν τὴν ἐκκλησίαν διέλυσεν εἰς νύκτα συγκλεισθεὶς ὁ χρόνος.
προθέντων δὲ πάλιν τῶν δημάρχων εἰς τρίτην
ἀγορὰν τὴν περὶ τοῦ νόμου διάγνωσιν καὶ συνελθόντος ἔτι πλείονος εἰς αὐτὴν ὄχλου τὸ παρα-
5 πλήσιον τῷ προτέρῳ συνέβη γενέσθαι πάθος. τοῦτο
συνιδὼν ὁ Πόπλιος ἔγνω μήτε τοῖς ὑπάτοις ἐπιτρέπειν ἔτι τοῦ νόμου κατηγορεῖν μήτε πατρικίους
ἐᾶν τῇ ψηφοφορίᾳ παρεῖναι· καθ' ἑταιρείας γὰρ
ἐκεῖνοι καὶ κατὰ συστροφὰς ἅμα τοῖς ἑαυτῶν
πελάταις οὐκ ὀλίγοις οὖσι πολλὰ μέρη τῆς ἀγορᾶς
κατεῖχον, ἐπικελεύοντές τε τοῖς κατηγοροῦσι τοῦ
νόμου καὶ θορυβοῦντες τοὺς ἀπολογουμένους καὶ

---

[1] Reiske : ἱερῶν O.   [2] Sylburg : ταῦτα AB.

after both these votes the heavenly signs and omens should offer no opposition ; whereas, in the case of the voting of the tribal assembly, neither the preliminary decree of the senate was necessary nor the sanction of the priests and augurs, but it was only necessary that it should be carried through and completed by the members of the tribes in a single day. Now of the other four tribunes there were two who joined with Volero in proposing this law ; and by enlisting the co-operation of these two he carried the day, as those who were not of the same mind were in the minority. But the consuls, the senate, and all the patricians sought to prevent the law from passing ; and coming to the Forum in great numbers on the day appointed by the tribunes for ratifying the law, they delivered all kinds of speeches, the consuls, the oldest senators and everyone else who so desired enumerating the absurdities inherent in the law. When the tribunes had argued on the other side and the consuls had spoken a second time and the verbal skirmishing had lasted a long while, that assembly at least was dispersed by the closing in of night-time. The tribunes having again appointed the third market-day for the consideration of the law and an even greater throng flocking to the Forum on that day, the same thing happened as before. Publius, perceiving this, resolved neither to permit the consuls to inveigh against the law again nor to allow patricians to be present at the voting. For the patricians in their partisan bands and in groups together with their clients, who were numerous, occupied many parts of the Forum, shouting encouragement to those who inveighed against the law and noisily interrupting those who defended it, and doing many other things

ἄλλα πολλὰ πράττοντες ἀκοσμίας τε καὶ βίας τῆς
ἐν ταῖς ψήφοις ἐσομένης[1] μηνύματα.

XLII. Ἐπέσχε δ' αὐτοῦ τὰ βουλεύματα ὄντα
τυραννικὰ ἑτέρα συμπεσοῦσα θεήλατος συμφορά.
νόσος γὰρ ἥψατο λοιμικὴ τῆς πόλεως, γενομένη μὲν
καὶ κατὰ τὴν ἄλλην Ἰταλίαν, μάλιστα δὲ πλεονά-
σασα κατὰ τὴν Ῥώμην· καὶ οὔτε ἀνθρωπίνη βοήθεια ἧκει τοῖς κάμνουσιν οὐδεμία, ἀλλ' ἐν τῷ
ἴσῳ οἵ τε σὺν πολλῇ θεραπευόμενοι φροντίδι καὶ
οἷς μηδὲν ἐγίνετο τῶν δεόντων ἀπέθνησκον· οὔτε
λιτανεῖαι θεῶν καὶ θυσίαι καὶ ἐφ' οὓς ἄνθρωποι
τελευταίους[2] ἐν ταῖς τοιαῖσδε ἀναγκάζονται καταφεύγειν συμφοραῖς, οἱ κατ' ἄνδρα τε γινόμενοι καὶ
ὑπὲρ τοῦ κοινοῦ καθαρμοί, τότε προσωφέλουν,
διέκρινέ τε τὸ πάθος οὐχ ἡλικίαν, οὐ φύσιν, οὐ
ῥώμην ἢ ἀσθένειαν σωμάτων, οὐ τέχνην, οὐκ ἄλλο
τι τῶν δοκούντων κουφίζειν τὴν νόσον,[3] ἀλλὰ γυ-
ναιξί τε ἐνέπιπτε καὶ ἀνδράσι καὶ γηραιοῖς καὶ
2 νέοις. οὐ μὴν πολὺν[4] κατέσχε χρόνον, ὅπερ αἴτιον
ἐγένετο τοῦ μὴ σύμπασαν διαφθαρῆναι τὴν πόλιν·
ἀλλὰ ποταμοῦ δίκην ἢ πυρὸς ἀθρόα τοῖς ἀνθρώποις ἐμπεσοῦσα τήν τε προσβολὴν ὀξεῖαν καὶ τὴν
ἀπαλλαγὴν ταχεῖαν ἔλαβεν. ὡς δὲ τὸ δεινὸν

[1] ἐσομένης Gelenius : ἐχομένης R, Jacoby, om. B, ἀρχομένης Sintenis, ἐρχομένης (or ἐπερχομένης) Post.

[2] ἐφ' οὓς ἄνθρωποι τελευταίους B : ἐφ' οἷς ἄνθρωποι τελευταῖον AC.

[3] Reiske transposed the words οὐκ ἄλλο τι τῶν δοκούντων
κουφίζειν τὴν νόσον to follow προσωφέλουν. Kiessling, accepting this transposition, proposed οὔτε ἄλλο τι, and, in place
of οὐ τέχνην, either (a) οὔτε τέχνη, to stand between προσωφέλουν and οὔτε ἄλλο τι, or (b) οὐ τύχην (cf. vii. 12, 4),
to follow σωμάτων.

[4] οὐ μὴν πολὺν A : οὐ πολὺν δὲ B.

that were indications of the disorder and violence
that there would be in the voting.

XLII. These designs of Publius, pointing toward
a tyranny, were checked by a fresh calamity sent
from Heaven. For the city was visited with a pestilence, which occurred, indeed, in the rest of Italy also,
but was especially prevalent in Rome. No human
assistance could relieve the sick ; but alike whether
they were attended with great care or received none
of the necessary attentions, they died all the same.
No supplications to the gods nor sacrifices nor the
final refuge to which men under such calamities are
compelled to have recourse—private and public
expiations—contributed any help at that time ; and
the disease made no distinction of age or sex, of
strong or weak constitutions, of skill, or of any other of
the agencies supposed to lighten the malady,[1] but attacked both men and women, old and young. However, it did not last long—a circumstance which saved
the city from utter destruction ; but, like a river in
flood or a conflagration, falling upon the people with
full force, it made a sharp attack and a speedy departure. As soon as the calamity abated, Publius,

---

[1] The phrases " of skill " and " of any other of the agencies
supposed to lighten the malady " seem to be out of their
proper place. According to Kiessling's transposition we
should have, following " contributed any help at that time,"
either (1), retaining τέχνη, " nor did skill, nor any of the
other agencies supposed to lighten the malady " ; or (2),
substituting τύχην for τέχνην and retaining in its present position, " nor did any of the other agencies supposed to lighten
the malady ; and the disease made no distinction of age or
sex, of strong or weak constitutions, or of one's circumstances (one's station in life), but attacked both men and
women," etc.

ἐλώφησεν, ἐπ' ἐξόδῳ τῆς ἀρχῆς ὢν ὁ Πόπλιος,
ἐπειδὴ οὐκ ἐδύνατο κυρῶσαι τὸν νόμον ἐν τῷ περι-
ιόντι χρόνῳ τῶν ἀρχαιρεσίων ἐπιστάντων, μετῄει
πάλιν τὴν δημαρχίαν εἰς τὸν ἐπιόντα ἐνιαυτόν, πολλὰ
καὶ μεγάλα τοῖς δημόταις ὑπισχνούμενος· καὶ
ἀποδείκνυται πάλιν δήμαρχος ὑπ' αὐτῶν καὶ δύο
3 τῶν συναρχόντων. οἱ δὲ πατρίκιοι πρὸς τοῦτο
ἀντεμηχανήσαντο πικρὸν ἄνδρα καὶ μισόδημον καὶ
μηδὲν ἐλαττώσοντα τῆς ἀριστοκρατίας ἐπὶ τὴν
ὑπατείαν προαγαγεῖν, Ἄππιον Κλαύδιον, υἱὸν
Ἀππίου τοῦ πλεῖστα τῷ δήμῳ περὶ τὴν κάθοδον
ἐναντιωθέντος. καὶ αὐτὸν πολλὰ ἀντειπόντα καὶ
οὐδ' εἰς τὸ πεδίον ἐλθεῖν βουληθέντα ἕνεκα τῶν
ἀρχαιρεσίων, οὐδὲν ἧττον προὐβούλευσάν τε καὶ
ἐψηφίσαντο ἀπόντα ὕπατον.

XLIII. Τελεσθέντων δὲ τῶν ἀρχαιρεσίων κατὰ
πολλὴν εὐπέτειαν, οἱ γὰρ πένητες ἐξέλιπον τὸ
πεδίον ἐπειδὴ τὸν ἄνδρα τόνδε ὀνομασθέντα ἤκου-
σαν, παραλαμβάνουσι τὴν ὑπατείαν Τίτος Κοΐντιος
Καπιτωλῖνος καὶ Ἄππιος Κλαύδιος Σαβῖνος, οὔτε
τὰς φύσεις οὔτε τὰς προαιρέσεις ἔχοντες ὁμοίας.
2 Ἀππίου μὲν γὰρ ἦν γνώμη περισπᾶν περὶ τὰς ἔξω
στρατείας τὸν ἀργὸν καὶ πένητα δῆμον, ἵνα τῶν τε
καθ' ἡμέραν ἀναγκαίων ἐκ τῆς πολεμίας εὐπορῶν
τοῖς αὑτοῦ πόνοις ὢν ἐν χρείᾳ μάλιστα ὑπῆρχε
καὶ τὰ συμφέροντα τῇ πόλει διαπραττόμενος,

---

[1] See vi. 59 ff. The reference is to the return from the
Sacred Mount.

whose magistracy was near expiring, since he could
not get the law confirmed during the remainder of
his term, as the election of magistrates was at hand,
stood again for the tribuneship for the following year,
making many big promises to the plebeians ; and he
was again chosen tribune by them, together with two
of his colleagues. The patricians, to meet this situation, contrived to advance to the consulship a man of
stern disposition and an enemy of the populace, one
who would not diminish in any respect the power of
the aristocracy, namely, Appius Claudius, the son
of that Appius who had most strongly opposed the
populace in the matter of their return.[1] And though
he protested much and even refused to go to the
field [2] for the election, they nevertheless passed the
preliminary vote and appointed him consul [3] in his
absence.

XLIII. After the election [4] had been carried
through quite easily [5]—for the poorer people left the
field [2] as soon as they heard Appius named [6]—Titus
Quintius Capitolinus and Appius Claudius Sabinus
succeeded to the consulship, men alike neither in
their dispositions nor in their principles. For it was
the opinion of Appius that the idle and needy populace should be kept employed in military expeditions
abroad, in order that. while supplying themselves
from the enemy's country by their own toils with an
abundance of the daily necessaries of which they
were in the greatest need and at the same time
accomplishing results advantageous to the common-

[2] The Campus Martius.
[3] *i.e.* they named him as their candidate for the consulship.
[4] For chaps. 43-49 *cf.* Livy ii. 56, 5-58, 2.
[5] Dionysius is speaking from the patricians' point of view.
[6] *i.e.* heard his candidacy announced.

ἥκιστα τοῖς ἐκ τοῦ συνεδρίου διοικοῦσι[1] τὰ κοινὰ
δυσμενής τε καὶ χαλεπὸς ᾖ· πολέμου δὲ πᾶσαν
ἔσεσθαι πρόφασιν εὔλογον ἀπέφαινεν ἡγεμονίας
ἀντιποιουμένῃ πόλει καὶ ὑπὸ πάντων ἐπιφθονου-
μένῃ, κατά τε τὸ εἰκὸς τοῖς γεγονόσιν ἤδη τὰ
μέλλοντα εἰκάζειν ἠξίου, ἐπιλεγόμενος, ὅσαι ἤδη
κινήσεις ἐγένοντο ἐν τῇ πόλει, ὅτι πᾶσαι κατὰ
3 τὰς ἀναπαύλας ἐγένοντο τῶν πολέμων. Κοϊντίῳ
δ' οὐκ ἐδόκει πόλεμον ἐκφέρειν οὐδένα, ἀγαπητὸν
ἀποφαίνοντι εἰ πρὸς τοὺς ἀναγκαίους τε καὶ ἔξωθεν
ἐπαγομένους κινδύνους καλούμενος ὁ δῆμος εὐπει-
θὴς γένοιτο, καὶ διδάσκοντι ὡς εἰ βίαν προσάξουσι
τοῖς μὴ πειθομένοις εἰς ἀπόνοιαν ἀναγκάσουσιν
ἐλθεῖν τὸ δημοτικόν, ὥσπερ καὶ οἱ πρὸ αὐτῶν
ἐποίησαν ὕπατοι· ἐξ ὧν κινδυνεύσειν αὐτοὺς δυεῖν
θάτερον, ἢ δι' αἵματος καὶ φόνων καταπαῦσαι τὴν
στάσιν ἢ θεραπεύειν αἰσχρῶς ὑπομεῖναι τὸ δημοτι-
4 κόν. ἦν δ' ἡ τοῦ μηνὸς ἐκείνου ἡγεμονία τῷ
Κοϊντίῳ προσήκουσα, ὥστε ἀναγκαῖον ἦν τὸν ἕτερον τῶν ὑπάτων μηδὲν ἄκοντος ἐκείνου ποιεῖν. οἱ
δὲ περὶ τὸν Πόπλιον δήμαρχοι οὐθὲν ἔτι διαμελλήσαντες τὸν ἐν τῷ πρόσθεν ἐνιαυτῷ οὐ δυνηθέντα
νόμον ἐπικυρωθῆναι[2] πάλιν εἰσέφερον, προσγρά-
ψαντες αὐτῷ καὶ τὸ τῶν ἀγορανόμων ἀρχεῖον ἐν
ταῖς αὐταῖς ψηφοφορεῖσθαι ἐκκλησίαις, καὶ πάντα
τἆλλα ὅσα ἐν τῷ δήμῳ πράττεσθαί τε καὶ ἐπι-
κυροῦσθαι δεήσει ὑπὸ τῶν φυλετῶν ἐπιψηφίζεσθαι

---

[1] Sylburg : συνδιοικοῦσι A, συνοικοῦσι BC.
[2] νόμον ἐπικυρωθῆναι B : ἐπικυρωθῆναι νόμον R.

wealth, they might be least likely to be hostile and
troublesome to the senators who were administering
public affairs. He declared that any excuse for
making war would be justifiable for a state that laid
claim to supremacy and was envied by all ; and he
asked them, applying the principle of probability, to
judge what was to happen in the future by what
had already taken place in the past, adding that all
the commotions which had occurred in the commonwealth in the past had happened during the respites
from war. Quintius, on the other hand, thought
they ought not to wage any war. He declared they
ought to be satisfied if the populace, when called
upon to face the inevitable dangers brought upon
them from outside, yielded ready obedience ; and he
showed that if they attempted to use force with the
disobedient they would drive the plebeians to desperation, as the consuls before them had done. As a
result, they would run the risk either of putting down
the sedition with bloodshed and slaughter or of submitting to a shameful courting of the plebeians. In
that month the command belonged to Quintius, so
that the other consul was bound to do nothing without his consent. In the meantime Publius and the
other two tribunes without further delay were again
proposing the law which they had been unable to get
ratified the year before, with this additional provision
that the college of aediles [1] should also be chosen in
the same assemblies,[2] and that everything else that
was to be done and ratified by the populace should
be voted on in like manner by the members of the

---

[1] For the relation of the (plebeian) aediles to the tribunes
see vi. 90, 2 f. Curule aediles were not appointed until a
century later.   [2] See chap. 41, 2 ff.

κατὰ τὸ αὐτό· ὅπερ ἦν ἄρα τῆς μὲν βουλῆς κατάλυσις φανερά, τοῦ δὲ δήμου δυναστεία.

XLIV. Τοῦτο μαθοῦσι τοῖς ὑπάτοις φροντὶς εἰσ-
ήει καὶ λογισμὸς[1] ὅπως ἂν ἐν τάχει καὶ σὺν τῷ
ἀσφαλεῖ τὸ παρακινοῦν καὶ στασιάζον ἐξαιρεθῇ.
ὁ μὲν οὖν Ἄππιος ἐπὶ τὰ ὅπλα καλεῖν γνώμην
ἐδίδου τοὺς βουλομένους[2] σῴζεσθαι τὴν πάτριον
πολιτείαν· εἰ δέ τινες ἐναντιωθήσονται[3] σφίσι,[4] τού-
2 τους ἐν πολεμίων ποιεῖσθαι μοίρᾳ. ὁ δὲ Κοΐντιος
λόγῳ πείθειν ᾤετο δεῖν τοὺς δημοτικοὺς καὶ μετα-
διδάσκειν ὡς δι' ἄγνοιαν τοῦ συμφέροντος εἰς
ὀλέθρια βουλεύματα φερομένους· ἐσχάτης μανίας
ἔργον εἶναι λέγων, ἃ παρ' ἑκόντων ἔξεστι φέρεσθαι τῶν συμπολιτευομένων, ταῦτα παρ' ἀκόντων
3 βούλεσθαι λαμβάνειν. ἐπαινεσάντων δὲ καὶ τῶν
ἄλλων τῶν συμπαραληφθέντων εἰς τὸ συνέδριον
τὴν Κοϊντίου γνώμην παρελθόντες εἰς τὴν ἀγορὰν
οἱ ὕπατοι λόγον ᾐτοῦντο παρὰ τῶν δημάρχων καὶ
χρόνον. μόλις δ' ἀμφοῖν τυχόντες, ἐπειδὴ καθῆκεν
ἣν ᾐτήσαντο παρ' αὐτῶν ἡμέραν, ὄχλου παντοδα-
ποῦ συνεληλυθότος εἰς τὴν ἀγοράν, ὃν ἀμφότεραι
παρεσκευάσαντο σύμμαχον ἑαυταῖς ἐκ παρακλήσεως αἱ ἀρχαί, παρῆσαν ὡς κατηγορήσοντες τοῦ
4 νόμου. ὁ μὲν οὖν Κοΐντιος, τά τε ἄλλα ἐπιεικὴς
ὢν ἀνὴρ καὶ δῆμον οἰκειώσασθαι λόγῳ πιθανώ-
τατος, πρῶτος αἰτησάμενος λόγον,[5] ἐπιδέξιόν τινα
καὶ κεχαρισμένην ἅπασι διεξῆλθε δημηγορίαν, ὥστε
τοὺς ὑπὲρ τοῦ νόμου λέγοντας εἰς πολλὴν ἐλθεῖν

---

[1] Kiessling : λόγος O.
[2] τοὺς βουλομένους A : τοῖς βουλομένοις R.
[3] ἐναντιωθήσονται R : ἐναντία θήσονται Ba, Jacoby.

tribes. This, now, clearly meant the overthrow of the senate and the dominance of the populace.

XLIV. When the consuls were informed of this, they grew anxious and considered by what means the commotion and sedition might speedily and safely be removed. Appius advised summoning to arms all who wished the constitution of their fathers to be preserved, and if any opposed them, to look upon them as enemies. But Quintius thought they ought to use persuasion with the plebeians and convince them that through ignorance of their own interest they were being led into pernicious counsels. He said that it was the extreme of folly to wish to obtain from their fellow citizens against their will the things which they might receive by their consent. The advice of Quintius being approved of by the other members of the senate, the consuls went to the Forum and asked the tribunes to give them a hearing and to appoint a time for it. And having obtained both requests with difficulty, when the day they had asked of them had come, the Forum being filled with a great concourse of people of all sorts, which the magistrates on both sides had got together under instructions to support them, the consuls presented themselves with the intention of speaking against the law. Quintius, accordingly, who was a fair-minded man in all respects and most capable of winning over the populace by his eloquence, first desired leave to speak, and then made an adroit speech that was acceptable to everybody, with the result that those who spoke in favour of the law were

---

[4] σφίσι Kiessling : σφίσι τὰ ὅπλα Ba, Jacoby, σφίσι πρὸς τὰ ὅπλα R.

[5] τὸν before λόγον deleted by Cobet.

ἀμηχανίαν, οὔτε δικαιότερα λέγειν ἔχοντας οὔτε
5 ἐπιεικέστερα. κ̓αὶ εἰ μηδὲν ἔτι πολυπραγμονεῖν ὁ
συνύπατος αὐτοῦ προείλετο, συγγνοὺς ἂν ὁ δῆμος
ὡς οὔτε δίκαια οὔθ᾽ ὅσια ἀξιῶν ἔλυσε τὸν νόμον·
νῦν δ᾽ ἐκείνου λόγον διελθόντος ὑπερήφανον καὶ
βαρὺν ἀκουσθῆναι πένησι χαλεπὸς εἰς ὀργὴν ἐγένετο καὶ ἀμείλικτος καὶ εἰς ἔριν ἦλθεν ὅσην οὔπω
6 πρότερον. οὐ γὰρ ὡς ἐλευθέροις τε καὶ πολίταις
ὁ ἀνὴρ διαλεγόμενος, οἷ τοῦ θεῖναι τὸν νόμον ἢ
λῦσαι κύριοι ἦσαν, ἀλλ᾽ ὡς ἐν ἀτίμοις ἢ ξένοις
ἢ μὴ βεβαίως ἔχουσι τὴν ἐλευθερίαν ἐξουσιάζων,
πικρὰς καὶ ἀνυπομονήτους ἐποιήσατο κατηγορίας,
τῶν τε χρεῶν τὰς ἀποκοπὰς αὐτοῖς ὀνειδίζων καὶ
τῶν ὑπάτων τὴν ἀπόστασιν προφέρων, ὅτε τὰ ἱερὰ
σημεῖα ἁρπάσαντες ᾤχοντο ἐκ τοῦ στρατοπέδου
φυγὴν ἐπιβάλλοντες ἑαυτοῖς ἑκούσιον· τούς θ᾽ ὅρκους ἀνακαλούμενος οὓς ὤμοσαν τὰ ὅπλα περὶ τῆς
γεινομένης[1] αὐτοὺς[2] γῆς ἀναλαμβάνοντες, οἷς κατ᾽
7 αὐτῆς ἐκείνης ἐχρήσαντο. τοιγάρτοι θαυμαστὸν
οὐδὲν ἔφησεν αὐτοὺς ποιεῖν, εἰ θεοὺς μὲν ἐπιορκή-
σαντες, ἡγεμόνας δὲ καταλιπόντες, πόλιν δ᾽ ἔρημον
τὸ καθ᾽ ἑαυτοὺς εἶναι[3] μέρος ἀφέντες, ἐπὶ δὲ
πίστεως συγχύσει καὶ νόμων ἀνατροπῇ καὶ πολι-
τεύματος πατρίου φθορᾷ ποιησάμενοι τὴν κάθοδον,
οὐ μετριάζουσιν οὐδὲ χρηστοὺς δύνανται πολίτας
ἑαυτοὺς παρασχεῖν, ἀλλ᾽ αἰεί τινος ὀρέγονται πλεονεξίας καὶ παρανομίας, τοτὲ μὲν ἀρχὰς ἐξεῖναι σφίσιν ἀξιοῦντες αὐτοὺς ἐφ᾽ ἑαυτῶν ἀποδεικνύναι καὶ

---

[1] περὶ τῆς γεινομένης Steph. : περὶ τῆς γινομένης Α, περι-
γινομένης Β.
[2] αὐτοὺς Steph. : αὐτοῖς ΑΒ.
[3] εἶναι placed here by Cobet : after ἔρημον Ο.

reduced to great embarrassment, finding nothing to
say that was more just or more reasonable.   And if
his colleague had not chosen to continue his officiousness, the populace, being fully aware that their
demands were neither just nor right, would have
rejected the law.   But as it was, he delivered a speech
that was haughty and offensive to the ears of the
poor, so that they became exasperated and implacable and fell into greater strife than ever before.
For he did not talk to them as if they were free men
and his fellow citizens who had power to confirm or
reject the law, but domineering over them as if they
were outcasts or foreigners or men whose liberty
was precarious, he uttered bitter and intolerable reproaches, upbraiding them with the abolition of their
debts and with their desertion of the consuls when
they snatched up the standards and quit the camp,
imposing voluntary banishment upon themselves [1];
and he appealed to the oaths they had sworn when
they took up arms in defence of the country which
had given them birth, only to turn them against that
very country.   Therefore their conduct was not at
all strange, he said, if, after being guilty of perjury
to the gods, deserting their generals, leaving the
city undefended as far as in them lay, and returning
home in order to violate the public faith, subvert the
laws and overthrow the constitution of their fathers,
they showed no moderation and could not behave
themselves like good citizens, but were always aiming at some selfish encroachment and violation of
the laws.   At one time they were demanding the
right to choose for themselves their own magis-

[1] At the time of the secession to the Sacred Mount; see
vi. 45.

ταύτας ἀνυπευθύνους ποιοῦντες καὶ παναγεῖς· τοτὲ
δ' εἰς ἀγῶνας ὑπὲρ τῶν¹ ἐσχάτων² κινδύνων³ καθ-
ιστάντες οὓς αὐτοῖς δόξειε τῶν πατρικίων, καὶ τὰ
νόμιμα δικαστήρια, οἷς περὶ θανάτου καὶ φυγῆς ἡ
πόλις πρότερον ἔδωκε κρίνειν,⁴ μεταφέροντες ἐκ
τῆς καθαρωτάτης βουλῆς⁵ ἐπὶ τὸν ῥυπαρώτατον
ὄχλον· τοτὲ δὲ νόμους εἰσφέροντες οἱ θῆτες καὶ
ἀνέστιοι κατὰ τῶν εὐπατριδῶν τυραννικοὺς καὶ
ἀνίσους, καὶ οὐδὲ τοῦ προβουλεῦσαι περὶ αὐτῶν
ἐξουσίαν τῇ βουλῇ καταλείποντες,⁶ ἀλλ' ἀφαιρούμενοι καὶ ταύτην αὐτῆς τὴν τιμήν, ἣν ἐκ τοῦ παντὸς
εἶχεν ἀναμφίλεκτον χρόνου βασιλευομένης τε καὶ
8 τυραννουμένης τῆς πόλεως. πολλὰ δὲ καὶ ἄλλα

---

¹ τῶν om. B. ² Gelenius : αἰσχίστων O.
³ κινδύνων B : om. R.
⁴ ἔδωκε κρίνειν (cf. chap. 46, 4) ACmg : ἐχρῆτο B.
⁵ βουλῆς Capps, Post : φυλῆς O, Jacoby.
⁶ Reiske : καταλιπόντες O.

---

¹ This passage has not been properly understood hitherto.
Instead of " senate " the MSS. read " tribe ", a manifest
corruption ; and the editors and translators seem to have
thought of the centuriate assembly, whatever may have
been the actual word used by Dionysius. The true reading
becomes evident when we compare this account of the suc-
cessive gains made by the plebeians, and the parallel account
just below, in chap. 46, 4, with the report of the trial of
Coriolanus as given in Book VII. For just as the first
concessions to the plebeians enumerated here and in chap. 46
obviously belong to the time of the secession of the plebs
to the Sacred Mount, so those named later correspond perfectly with the account of the trial of Coriolanus. Concerning
that trial we were informed that the tribunes, after first
insisting upon trying the accused before the people without
the previous sanction of the senate (vii. 25, 3 ; 26 ; 38),
finally agreed that the senate should pass a preliminary

trates and making these unaccountable for their
actions and sacrosanct ; again, they were putting on
trial for their lives such of the patricians as they saw
fit, and transferring the legitimate courts, to which
the commonwealth had formerly entrusted the trial
of causes involving death or banishment, from the
most incorruptible senate [1] to the vilest mob ; and
yet again, the labourers for hire and the homeless
were introducing tyrannical and unfair laws against
the men of noble birth, without leaving to the senate
the power even of passing the preliminary decree
concerning those laws, but depriving that body of
this honour also, which it had always enjoyed undis-
puted under both kings and tyrants.   After he had

decree (to be ratified afterwards by the people), permitting
Coriolanus to be tried by the people (vii. 39, 58) ; and a
subsequent concession permitted the summoning, for that
purpose, of the tribal instead of the centuriate assembly
(vii. 59 ; 60, 1).   It is the combined effect of these two
" laws " (ix. 46, 4), then, that is mentioned with such scorn
in the present passage.   At the outset of their controversy
with the plebeians over Coriolanus the senators had maintained that the senate was the normal tribunal for the trial
of patricians (vii. 52, 6 and 8) ; and they declared that no
patrician had as yet been tried by the popular court, which
had been instituted for the benefit of plebeians oppressed
by the patricians (vii. 52, 1 f. ; 41, 1 f.).   There is no real
contradiction between this claim of the senators and the
declaration of Coriolanus (viii. 6, 2) that the normal court
for these trials was the centuriate assembly ; his statement
really applies simply to trials of plebeians, as only plebeians
had been tried by the popular court.   A further argument
for understanding the senate as the tribunal from whose
jurisdiction these trials had been taken away is to be seen
in the highly complimentary adjective applied to that tribunal, an adjective which neither Dionysius nor the senators
would ever have thought of applying even to the centuriate
assembly, however it might be composed.

τούτοις ὅμοια προσθεὶς καὶ οὐδενὸς οὔτε πικροῦ
πράγματος οὔτε βλασφήμου ὀνόματος φεισάμενος,
τελευτῶν ἐκεῖνον ἔτι προσέθηκεν τὸν λόγον, ἐφ᾽ ᾧ
μάλιστα ἡ πληθὺς ἠγανάκτησεν, ὅτι χρόνον οὐδένα
παύσεται στασιάζουσα περὶ παντὸς χρήματος ἡ
πόλις, ἀλλ᾽ αἰεί τινα καινὴν ἐπὶ παλαιᾷ νοσήσει
νόσον ἕως ἂν ἡ τῶν δημάρχων ἐξουσία διαμένῃ·
διδάσκων ὅτι πράγματος παντὸς πολιτικοῦ καὶ
κοινοῦ τὰς ἀρχὰς προσήκει σκοπεῖν, ὅπως εὐσεβεῖς
ἔσονται καὶ δίκαιοι. φιλεῖν γὰρ ἐκ μὲν τῶν ἀγαθῶν
σπερμάτων χρηστοὺς γίγνεσθαι καὶ εὐτυχεῖς τοὺς
καρπούς, ἐκ δὲ τῶν πονηρῶν κακοὺς καὶ ὀλεθρίους.

XLV. "Εἰ μὲν οὖν," ἔφη, "ἥδε ἡ ἀρχὴ μεθ᾽
ὁμονοίας εἰσῆλθεν εἰς τὴν πόλιν ἐπὶ τῷ πάντων
ἀγαθῷ, παροῦσα σὺν οἰωνοῖς τε καὶ ὀττείαις, πολλῶν ἂν ἡμῖν ἐγίνετο καὶ μεγάλων ἀγαθῶν αἰτία,
χαρίτων, ὁμοφροσύνης, εὐνομίας, ἐλπίδων χρηστῶν
παρὰ τοῦ δαιμονίου, μυρίων ἄλλων· νῦν δέ, βία
γὰρ[1] αὐτὴν εἰσήγαγε καὶ παρανομία καὶ στάσις καὶ
πολέμου δέος ἐμφυλίου καὶ πάντα τὰ ἔχθιστα ἐν
ἀνθρώποις, τί οὖν ἔτι καὶ μέλλει χρηστὸν ἔσεσθαί
ποτε[2] ἢ σωτήριον τοιαύτας λαβούσης τὰς ἀρχάς;
ὥστε περιττόν ἐστιν[3] ἡμῖν ἴασιν καὶ ἀλεξήματα τῶν
ἀναβλαστανόντων ἐξ αὐτῆς κακῶν ζητεῖν, ὁπόσα
εἰς ἀνθρώπινον πίπτει λογισμόν, μενούσης ἔτι τῆς
2 πονηρᾶς ῥίζης. οὐ γὰρ ἔσται πέρας οὐδ᾽ ἀπαλλαγὴ
τῶν δαιμονίων χόλων ἕως ἂν ἥδε ἡ βάσκανος ἐρινὺς
καὶ φαγέδαινα ἐγκαθημένη πάντα σήπῃ καὶ δια-
φθείρῃ τὰ καλά. ἀλλ᾽ ὑπὲρ μὲν τούτων ἕτερος ἔσται
λόγος καὶ καιρὸς ἐπιτηδειότερος, νῦν δ᾽ ἐπεὶ τὰ

---

[1] βία γὰρ Ba : ἐπεὶ βία R.   [2] ποτε B : om. R.
[3] περιττόν ἐστιν Sintenis : περίεστιν O, Jacoby.

uttered many other reproaches of like nature and
withheld neither any bitter fact nor any opprobrious
word, he concluded with this declaration—which
gave greater offence to the multitude than all the
rest—that the commonwealth would never cease
being divided into factions over every matter, but
would always suffer from some fresh distemper following the old as long as the tribunician power should
last.   He pointed out that it is important to examine
the beginnings of every political and public institu-
tion, to see that they shall be righteous and just ;
for from good seeds are wont to come good and wholesome fruit, and from bad seeds evil and deadly fruit.

XLV. " If, now," he said, " this magistracy had
been introduced into the commonwealth harmoni-
ously, for the good of all, entering in with the sanction
of both omens and religious rites, it would have been
the source of many blessings to us—kindly services,
harmony, wholesome laws, hopes of blessings from
Heaven, and countless other benefits.   But as it is,
since it was introduced by violence, lawlessness,
sedition, the fear of civil war, and by everything
mankind most abhors, what good or salutary thing
can one now expect will ever come of it when it had
such beginnings ?   So that it is in vain for us to seek
for a cure and for the aids which human reason suggests against the evils that are continually springing
out of it, so long as the pernicious root remains.   For
we shall have no end of outbursts of the divine wrath,
no deliverance from them, while this malignant curse
and cancer, firmly imbedded in our body politic,
corrupts and destroys all that is wholesome.   But for
the discussion of this subject another occasion will be
more suitable.   For the moment, since it is necessary

παρόντα εὖ τίθεσθαι χρή, πᾶσαν εἰρωνείαν ἀφεὶς
τάδε ὑμῖν λέγω· οὔτε ὅδε ὁ νόμος οὔτ' ἄλλος οὐδεὶς ὃν οὐχ ἡ βουλὴ προβουλεύσει κύριος ἐπὶ τῆς
ἐμῆς ὑπατείας γενήσεται, ἀλλὰ καὶ λόγοις ἀγω-
νιοῦμαι περὶ τῆς ἀριστοκρατίας, κἂν εἰς τὰ ἔργα
δέῃ χωρεῖν οὐδ' ἐν¹ τούτοις² τῶν ἐναντιουμένων
λελείψομαι· καὶ εἰ μὴ πρότερον ἔγνωτε ὅσην ἰσχὺν
ἔχει τὸ τῶν ὑπάτων κράτος, ἐπὶ τῆς ἐμῆς ἀρχῆς
μαθήσεσθε.''

XLVI. Ἄππιος μὲν δὴ ταῦτ' εἶπεν, ἐκ δὲ τῶν
δημάρχων ὁ πρεσβύτατος καὶ πλείστου ἀξιώματος
τυγχάνων, Γάιος Λαιτώριος, ἀνὴρ ἔν τε τοῖς πολέμοις ἐγνωσμένος εἶναι ψυχὴν οὐ κακὸς καὶ τὰ
πολιτικὰ πράττειν οὐκ ἀδύνατος, ἀνίσταται πρὸς
ταῦτ' ἀπολογησόμενος· καὶ διῆλθεν ὑπὲρ τοῦ δήμου
λόγον πολὺν ἀπὸ τῶν ἄνωθεν ἀρξάμενος· ὡς πολλὰς
μὲν καὶ χαλεπὰς στρατείας οἱ βλασφημούμενοι
πρὸς αὐτοῦ πένητες ἐστρατεύσαντο, οὐ μόνον ἐπὶ
τῶν βασιλέων, ὅτε τὴν ἀνάγκην ἄν³ τις ᾐτιά-
σατο, ἀλλὰ καὶ μετὰ τὴν ἐκείνων ἐκβολὴν ἐλευ-
2 θερίαν κτώμενοι τῇ πατρίδι καὶ ἡγεμονίαν· ἀμοιβὴν
δ' οὐδεμίαν ἐκομίσαντο παρὰ τῶν πατρικίων οὐδ'
ἀπήλαυσαν οὐδενὸς τῶν κοινῶν ἀγαθῶν, ἀλλ' ὡς
πολέμῳ ἁλόντες ἀφῃρέθησαν ὑπ' αὐτῶν καὶ τὴν
ἐλευθερίαν, ἣν ἀνασώσασθαι βουλόμενοι καταλιπεῖν
ἠναγκάσθησαν τὴν πατρίδα πόθῳ γῆς ἑτέρας ἐν ᾗ
τὸ μὴ ὑβρίζεσθαι αὐτοῖς ἐλευθέροις οὖσιν ὑπάρξει·
καὶ οὔτε βιασάμενοι τὴν βουλὴν οὔτε πολέμῳ
προσαναγκάσαντες εὕροντο τὴν ἐπὶ τὰ σφέτερα
κάθοδον, ἀξιούσῃ δὲ καὶ δεομένῃ τὰ ἐκλειφθέντα

---

¹ οὐδ' ἐν Reiske : οὐδὲν AB.

² τούτοις B : τούτων R.   ³ ἄν B : om. R.

to compose the present disturbances, I put aside all
equivocation and say this to you : Neither this nor
any other law shall become valid during my consulship without a preliminary decree of the senate ; on
the contrary, I will fight for the aristocracy not only
with words, but, if it shall be necessary to proceed to
deeds, I shall not be outdone by its opponents even
in these.   And if you did not know before the extent
of the consular power, you shall learn it during my
term of office."

XLVI. Thus Appius spoke ; and, on the side of the
tribunes, the oldest and most highly respected, Gaius
Laetorius, a man acknowledged to be of no mean
courage in warfare and not without ability in public
affairs, rose up to answer him ; and he delivered a
long speech in behalf of the populace, beginning with
the earliest times.   He showed that the poor whom
Appius maligned had made many hard campaigns not
only under their kings, when one might say their
action was due to compulsion, but also after the expulsion of the kings, when they were acquiring liberty
and supremacy for the fatherland.   But they had
received no recompense from the patricians nor
enjoyed any of the public advantages, but, like
captives taken in war, had been deprived by them
even of their liberty, to recover which they had been
compelled to leave their country in their yearning
for another land in which they might live as free men
without being insulted.   And they had obtained their
return to their possessions neither by offering violence
to the senate nor by resorting to the compulsion of
war, but by yielding to it when it asked and implored

75

3 ἀπολαβεῖν εἴξαντες.[1] τούς τε ὅρκους διεξήει καὶ τὰς
συνθήκας τὰς ἐπὶ τῇ καθόδῳ γενομένας ἀνεκαλεῖτο·
ἐν αἷς ἦν ἀμνηστία μὲν πρῶτον ἁπάντων,[2] ἔπειτα
ἐξουσία τοῖς πένησιν ἀρχὰς ἀποδεικνύναι, τιμωροὺς
μὲν ἐσομένας σφίσιν αὐτοῖς, τοῖς δὲ κατισχύειν
4 βουλομένοις ἀντιπάλους. διεξελθὼν δὲ ταῦτα τοὺς
νόμους ἐπεδείκνυτο οὓς ὁ δῆμος ἐπεκύρωσεν οὐ
πρὸ πολλοῦ, τόν τε περὶ τῶν δικαστηρίων τῆς
μεταγωγῆς, ὡς[3] ἔδωκεν ἡ βουλὴ τῷ δήμῳ τὴν
ἐξουσίαν κρίνειν οὓς ἂν αὐτοῖς δόξειε τῶν πατρικίων, καὶ τὸν ὑπὲρ τῆς ψηφοφορίας, ὃς οὐκ ἔτι[4]
τὴν λοχῖτιν[5] ἐκκλησίαν,[6] ἀλλὰ τὴν φυλετικὴν[7] ἐποίει
τῶν ψήφων κυρίαν.

XLVII. Διεξελθὼν δὲ τὸν ὑπὲρ τοῦ δήμου λόγον,
ἐπιστρέψας ἐπὶ τὸν Ἄππιον, " Ἔπειτα σὺ τολμᾷς," εἶπε, " λοιδορεῖσθαι τούτοις δι' οὓς μεγάλη
μὲν ἐκ μικρᾶς, ἐπιφανὴς δ' ἐξ ἀδόξου γέγονεν ἡ
πόλις; καὶ στασιαστὰς ἑτέρους ἀποκαλεῖς καὶ
φυγαδικήν τινα τύχην ὀνειδίζεις, ὥσπερ οὐχ ἁπάντων ἔτι τούτων μεμνημένων τὸ καθ' ὑμᾶς, ὅτι
στασιάσαντες οἱ σοὶ πρόγονοι πρὸς τοὺς ἐν τέλει
καὶ τὴν ἑαυτῶν πατρίδα καταλιπόντες ἐνθάδ' ἱδρύ-
θησαν ἱκέται; εἰ μὴ ἄρα ὑμεῖς μὲν ἐκλιπόντες
τὴν ἑαυτῶν πατρίδα πόθῳ τῆς ἐλευθερίας καλὸν
ἔργον ἐπράττετε, Ῥωμαῖοι δὲ τὰ ὅμοια ὑμῖν δεδρα-
2 κότες οὐ καλόν. τολμᾷς δὲ καὶ τὴν τῶν δημάρχων

---

[1] After εἴξαντες ACmg add ἔδωκαν.
[2] Kiessling : πάντων O.
[3] ὥς O : ᾧ Portus.
[4] ἔτι R (?) : εἶχε AB.
[5] κουριάτην Reiske.
[6] ἐκκλησίαν A : ἐξουσίαν B.
[7] Reiske : κουριᾶτιν O, Jacoby.

them to receive back their abandoned possessions. He mentioned the oaths and appealed to the terms of the compact which had been made to induce them to return, among which there was, first, a general amnesty, and then for the poor the power of choosing magistrates who should assist them and oppose those who wished to do violence to them. After recounting these matters, he cited the laws which the people had not long before ratified, both the one concerning the transfer of the courts, by which the senate had granted to the people the power to try any of the patricians they should think fit, and also the one concerning the manner of their voting, which no longer made the centuriate assembly, but rather the tribal assembly, responsible for the voting.[1]

XLVII. When he had finished his defence of the populace, he turned to Appius and said : " After this do *you* dare revile these men through whom the commonwealth, once small, has become great, and, once obscure, illustrious ? And do you call your opponents seditious and reproach them for a fate akin to exile, as if all these men here did not still remember what befel your own family—that your ancestors, having raised a sedition against the authorities and abandoned their country, settled here as suppliants ? [2] Unless, indeed, your folk, when they forsook their country through a desire for liberty, did a noble thing, but Romans, when they did the same thing as you, did an ignoble thing ! Do you dare also to revile the

---

[1] See the note on chap. 44, 7. Reiske's proposal to read " curiate assembly " for " centuriate assembly " was evidently based on the assumption that the reference is to the tribunician elections (chap. 41, 2) ; but the people did not ratify that proposed change until later (chap. 49, 4 f.).

[2] See v. 40, 3-5.

ἐξουσίαν ὡς ἐπὶ κακῷ παρεληλυθυῖαν εἰς τὴν πόλιν
λοιδορεῖν καὶ πείθεις τουτουσὶ καταλῦσαι τὴν τῶν
πενήτων ἐπικουρίαν τὴν ἱερὰν καὶ ἀκίνητον καὶ
μεγάλαις ἠσφαλισμένην ἐκ θεῶν τε καὶ ἀνθρώπων
ἀνάγκαις, ὦ μισοδημότατε καὶ τυραννικώτατε;
καὶ οὐδὲ τοῦτο ἄρα ἐδυνήθης μαθεῖν, ὅτι τῇ τε
βουλῇ καὶ τῇ σεαυτοῦ ἀρχῇ ταῦτα λέγων λοιδορῇ;
καὶ γὰρ ἡ βουλὴ διαναστᾶσα[1] πρὸς[2] τοὺς βασιλεῖς,
ὧν οὐκέτι τὰς ὑπερηφανίας καὶ τὰς ὕβρεις ὑπο-
φέρειν ἠξίου, τὸ τῶν ὑπάτων ἀρχεῖον κατεστήσατο,
καὶ πρὶν ἐκείνους ἐξελάσαι τῆς πόλεως ἑτέρους
3 ἐποίησε τῆς βασιλικῆς ἐξουσίας κυρίους. ὥστε ἃ
περὶ τῆς δημαρχίας λέγεις ὡς ἐπὶ κακῷ παρελη-
λυθυίας, ἐπειδὴ τὴν ἀρχὴν ἀπὸ διχοστασίας ἔλαβε,
ταῦτα καὶ κατὰ τῆς ὑπατείας λέγεις. οὐδὲ γὰρ
ἐκείνην ἄλλη τις εἰσήγαγε πρόφασις ἀλλ' ἡ πρὸς
4 τοὺς βασιλεῖς τῶν πατρικίων στάσις. ἀλλὰ τί
ταῦτά σοι διαλέγομαι ὡς χρηστῷ καὶ μετρίῳ
πολίτῃ, ὃν ἅπαντες ἴσασιν οὗτοι σκαιὸν ὄντα διὰ
γένος καὶ πικρὸν καὶ μισόδημον καὶ τὸ θηριῶδες
ὑπὸ φύσεως οὐδέποτε ἐξημερῶσαι δυνάμενον, ἀλλ'
οὐχ ὁμόσε χωρῶ σοι τὰ ἔργα ἐπίπροσθεν ποιησάμενος τῶν λόγων, καὶ δείκνυμι ὅσην ἰσχὺν ὁ δῆμος
ἔχων λέληθέ σε, ὃν οὐκ ἠσχύνθης ἀνέστιον καὶ
ῥυπαρὸν καλῶν, καὶ ὅσον ἥδε ἡ ἀρχὴ δυναμένη,[3]
ἣν σε ὁ νόμος ἐκτρέπεσθαι καὶ εἴκειν ἀναγκάζει;
παρεὶς δὲ καὶ αὐτὸς ἅπασαν εἰρωνείαν ἔργου
ἔξομαι.''[4]

XLVIII. Ταῦτ' εἰπών, ὅρκον ὅσπερ μέγιστος
αὐτοῖς ἦν διομοσάμενος ἢ τὸν νόμον ἐπικυρώσειν

---

[1] διαναστᾶσα R : διαστᾶσα C.
[2] πρὸς B : om. C, πᾶσα πρὸς R.

tribunician power as having been introduced into the
commonwealth for a mischievous purpose and do you
attempt to persuade these men here to abrogate this
sacred and inviolable protection of the poor, safe-
guarded as it is by powerful sanctions which stem
from both gods and men, O greatest enemy of
the populace and most tyrannical of men ? Have
you not been able, then, to learn even this, that in
saying these things you traduce both the senate and
your own magistracy ? For the senate, having risen
against the kings, whose arrogance and insults they
resolved to bear no longer, established the consulship,
and before they had expelled the kings, invested
others with the royal authority. So that everything
you say against the tribunician power as having been
introduced for a mischievous purpose, since it had its
origin in sedition, you say against the consulship also ;
for there was no other ground for introducing that
magistracy than the sedition of the patricians against
the kings. But why do I talk thus with you as with
a good and fair-minded citizen, when all these men
here know that you are by inheritance mischievous,
harsh and an enemy of the populace, and that you
can never tame your inborn savagery ? Why do I not
rather come to grips with you, preferring actions to
words, and show you how great is the strength, all
unknown to you, of the populace, whom you were
not ashamed to call homeless and vile, and how great
is the power of *this* magistracy, to which the law
obliges you to give way and submit ? I too shall lay
aside all equivocation and set to work."

XLVIII. Having said this and sworn the strongest
oath in use among the Romans that he would either

---

[3] δυναμένη deleted by Kayser. [4] Cobet : ἄρξομαι O.

ἢ τοῦ ζῆν μεθήσεσθαι, σιωπῆς γενομένης ἐκ τοῦ
πλήθους καὶ ἐναγωνίου προσδοκίας ἐφ᾽ ᾧ μέλλει
δρᾶν, ἐκέλευσε μεταχωρεῖν ἐκ τῆς ἐκκλησίας τὸν
Ἄππιον. ὡς δ᾽ οὐκ ἐπείθετο, ἀλλὰ τοὺς ῥαβδούχους παραστησάμενος καὶ τὸν ὄχλον ὃν ἦγε παρα-
σκευασάμενος οἴκοθεν ἀπεμάχετο μὴ παραχωρῆσαι
τῆς ἀγορᾶς, σιωπὴν ὑποκηρυξάμενος ὁ Λαιτώριος
ἀνεῖπεν ὅτι τὸν ὕπατον εἰς φυλακὴν κελεύουσιν
2 ἀπάγειν¹ οἱ δήμαρχοι. καὶ ὁ μὲν ὑπηρέτης κελευσθεὶς ὑπ᾽ αὐτοῦ προσῆγεν ὡς τοῦ σώματος ἐπι-
ληψόμενος· τῶν δὲ ῥαβδούχων ὁ πρῶτος ἐπιτυχὼν
παίων αὐτὸν ἀπήλασε. κραυγῆς δ᾽ ἐκ τῶν παρόντων γενομένης μεγάλης καὶ ἀγανακτήσεως ἵεται
αὐτὸς ὁ Λαιτώριος παρακελευσάμενος τοῖς ὄχλοις
ἀμύνειν, καὶ οἱ περὶ τὸν Ἄππιον στῖφος ἔχοντες
νέων πολὺ καὶ καρτερὸν ὑφίστανται. καὶ μετὰ
τοῦτο λόγοι τε ἀσχήμονες ἐγένοντο εἰς ἀλλήλους
καὶ καταβοαὶ καὶ σωμάτων ὠθισμοί· καὶ τελευτῶσα
εἰς χεῖρας ἀπέσκηψεν ἡ ἔρις καὶ εἰς λίθων ἤρξατο
3 προβαίνειν βολάς. ἐπέσχε δὲ ταῦτα καὶ τοῦ μὴ
προσωτέρω χωρῆσαι τὰ δεινὰ Κοΐντιος ἅτερος τῶν
ὑπάτων αἴτιος ἐγένετο, δεόμενός τε ἁπάντων καὶ
λιπαρῶν σὺν τοῖς πρεσβυτάτοις τῶν ἐκ τοῦ συνεδρίου καὶ εἰς μέσους τοὺς ἁψιμαχοῦντας ὠθού-
μενος. ἦν δὲ καὶ τῆς ἡμέρας τὸ λειπόμενον βραχὺ
μέρος, ὥστε ἀκούσιοι ἀπ᾽ ἀλλήλων διελύθησαν.
4   Ταῖς δ᾽ ἑξῆς ἡμέραις αἵ τ᾽ ἀρχαὶ ἀλλήλαις ἐν-
εκάλουν, ὁ μὲν ὕπατος τοῖς δημάρχοις ὅτι καταλύειν αὐτοῦ τὴν ἀρχὴν ἠξίουν ἐς τὸ δεσμωτήριον
τὸν ὕπατον ἀπάγειν κελεύσαντες, τῷ δ᾽ ὑπάτῳ οἱ
δήμαρχοι ὡς ἐμβεβληκότι πληγὰς σώμασιν ἱεροῖς

¹ ἀπάγειν ACmg : om. R.

get the law ratified or abandon life, the multitude meanwhile having become silent and being in an agony of expectation concerning what he was going to do, he ordered Appius to leave the assembly. And when Appius, instead of obeying, placed the lictors about him, together with the crowd which he had brought from home for that purpose, and obstinately refused to leave the Forum, Laetorius, after bidding the heralds to command silence, announced that the tribunes ordered the consul to be led away to prison. Upon this the assistant by his command advanced in order to seize the person of Appius, but the foremost lictor with a successful blow drove him back. When those present raised a great outcry and showed their resentment, Laetorius himself rushed forward after appealing to the crowds to assist him, while Appius, supported by a numerous and vigorous body of young men, stood his ground. There followed unseemly words between the factions and shouting and the pushing of body against body ; and at last the strife broke out into blows and they began to throw stones. But a stop was put to this and the mischief was prevented from proceeding farther by Quintius, the other consul, who together with the oldest senators implored and entreated them all to desist, and thrust himself into the midst of the contending parties. Moreover, there was little of the day left, so that, albeit reluctantly, they separated.

During the following days not only did the magistrates indulge in accusations against one another, the consul charging the tribunes with a desire to invalidate his authority by ordering a consul to be led away to prison, and the tribunes charging the consul with having struck those whose persons were

καὶ καθωσιωμένοις ὑπὸ τοῦ νόμου (καὶ ὁ Λαιτώριος
τὰ ἴχνη τῶν πληγῶν εἶχεν ἐπὶ τῆς ὄψεως ἔτι
φανερά), ἥ τε πόλις ὅλη διοιδοῦσα καὶ ἀγριαινομένη
5 διειστήκει. ἔπειτα ὁ μὲν δῆμος ἐφρούρει τὸ Καπιτώλιον ἅμα τοῖς δημάρχοις, οὔτε ἡμέρας οὔτε
νυκτὸς ἐκλείπων τὴν¹ φυλακήν· ἡ δὲ βουλὴ συνιοῦσα
πολλὴν καὶ ἐπίπονον ἐποιεῖτο ζήτησιν ὅπως χρὴ
παῦσαι τὴν διχοστασίαν, τοῦ τε κινδύνου τὸ μέγεθος ἐνθυμουμένη καὶ ὅτι οὐδὲ τοῖς ὑπάτοις τὰ
αὐτὰ παρεστήκει φρονεῖν. ὁ μὲν γὰρ Κοΐντιος
εἴκειν τῷ δήμῳ τὰ μέτρια ἠξίου, ὁ δ' Ἄππιος
μέχρι θανάτου ἀντέχειν.²

XLIX. Ὡς δ' οὐδὲν ἐγίνετο πέρας, χωρὶς ἑκάστους ἀπολαμβάνων ὁ Κοΐντιος, τούς τε δημάρχους
καὶ τὸν Ἄππιον, ἐδεῖτο καὶ ἐλιπάρει καὶ τὰ κοινὰ
τῶν ἰδίων ἀναγκαιότερα ἡγεῖσθαι ἠξίου. ὁρῶν δὲ
τοὺς μὲν ἤδη πεπειροτέρους γεγονότας, τὸν δὲ συνάρχοντα ἐπὶ τῆς αὐτῆς αὐθαδείας μένοντα, πείθει
τοὺς ἀμφὶ Λαιτώριον ὑπὲρ ἁπάντων τῶν τε ἰδίων
ἐγκλημάτων καὶ τῶν δημοσίων τὴν βουλὴν ποιῆσαι
2 κυρίαν. ἐπεὶ δὲ τοῦτο διεπράξατο, συνεκάλει
τὴν βουλὴν καὶ τοὺς δημάρχους πολλὰ ἐπαινέσας
καὶ τοῦ συνάρχοντος δεηθεὶς μὴ ἀντιπράττειν τῇ
σωτηρίᾳ τῆς πόλεως ἐκάλει τοὺς εἰωθότας ἀπο-
3 φαίνεσθαι γνώμας. πρῶτος δὲ κληθεὶς Πόπλιος
Οὐαλέριος Ποπλικόλας γνώμην ἀπεφήνατο τήνδε·
ὅσα μὲν ἀλλήλοις ἐγκαλοῦσιν οἵ τε δήμαρχοι καὶ ὁ
ὕπατος, ὑπὲρ ὧν ἔπαθον ἢ ἔδρασαν ἐν τῇ ταραχῇ,
ἐπειδὴ οὐκ ἐξ ἐπιβουλῆς οὐδ' οἰκείας πλεονεξίας

¹ τὴν B : αὐτοῦ τὴν R.   ² Kiessling : ἀντεῖχεν O.

sacred and made inviolate by the law—Laetorius, indeed, bore on his face the marks, still visible, of the blows—but the whole city, filled with rage and fury, was rent with faction. Then the populace together with the tribunes proceeded to guard the Capitol both day and night without intermission. The senate assembled and entered into a long and difficult consideration of the proper means of putting a stop to the sedition, being sensible not only of the magnitude of the danger but also that not even the consuls had succeeded in being of one mind ; for Quintius advised yielding to the populace in everything that was reasonable, whereas Appius proposed to resist till death.

XLIX. When no end would come to the strife, Quintius took each party aside separately, the tribunes and Appius, and begged, besought and implored them to regard the public interests as more vital than their private concerns. And observing that the tribunes had become milder but that his colleague persisted in the same arrogance, he undertook to persuade Laetorius and his colleagues to refer all their complaints, both private and public, to the determination of the senate. When he had accomplished this, he assembled the senate, and after bestowing great praise upon the tribunes and begging his colleague not to act against the safety of the state, he then proceeded to call upon those who were wont to express their opinions.[1] Publius Valerius Publicola, who was called upon first, expressed the following opinion : That the mutual accusations of the tribunes and the consul relating to what they had suffered or done in the tumult, since they had gone so far, not

---

[1] i.e., the older members; cf. chap. 51, 3.

ἕνεκεν εἰς αὐτὰ κατέστησαν, ἀλλ' ὑπὸ[1] τῆς εἰς τὰ κοινὰ φιλοτιμίας, ἀφεῖσθαι δημοσίᾳ καὶ μηδεμίαν ὑπὲρ αὐτῶν εἶναι δίκην· περὶ δὲ τοῦ νόμου, ἐπειδὴ ὁ ὕπατος[2] οὐκ ἐᾷ νόμον ἀπροβούλευτον εἰς τὴν ἐκκλησίαν ἐκφέρειν, προβουλεῦσαι μὲν περὶ τούτου τὸ συνέδριον· τοὺς δὲ δημάρχους ἅμα τοῖς ὑπάτοις ἐπιμέλειαν ποιήσασθαι τῆς τε ὁμονοίας τῶν πολιτῶν, ὅταν ἡ ψῆφος περὶ αὐτοῦ διαφέρηται, καὶ τῆς 4 εὐκοσμίας. ἐπαινεσάντων δὲ τὴν γνώμην ἁπάντων εὐθὺς ἀνέδωκε τὴν ὑπὲρ τοῦ νόμου ψῆφον ὁ Κοΐντιος τῷ συνεδρίῳ, καὶ πολλὰ μὲν Ἀππίου κατηγορήσαντος, πολλὰ δὲ τῶν δημάρχων ἀντιλεξάντων, ἐνίκα παρὰ πολλὰς ψήφους ἡ τὸν νόμον εἰσφέρειν ἀξιοῦσα γνώμη. ἐπικυρωθέντος δὲ τοῦ προβουλεύματος αἵ τε ἴδιαι τῶν ἀρχόντων διαφοραὶ διελύθησαν καὶ ὁ δῆμος ἀγαπητῶς δεξάμενος τὸ συγχώρημα τῆς βουλῆς ἐπεψήφισε τὸν 5 νόμον. ἀπ' ἐκείνου τοῦ χρόνου τὰ τῶν δημάρχων καὶ ἀγορανόμων ἀρχαιρέσια μέχρι τοῦ καθ' ἡμᾶς χρόνου δίχα οἰωνῶν τε καὶ τῆς ἄλλης ὀττείας ἁπάσης αἱ φυλετικαὶ ψηφοφοροῦσιν ἐκκλησίαι. αὕτη λύσις ἐγένετο τῆς τότε κατασχούσης ταραχῆς τὴν πόλιν.

L. Καὶ μετ' οὐ πολὺ στρατιὰς ἐδόκει Ῥωμαίοις καταγράφειν καὶ τοὺς ὑπάτους ἐκπέμπειν ἀμφοτέρους ἐπί τε Αἰκανοὺς καὶ Οὐολούσκους. δυνάμεις γὰρ ἐξ[3] ἑκατέρων τῶν ἐθνῶν ἐξεληλυθέναι ἠγγέλλοντο μεγάλαι καὶ προνομεύειν τοὺς Ῥωμαίων συμμάχους. παρασκευασθεισῶν δὲ τῶν δυνάμεων

---

[1] Sylburg : ὑπὲρ O.
[2] Ἄππιος after ὕπατος deleted by Cobet.
[3] ἐξ B : ἀφ' AC.

with malice aforethought or for personal advantage, but out of rivalry in their zeal for the public welfare, should be publicly dismissed and that no suit should be brought because of them. As to the proposed law, since the consul would not allow any law to be presented to the assembly without a preliminary vote of the senate, he advised that the senate should vote upon it first ; also that the tribunes together with the consuls should take care to preserve harmony and decorum among the citizens when the vote should be taken concerning it. This advice being approved of by all, Quintius immediately put the question to the senate concerning the law, and after many objections offered by Appius and many rejoinders made by the tribunes the motion to lay it before the populace was carried by a large majority. The preliminary decree having been thus passed, the private differences of the magistrates were composed ; and the populace, gladly accepting this concession of the senate, ratified the law. From that time down to our own the tribunes and the aediles have been chosen in the tribal assemblies [1] without auspices or any other religious observances. This was the end of the tumult which disturbed the commonwealth at that time.

L. Not long afterwards [2] the Romans decided to enrol armies and to send out both consuls against the Aequians and the Volscians ; for it was reported that large forces from both these nations had taken the field and were then pillaging the territories of the Romans' allies. The armies being soon ready, Quin-

---

[1] See the note on chap. 41, 2.
[2] *Cf.* Livy ii. 58, 3–60, 5.

σὺν τάχει Κοίντιος μὲν Αἰκανοῖς πολεμήσων ᾤχετο,
Ἄππιος δὲ Οὐολούσκοις, κλήρῳ διαλαχόντες τὰς
ἀρχάς. συνέβη δὲ τῶν ὑπάτων ἑκατέρῳ τὰ εἰκότα
2 πάσχειν. ἡ μὲν γὰρ τῷ Κοιντίῳ προσνεμηθεῖσα
στρατιὰ τὴν ἐπιείκειάν τε καὶ μετριότητα τοῦ
ἀνδρὸς ἀσπαζομένη πρόθυμος ἦν εἰς ἅπαντα τὰ
ἐπιταττόμενα, καὶ τὰ πλεῖστα αὐτοκέλευστος ὑφ-
ίστατο κινδυνεύματα δόξαν τῷ ἡγεμόνι καὶ τιμὴν
πράττουσα· καὶ διεξῆλθε πολλὴν τῆς Αἰκανῶν
χώρας λεηλατοῦσα οὐ τολμώντων εἰς χεῖρας ἐλθεῖν
τῶν πολεμίων, ἐξ ἧς λάφυρα πολλὰ καὶ ὠφελείας
μεγάλας ἐκτήσατο. χρόνον δ' οὐ πολὺν ἐν τῇ
πολεμίᾳ διατρίψασα παρῆν εἰς τὴν πόλιν ἀπαθὴς
κακῶν, λαμπρὸν ἐπὶ τοῖς ἔργοις τὸν στρατηγὸν
3 ἄγουσα. ἡ δὲ τῷ Ἀππίῳ συνεξελθοῦσα[1] δύναμις
μίσει τῷ πρὸς αὐτὸν πολλὰ ὑπερεῖδε τῶν πατρίων.
τά τε γὰρ ἄλλα ἐθελοκακοῦσα ἐν ὅλῃ τῇ στρατείᾳ
καὶ ὀλιγωροῦσα τοῦ ἡγεμόνος διετέλεσε, καὶ ἐπειδὴ μάχεσθαι ἔδει τῇ Οὐολούσκων στρατιᾷ, κατα-
σταθεῖσα ὑπὸ τῶν ἡγεμόνων εἰς τάξιν οὐκ ἠξίωσε
τοῖς πολεμίοις εἰς χεῖρας ἰέναι· ἀλλ' οἵ τε λοχαγοὶ
καὶ οἱ πρόμαχοι αὐτῶν, οἱ μὲν[2] τὰ σημεῖα ῥίψαντες,
οἱ δὲ τὴν τάξιν[3] ἐγκαταλιπόντες ἐπὶ τὸν χάρακα
4 ἔφευγον. καὶ εἰ μὴ θαυμάσαντες τὸ παράλογον
τῆς φυγῆς αὐτῶν οἱ πολέμιοι καὶ δείσαντες μὴ
ἐνέδρα τις ᾖ, τῆς ἐπὶ πλεῖον διώξεως ἀπετράποντο,
τὸ πλεῖον ἂν μέρος τῶν Ῥωμαίων διέφθαρτο.
ἐποίουν δὲ ταῦτα φθόνῳ τοῦ ἡγεμόνος, ἵνα μὴ

---

[1] Reiske : συνελθοῦσα O.

[2] οἱ μὲν om. B.　　　　[3] οἱ δὲ τὴν τάξιν om. BC.

tius set out to make war against the Aequians and
Appius against the Volscians, these commands having
fallen to them by lot. And the fortunes of each of
the consuls were such as might have been expected.
The army assigned to Quintius, pleased with the
fairness and moderation of their general, were eager
to carry out all his orders, and undertook most of
the hazards unbidden, thereby achieving glory and
honour for their commander. They overran a large
part of the country of the Aequians and plundered
it, the enemy not daring to come to an engagement ;
and from it they acquired great booty and rich
spoils. After tarrying a short time in the enemy's
country they returned to the city without any losses,
bringing their general home illustrious because of
his exploits. But the army that went out with
Appius because of their hatred of him disregarded
many of the principles of their ancestors. In fact,
during the whole campaign they not only played the
coward deliberately and treated their general with
contempt, but particularly when they were to engage
the army of the Volscians and their commanders
had drawn them up in order of battle, they refused
to come to grips with the enemy, but both the centurions and the *antesignani*,[1] some throwing away
their standards and others quitting their posts, fled
to the camp. And if the enemy, wondering at their
unexpected flight and fearing there might be an
ambush, had not turned back from pursuing them
farther, the greater part of the Romans would have
been destroyed. The troops acted thus because of
the grudge they bore to their general, lest he should

[1] The soldiers, specially chosen, who fought before the
standards.

καλὸν ἀγώνισμα ὁ ἀνὴρ διαπραξάμενος θριάμβῳ τε
5 καὶ ταῖς ἄλλαις ἐπιλαμπρυνθῇ τιμαῖς. τῇ δὲ κατόπιν ἡμέρᾳ τὰ μὲν ἐπιτιμῶντος αὐτοῖς τοῦ ὑπάτου
τῆς ἀδόξου φυγῆς, τὰ δὲ παρακαλοῦντος αἴσχιστον
ἔργον ἀναλύσασθαι καλῷ ἀγῶνι, τὰ δ' ἀπειλοῦντος,
εἰ μὴ στήσονται παρὰ τὰ δεινά, χρήσεσθαι τοῖς
νόμοις, ἀπειθείᾳ τε διεχρῶντο καὶ καταβοῇ καὶ
ἀπάγειν σφᾶς ἐκέλευον ἐκ τῆς πολεμίας ὡς ἀδύνατοι ἔτι ὄντες ὑπὸ τραυμάτων ἀντέχειν· κατ-
εδήσαντο γὰρ αὐτῶν οἱ πολλοὶ τοὺς ὑγιεῖς χρῶτας
ὡς τραυματίαι· ὥστε ὁ Ἄππιος ἠναγκάσθη ἀπάγειν
τὸν στρατὸν ἐκ τῆς πολεμίας, καὶ οἱ Οὐολοῦσκοι
ἀπιοῦσιν ἑπόμενοι πολλοὺς αὐτῶν ἀπέκτειναν.
6 ὡς δ' ἐν τῇ φιλίᾳ ἐγένοντο, συναγαγὼν εἰς ἐκκλησίαν αὐτοὺς ὁ ὕπατος καὶ πολλὰ ὀνειδίσας ἔφη
χρήσεσθαι τῇ κατὰ τῶν λιποτακτῶν[1] κολάσει. καὶ
πολλὰ δεομένων τῶν πρεσβευτῶν καὶ τῶν ἄλλων
τῶν ἐν τέλει μετριάσαι καὶ μὴ συμφορὰν ἐπὶ
συμφορᾷ προσθεῖναι τῇ πόλει, λόγον οὐδενὸς αὐτῶν
7 ποιησάμενος ἐκύρωσε τὴν κόλασιν. καὶ μετὰ τοῦτο
οἱ λοχαγοί τε ὧν οἱ λόχοι ἔφυγον, καὶ οἱ πρόμαχοι
τῶν σημείων ὅσοι τὰ σημεῖα ἀπολωλέκεσαν, οἱ μὲν
πελέκει τοὺς αὐχένας ἀπεκόπησαν, οἱ δὲ ξύλοις
παιόμενοι διεφθάρησαν· ἐκ δὲ τοῦ ἄλλου πλήθους
ἀπὸ δεκάδος ἑκάστης εἷς ἀνὴρ ὁ λαχὼν κλήρῳ
πρὸ τῶν ἄλλων ἀπέθνησκεν. αὕτη Ῥωμαίοις
πάτριός ἐστι κατὰ τῶν λιπόντων τὰς τάξεις ἢ
προεμένων τὰς σημείας ἡ κόλασις. καὶ μετὰ ταῦτ'
αὐτός τε μισούμενος ὁ στρατηγὸς καὶ τῆς στρατιᾶς
ὅσον ἔτι περιῆν κατηφὲς καὶ ἄτιμον ἐπαγόμενος,

---

[1] λιποτακτῶν Ba : λειποτακτῶν R.

win a brilliant engagement and so obtain the distinction of a triumph and the other honours. And the following day, when the consul alternately upbraided them for their inglorious flight, exhorted them to redeem their most disgraceful conduct by a noble effort, and threatened to invoke the laws against them if they would not stand firm in the face of danger, they broke out into disobedience, clamoured against him and bade him lead them out of the enemy's country, alleging that they were no longer able to hold out by reason of their wounds; for most of them had bound up the sound parts of their bodies as if they had been wounded. Hence Appius was obliged to withdraw his army from the enemy's country, and the Volscians, pursuing them as they retreated, killed many of them. As soon as they were in friendly territory, the consul assembled the troops, and after uttering many reproaches said that he would inflict upon them the punishment ordained against those who quit their posts. And though the legates and the other officers earnestly besought him to use moderation and not to heap one calamity after another upon the commonwealth, he paid no heed to any of them but confirmed the punishment. Thereupon the centurions whose centuries had run away and the *antesignani* who had lost their standards were either beheaded with an axe or beaten to death with rods; as for the rank and file, one man chosen by lot out of every ten was put to death for the rest. This is the traditional punishment among the Romans for those who desert their posts or yield their standards. Afterwards, the general, an object of hatred himself and leading back, dejected and disgraced, what was left of his army,

DIONYSIUS OF HALICARNASSUS

τῶν ἀρχαιρεσίων καθηκόντων ἀνέστρεψεν εἰς τὴν πατρίδα.

LI. Ἀποδειχθέντων δὲ μετ᾽ ἐκείνους ὑπάτων Λευκίου Οὐαλερίου τὸ δεύτερον καὶ Τιβερίου Αἰμιλίου βραχύν τινα χρόνον ἐπισχόντες οἱ δήμαρχοι τὸν ὑπὲρ κληρουχίας πάλιν εἰσῆγον λόγον· καὶ προσιόντες τοῖς ὑπάτοις ἠξίουν βεβαιῶσαι τῷ δήμῳ τὰς ὑποσχέσεις ἃς ἐποιήσατο ἡ βουλὴ Σπορίου Κασσίου καὶ Πρόκλου Οὐεργινίου ὑπατευόντων, 2 δεόμενοί τε καὶ λιπαροῦντες. καὶ οἱ ὕπατοι αὐτοῖς συνελάμβανον ἀμφότεροι, Τιβέριος μὲν Αἰμίλιος κότον τινὰ παλαιὸν εἰς τὴν βουλὴν οὐκ ἄλογον ἀναφέρων ὅτι τῷ πατρὶ αὐτοῦ θρίαμβον αἰτουμένῳ κατάγειν οὐκ ἐπέτρεψεν, ὁ δὲ Οὐαλέριος ἀποθεραπεῦσαι τοῦ δήμου τὴν ὀργὴν βουλόμενος ἣν εἶχε πρὸς αὐτὸν ἐπὶ τῷ Σπορίου Κασσίου θανάτῳ, ὃν ἀπέκτεινεν ὡς ἐπιχειροῦντα βασιλείᾳ ταμίας τότε ὢν Οὐαλέριος, ἄνδρα τῶν κατὰ τὴν αὐτὴν ἡλικίαν γενομένων ἐπιφανέστατον ἐν ἡγεμονίαις τε πολέμων καὶ πολιτικαῖς πράξεσιν, ὃς καὶ τὸ περὶ τῆς κληρουχίας πολίτευμα πρῶτος εἰσήγαγεν εἰς τὴν πόλιν, καὶ δι᾽ αὐτὸ μάλιστα ὑπὸ τῶν πατρικίων, ὡς δῆμον 3 αἱρούμενος[1] πρὸ[2] αὐτῶν, ἐμισήθη. τότε δ᾽ οὖν ὑποσχομένων τῶν ὑπάτων αὐτοῖς προθήσειν ἐν τῇ βουλῇ τὸν ὑπὲρ τῆς διανομῆς τῶν δημοσίων κλήρων λόγον καὶ τῆς ἐπικυρώσεως τοῦ νόμου συναρεῖσθαι,[3] πιστεύσαντες αὐτοῖς οἱ δήμαρχοι παρῆσαν ἐπὶ τὴν βουλὴν καὶ λόγους διεξῆλθον ἐπιεικεῖς. οἷς οὐδὲν ἀντιλέξαντες οἱ ὕπατοι ὡς μὴ φιλονεικίας δόξαν ἀπενέγκαιντο, γνώμην ἀποδείκνυσθαι τοὺς πρεσβυ-

---

[1] αἱρούμενος R : ἀναιρούμενος A, Jacoby.
[2] Steph.[2] : πρὸς AB.   [3] Reiske : συναιρεῖσθαι O.

the elections being now at hand, returned to the fatherland.

LI. When Lucius Valerius [1] (for the second time) and Tiberius Aemilius had been appointed as the next consuls, the tribunes after a short delay brought up again the question of the land-allotment ; and coming to the consuls, they asked them, with prayers and entreaties, to fulfil for the populace the promises which the senate had made in the consulship of Spurius Cassius and Proculus Verginius. [2] Both consuls favoured their request, Tiberius Aemilius bringing up an old and not unreasonable grudge against the senate because it had refused a triumph to his father when he asked for it, and Valerius from a desire to heal the anger of the populace directed against him because of the death of Spurius Cassius, whom he, being quaestor at the time, had caused to be put to death for aiming at tyranny. Cassius had been the most distinguished of his contemporaries both in military commands and in civil affairs ; moreover, he was the first to introduce into the commonwealth the measure concerning the allotment of lands and for that reason in particular was hated by the patricians as one who preferred the populace to them. At the time in question, at any rate, when the consuls promised them to bring up in the senate the question of the division of the public lands and to assist in securing the ratification of the law, the tribunes trusted them, and going to the senate, they spoke with moderation. And the consuls, desiring to avoid any appearance of contention, said nothing in opposition, but asked the oldest

---

[1] For chaps. 51-54 cf. Livy ii. 61.
[2] 484 B.C. ; see viii. 76.

4 τάτους ἠξίουν. ἦν δ᾽ ὁ πρῶτος ὑπ᾽ αὐτῶν κληθεὶς
Λεύκιος Αἰμίλιος θατέρου τῶν ὑπάτων πατήρ· ὃς
ἔφη δοκεῖν αὐτῷ καὶ δίκαιον καὶ συμφέρον ἔσεσθαι
τῇ πόλει πάντων εἶναι τὰ κοινὰ καὶ μὴ ὀλίγων, τῷ
τε δήμῳ πείθοντι ὑπουργεῖν συνεβούλευεν, ἵνα χάρις
ἡ παραχώρησις αὐτῶν γένηται. πολλὰ γὰρ καὶ
ἄλλα μὴ δόντας αὐτῷ κατὰ προαίρεσιν, ὑπ᾽ ἀνάγκης
συγκεχωρηκέναι· τούς τε κατέχοντας τὰς κτήσεις
ὧν ἐκαρπώσαντο χρόνων λαθόντες ἠξίου χάριν
5 εἰδέναι, κωλυομένους δὲ μὴ φιλοχωρεῖν. ἔφη τε
σὺν τῷ δικαίῳ, ὃ πάντες ἂν[1] ὁμολογήσειαν ἰσχυρὸν
εἶναι, τὰ μὲν δημόσια κοινὰ πάντων εἶναι, τὰ δ᾽
ἴδια ἑκάστου τῶν νόμῳ κτησαμένων, καὶ ἀναγκαῖον
ἤδη τὸ πρᾶγμα ὑπὸ τῆς[2] βουλῆς γεγονέναι πρὸ
ἐτῶν ἑπτακαίδεκα τὴν γῆν διανέμειν ψηφισαμένης.
καὶ τοῦτ᾽ ἀπέφηνεν ἐπὶ τῷ συμφέροντι τότε αὐτὴν
βεβουλεῦσθαι, ἵνα μήτε γῆ χέρσος ᾖ καὶ ὁ τὴν
πόλιν οἰκουρῶν πένης ὄχλος[3] μὴ ἀργός, ὥσπερ νῦν,
τοῖς ἀλλοτρίοις ἀγαθοῖς φθονῶν, ἐπιτρέφηται δὲ[4] τῇ
πόλει νεότης ἐν ἐφεστίοις καὶ κλήροις πατρῴοις,[5]
ἔχουσά τι καὶ ἐπὶ τῷ καλῶς τεθράφθαι[6] μέγα
6 φρονεῖν· ἐπεὶ τοῖς γε ἀκλήροις καὶ ἐκ τῶν ἀλλο-
τρίων κτημάτων,[7] ἃ μισθοῦ ἐργάζονται, γλίσχρως
διατρεφομένοις ἢ ἀρχῆθεν μὴ ἐμφύεσθαι ἔρωτα

---

[1] ἂν added by Cobet. [2] τῆς added by Reiske.
[3] ὄχλος ACmg : om. R. [4] δὲ Steph. : om. AB.
[5] πατρίοις B. [6] Cobet : τετράφθαι O.
[7] Sylburg : χρημάτων O.

senators to express their opinions. The first person
called upon was Lucius Aemilius, the father of one of
the consuls, who said it seemed to him that it would
be both just and for the interest of the commonwealth
that the possessions of the public should belong to all
and not to a few, and he advised them to support the
plea of the populace, in order that this concession on
their part might be regarded as a favour ; for many
other things which they had not granted them by
choice they had yielded through necessity. He felt
also that those who were occupying these possessions ought to be grateful for the time they had
enjoyed them without being detected, and when
prevented from using them longer should not cling
to them obstinately. He added that, along with the
principle of justice, the force of which all would
acknowledge, according to which the public possessions are the common property of all and private
possessions the property of the one who has acquired
them according to law, the action had also become
unavoidable now through the action of the senate,
which seventeen years before had ordered that the
land be divided. And he declared that it had
reached this decision at that time in the public
interest, to the end that neither the land should
go uncultivated nor the multitude of poor people
dwelling in the city should live in idleness, envying
the advantages of the others, as was now the case,
and that young men might be reared up for the state
in the homes and on the lands of their fathers, deriv-
ing also some pride of spirit from this very rearing.
For such as have no lands of their own and live miser-
ably off the possessions of others which they culti-
vate for hire either do not feel any desire at all to

γενεᾶς τέκνων ἢ ἐμφύντα πονηρὸν ἐκφέρειν καρπὸν
καὶ οὐδ᾽ εὐτυχῆ, ἐκ ταπεινῶν τε συμπορισθέντα οἷα
εἰκὸς γάμων καὶ ἐν κατεπτωχευμέναις τραφέντα
7 τύχαις. '' Ἐγὼ μὲν οὖν,'' ἔφη, '' γνώμην ἀπο-
δείκνυμαι, τά τε προβουλευθέντα ὑπὸ τοῦ συνεδρίου
καὶ διὰ τὰς μεταξὺ ταραχὰς παρειλκυσμένα ἐμ-
πεδοῦν τοὺς ὑπάτους, καὶ τοὺς ποιησομένους τὴν
διανομὴν ἄνδρας ἀποδεικνύναι.''

LII. Ταῦτ᾽ εἰπόντος Αἰμιλίου δεύτερος κληθεὶς
Ἄππιος Κλαύδιος, ὁ τῷ πρόσθεν ὑπατεύσας ἔτει,
τὴν ἐναντίαν γνώμην ἀπεφήνατο, διδάσκων ὡς
οὔθ᾽ ἡ βουλὴ διανεῖμαι τὰ δημόσια¹ προαίρεσιν
ἔσχε (πάλαι γὰρ ἂν εἰληφέναι τὰ δόξαντ᾽ αὐτῇ
τέλος), ἀλλ᾽ εἰς χρόνον καὶ διάγνωσιν ἑτέραν² ἀνε-
βάλετο, παῦσαι προθυμουμένη τὴν τότε κατασχοῦ-
σαν στάσιν, ἣν εἰσῆγεν ὁ τῇ τυραννίδι ἐπιχειρῶν
2 ὕπατος καὶ μετὰ ταῦτα δίκας δοὺς καλάς· οὔτε οἱ
μετὰ τὸ προβούλευμα λαχόντες³ ὕπατοι τέλος τοῖς
ἐψηφισμένοις ἐπέθεσαν, ὁρῶντες ὅσων εἰσελεύσεται
κακῶν εἰς τὴν πόλιν ἀρχὴ συνεθισθέντων τὰ κοινὰ
τῶν πενήτων διαλαγχάνειν· αἵ τε μετ᾽ ἐκείνους
πεντεκαίδεκα ὑπατεῖαι πολλῶν αὐταῖς⁴ ἐπαχθέν-
των ὑπὸ τοῦ δήμου κινδύνων οὐδὲν ὑπέμειναν ὃ
μὴ συνέφερε τῷ⁵ κοινῷ⁶ πράττειν, διὰ τὸ μηδ᾽ ἐξεῖναι σφίσι κατὰ τὸ προβούλευμα τοὺς γεωμόρους⁷
ἀποδεικνύειν, ἀλλὰ τοῖς πρώτοις ἐκείνοις ὑπάτοις.

---

¹ δημόσια B : δημόσια πράγματα R.
² εἰς χρόνον ἕτερον καὶ διάγνωσιν Steph.²
³ λαχόντες C : λαβόντες R : λαβόντες ὑπατείαν Sylburg.
⁴ Sylburg : αὐτοῖς AB.   ⁵ συνέφερε τῷ B : συνεφέρετο A.
⁶ κοινῷ added by Kiessling.   ⁷ γε ὠμόρους B : τε ὁμόρους AC.

---

¹ The word γεωμόροι (Doric γαμόροι) usually means " land-

beget children, or, if they do, produce a sorry and wretched offspring, such as might be expected of those who are the fruit of humble marriages and are reared in beggared circumstances. "As for me, then," he said, "the motion I make is that the consuls should carry out the preliminary decree which was then passed by the senate and has since been delayed by reason of the intervening disturbances, and appoint the men to divide the land."

LII. Aemilius having spoken thus, Appius Claudius, who had been consul the preceding year, being the second person called upon, expressed the contrary opinion, pointing out that neither the senate had had any intention of dividing the public possessions—for in that case its decree would long since have been carried out—but had deferred it to a later time for further consideration, its concern being to put a stop to the sedition then raging, which had been stirred up by the consul who was aiming at tyranny and afterwards suffered deserved punishment ; nor had the first consuls chosen after the preliminary decree put the vote into effect, when they saw what a source of evils would be introduced into the state if the poor were once accustomed to get by allotment the public possessions ; nor did the consuls of the following fifteen years, though they were threatened with many dangers from the populace, consent to do anything that was not in the public interest, for the reason that no authority even was given to them by the preliminary decree to appoint the land commissioners,[1] but only to those first con-

owners " ; but here it clearly refers to the men who were to make the allotments. The word is somewhat corrupted in our MSS., though all the readings point to γεωμόρους. Dionysius uses the word again in x. 38, 4 in the same sense.

3 " "Ὥστε οὐδ' ὑμῖν," ἔφησεν, "ὦ Οὐαλέριε, καὶ
σύ, Αἰμίλιε, γῆς ἀναδασμοὺς εἰσφέρειν οὓς οὐκ
ἐπέταξεν ὑμῖν τὸ συνέδριον οὔτε καλῶς ἔχει,
προγόνων οὖσιν ἀγαθῶν, οὔτ' ἀσφαλῶς. καὶ περὶ
μὲν τοῦ προβουλεύματος, ὡς οὐ κρατεῖσθε ὑπ'
αὐτοῦ οἱ τοσούτοις ὕστερον ὑπατεύσαντες χρόνοις,
4 ταῦθ' ἱκανά. περὶ δὲ τοῦ βιασαμένους τινὰς ἢ
λαθόντας σφετερίσασθαι τὰ δημόσια βραχὺς ἀπ-
αρκεῖ μοι λόγος. εἰ γάρ τις οἶδε καρπούμενόν τινα
ὧν οὐκ ἔχει κτῆσιν ἀποδεῖξαι νόμῳ, μήνυσιν ἀπ-
ενεγκάτω πρὸς τοὺς ὑπάτους καὶ κρινάτω κατὰ
τοὺς νόμους, οὓς οὐ νεωστὶ δεήσει γράφειν· πάλαι
γὰρ ἐγράφησαν, καὶ οὐδεὶς αὐτοὺς ἠφάνικε χρόνος.
5 ἐπεὶ δὲ καὶ περὶ τοῦ συμφέροντος ἐποιεῖτο λόγους
Αἰμίλιος, ὡς ἐπὶ τῷ πάντων ἀγαθῷ τῆς κληρουχίας
ἐσομένης, οὐδὲ τοῦτο τὸ μέρος ἀνέλεγκτον ἐᾶσαι
βούλομαι. ἐμοὶ γὰρ δοκεῖ τὸ αὐτόθι μόνον οὗτός
γε ὁρᾶν, τὸ δὲ μέλλον οὐ προσκοπεῖν, ὅτι τὸ[1]
μικρὸν εἶναι δοκοῦν, δοῦναί τι[2] τῶν δημοσίων τοῖς
ἀργοῖς καὶ ἀπόροις, πολλῶν ἔσται καὶ μεγάλων
6 κακῶν αἴτιον. τὸ γὰρ ἔθος τὸ συνεισπορευόμενον
ἅμα τούτῳ καὶ διαμένον ἐν τῇ πόλει καὶ[3] μέχρι
παντὸς ὀλέθριον ἔσται καὶ δεινόν· οὐ γὰρ ἐξαιρεῖ
τὰς πονηρὰς ἐπιθυμίας ἐκ τῆς ψυχῆς τὸ τυγχάνειν αὐτῶν, ἀλλ' αὔξει καὶ πονηροτέρας ποιεῖ.
τεκμήρια δ' ὑμῖν γενέσθω τούτων τὰ ἔργα· τί γὰρ
δεῖ τοῖς λόγοις ὑμᾶς τοῖς ἐμοῖς ἢ τοῖς Αἰμιλίου
προσέχειν;

---

[1] τὸ R : om. B, Jacoby.
[2] δοῦναί τι Post : εἴ τι Ba, ἔτι R, ἐπὶ Jacoby. Reiske read
ἔτι τὸ and added μεταδιδόναι after ἀπόροις.
[3] καὶ deleted by Smit. Reiske added προϊὸν after παντός.
Cobet proposed διαμενεῖ for διαμένον.

suls. " So that for you men also, Valerius, yes, and
you too, Aemilius, to propose allotments of land
which the senate did not direct you to carry out
is neither honourable, descended as you are from
worthy ancestors, nor is it safe. As regards the
preliminary decree, then, let this suffice to show
that you who have become consuls so many years
afterwards are not bound by it. As for any who
may, either forcibly or stealthily, have appropriated
to themselves the public possessions, a few words
will serve my purpose. If anyone knows that another is enjoying the use of property to which he
cannot support his title by law, let him give information of it to the consuls and prosecute him according
to the laws, which will not have to be drawn up
afresh ; for they were drawn up long since, and no
lapse of time has abrogated them. But since Aemilius has spoken also about the advantage of this
measure, asserting that the allotting of the land will
be for the good of all, I do not wish to leave this point
either unrefuted. For he, it seems to me, looks only
to the present, and does not foresee the future,
namely, that the granting of a portion of the public
possessions to the idle and the poor, which now seems
to him of small importance, will be the cause of many
great evils, since the custom thereby introduced will
not only continue in the state, but will for all time
prove pernicious and dangerous. For the gratifica-
tion of evil desires does not eradicate them from the
soul, but rather strengthens them and renders them
still more evil. Let the facts convince you of this ;
for why should you pay any attention to words,
either mine or those of Aemilius ?

LIII. '' Ἴστε δήπου πάντες ὅσους ἐχειρωσάμεθα
πολεμίους, καὶ ὅσην προενομεύσαμεν, καὶ ὅσα
λάφυρα ἐκ τῶν ἁλόντων χωρίων ἐλάβομεν, ὧν
οἱ πολέμιοι στερόμενοι τέως εὐδαίμονες ὄντες ἐν
πολλῇ νῦν καθεστήκασιν ἀπορίᾳ· καὶ ὅτι τούτων
οὐδενὸς ἀπηλάθησαν οὐδὲ μεῖον ἐκτήσαντο ἐν ταῖς
2 διανομαῖς[1] οἱ τὴν ἀπορίαν ὀδυρόμενοι. ἆρ᾽ οὖν διὰ
ταύτας τὰς ἐπικτήσεις ἐπανορθωσάμενοι φαίνονταί
τι τῆς παλαιᾶς τύχης καὶ προελελυθότες εἰς ἐπι-
φάνειαν τοῖς βίοις; ἐβουλόμην μὲν ἂν καὶ θεοῖς
εὐξάμην, ἵνα ἧττον ἦσαν ἐπίσκηνοι[2] λυπηροὶ τῇ
πόλει· νῦν δέ, ὁρᾶτε γὰρ καὶ ἀκούετε αὐτῶν ὀδυρο-
μένων ὅτι ἐν ἐσχάτῃ εἰσὶν ἀπορίᾳ. ὥστε οὐδ᾽ εἰ
ταῦτα ἃ νῦν αἰτοῦνται καὶ ἔτι πλείω[3] τούτων
3 λάβοιεν, ἐπανορθώσονται τοὺς βίους. οὐ γὰρ ἐν
ταῖς τύχαις αὐτῶν ἐνοικεῖ τὸ ἄπορον, ἀλλ᾽ ἐν τοῖς
τρόποις· οὓς οὐχ οἷον ὁ βραχὺς οὗτος ἐκπληρώσει
κλῆρος, ἀλλ᾽ οὐδ᾽ αἱ σύμπασαι βασιλέων τε καὶ
τυράννων δωρεαί. δράσομέν τε, εἰ καὶ ταῦτα
συγχωρήσομεν αὐτοῖς, ὅμοια τοῖς πρὸς ἡδονὴν
θεραπεύουσι τοὺς κάμνοντας ἰατροῖς. οὐ γὰρ τὸ
νοσοῦν ὑγιασθήσεται τῆς πολιτείας μέρος, ἀλλὰ
καὶ τὸ ὑγιαῖνον ἀπολαύσει τῆς νόσου. καθόλου
τε, ὦ βουλή, πολλῆς ὑμῖν δεῖ ἐπιμελείας τε καὶ
φροντίδος ὅπως ἂν σώσητε πάσῃ προθυμίᾳ δια-
4 φθειρόμενα τὰ ἤθη[4] τῆς πόλεως. ὁρᾶτε γὰρ εἰς ἃ
προελήλυθεν ἡ τοῦ δήμου ἀκοσμία καὶ ὡς οὐκέτι
ἄρχεσθαι πρὸς τῶν ὑπάτων ἀξιοῖ· ᾧ γε οὐ μετ-

---

[1] ἐν ταῖς διανομαῖς B : om. R.
[2] ἐπίσκηνοι B : οἱ ἐπίσκηνοι R.
[3] πλείω B : πλέον AC.
[4] Sylburg : ἔθη O.

LIII. "You all know, to be sure, how many enemies we have overcome, how much territory we have ravaged, and how great spoils we have taken from the towns we have captured, the loss of which has reduced the enemy from their former prosperity to great want, and that those who now bewail their poverty were excluded from none of these spoils nor had less than their share in the distribution of them. Do they appear, then, to have improved their former condition at all by these further acquisitions or to have attained to any distinction in their lives? I could wish and have prayed to the gods that they might do so, in order that they might have been to a less extent mere transients,[1] a nuisance to the city. But as it is, you see and hear them complaining that they are in the direst want. So that not even if they should receive what they now ask for—aye, still more than that—will they effect any improvement in their lives. For their poverty is not inherent in their condition in life, but in their character; and not only will this small portion of land not supply their lack of that, but not even all the largesses of kings and despots would do so. If we make this concession also to them, we shall be like those physicians whose treatment of the sick is to tickle their palates. For the diseased part of the commonwealth will not be cured, but even the sound part will catch the disease. In general, senators, you need to take much care and thought how you may preserve with all possible zeal the morals of the commonwealth which are being corrupted. For you see to what lengths the unruliness of the populace has gone and that they no longer care to be governed by the consuls; indeed, they

_____
[1] Literally, "billeted troops."

ἐμέλησε τῶν ἐνθάδε πραττομένων, ἀλλὰ καὶ ἐπὶ
στρατοπέδου τὴν αὐτὴν ἀπεδείξατο ἀκοσμίαν, ὅπλα
τε ῥίψας καὶ τάξεις ἐκλιπὼν καὶ σημεῖα πολεμίοις
προέμενος καὶ φυγῇ πρὶν εἰς χεῖρας ἐλθεῖν ἐπονει-
δίστῳ χρησάμενος, ὥσπερ ἐμοῦ μόνον ἀφαιρησόμενος τὴν ἐκ τῆς νίκης δόξαν, ἀλλ' οὐχὶ καὶ τῆς
5 πατρίδος τὸ κατὰ τῶν ἐχθρῶν κλέος.[1] καὶ νῦν
Οὐολούσκοις κατὰ Ῥωμαίων ἵσταται τρόπαια, καὶ
κοσμεῖται τοῖς ἡμετέροις[2] λαφύροις τἀκείνων ἱερὰ
καὶ ἐν αὐχήμασιν ἡλίκοις οὐπώποτε αἱ πόλεις
αὐτῶν εἰσιν, τέως ὑπὲρ ἀνδραποδισμοῦ τε καὶ κατα-
6 σκαφῆς τῶν ἡμετέρων[3] δεόμεναι ἡγεμόνων. ἆρά γε
δίκαιον ἢ καλὸν ἐπὶ τοιούτοις κατορθώμασι χάριν
αὐτοῖς ὑμᾶς εἰδέναι, καὶ δημοσίαις ἐπικοσμεῖν δω-
ρεαῖς κληρουχήσαντες τὴν γῆν ἧς πολέμιοι κρατοῦσι
τὸ κατὰ τούτους εἶναι μέρος; ἀλλὰ τί δεῖ τούτοις
ἐγκαλεῖν οἷς δι' ἀπαιδευσίαν τε καὶ δυσγένειαν
ὀλίγος ἐστὶ τῶν καλῶν λόγος, ὁρῶντας ὡς οὐδ' ἐν
τοῖς ὑμετέροις ἤθεσι πᾶσιν ἔτι τὸ ἀρχαῖον οἰκεῖ
φρόνημα, ἀλλ' αὐθάδεια μὲν ἡ σεμνότης καλεῖται
πρὸς ἐνίων, μωρία δ' ἡ δικαιοσύνη, μανικὸν δὲ τὸ
ἀνδρεῖον, καὶ ἠλίθιον τὸ σῶφρον; ἃ δὲ μισητὰ
παρὰ τοῖς προτέροις ἦν, ταῦτα πυργοῦταί τε νῦν
καὶ θαυμάσια ἡλίκα[4] φαίνεται τοῖς διεφθαρμένοις
ἀγαθά, ἀνανδρία καὶ βωμολοχία καὶ κακοήθεια καὶ
τὸ πανούργως σοφὸν καὶ τὸ πρὸς ἅπαντα[5] ἰταμὸν
καὶ τὸ μηδενὶ τῶν κρειττόνων εὐπειθές· ἃ πολλὰς
ἤδη πόλεις ἰσχυρὰς λαβόντα ἐκ βάθρων ἀνέτρεψε.
7 ταῦθ' ὑμῖν, ὦ βουλή, εἴτε ἡδέα ἐστὶν ἀκούειν εἴτε

---

[1] κλέος Reiske, κράτος Kiessling, τρόπαιον Casaubon, θάρσος
Post : πάθος O, Jacoby.
[2] Steph. : ὑμετέροις AB.   [3] Steph. : ὑμετέρων AB.

were so far from repenting of what they did here that
they showed the same unruliness in the field too,
throwing away their arms, quitting their posts,
abandoning their standards to the enemy and resorting to disgraceful flight before ever coming to grips
with them, as if they could rob me alone of the glory
of the victory without robbing the fatherland at the
same time of the renown it would gain at the expense
of its enemies. And now trophies are being erected
by the Volscians over the Romans, their temples are
being adorned with spoils taken from us and their
cities vaunt themselves as never before—those cities
which were wont aforetime to beseech our generals
to save them from slavery and total destruction. Is
it just, then, or becoming in you to feel gratitude to
them for such successes and to honour them with
public grants by dividing up the land which, so far
as they are concerned, is in the enemy's possession ?
Yet why should we accuse those who because of their
lack of education and because of their low birth pay
little regard to matters of honour, when we see that
no longer in the character of all even of your own
number does the ancient proud spirit dwell, but, on
the contrary, some call gravity haughtiness, justice
folly, courage madness, and modesty stupidity ? On
the other hand, those qualities that were held in de-
testation by the men of former times are now extolled
and appear to the corrupt as wonderful virtues, such
as cowardice, buffoonery, malignity, crafty wisdom,
rashness in undertaking everything and unwillingness
to listen to any of one's betters—vices which ere
now have laid hold on and utterly overthrown many
strong states. These words, senators, whether they

---

⁴ ἡλίκα B : om. R.   ⁵ Jacoby ; πάντα O,

ἀνιαρά, μετὰ πάσης ἀληθείας καὶ παρρησίας εἴρη-
ται, τοῖς μὲν πεισθησομένοις ὑμῶν, ἐὰν ἄρα πεισ-
θῆτε, ἔν τε τῷ παρόντι χρήσιμα καὶ εἰς τὸ μέλλον
ἀσφαλῆ· ἐμοὶ δέ, ὃς ὑπὲρ τοῦ κοινῇ[1] συμφέροντος
ἰδίας ἀπεχθείας ἀναιροῦμαι, πολλῶν ἐσόμενα κινδύνων αἴτια. προορᾶν γὰρ ἱκανός εἰμι τὰ συμβη-
σόμενα ἐκ λογισμοῦ, καὶ παραδείγματα ποιοῦμαι
τἀλλότρια πάθη τῶν ἐμαυτοῦ."

LIV. Ταῦτ' εἰπόντος Ἀππίου καὶ τῶν ἄλλων
ὀλίγου δεῖν πάντων τὴν αὐτὴν γνώμην ἀποφηνα-
μένων ἡ μὲν βουλὴ διελύετο. οἱ δὲ δήμαρχοι δι'
ὀργῆς ἔχοντες τὴν ἀποτυχίαν ἀπῄεσαν καὶ μετὰ
τοῦτ' ἐσκόπουν ὅπως τιμωρήσονται τὸν ἄνδρα·
ἔδοξεν οὖν αὐτοῖς πολλὰ βουλευσαμένοις δίκη τὸν
Ἄππιον ὑπαγαγεῖν θάνατον ἐχούσῃ τὸ τίμημα.
καὶ μετὰ ταῦτα ἐν ἐκκλησίᾳ τοῦ ἀνδρὸς κατηγορή-
σαντες παρεκάλουν ἥκειν ἅπαντας εἰς τὴν ἀπο-
δειχθησομένην ἡμέραν ὡς διοίσοντας ὑπὲρ αὐτοῦ
2 ψῆφον. ἃ δὲ κατηγορεῖν ἔμελλον ταῦτ' ἦν· ὅτι
πονηρὰς ἐτίθει κατὰ τοῦ δήμου γνώμας, καὶ στάσιν
εἰσῆγεν εἰς τὴν πόλιν, καὶ δημάρχῳ χεῖρας ἐπήνεγκε παρὰ τοὺς ἱεροὺς νόμους, καὶ στρατιᾶς
ἡγησάμενος σὺν βλάβῃ τε καὶ αἰσχύνῃ μεγάλῃ
ἀνέστρεψε. ταῦτα προειπόντες ἐν τῷ πλήθει καὶ
ῥητήν τινα ἀποδείξαντες ἡμέραν ἐν ᾗ τέλος ἔφησαν
ἐπιθήσειν τῇ δίκῃ, παρήγγειλαν αὐτῷ παρεῖναι
3 τότε ἀπολογησομένῳ. ἀγανακτούντων δ' ἁπάντων τῶν πατρικίων καὶ παρεσκευασμένων ἁπάσῃ
προθυμίᾳ σώζειν τὸν ἄνδρα καὶ τὸν Ἄππιον
παρακαλούντων εἶξαι τῷ καιρῷ καὶ σχῆμα ταῖς
παρούσαις τύχαις ἁρμόττον μεταλαβεῖν, οὐδὲν ἔφη

---

[1] κοινῇ Bb : κοινοῦ ABaC.

are pleasing to you to hear or vexatious, have been uttered in all sincerity and frankness. To those among you who will be persuaded—if indeed you will be persuaded—they will prove both useful at the present time and a source of security for the future ; but to me, who in the interest of the public good am bringing private hatreds upon myself, they will be the cause of great dangers. For reason enables me to foresee what will happen ; and I take the misfortunes of others as examples of my own."

LIV. After Appius had spoken thus and almost all the others had expressed the same opinion, the senate was dismissed. The tribunes, angry at their failure, departed and after that considered how they might take revenge on the man ; and they decided, after long deliberation, to bring him to trial on a capital charge. Then, having accused him before the popular assembly, they asked all to be present on the day they should appoint in order to give their votes concerning him. The charges they planned to bring against him were these : that he had been expressing mischievous opinions against the populace and introducing sedition into the commonwealth, that he had laid hands on a tribune contrary to the sacred laws, and that after taking command of the army he had returned home with great loss and disgrace. After announcing these accusations to the populace and appointing a definite day on which they said they would hold the trial, they summoned him to appear on the day named and make his defence. All the patricians resented this proceeding and were prepared to use every effort to save Appius, and they urged him to yield to the occasion and to assume a bearing suitable to his present fortunes ; but he declared

ποιήσειν ὁ ἀνὴρ οὔτ' ἀγεννὲς οὔτε τῶν προγεγονό-
των ἔργων ἀνάξιον, μυρίους δ' ἂν ὑπομεῖναι θανάτους πρότερον ἢ γονάτων ἅψασθαί τινος· τούς τε
ὑπὲρ αὐτοῦ δεῖσθαι παρεσκευασμένους διεκώλυεν,
εἰπὼν ὡς διπλασίως ἂν αἰδεσθείη ταῦτα ὑπὲρ
αὐτοῦ ποιοῦντας ἑτέρους ὁρῶν ἃ μηδ' αὐτὸν[1] ὑπὲρ
4 ἑαυτοῦ πράττειν πρέποντα ἡγεῖται. ταῦτά τε δὴ
καὶ πολλὰ ὅμοια τούτοις λέγων καὶ οὔτ' ἐσθῆτα
ἀλλάξας οὔτε τὸ τῆς ὄψεως γαῦρον ἀλλοιώσας
οὔτε φρονήματός τι ὑφέμενος, ὡς εἶδεν ὀρθὴν καὶ
μετέωρον ἐπὶ τῇ προσδοκίᾳ τοῦ ἀγῶνος τὴν πόλιν,
ὀλίγων ἔτι λειπομένων ἡμερῶν ἑαυτὸν διεχειρί-
5 σατο.[2] οἱ μὲν δὴ προσήκοντες αὐτῷ νόσον ἐσκήπ-
τοντο γενέσθαι τοῦ θανάτου αἰτίαν· προενεχθέντος
δὲ τοῦ σώματος εἰς τὴν ἀγορὰν ὁ μὲν υἱὸς αὐτοῦ
προσιὼν τοῖς δημάρχοις καὶ τοῖς ὑπάτοις ἠξίου
τὴν νόμιμον ἐκκλησίαν αὐτῷ συναγαγεῖν καὶ τὸν ἐν
ἔθει Ῥωμαίοις ὄντα ἐπὶ ταῖς ταφαῖς ἀγορεύεσθαι
τῶν ἀγαθῶν ἀνδρῶν λόγον ἐπιτρέψαι περὶ τοῦ
6 πατρὸς διελθεῖν. οἱ δὲ δήμαρχοι καλουμένης ἔτι
τῆς ἐκκλησίας ὑπὸ τῶν ὑπάτων ἐνίσταντο καὶ
παρήγγελλον τῷ μειρακίῳ τὸν νεκρὸν ἀποφέρειν.
οὐ μὴν ὁ δῆμός γε ἠνέσχετο οὐδὲ περιεῖδε τὴν
ὕβριν, ἄτιμον ἐκβληθῆναι τὸ σῶμα, ἀλλ' ἐπέτρεψε
τῷ μειρακίῳ τὰς νομιζομένας ἀποδοῦναι τῷ πατρὶ
τιμάς. Ἄππιος μὲν οὖν τοιαύτης τελευτῆς ἔτυχεν.

LV. Οἱ δ' ὕπατοι καταγράψαντες τὰς δυνάμεις
ἐξῆγον ἐκ τῆς πόλεως, Λεύκιος μὲν Οὐαλέριος
Αἰκανοῖς πολεμήσων, Τιβέριος δ' Αἰμίλιος Σαβίνοις. καὶ γὰρ οὗτοι κατὰ τὸν τῆς στάσεως καιρὸν

---

[1] αὐτὸν A : om. B, αὐτὸς Kiessling.
[2] διεχειρίσατο ABbC : διεχρήσατο Reiske, Jacoby.

that he would do nothing ignoble or unworthy of his former conduct, and that he would rather die a thousand deaths than cling to the knees of any man. And though his friends were prepared to make entreaties in his behalf, he would not permit it, saying that he would be doubly ashamed to see others doing for him things which he thought unbecoming even for him to do for himself. After he had said this and many other things of like nature and neither changed his dress, altered the haughtiness of his looks nor abated anything of his proud spirit, when now he saw the whole city intent upon his trial and on tiptoe with expectation, and only a few days were left, he made away with himself ; his relations, however, pretended that he had died a natural death. When his body was brought into the Forum, his son went to the tribunes and consuls and asked them to assemble the people for him in the manner usual upon such occasions and give him leave to deliver the eulogy over his father according to the practice of the Romans at the funerals of worthy men. But the tribunes, even while the consuls were calling the assembly, vetoed it and bade the youth take away the body. However, the people would not permit this nor allow the body to be cast out in dishonour and ignominy, but gave leave to the youth to render the customary honours to his father. Such was the end of Appius.

LV. The consuls,[1] having enrolled the armies, led them out of the city, Lucius Valerius to fight against the Aequians and Tiberius Aemilius against the Sabines ; for these nations had made an incursion

---

[1] Cf. Livy ii. 62.

DIONYSIUS OF HALICARNASSUS

ἐνέβαλον εἰς τὴν Ῥωμαίων χώραν καὶ πολλὴν
αὐτῆς κακώσαντες ἀπῆλθον λείαν ἄφθονον περι-
βαλόμενοι. Αἰκανοὶ μὲν οὖν πολλάκις εἰς χεῖρας
ἐλθόντες καὶ πολλὰς πληγὰς λαβόντες εἰς τὸν
χάρακα ἐν ἐχυρῷ χωρίῳ κείμενον κατέφυγον καὶ
2 τὸ λοιπὸν οὐκέτι προῄεσαν εἰς μάχην. ὁ δὲ Οὐαλέριος ἐπεχείρησε μὲν ἐκπολιορκεῖν αὐτῶν τὸ
στρατόπεδον ἐκωλύθη δ' ὑπὸ τοῦ δαιμονίου. προ-
ϊόντι γὰρ αὐτῷ καὶ ἤδη ἔργου ἐχομένῳ ζόφος ἐξ
οὐρανοῦ γίνεται καὶ ὄμβρος πολύς, ἀστραπαὶ δὲ
καὶ βρονταὶ σκληραί. διασκεδασθείσης δὲ τῆς
στρατιᾶς ὅ τε χειμὼν εὐθὺς ἐπαύσατο καὶ πολλὴ
κατέσχε τὸν τόπον αἰθρία. τοῦτό τε δὴ τὸ ἔργον
ὀττευσάμενος ὁ ὕπατος καὶ τῶν μάντεων κωλυόντων ἔτι[1] πολιορκεῖν τὸ χωρίον, ἀποτραπεὶς τὴν γῆν
αὐτῶν ἐκάκου, καὶ ὅση ἐπέτυχε λείᾳ τοῖς στρατιώταις ἅπασαν ὠφελεῖσθαι ἐφείς, ἀπῆγεν ἐπ' οἴκου
3 τὴν δύναμιν. Τιβερίῳ δ' Αἰμιλίῳ διεξιόντι τὴν
πολεμίαν σὺν πολλῇ καταφρονήσει κατ' ἀρχὰς καὶ
οὐδὲν ἔτι προσδοκῶντι ἀντίπαλον ἐπῆλθεν ἡ Σαβίνων δύναμις καὶ γίνεται μάχη αὐτῶν ἐκ παρατάξεως
μεσούσης μάλιστα τῆς ἡμέρας ἀρξαμένη μέχρι
δύσεως ἡλίου. σκότους δ' ἐπιλαμβάνοντος ἀνεχώρουν αἱ δυνάμεις ἐπὶ τοὺς ἑαυτῶν χάρακας οὔτε
4 νικῶσαι οὔτε λειπόμεναι. ταῖς δ' ἑξῆς ἡμέραις
νεκρούς τε τοὺς ἑαυτῶν ἐκήδευσαν οἱ ἡγεμόνες καὶ
χάρακας ἐξωρύξαντο· καὶ γνώμας τὰς αὐτὰς εἶχον
ἑκάτεροι, διὰ φυλακῆς τὰ οἰκεῖα ἔχειν καὶ μηκέτι
ἄρχειν μάχης. ἔπειτα σὺν χρόνῳ τὰς σκηνὰς
λύσαντες ἀπῆγον τὰς δυνάμεις.

[1] ἔτι Sintenis : ὅτι B, om. R.

106

into the Romans' country on the occasion of the
sedition and after plundering much of it had returned
home with rich booty. The Aequians came to an
engagement repeatedly ; but after receiving many
wounds they fled to their camp, which was situated
in a strong place, and from that time no longer came
out to fight. Valerius endeavoured to take their
camp by storm but was prevented by the gods from
doing so. For as he was advancing and already setting himself to the task darkness descended from
the sky, and a heavy rain, accompanied by lightning
and terrible thunder claps. Then, as soon as the
army had scattered, the storm ceased and the sky
over the place became perfectly clear. The consul
looking upon this as an omen and the augurs forbid-
ding him to besiege the place any longer, he desisted
and laid waste the enemy's country ; then, having
yielded as spoils to the soldiers all the booty he
came upon, he led the army home. As for Tiberius
Aemilius, while he was overrunning the enemy's
country with great contempt of them at first and no
longer expecting anyone to oppose him, the army of
the Sabines came upon him and a pitched battle took
place between them, beginning about noon and lasting till sunset ; but when darkness came on, the two
armies retired to their camps neither victorious nor
yet outmatched. During the following days the
commanders paid the final offices to their dead and
constructed ramparts for their camps ; and both of
them had the same intention, which was to defend
their own positions and not to engage in another
action. Then, after a time, they struck their tents
and withdrew their forces.

LVI. Ἐν δὲ τῷ μετὰ τούτους τοὺς ὑπάτους ἔτει, κατὰ τὴν ἑβδομηκοστὴν καὶ ὀγδόην ὀλυμπιάδα, ἣν ἐνίκα στάδιον Παρμενίδης Ποσειδωνιάτης, Ἀθήνησι[1] τὴν ἐνιαύσιον ἀρχὴν ἔχοντος Θεαγενίδου, κατεστάθησαν ὕπατοι Ῥωμαίων Αὖλος Οὐεργίνιος Καιλιμοντανὸς[2] καὶ Τίτος Νομίκιος Πρίσκος. ἄρτι δ᾽ αὐτῶν τὴν ἀρχὴν παρειληφότων ἀγγέλλεται στρατιὰ Οὐολούσκων πολλὴ παροῦσα. καὶ μετ᾽ οὐ πολὺ τῶν περιπολίων τι τῶν Ῥωμαϊκῶν ἐξ ἐφόδου[3] καταληφθὲν ἐκαίετο· ἦν δ᾽ οὐ διὰ μακροῦ τῆς Ῥώμης καὶ ὁ καπνὸς ἤγγελλε τοῖς ἐν τῇ πόλει 2 τὸ πάθος. τότε μὲν οὖν, καὶ γὰρ ἦν ἔτι νύξ, ἱππεῖς τινας ἀποστείλαντες ἐπὶ κατασκοπὴν οἱ ὕπατοι καὶ φυλακὰς καταστήσαντες ἐπὶ τοῖς τείχεσι καὶ αὐτοὶ ταξάμενοι πρὸ τῶν πυλῶν σὺν τοῖς εὐζωνοτάτοις, ἐξεδέχοντο τὰς παρὰ τῶν ἱππέων ἀγγελίας· ὡς δ᾽ ἡμέρα τε ἐγένετο καὶ συνήθροιστο αὐτοῖς ἡ ἐν τῇ πόλει δύναμις, ἦγον ἐπὶ τοὺς πολεμίους. οἱ δὲ διαρπάσαντες καὶ κατακαύσαντες τὸ φρούριον ἀπ- 3 ῇεσαν διὰ τάχους. τότε μὲν οὖν οἱ ὕπατοι σβέ- σαντες τὰ ἔτι καιόμενα καὶ τοῦ χωρίου φυλακὴν καταλιπόντες ἀπῇεσαν εἰς τὴν πόλιν· ὀλίγαις δ᾽ ὕστερον ἡμέραις τάς τε οἰκείας ἔχοντες δυνάμεις καὶ τὰς παρὰ τῶν συμμάχων ἐξῇεσαν ἀμφότεροι, Οὐεργίνιος μὲν ἐπὶ τὴν Αἰκανῶν, Νομίκιος δ᾽ ἐπὶ τὴν Οὐολούσκων· καὶ αὐτοῖς ἀμφοτέροις κατὰ 4 γνώμην τὰ τοῦ πολέμου ἐχώρησεν. Οὐεργινίῳ τε γὰρ Αἰκανοὶ δῃοῦντι τὴν χώραν αὐτῶν οὐκ ἐτόλμησαν εἰς χεῖρας ἐλθεῖν, ἀλλὰ καὶ λόχον τινὰ ὑποκαθίσαντες ἐν ὕλαις ἐπιλέκτων ἀνδρῶν οἱ

---

[1] ἀθήνησι A : ἀθήνησι δὲ R.

[2] Gelenius : νομεντανὸς O.   [3] ἐξ ἐφόδου B : om. R.

LVI. The year following [1] their consulship, in the seventy-eighth Olympiad (the one at which Parmenides of Posidonia won the foot-race), Theagenides being annual archon at Athens, Aulus Verginius Caelimontanus and Titus Numicius Priscus were made consuls. They had no sooner entered upon their magistracy than news was brought that a numerous army of Volscians was at hand. And not long afterwards one of the guard-houses of the Romans was on fire after being taken by assault; it was not far from Rome and the smoke informed the people in the city of the disaster. Thereupon, it being still night, the consuls sent some horsemen out to reconnoitre, and stationing guards upon the walls and posting themselves before the gates with the troops which were most lightly equipped, they waited for the report of the horsemen. Then, as soon as it was day and the forces in the city had joined them, they marched against their foes. These, however, after plundering and burning the fort, had retired in haste. The consuls extinguished what was still burning, and leaving a guard over the place, returned to the city. A few days later they both took the field with not only their own forces but those of the allies as well, Verginius marching against the Aequians and Numicius against the Volscians; and the campaigns of both proceeded according to plan. The Aequians, when Verginius was laying waste their country, not only did not dare come to an engagement, but even when they placed an ambush of chosen men in the woods with

---

[1] Cf. Livy ii. 63. The year was 467 B.C.

ἔμελλον ἐσκεδασμένοις ἐπιθήσεσθαι τοῖς πολεμίοις, διήμαρτον τῆς ἐλπίδος, ταχείας γενομένης τοῖς
Ῥωμαίοις αἰσθήσεως καὶ μάχης καρτερᾶς ἐξ ἧς
πολλοὺς τῶν σφετέρων οἱ Αἰκανοὶ ἀπέβαλον· ὥστε
5 οὐδ᾽ εἰς πεῖραν ἑτέρας μάχης ἔτ᾽ ἤρχοντο. Νο-
μικίῳ τ᾽ ἄγοντι τὴν στρατιὰν ἐπὶ τὴν Ἀντιατῶν
πόλιν, ἣ ἐν ταῖς πρώταις τότε τῶν Οὐολούσκων
πόλεσιν ἦν, οὐδεμία ἠναντιώθη δύναμις, ἀλλ᾽ ἀπὸ
τῶν τειχῶν ἠναγκάζοντο ἑκάστοτ᾽[1] ἀμύνεσθαι. ἐν
δὲ τούτῳ ἥ τε γῆ αὐτῶν ἡ πολλὴ ἐτμήθη, καὶ
πολίχνη τις ἐπιθαλάττιος ἑάλω[2] ᾗ ἐπινείῳ τε καὶ
ἀγορᾷ τῶν εἰς τὸν βίον ἀναγκαίων ἐχρῶντο, ἐκ
θαλάττης τε καὶ διὰ λῃστηρίων τὰς πολλὰς ἐπαγόμενοι ὠφελείας. ἀνδράποδα μὲν οὖν καὶ χρήματα
καὶ βοσκήματα καὶ τοὺς ἐμπορικοὺς φόρτους ἡ
στρατιὰ συγχωρήσει τοῦ ὑπάτου διήρπασε, τὰ
δ᾽ ἐλεύθερα σώματα ὁπόσα μὴ ὁ πόλεμος ἔφθη
διειργασμένος ἐπὶ τὸ λαφυροπώλιον ἀπήχθη. ἐλήφ-
θησαν δὲ καὶ νῆες τῶν Ἀντιατῶν εἴκοσι καὶ δύο
μακραὶ καὶ ἄλλα[3] νεῶν ὅπλα τε καὶ παρασκευαί.
6 μετὰ ταῦτα κελεύσαντος τοῦ ὑπάτου τάς τε οἰκίας
ἐνεπίμπρασαν οἱ Ῥωμαῖοι καὶ τοὺς νεωσοίκους
κατέσκαπτον καὶ τὸ τεῖχος ἤρειπον ἐκ θεμελίων,
ὥστε μηδ᾽ ἀπελθόντων σφῶν χρηστὸν ἔτι τοῖς
Ἀντιάταις εἶναι τὸ φρούριον. ταῦτά τε δὴ ἐπράχθη
χωρὶς ἑκατέρῳ τῶν ὑπάτων, καὶ ἀμφοτέροις ἔτι
κοινὴ στρατεία τοῖς ἀνδράσιν ἐπὶ τὴν Σαβίνων γῆν,
ἣν δῃώσαντες ἀπῆγον ἐπ᾽ οἴκου τὴν δύναμιν· καὶ
ὁ ἐνιαυτὸς οὗτος ἐτελεύτα.

---

[1] Post : ἕκαστοι O, ἐκεῖνον Hertlein.
[2] ἑάλω Cmg : om. ABC.
[3] ἄλλων Enthoven.

orders to fall upon their enemies when they were
scattered, they were disappointed of their hopes,
inasmuch as the Romans soon became aware of their
design and a sharp action ensued, in which the
Aequians lost many of their men ; the result was
that they would no longer even try the fortune of
another engagement. Neither did any army oppose
Numicius as he was marching on Antium, which
was at that time among the foremost cities of the
Volscians ; but the people were forced in every
instance to defend themselves from their walls. In
the meantime not only was the greater part of their
country laid waste, but also a small town on the coast
was taken which they used as a station for their ships
and a market for the necessaries of life, bringing
thither the many spoils they took both from the sea
and by raids on land. The slaves, goods, cattle and
merchandise were seized as plunder by the army
with the consul's permission ; but all the free men
who had not lost their lives in the war were taken
away to be sold at an auction of spoils. There were
also captured twenty-two warships belonging to the
Antiates together with rigging and equipment for
ships besides. After that at the consul's command
the Romans set fire to the houses, destroyed the
docks and demolished the wall to its foundations,
so that even after their departure the fortress could
be of no use to the Antiates. These were the exploits of the two consuls while they acted separately.
They afterwards joined forces and made an incursion
into the territory of the Sabines ; and having laid
it waste, they returned home with the army. Thus
that year ended.

DIONYSIUS OF HALICARNASSUS

LVII. Τῷ δ᾽ ἑξῆς ἔτει Τίτου[1] Κοϊντίου Καπιτω-λίνου[2] καὶ Κοΐντου Σερουϊλίου Πρίσκου τὴν ὕπατον ἀρχὴν παρειληφότων ἥ τε οἰκεία δύναμις Ῥωμαίων ἅπασα ἐν τοῖς ὅπλοις ἦν καὶ τὰ συμμαχικὰ ἑκούσια παρῆν πρὶν ἐπαγγελθῆναι αὐτοῖς στρατιάν.[3] καὶ μετὰ τοῦτο εὐχάς τε ποιησάμενοι τοῖς θεοῖς οἱ ὕπατοι καὶ καθήραντες τὸν στρατὸν ἐξῄεσαν ἐπὶ 2 τοὺς πολεμίους. Σαβῖνοι μὲν οὖν, ἐφ᾽ οὓς ὁ Σερ-ουΐλιος ἤλασεν, οὔτ᾽ εἰς μάχην κατέστησαν οὔτ᾽ ἐξῆλθον εἰς τὴν ὕπαιθρον, μένοντες δ᾽ ἐν τοῖς φρου-ρίοις ἠνείχοντο γῆς τε αὐτοῖς τεμνομένης[4] καὶ οἰκιῶν ἐμπιμπραμένων θεραπείας τε αὐτομολούσης· ὥστε κατὰ πολλὴν εὐπέτειαν ἀπελθεῖν ἐκ τῆς χώρας αὐτῶν τοὺς Ῥωμαίους ὠφελείαις τε βαρεῖς καὶ αὐχήμασι λαμπρούς· καὶ ἡ μὲν Σερουϊλίου στρατεία τοῦτ᾽ ἔσχε τὸ τέλος. 3 Οἱ δὲ σὺν τῷ Κοϊντίῳ στρατεύσαντες ἐπί τ᾽ Αἰκανοὺς καὶ Οὐολούσκους (συνεληλύθεσαν γὰρ εἰς τὸν αὐτὸν τόπον ἐξ ἀμφοτέρων τῶν ἐθνῶν οἱ προ-αγωνιούμενοι τῶν ἄλλων καὶ πρὸ τῆς Ἀντιατῶν πόλεως ἀντεστρατοπεδεύσαντο) θᾶττον ἢ βάδην χωροῦντες ἐπιφαίνονται αὐτοῖς· καὶ οὐ πολὺν τόπον τοῦ χάρακος αὐτῶν ἀποσχόντες, ἐν ᾧ πρῶτον ὤφθησάν τε καὶ εἶδον ἐκείνους χωρίῳ ταπεινῷ ὄντι τὰς ἀποσκευὰς ἔθεντο, τοῦ μὴ δεδοικέναι τὰ πο-λέμια πλήθει μακρῷ προὔχοντα δόξαν ποιῆσαι 4 βουλόμενοι. ὡς δ᾽ εὐτρεπῆ τὰ εἰς μάχην ἑκατέροις ἅπαντα ἦν, ἐξῄεσαν εἰς τὸ πεδίον καὶ συμπεσόντες ἠγωνίζοντο μέχρι μεσούσης ἡμέρας, οὔτε εἴκοντες

[1] Τίτου added by Sylburg.
[2] Καπιτωλίνου Cary, Καπετωλίνου Sylburg, Jacoby : καπε-τωλίου O.

LVII. The next year,[1] when Titus Quintius Capitolinus and Quintus Servilius Priscus had succeeded
to the consulship, not only were the Romans' forces
all under arms, but the allied contingents as well
presented themselves of their own accord before
they were notified of the expedition. Thereupon
the consuls, after they had offered up their vows to
the gods and performed the lustration of the army,
set out against their enemies. The Sabines, against
whom Servilius marched, neither drew up for battle
nor came out into the open, but remaining in their
fortresses, permitted their land to be laid waste, their
houses to be burned and their slaves to desert, so that
the Romans retired from their country entirely at
their ease, loaded down with spoils and exulting in
their success. This was the outcome of the expedition led by Servilius.

The forces which had marched under Quintius
against the Aequians and the Volscians—for the
contingents from both nations who were to fight
in behalf of the rest had joined together and had
encamped before Antium—advancing at a quick
pace, suddenly appeared before them and set down
their baggage not far from the enemy's camp in
the place where they had first been visible to each
other, even though it was a low position ; for they
wished to avoid the appearance of fearing the enemy's
numbers, which were much larger than their own.
When everything was ready for battle on both sides,
they advanced into the plain, and engaging, fought
till midday, neither yielding to nor charging their

[1] For chaps. 57 f. cf. Livy ii. 64 f.

---

[3] στρατιάν O (cf. ch. 59 ad fin.) : στρατείαν Sylburg, Jacoby.
[4] Cobet : ἐκτεμνομένης O.

τοῖς πολεμίοις οὔτε ἐπιβαίνοντες, ἀεί τε τὸ κάμνον
μέρος ἀνισοῦντες τοῖς ἐπὶ ταῖς ἐφεδρείαις[1] τεταγ-
μένοις ἑκάτεροι. ἐν δὲ τούτῳ μάλιστα οἱ Αἰκανοὶ
καὶ Οὐολοῦσκοι πλήθει τῶν Ῥωμαίων προὔχοντες
ἀνέφερον καὶ περιῆσαν, τῶν πολεμίων οὐκ ἐχόντων
5 ἴσον τῇ προθυμίᾳ τὸ πλῆθος. ὁ δὲ Κοΐντιος ὁρῶν
νεκρούς τε πολλοὺς τῶν σφετέρων καὶ τῶν περι-
όντων τοὺς πλείους τραυματίας ἐμέλλησε μὲν
ἀνακαλεῖσθαι τὴν δύναμιν, δείσας δὲ μὴ δόξαν
παράσχῃ τοῖς πολεμίοις φυγῆς, παρακινδυνευτέον
σφίσιν εἶναι ἔγνω. ἐπιλεξάμενος δὲ τῶν ἱππέων τοὺς
κρατίστους κατὰ τὸ δεξιόν, ὃ μάλιστα ἔκαμνεν,[2]
6 τοῖς σφετέροις παρεβοήθει. καὶ τὰ μὲν ἐπιτιμῶν
τοῖς ἡγεμόσιν αὐτοῖς τῆς ἀνανδρίας, τὰ ὑπομιμνή-
σκων τῶν προτέρων ἀγώνων, τὰ δὲ τὴν αἰσχύνην
ἐπιλεγόμενος καὶ τὸν κίνδυνον ὃς καταλήψεσθαι
αὐτοὺς ἔμελλεν ἐν τῇ φυγῇ, τελευτῶν εἶπέ τι[3] οὐκ
ἀληθές,[4] ὃ μάλιστα μὲν τοῖς σφετέροις θάρσος
παρέστησε, τοῖς δὲ πολεμίοις δέος. ἔφη γὰρ ὅτι
θάτερον αὐτῶν ἤδη κέρας ἐξέωσε τοὺς πολεμίους
7 καὶ ἐγγὺς ἤδη ἐστὶ τοῦ ἐκείνων χάρακος. ταῦτ᾽
εἰπὼν ἐνσείει τοῖς πολεμίοις, καὶ καταβὰς ἀπὸ τοῦ
ἵππου σὺν τοῖς ἀμφ᾽ αὐτὸν ἐπιλέκτοις τῶν ἱππέων
συστάδην ἐμάχετο. ἐκ δὲ τούτου τόλμα τις ἐμ-
πίπτει τοῖς κάμνουσι τέως, καὶ ὠθοῦνται ἅπαντες
ὥσπερ ἕτεροί τινες γεγονότες· καὶ οἱ Οὐολοῦσκοι,
τῇδε γὰρ ἐκεῖνοι ἐτάξαντο, μέχρι πολλοῦ διακαρ-
τερήσαντες ἐνέκλιναν. ὡς δὲ τούτους ὁ Κοΐντιος
ἀπεώσατο, ἀναβὰς ἐπὶ τὸν ἵππον παρήλαυνεν ἐπὶ

---

[1] τοῖς ἐπὶ ταῖς ἐφεδρίαις A : τοῖς σφετέροις B.
[2] ὃ μάλιστα ἔκαμνεν Ba, Sylburg : ᾧ μ. ἔκαμνον R.
[3] εἶπέ τι Cary : εἶπεν O, Jacoby.

opponents, and both sides continually bringing up
to equal strength with the enemy, by means of the
troops held in reserve, any part of their line that
was in distress. In this respect particularly the
Aequians and Volscians, being more numerous than
the Romans, rallied and had the advantage, since
their foes' numbers were not equal to their ardour.
Quintius, seeing many of his men dead and the
greater part of the survivors wounded, was on the
point of recalling his forces, but fearing that this
would give the enemy the impression of a flight, he
decided that they must make a bold stroke. Choosing, therefore, the best of his horse, he hastened
to the aid of his men on the right wing, which was
hardest pressed. And upbraiding the officers themselves for their want of courage, reminding them of
their former exploits, and showing them to what
shame and danger they would be exposed in fleeing,
he ended with an untruth, which more than anything
else inspired his own men with confidence and the
enemy with fear. For he told them that their other
wing had already put the enemy to flight and was
by now close to their camp. Having said this, he
charged the enemy, and dismounting from his horse,
he and the chosen horsemen with him fought hand
to hand. Upon this a kind of daring came to those
whose spirits till then had flagged, and as if they
had become different men, all pressed forward ; and
the Volscians—for these stood opposite to them—
after holding out for a long time, gave way. Quintius,
having repulsed these opponents, mounted his horse

---

[4] ἀληθές C, by correction : ἀληθῆ BbC.

τὴν ἑτέραν τάξιν, καὶ ἐδείκνυε τοῖς ἐκεῖ πεζοῖς τὸ
ἡττώμενον τῶν πολεμίων μέρος καὶ παρεκελεύετο
μὴ λείπεσθαι ἀρετῇ τῶν ἑτέρων.

LVIII. Καὶ μετὰ τοῦτο οὐδὲν ἔτι διέμενε τῶν
πολεμίων, ἀλλὰ πάντες εἰς τὸν χάρακα ξυνέφευγον.
οὐ μέντοι δίωξίς γε αὐτῶν ἐπὶ πολὺ ἐγένετο, ἀλλ'
εὐθὺς οἱ Ῥωμαῖοι ἀπετράποντο, ὑπὸ κόπου τὰ
σώματα παρειμένοι καὶ οὐδὲ τὰ ὅπλα ἔτι ὅμοια
ἔχοντες. ὀλίγων δὲ διελθουσῶν ἡμερῶν, ἃς ἐσπεί-
σαντο ταφῆς τε τῶν οἰκείων νεκρῶν[1] καὶ θεραπείας
τῶν κεκμηκότων ἕνεκα, παρεσκευασμένοι τὰ εἰς
τὸν πόλεμον ἐλλείποντα, ἑτέραν ἠγωνίσαντο μάχην
2 περὶ τῷ Ῥωμαίων χάρακι. προσελθούσης γὰρ
ἄλλης δυνάμεως τοῖς Οὐολούσκοις τε καὶ Αἰκανοῖς
ἐκ τῶν πέριξ χωρίων οὐ διὰ μακροῦ ὄντων, ἐπαρθεὶς ὁ στρατηγὸς αὐτῶν ὅτι καὶ πενταπλάσιοι τῶν
πολεμίων ἦσαν οἱ σφέτεροι, τήν τε παρεμβολὴν
τῶν Ῥωμαίων οὐκ ἐν ἐχυρῷ οὖσαν ὁρῶν, κράτιστον
ὑπέλαβεν εἶναι καιρὸν ἐπιχειρεῖν αὐτοῖς. ἐνθυμη-
θεὶς δὲ ταῦτα περὶ μέσας νύκτας ἦγε τὴν δύναμιν
ἐπὶ τὸν χάρακα τῶν Ῥωμαίων, καὶ κύκλῳ περι-
3 στήσας ἐφρούρει, μὴ λάθοιεν ἀπιόντες. ὁ δὲ
Κοΐντιος, ὡς ἔμαθε τῶν πολεμίων τὸ πλῆθος,
ἀγαπητῶς ἐδέξατο καὶ περιμείνας ἕως ἡμέρα τε
ἐγένετο καὶ ὥρα πληθυούσης μάλιστα ἀγορᾶς,
κάμνοντας ἤδη τοὺς πολεμίους αἰσθόμενος ὑπό τε
ἀγρυπνίας καὶ ἀκροβολισμῶν καὶ οὐ κατὰ λόχους
οὐδὲ ἐν τάξει προσάγοντας ἀλλὰ πολλαχῇ κεχυ-
μένους καὶ σποράδας, ἀνοίξας τὰς πύλας τοῦ
χάρακος ἐξέδραμεν ἅμα τοῖς ἐπιλέκτοις τῶν ἱπ-
πέων· καὶ οἱ πεζοὶ πυκνώσαντες τοὺς λόχους ἠκο-

[1] νεκρῶν B : om. R.

and, riding along to the other wing, showed to the foot posted there the part of the enemy which was defeated, and exhorted them not to be behind the others in valour.

LVIII. After this no part of the enemy stood their ground but all fled together to their camp. The Romans, however, did not pursue them far, but promptly turned back, as their bodies were spent with toil and their weapons no longer what they had been. But after a few days had passed, for which they had made a truce in order to bury their dead and care for their sick, and they had supplied themselves with whatever was lacking for the war, they fought another battle, this time about the camp of the Romans. For, reinforcements having come to the Volscians and Aequians from the neighbouring forts round about, their general grew elated because his forces were actually five times as large as those of the enemy, and observing that the Romans' camp was not strongly situated, he thought this was a most excellent opportunity for attacking them. Having so reasoned, he led his army to their camp about midnight, and surrounding it with his men, kept it under guard so that the Romans should not steal away. Quintius, upon being informed of the numbers of the enemy, welcomed this move and bided his time till it was day and about the hour of full market. Then, perceiving that the enemy were already suffering both from lack of sleep and from the skirmishing and that they were advancing neither by centuries nor by ranks but widely extended and scattered, he opened the gates of the camp and sallied out with the flower of the horse ; and the foot, closing their ranks,

4 λούθουν. οἱ δὲ Οὐολοῦσκοι καταπλαγέντες αὐτῶν
τὸ θράσος καὶ τὸ μανικὸν τῆς ἐφόδου βραχὺν ἀνασχόμενοι χρόνον ἀνακρούονταί τε[1] καὶ ἅμα[2] ὑπο-
χωροῦσιν ἀπὸ τοῦ χάρακος· καί, ἦν γάρ τις οὐ
πρόσω τοῦ στρατοπέδου λόφος ὑψηλὸς ἐπιεικῶς,
εἰς τοῦτον οὖν ἀνατρέχουσιν ὡς ἀναπαυσόμενοί τε
καὶ αὖθις[3] εἰς τάξιν καταστησόμενοι. ἀλλ' οὐ
γὰρ αὐτοῖς ἐξεγένετο καταστῆναί τε[4] καὶ ἑαυτοὺς
ἀναλαβεῖν, ἀλλ' ἐκ ποδὸς ἠκολούθησαν αὐτοῖς οἱ
πολέμιοι πιλήσαντες ὡς μάλιστα ἦν δυνατὸν τοὺς
λόχους ἵνα μὴ καταραχθῶσι πρὸς ἄναντες χωρίον
5 βιαζόμενοι. καὶ γίνεται μέγας ἀγὼν ἐπὶ πολὺ
μέρος τῆς ἡμέρας, νεκροί τε πίπτουσι πολλοὶ ἀφ'
ἑκατέρων. καὶ Οὐολοῦσκοι πλήθει τε ὑπερέχοντες
καὶ τὸ ἐκ τοῦ τόπου προσειληφότες ἀσφαλές, οὐδετέρου τούτων οὐδὲν ἀγαθὸν ἀπήλαυσαν, ἀλλ' ὑπὸ
τῆς Ῥωμαίων προθυμίας καὶ ἀρετῆς ἐκβιασθέντες
τόν τε λόφον ἐξέλιπον καὶ ἐπὶ τὸν χάρακα φεύ-
6 γοντες οἱ πολλοὶ ἀπέθνησκον. οὐ γὰρ εἴασαν[5]
αὐτοὺς οἱ Ῥωμαῖοι διώκοντες ἀλλ' ἐκ ποδὸς
ἠκολούθησαν καὶ οὐ πρότερον ἀπετράποντο ἢ τὴν
παρεμβολὴν αὐτῶν ἑλεῖν κατὰ κράτος. γενόμενοι
δὲ σωμάτων τ'[6] ἐγκρατεῖς[7] ὅσα ἐγκατελείφθη[8] ἐν[9]
τῷ χάρακι καὶ ἵππων καὶ ὅπλων καὶ χρημάτων
παμπόλλων κύριοι, τὴν μὲν νύκτα ἐκείνην αὐτόθι
κατεστρατοπέδευσαν, τῇ δ' ἐπιούσῃ ἡμέρᾳ τὰ εἰς
πολιορκίαν ἐπιτήδεια παρεσκευασμένος ὁ ὕπατος
ἐπὶ τὴν Ἀντιατῶν πόλιν οὐ πλείω ἀπέχουσαν
7 τριάκοντα σταδίων ἦγε τὴν δύναμιν. ἔτυχον δὲ
φυλακῆς ἔνεκα τοῖς Ἀντιάταις Αἰκανῶν τινες ἐπί-

---

[1] τε R : om. B. [2] ἅμα R : om. B.
[3] καὶ αὖθις Hertlein : αὖθις καὶ O. [4] τε B om. R.

118

followed. The Volscians were astonished at their
boldness and at the madness of their onset and, after
holding out for a brief time, were repulsed and at the
same time began to retire from the camp ; and, as
there stood not far from it a hill of moderate height,
they hastened up this hill with the intention of both
resting themselves and forming in line of battle again.
But they were unable to form their lines and to
recover themselves, for the enemy followed at their
heels, closing their ranks as much as possible in order
not to be hurled back while trying to force their way
up-hill. There followed a mighty struggle which
lasted a large part of the day, and many fell on both
sides. The Volscians, though superior in numbers and
having the added security of their position, got no
benefit from either circumstance; but being forced
from their position by the ardour and bravery of the
Romans, they abandoned the hill and while fleeing
toward their camp the greater part of them were
killed. For the Romans never left them as they pursued, but followed at their heels and did not desist
till they had taken their camp by storm. Then, having seized all the persons who had been left behind
in the camp and taken possession of the horses and
arms and huge quantities of baggage, they encamped
there that night. The next day the consul, having
prepared everything that was necessary for a siege,
marched with his army to Antium, which was not
more than thirty stades distant. It chanced that
some reinforcements sent by the Aequians to the

---

⁵ εἴασαν O : ἀνίεσαν Smit. ⁶ τ' om. A.

⁷ ἐγκρατεῖς Post : ἐγκρατεῖς καὶ R, Jacoby, om. B

⁸ ἐγκατελείφθη R : ἐγκατελήφθη Ba.

⁹ ἐν Capps : om. O, Jacoby.

κουροι παρόντες καὶ φυλάττοντες τὰ τείχη· οἳ τότε
δείσαντες τὸ 'Ρωμαίων τολμηρὸν δρασμὸν ἐκ τῆς
πόλεως ἐπεχείρουν ποιεῖσθαι. γενομένης δὲ τοῖς
'Αντιάταις γνώσεως κωλυόμενοι πρὸς αὐτῶν ἀπιέναι γνώμην ἐποιοῦντο παραδοῦναι 'Ρωμαίοις
8 ἐπιοῦσι τὴν πόλιν. τοῦτο μαθόντες ἐκ μηνύσεως
οἱ 'Αντιάται τῷ τε καιρῷ εἴκουσι, καὶ κοινῇ μετ'
ἐκείνων βουλευσάμενοι παραδιδόασι τῷ Κοϊντίῳ
τὴν πόλιν ἐφ' ᾧ Αἰκανοὺς μὲν ὑποσπόνδους ἀπελθεῖν, 'Αντιάτας δὲ φρουρὰν δέξασθαι καὶ τὰ
κελευόμενα ὑπὸ 'Ρωμαίων ποιεῖν. ἐπὶ τούτοις
κύριος γενόμενος τῆς πόλεως ὁ ὕπατος καὶ λαβὼν
ὀψώνιά τε καὶ τἆλλα ὅσων ἔδει τῇ στρατιᾷ καὶ
φρουρὰν ἐγκαταστήσας, ἀπῆγε τὴν δύναμιν· ἀνθ'
ὧν αὐτὸν ἡ βουλὴ ὑπαντήσει τε φιλανθρώπῳ
ἐδέξατο καὶ θριάμβου πομπῇ ἐτίμησεν.

LIX. Ἐν δὲ τῷ μετὰ τούτους ἔτει ὕπατοι μὲν
ἦσαν Τιβέριος Αἰμίλιος τὸ δεύτερον καὶ Κόιντος
Φάβιος, ἑνὸς τῶν τριῶν ἀδελφῶν υἱὸς τῶν ἡγησα-
μένων τε τῆς ἀποσταλείσης φρουρᾶς εἰς Κρεμέραν[1]
καὶ διαφθαρέντων ἐκεῖ σὺν τοῖς πελάταις. ἡ δὲ
βουλή, τῶν δημάρχων ἀνακινούντων πάλιν τὸ πλῆθος ἐπὶ τῇ κληρουχίᾳ καὶ συναγωνιζομένου θατέρου
τῶν ὑπάτων αὐτοῖς Αἰμιλίου, δόγμα ἐπεκύρωσε,
θεραπεῦσαί τε καὶ ἀναλαβεῖν τοὺς πένητας βουλο-
μένη, διανεῖμαί τινα μοῖραν αὐτοῖς ἐκ τῆς 'Αντια-
τῶν χώρας ἣν τῷ προτέρῳ ἔτει δόρατι ἑλόντες
2 κατέσχον. καὶ ἀπεδείχθησαν ἡγεμόνες τῆς κληρουχίας Τίτος Κοΐντιος Καπιτωλῖνος, ᾧ παρέδοσαν

---

[1] Portus : κρέμερα ABC.

Antiates for their protection were in the city and were guarding the walls. These men, dreading the boldness of the Romans, were now attempting to escape from the city; but being prevented from leaving by the Antiates, who had notice of their intention, they resolved to deliver up the city to the Romans when they should attack it. The Antiates, being informed of this, yielded to the situation, and concerting measures with the Aequians, surrendered the city to Quintius upon the terms that the Aequians should have leave to depart under a truce and that the Antiates should receive a garrison and obey the commands of the Romans. The consul, having made himself master of the city upon these terms and having received provisions and everything that was needed for the army, placed a garrison there and then led his forces home. In consideration of his success the senate came out to meet him, gave him a cordial welcome and honoured him with a triumph.

LIX. The following year [1] the consuls were Tiberius Aemilius (for the second time) and Quintus Fabius, the son of one of the three brothers who had commanded the garrison that was sent out to Cremera and had perished there together with their clients.[2] As the tribunes, supported by Aemilius, one of the consuls, were again stirring up the populace over the land-allotment, the senate, wishing both to court and to relieve the poor, passed a decree to divide among them a certain part of the territory of the Antiates which they had taken by the sword the year before and now held. Those appointed as leaders in the allotting of the land were Titus Quintius Capitolinus,

[1] Cf. Livy iii. 1.　　　　[2] See ix. 15 ff.

Ἀντιᾶται σφᾶς αὐτούς, καὶ σὺν αὐτῷ Λεύκιος
Φούριος καὶ Αὖλος Οὐεργίνιος. ἦν δ' οὐκ ἀγαπῶσι[1] τοῖς πολλοῖς καὶ πένησι Ῥωμαίων ἡ διανομὴ
τῆς χώρας ὡς ἀπελαυνομένοις τῆς πατρίδος, ὀλίγων
τε ἀπογραψαμένων ἔδοξε τῇ βουλῇ, ἐπειδὴ οὐκ
ἀξιόχρεως ἦν ὁ ἀπόστολος, ἐπιτρέψαι Λατίνων τε
καὶ Ἑρνίκων τοῖς βουλομένοις τῆς ἀποικίας μετέχειν. οἱ μὲν δὴ εἰς Ἄντιον ἀποσταλέντες κατένεμον
τὴν γῆν τοῖς σφετέροις, μοῖράν τινα ἐξ αὐτῆς τοῖς
Ἀντιάταις ὑπολειπόμενοι.

3   Ἐν δὲ τῷ μεταξὺ χρόνῳ στρατεία τῶν ὑπάτων
ἀμφοτέρων ἐγένετο, Αἰμιλίου μὲν εἰς τὴν Σαβίνων
χώραν, Φαβίου δ' εἰς τὴν Αἰκανῶν. καὶ τῷ μὲν
Αἰμιλίῳ πολὺν ἐν τῇ πολεμίᾳ μείναντι χρόνον
οὐδεμία δύναμις ὑπήντησε μαχουμένη περὶ τῆς γῆς,
ἀλλ' ἀδεῶς αὐτὴν κείρας, ἐπειδὴ καθῆκεν ὁ χρόνος
τῶν ἀρχαιρεσίων, ἀπῆγε τὰς δυνάμεις. Φαβίῳ δ'
Αἰκανοί, πρὶν εἰς ἀνάγκην ἐλθεῖν στρατιᾶς δια-
φθαρείσης ἢ τειχῶν ἁλισκομένων, ἐπεκηρυκεύσαντο
4 περὶ διαλλαγῶν καὶ φιλίας. ὁ δ' ὕπατος δύο τε
μηνῶν τροφὰς τῇ στρατιᾷ καὶ δύο χιτῶνας κατ'
ἄνδρα καὶ ἀργύριον εἰς ὀψωνιασμὸν ἐξαμήνου
καὶ εἴ τι ἄλλο κατήπειγεν εἰσπραξάμενος, ἀνοχὰς
ἐποιήσατο πρὸς αὐτοὺς ἕως ἂν εἰς Ῥώμην ἀφικόμενοι παρὰ τῆς βουλῆς εὕρωνται τὰς διαλύσεις. ἡ
μέντοι βουλὴ ταῦτα μαθοῦσα τῷ Φαβίῳ ἐπέτρεψεν
αὐτοκράτορι διαλύσασθαι πρὸς τοὺς Αἰκανοὺς ἐφ'
5 οἷς ἂν αὐτὸς προαιρῆται. μετὰ τοῦτο συνθῆκαι
γίνονται ταῖς πόλεσι μεσιτεύσαντος αὐτὰς τοῦ

---

[1] οὐκ ἀγαπῶσι Kiessling, οὐκ ἄγαν ἀσπαστῇ Reiske, οὐκ
ἀσμένοις ἀκούσασι Kayser, οὐκ ἀγώνισμα πᾶσι Jacoby : οὐκ
ἀγὼν πᾶσιν ἀλλὰ Α, οὐκ ἀγὼν πᾶσι (or ῶᾶσι) Β.

to whom the Antiates had surrendered themselves, together with Lucius Furius and Aulus Verginius. But the masses and the poor among the Romans were dissatisfied with the proposed assignment of land, feeling that they were being banished from the fatherland [1] ; and when few gave in their names, the senate resolved, since the list of colonists was insufficient, to permit such of the Latins and Hernicans as so desired to join the colony. The triumvirs, accordingly, who were sent to Antium divided the land among their people, leaving a certain part of it to the Antiates.

Meanwhile both consuls took the field, Aemilius marching into the country of the Sabines and Fabius into that of the Aequians. Aemilius, though he remained a long time in the enemy's country, encountered no army ready to fight for it, but ravaged it with impunity ; then, when the time for the elections was at hand, he led his forces home. To Fabius the Aequians, even before they were compelled to do so by the destruction of their army or the capture of their walls, sent heralds to sue for a reconciliation and friendship. The consul, after exacting from them two months' provisions for his army, two tunics for every man and six months' pay, and whatever else was urgently required, concluded a truce with them till they should go to Rome and obtain the terms of peace from the senate. The senate, however, when informed of this, gave Fabius full power to make peace with the Aequians upon such terms as he himself should elect. After that the two nations by the mediation of the consul made a

[1] The majority preferred, as Livy says, to get land at Rome.

ὑπάτου τοιαίδε· Αἰκανοὺς εἶναι Ῥωμαίων ὑπηκόους
πόλεις τε καὶ χώρας τὰς ἑαυτῶν ἔχοντας, ἀποστέλλειν δὲ Ῥωμαίοις μηδὲν ὅτι μὴ στρατιάν, ὅταν
αὐτοῖς παραγγελῇ,[1] τέλεσι τοῖς ἰδίοις ἐκπέμποντας.[2]
ταῦτα συνθέμενος ἀπῆγε τὴν δύναμιν Φάβιος καὶ
εἰς τὸν ἐπιόντα ἐνιαυτὸν ἀρχὰς ἅμα τῷ συνυπάτῳ
κατέστησεν.

LX. Ἦσαν δ' ὑπ' αὐτῶν ἀποδειχθέντες ὕπατοι
Σπόριος Ποστόμιος Ἀλβῖνος[3] καὶ Κόιντος Σερουΐλιος Πρίσκος τὸ δεύτερον. ἐπὶ τούτων ἔδοξαν
Αἰκανοὶ παραβαίνειν τὰς πρὸς Ῥωμαίους νεωστὶ
2 γενομένας ὁμολογίας ἀπὸ τοιαύτης αἰτίας· Ἀντιατῶν ὅσοι μὲν εἶχον ἐφέστια καὶ κλήρους ἔμειναν ἐν
τῇ γῇ, τά τε ἀπομερισθέντα σφίσι καὶ τὰ ὑπὸ τῶν
κληρούχων ἀφορισθέντα κτήματα γεωργοῦντες ἐπὶ
ῥηταῖς τισι καὶ τεταγμέναις μοίραις ἃς ἐκ τῶν
καρπῶν αὐτοῖς ἐτέλουν· οἷς δ' οὐδὲν τούτων ἦν
ἐξέλιπον τὴν πόλιν, καὶ ὑποδεχομένων αὐτοὺς προθύμως τῶν Αἰκανῶν ἐκεῖθεν ὁρμώμενοι τοὺς Λατίνων ἀγροὺς ἐλήστευον. ἐκ δὲ τούτου καὶ τῶν
Αἰκανῶν ὅσοι τολμηροί τε καὶ ἄποροι ἦσαν συν-
3 ελάμβανον αὐτοῖς τῶν ληστηρίων. ταῦτα Λατίνων
ἀποδυρομένων ἐπὶ τῆς βουλῆς καὶ ἀξιούντων ἢ
στρατιὰν πέμπειν ἢ συγχωρῆσαι[4] σφίσιν αὐτοῖς
τοὺς ἄρξαντας πολέμου ἀμύνασθαι, μαθόντες οἱ
σύνεδροι στρατιὰν μὲν οὔτ' αὐτοὶ ἐψηφίσαντο πέμπειν οὔτε Λατίνοις ἐπέτρεψαν ἐξάγειν, πρεσβευτὰς
δ' ἑλόμενοι[5] τρεῖς, ὧν ἡγεῖτο Κόιντος Φάβιος ὁ τὰς

[1] Jacoby : παραγγέλῃ Bb, παραγγέλλῃ A, παραγγελθῇ Sylburg.   [2] αὐτάς after ἐκπέμποντας deleted by Kiessling.
[3] Lapus, Sigonius : λαουίνιος AC, λαβίνιος B.
[4] συγχωρῆσαι B : συγχωρήσειν R.

treaty as follows : the Aequians were to be subject to
the Romans while still possessing their cities and
lands, and were not to send anything to the Romans
except troops, when so ordered, these to be maintained at their own expense. Fabius, having made
this treaty, returned home with his army and together with his fellow consul nominated magistrates
for the following year.

LX. The consuls [1] named by them were Spurius
Postumius Albinus and Quintus Servilius Priscus, the
latter for the second time. In their consulship the
Aequians were held to be violating the agreements
lately made with the Romans, and this for the following reason. All the Antiates who possessed homes
and allotments of land remained in the country cultivating not only the lands assigned to them but also
those which had been taken from them by the colonists,[2] tilling the latter on the basis of certain fixed
shares which they paid to the colonists out of the
produce. But those who had no such possessions left
the city, and being heartily welcomed by the Aequians, were using their country as a base from which
to ravage the fields of the Latins. As a consequence,
such of the Aequians too as were bold and needy
joined with them in their raids. When the Latins
complained before the senate of their situation and
asked them either to send an army to their relief or to
permit them to take vengeance themselves on those
who had begun the war, the senators, on hearing
their complaint, neither voted to send an army themselves nor permitted the Latins to lead out theirs,
but choosing three ambassadors, of whom Quintus

---

[1] Cf. Livy iii. 2, 1.   [2] See chap. 59, 1 f.

[5] ἑλόμενοι O : ἔπεμψαν Portus, ἀπέστειλαν Kiessling.

πρὸς τὸ ἔθνος συνθήκας ποιησάμενος, ἔπεμψαν[1]
ἐντολὰς αὐτοῖς δόντες πυνθάνεσθαι παρὰ τῶν ἡγουμένων τοῦ ἔθνους πότερα κοινῇ γνώμῃ τὰ ληστήρια
ἐξαποστέλλουσιν εἴς τε τὴν τῶν συμμάχων καὶ εἰς[2]
τὴν τῶν Ῥωμαίων γῆν (ἐγένοντο γάρ τινες καὶ εἰς
αὐτὴν καταδρομαὶ τῶν φυγάδων) ἢ τῶν πραττομένων οὐδενός ἐστι τὸ κοινὸν αἴτιον· καὶ ἐὰν φῶσιν
ἰδιωτῶν ἔργα εἶναι μὴ ἐπιτρέψαντος τοῦ δήμου,
τά τε ἡρπασμένα ἀπαιτεῖν καὶ τοὺς ἐργασαμένους
4 τἀδικήματα ἐκδότους αἰτεῖν.[3] ἀφικομένων δὲ τῶν
πρεσβευτῶν ἀκούσαντες τοὺς λόγους οἱ[4] Αἰκανοὶ
πλαγίας αὐτοῖς ἔδοσαν ἀποκρίσεις, τὸ μὲν ἔργον
οὐκ ἀπὸ κοινῆς λέγοντες γνώμης γεγονέναι, τοὺς
δὲ δράσαντας οὐκ ἀξιοῦντες ἐκδιδόναι, πόλιν τε
ἀπολωλεκότας καὶ ἀλήτας γεγονότας σφῶν τε ἐν
5 τῇ πενίᾳ[5] ἱκέτας. ἐφ' οἷς ὁ Φάβιος ἀγανακτῶν καὶ
τὰς ψευσθείσας πρὸς αὐτῶν[6] ὁμολογίας ἀνακαλούμενος, ὡς εἶδεν εἰρωνευομένους τοὺς Αἰκανοὺς καὶ
εἰς βουλὴν χρόνον αἰτουμένους ξενισμοῦ τε χάριν
ἐπικατέχοντας αὐτόν, ὑπέμεινέ τε κατοπτεῦσαι τὰ
ἐν τῇ πόλει πράγματα βουλόμενος· καὶ διεξιὼν
ἅπαντα τόπον κατὰ πρόφασιν θεωρίας δημόσιόν τε
καὶ ἱερόν,[7] τά τε ἐργαστήρια πληθύνθ' ὁρῶν[8]
ἅπαντα πολεμικῶν ὅπλων, τῶν μὲν ἤδη συντετε-

---

[1] ἔπεμψαν added here by Cary, ἀπέστειλαν by Sintenis,
Jacoby (cf. n. 5 on preceding page).
[2] εἰς B : om. R.
[3] αἰτεῖν O : παραλαβεῖν Reiske, ἄγειν Sintenis, om. Jacoby.
[4] οἱ B : om. R.
[5] ἐν τῇ πενίᾳ Sintenis, ἐν τῷ πένθει Post : ἐν τῷ πεδίῳ O.
[6] Sylburg : αὐτὸν O.
[7] δημόσιον . . . ἱερόν Sintenis : δημοσίων . . . ἱερῶν O.

Fabius, who had concluded the treaty with the
Aequian nation, was the leader, they sent [1] them out
with instructions to inquire of the leaders of the
nation whether it was by general consent that they
were sending out these bands of brigands into the
territory of the allies and also into that of the Romans
—for there had been some raids into the latter too
by the fugitive Antiates—or whether the state had
no hand in any of the things that were going on ; and
if they should say that the acts complained of were
the work of private persons without the consent of
the people, they were to demand restitution of the
stolen property and ask for the surrender of those who
had committed the wrongs. Upon the arrival of the
ambassadors the Aequians, having heard their demands, gave them an evasive answer, saying, indeed,
that the plundering had not been done by public consent, yet refusing to deliver up the perpetrators,
who, after losing their own city and becoming wan-
derers, had in their destitution [2] become suppliants of
the Aequians. Fabius resented this and appealed
to the treaty which they had violated ; but seeing
that the Aequians were dissembling, asking time for
deliberation and seeking to detain him under the
pretence of hospitality, he remained there in order
to spy upon what was going on in the city. And
visiting every place, both profane and sacred, on the
pretext of seeing the sights, and observing the shops
full of weapons of war, some already completed and

---

[1] This verb is wanting in the MSS.
[2] Or, following Post's emendation, "in their misfortune."

[8] πληθύονθ' ὁρῶν (cf. chap. 71, 1) added by Cary, πλήρη
ὁρῶν by Sintenis, Jacoby ; Post would add ἰδὼν μεστὰ after
ἅπαντα.

λεσμένων τῶν δ' ἔτι ἐν χερσὶν ὄντων, ἔγνω τὴν
6 διάνοιαν αὐτῶν. καὶ ἀφικόμενος εἰς τὴν Ῥώμην
ἀπήγγειλε πρὸς τὴν βουλὴν ἅ τε ἤκουσε καὶ ἃ εἶδε.
κἀκείνη οὐδὲν ἔτι ἐνδοιάσασα τοὺς εἰρηνοδίκας
ἐψηφίσατο πέμπειν καταγγελοῦντας[1] Αἰκανοῖς τὸν
πόλεμον ἐὰν μὴ τούς τε Ἀντιατῶν φυγάδας ἀπ-
ελάσωσιν ἐκ τῆς πόλεως καὶ δίκας τοῖς ἠδικημέ-
νοις ὑπόσχωνται.[2] οἱ δ' Αἰκανοὶ θρασυτέρας πρὸς
τοὺς ἄνδρας ἐποιήσαντο τὰς ἀποκρίσεις, καὶ τὸν
7 πόλεμον οὐκ ἀκούσιοι δέχεσθαι ὡμολόγησαν. ἀλλὰ
γὰρ οὐκ ἐξεγένετο Ῥωμαίοις στρατιὰν ἐν ἐκείνῳ
τῷ ἐνιαυτῷ ἐπ' αὐτοὺς ἀποστεῖλαι, εἴτε τοῦ δαιμονίου κωλύοντος εἴτε διὰ τὰς νόσους αἳ κατέσχον τὴν πληθὺν ἐπὶ πολὺ μέρος τοῦ ἔτους·
ἀλλὰ φυλακῆς ἕνεκα τῶν συμμάχων ὀλίγη τις
ἐξελθοῦσα δύναμις, ἧς ἡγεῖτο Κόιντος Σερουίλιος
ἅτερος τῶν ὑπάτων, ἐν τοῖς Λατίνων ὅροις διέτριψεν.

8   Ἐν δὲ τῇ πόλει τὸν νεὼν τοῦ Πιστίου Διὸς
Σπόριος Ποστόμιος ὁ συνύπατος αὐτοῦ καθιέρωσε
μηνὸς Ἰουνίου ταῖς καλουμέναις νώναις ἐπὶ τοῦ
Ἐνναλίου λόφου, κατασκευασθέντα μὲν ὑπὸ τοῦ
τελευταίου βασιλέως Ταρκυνίου, τῆς δὲ νομιζομένης
παρὰ Ῥωμαίοις ἀνιερώσεως οὐ τυχόντα ὑπ'[3] ἐκείνου. τότε δὲ[4] τῇ βουλῇ δόξαν ὁ Ποστόμιος ἔλαβεν
αὐτοῦ τὴν ἐπιγραφήν. ἄλλο δ' οὐδὲν ἐπὶ τῶν
ὑπάτων τούτων λόγου ἄξιον ἐπράχθη.

LXI. Ἐπὶ δὲ τῆς ἐνάτης καὶ ἑβδομηκοστῆς
ὀλυμπιάδος, ἣν ἐνίκα Ξενοφῶν Κορίνθιος, ἄρχον-

---

[1] καταγγελοῦντας Cmg : καταγγέλλοντας ABC.
[2] ὑπόσχωσιν Cobet.
[3] ὑπ' AB : παρ' C, ἐπ' Portus.

others still in the making, he perceived their intention. And returning to Rome, he reported to the senate both what he had heard and what he had seen. The senate, without hesitating any longer, voted to send the *fetiales* [1] to declare war against the Aequians unless they expelled the Antiate fugitives from the city and promised satisfaction to the injured. The Aequians gave a rather bold answer to the *fetiales* and admitted that they not unwillingly accepted war. But the Romans were unable to send an army against them that year, either because Heaven forbade it or because of the maladies with which the population was afflicted during a great part of the year ; however, for the protection of their allies a small army marched forth under Quintus Servilius, one of the consuls, and remained on the frontiers of the Latins.

At Rome his colleague, Spurius Postumius, consecrated the temple of Dius Fidius upon the Quirinal hill on the day called the nones of June. This temple had been built by Tarquinius, the last king, but had not received at his hands the dedication customary among the Romans. At this time by order of the senate the name of Postumius was inscribed on the temple. Nothing else worth relating happened during that consulship.

LXI. In the seventy-ninth Olympiad [2] (the one at which Xenophon of Corinth won the foot-race),[3]

---

[1] *Cf*. ii. 72.

[2] *Cf*. Livy iii. 2, 2–3, 10. The year was 463 B.C.

[3] This victory of Xenophon is celebrated by Pindar in the 13th Olympian ode.

---

[4] δὲ A : om. R.

τος Ἀθήνησιν Ἀρχεδημίδου, παραλαμβάνουσι τὴν
ὑπατείαν Τίτος Κοΐντιος Καπιτωλῖνος καὶ Κόιντος
Φάβιος Οὐιβουλανός,[1] Κοΐντιος μὲν τὸ τρίτον ἐπὶ
τὴν ἀρχὴν ἀποδειχθεὶς ὑπὸ τοῦ δήμου, Φάβιος δὲ
τὸ δεύτερον. οἷς ἡ βουλὴ ἀμφοτέροις στρατιὰς
μεγάλας καὶ εὖ παρεσκευασμένας παραδοῦσα ἐξ-
2 έπεμψε. Κοΐντιος μὲν οὖν ἐτάχθη φυλάττειν τὴν
σφετέραν γῆν ὅση τοῖς πολεμίοις ὅμορος ἦν,
Φάβιος δὲ τὴν Αἰκανῶν δῃοῦν· καὶ καταλαμβάνει
τοὺς Αἰκανοὺς ἐπὶ τοῖς μεθορίοις ὑπομένοντας
αὐτὸν σὺν δυνάμει πολλῇ. καὶ ἐπειδὴ τὰς παρ-
εμβολὰς ἐν τοῖς κρατίστοις ἑκάτεροι χωρίοις
κατεστήσαντο, προῄεσαν εἰς τὸ πεδίον Αἰκανῶν
προκαλεσαμένων καὶ ἀρξάντων τῆς μάχης, καὶ
διέμειναν ἐπὶ πολὺ τῆς ἡμέρας ἐκθύμως καὶ φιλο-
πόνως ἀγωνιζόμενοι, καὶ τὸ νικᾶν οὐ παρ' ἄλλον
3 τινὰ ἢ παρ' ἑαυτὸν ἕκαστος τιθέμενος. ὡς δὲ τὰ
ξίφη τοῖς πλείοσιν αὐτῶν διὰ τὰς συνεχεῖς πληγὰς
ἄχρηστα ἐγεγόνει, σημηνάντων τὸ ἀνακλητικὸν τῶν
ἡγεμόνων ἀπῆλθον ἐπὶ τοὺς χάρακας. καὶ μετὰ
τοῦτο τὸ ἔργον ἀγὼν μὲν ἐκ παρατάξεως οὐκέτ'
αὐτῶν ἐγένετο, ἀκροβολισμοὶ δέ τινες καὶ συμπλο-
καὶ ψιλῶν περί τε ὕδασι καὶ ἐν ἀγορᾶς παραπομπαῖς
συνεχεῖς· κἂν τούτοις μέντοι τὰ πολλὰ ἦσαν ἰσόρ-
4 ροποι. ἐν ᾧ δὲ ταῦτ' ἐγίνετο χρόνῳ μοῖρά τις
ἀπὸ τῆς Αἰκανῶν στρατιᾶς παρελθοῦσα καθ' ἑτέρας
ὁδοὺς[2] ἐνέβαλεν εἰς τὴν Ῥωμαίων γῆν ἢ πλεῖστον
ἀφειστήκει τῆς ὁμόρου καὶ διὰ τοῦτο ἀφύλακτος
ἦν· ἐξ ἧς ἀνθρώπους τε πολλοὺς συνήρπασε καὶ

---

[1] Sylburg : βωλανὸς ACmg, ιουλανὸς BC.

[2] ὁδοὺς Jacoby : ἀφύλακτος ὁδοὺς Ba, ἀφύλάκτους ὁδοὺς Bb, ὁδοὺς ἀφυλάκτους R.

Archedemides being archon at Athens, Titus Quintius
Capitolinus and Quintus Fabius Vibulanus succeeded
to the consulship, Quintius being elected by the
people to that office for the third time and Fabius
for the second. Both of them the senate sent into
the field, giving them large and well-equipped armies.
Quintius was ordered to defend the part of their
territory which adjoined that of the enemy, and Fabius to plunder the country of the Aequians. Fabius
found the Aequians waiting for him on their own
borders with a large force. After both sides had
placed their camps in the most advantageous positions, they advanced into the plain, the Aequians
being the challengers and beginning the battle ; and
they continued fighting spiritedly and with perseverance for a great part of the day, each man placing his
hopes of victory in no one but himself. But when
the swords of the greater part of them had become
useless from repeated blows, the generals ordered
the retreat to be sounded and the men returned to
their camps. After this action no pitched battle was
again fought by them, but there were sundry skirmishes and constant clashes of the light-armed troops
as they went to fetch water and escorted convoys of
provisions ; and in these encounters, moreover, they
were as a rule evenly matched. While this was going
on, a detachment of the Aequians' army, marching
by other roads, made an irruption into the part of
the Roman territory which lay at a very great distance from the common boundary and was for that
reason unguarded ; and seizing there many persons
and goods, they returned to their homes without

χρήματα, λαθοῦσά τε τοὺς σὺν τῷ Κοϊντίῳ περι-
πόλους τῆς σφετέρας γῆς ἀπῆλθεν ἐπὶ τὰ οἰκεῖα.
τοῦτο συνεχῶς ἐγίνετο καὶ πολλὴν παρεῖχεν αἰσχύ-
5 νην τοῖς ὑπάτοις. ἔπειτα μαθὼν διὰ κατασκόπων
τε καὶ αἰχμαλώτων ὁ Φάβιος ἐξεληλυθυῖαν ἐκ τοῦ
χάρακος τῶν Αἰκανῶν τὴν κρατίστην δύναμιν, ἐν
τῇ παρεμβολῇ καταλιπὼν τοὺς πρεσβυτάτους αὐτὸς
ἐξῆλθε νύκτωρ ἱππέων ἐπαγόμενος καὶ τοῦ πεζοῦ
τὸ ἀκμαιότατον. οἱ μὲν οὖν Αἰκανοί, διηρπακότες
τὰ χωρία οἷς ἐνέβαλον, ἀπῄεσαν ἐπαγόμενοι πολλὰς
ὠφελείας, ὁ δὲ Φάβιος οὐ πολὺ προελθοῦσιν αὐτοῖς
ἐπιφαίνεται καὶ τήν τε λείαν ἀφαιρεῖται καὶ μάχῃ
τοὺς ὑπομείναντας νικᾷ γενομένους ἄνδρας ἀγα-
θούς· οἱ δὲ λοιποὶ σποράδες ἐμπειρίᾳ ὁδῶν λαθόντες
6 τοὺς διώκοντας κατέφυγον εἰς τὸν χάρακα. ἐπεὶ
δὲ ταύτῃ ἀνεκρούσθησαν οἱ Αἰκανοὶ τῇ συμφορᾷ
παρὰ δόξαν σφίσι γενομένῃ, λύσαντες τὴν παρεμβολὴν ὑπὸ νύκτα ᾤχοντο καὶ οὐκέτι τὸ λοιπὸν
ἐξῄεσαν ἐκ τῆς πόλεως· ἀλλ' ἠνείχοντο σῖτόν τε,
ὃς ἐν ἀκμῇ τότε ἦν, συγκομιζόμενον ὑπὸ τῶν
πολεμίων καὶ ἀγέλας βοσκημάτων ἀπελαυνομένας
ὁρῶντες, χρήματά τε διαρπαζόμενα καὶ αὐλὰς πυρὶ
διδομένας καὶ αἰχμαλώτους πολλοὺς ἀγομένους.
τοῦτο διαπραξάμενος ὁ Φάβιος, ἐπειδὴ παραδοῦναι
τὰς ἀρχὰς ἑτέροις ἔδει, τὴν δύναμιν ἀναστήσας
ἀπῆγε· τὸ δ' αὐτὸ καὶ Κοΐντιος ἐποίει.

LXII. Ἀφικόμενοι δ' εἰς τὴν Ῥώμην ἀπέδειξαν
ὑπάτους Αὖλον Ποστόμιον Ἄλβον καὶ Σερούιον
Φούριον. οἱ μὲν δὴ νεωστὶ παρειλήφεσαν τὴν ἀρχήν, παρὰ δὲ τῶν συμμάχων Λατίνων ἄγγελοι
Ῥωμαίοις κατὰ σπουδὴν διαπεμφθέντες ἧκον. οὗτοι καταστάντες ἐπὶ τὴν βουλὴν διεσάφουν Ἀντια-

being discovered by the patrols under Quintius who were guarding their own territory. This happened continually and brought much disgrace upon the consuls. Later Fabius, learning through scouts and prisoners that the best of the Aequians' forces had gone out of their camp, set out himself in the night with the flower of the horse and foot, leaving the oldest men in the camp. The Aequians, after plundering the regions which they had invaded, were returning home with many spoils. But they had not proceeded far when Fabius suddenly appeared before them, took away their booty, and defeated in battle those who valiantly withstood him; the rest scattered, and being familiar with the roads, escaped their pursuers and fled to their camp for refuge. When the Aequians had been checked by this unexpected disaster, they broke camp and departed as night came on; and after that they ventured out no more from their city, but submitted to seeing their corn, which was then ripe, carried off by the enemy, their herds of cattle driven away, their effects seized, their farmhouses given to the flames and many prisoners led away. After these achievements Fabius, the time having come for the consuls to hand over their power to their successors, took his army and returned home; and Quintius did the same.

LXII. When they came to Rome,[1] they named Aulus Postumius Albus and Servius Furius consuls. These had just taken over their magistracy when messengers from the Latin allies, sent in haste to the Romans, arrived. These, being introduced into the senate, informed them that the situation at Antium

---

[1] For chaps. 62-66 cf. Livy iii. 4-5. Livy's name for the second consul is Spurius Furius Fusus.

τῶν τὰ πράγματα οὐ βέβαια εἶναι, κρύφα τε
διαπρεσβευομένων πρὸς αὐτοὺς Αἰκανῶν καὶ ἀνα-
φανδὸν εἰσιόντων εἰς τὴν πόλιν ἀγορᾶς προφάσει
πολλῶν Οὐολούσκων, οὓς ἐπήγοντο οἱ πρότερον
ἐκλιπόντες τὴν πόλιν Ἀντιατῶν, ὅτ' ἐκληρουχεῖτο,
διὰ πενίαν καὶ πρὸς Αἰκανοὺς ἀπαυτομολήσαντες,
2 ὥσπερ ἔφην. συνδιεφθάρθαι τε τοῖς ἐπιχωρίοις
ἅμα ἤγγελλον καὶ τῶν ἐποίκων συχνούς· καὶ εἰ μὴ
προκαταληφθήσονται φυλακῇ ἀξιόχρεω, ἀναστήσε-
σθαί τινα ἔλεγον κἀκεῖθεν ἀπροσδόκητον Ῥωμαίοις
πόλεμον. τούτων οὐ πολλῷ ὕστερον ἕτεροι πεμφ-
θέντες ὑφ' Ἑρνίκων ἤγγελλον ἐξεληλυθέναι μεγάλην δύναμιν Αἰκανῶν καὶ ἐγκαθεζομένην ἐν τῇ
σφετέρᾳ γῇ φέρειν τε πάντα καὶ ἄγειν, στρατεύειν
δ' ἅμα τοῖς Αἰκανοῖς καὶ Οὐολούσκους τὴν πλείω
3 τοῦ στρατοῦ μοῖραν παρεχομένους. πρὸς ταῦτα
ἐψηφίσατο ἡ βουλὴ τοῖς μὲν Ἀντιατῶν ταράττουσι
τὰ πράγματα (ἧκον γὰρ ἀπολογησόμενοί τινες ἐξ
αὐτῶν καὶ καταφανεῖς ἐγένοντο οὐδὲν ὑγιὲς φρο-
νοῦντες) φυλακὴν ἑτέραν πέμψαι ἢ ἔμελλε δι'
ἀσφαλείας ἕξειν τὴν πόλιν· ἐπὶ δ' Αἰκανοὺς ἄγειν
τὴν στρατιὰν τὸν ἕτερον τῶν ὑπάτων Σερούιον
4 Φούριον· καὶ ἐγίνετο ταχεῖα ἀμφοῖν ἡ ἔξοδος. οἱ
δ' Αἰκανοὶ μαθόντες ἐξεληλυθυῖαν τὴν Ῥωμαίων
στρατιάν, ἀναστάντες ἐκ τῆς¹ Ἑρνίκων ἐχώρουν
αὐτοῖς ὁμόσε. ἐπεὶ δ' εἶδον ἀλλήλους, ἐκείνην μὲν
τὴν ἡμέραν οὐ πολὺ διαστάντες κατεστρατοπέδευσαν, τῇ δ' ἐξῆς ἐπὶ τὸν χάρακα τῶν Ῥωμαίων
οἱ πολέμιοι ἧκον διάπειραν αὐτῶν τῆς γνώμης

---

¹ ἐκ τῆς Gelenius : εἰς τὴν O.

---

¹ In chap. 60, 2.

was precarious, since the Aequians were sending envoys thither in secret and large numbers of Volscians were resorting to the city openly on the pretext of trading ; they were being brought there by those who had left Antium earlier because of poverty, when their lands were allotted among the Roman colonists, and had deserted to the Aequians, as I have related.[1] At the same time they reported that along with the natives many also of the colonists had been corrupted, and that unless their purpose were forestalled by means of an adequate garrison an unexpected war would break out in that quarter also against the Romans. Not long after this other messengers, sent by the Hernicans, brought word that a large force of Aequians had set out and now lay encamped in the Hernicans' country, where they were plundering everything, and that the Volscians were joining with the Aequians in the expedition, contributing the larger part of the army. In view of all this the senate voted, first, with reference to those among the Antiates who were creating the disturbances—for some of them had come to Rome to defend their conduct and had made it clear that they had no honest purpose—to send another garrison to keep the city safe ; and second, with reference to the Aequians, that Servius Furius, one of the consuls, should lead the army against them ; and both forces promptly set out. The Aequians, upon learning that the Roman army had taken the field, departed from the country of the Hernicans and went to meet it. When the two armies came in sight of one another, they encamped that day not far apart ; and the next day the enemy advanced toward the camp of the Romans in order to ascertain their intentions. Then, when the

5 ληψόμενοι. ὡς δ᾽ οὐκ ἐξῆεσαν εἰς μάχην, ἀκρο-
βολισμοῖς χρησάμενοι καὶ οὐδὲν ἀξιόλογον δρά-
σαντες σὺν μεγάλῳ αὐχήματι ἀπῆλθον. ὁ μέντοι
Ῥωμαίων ὕπατος ἐκλιπὼν τὸν χάρακα τῇ ἐπιούσῃ
(τὸ γὰρ χωρίον οὐ λίαν ἀσφαλὲς ἦν) μετεστρατοπε-
δεύσατο ἐν ἐπιτηδειοτέρῳ, ἔνθα τάφρον τ᾽ ὠρύξατο
βαθυτέραν καὶ χάρακα ἐβάλετο ὑψηλότερον. τοῖς
δὲ πολεμίοις ταῦθ᾽ ὁρῶσι πολὺ θράσος προσεγένετο·
καὶ ἔτι μᾶλλον ἐπειδὴ σύμμαχος αὐτοῖς ἀφίκετο
στρατιὰ παρὰ τοῦ Οὐολούσκων τε καὶ Αἰκανῶν
ἔθνους, οὐδὲν ἔτι διαμελλήσαντες ἐπῆγον τῷ Ῥωμαίων χάρακι.

LXIII. Ὁ δ᾽ ὕπατος, ἐνθυμούμενος ὅτι οὐκ ἀξιό-
μαχος ἔσται ἡ σὺν αὐτῷ δύναμις ἀγωνιζομένη πρὸς
ἀμφότερα τὰ ἔθνη, πέμπει τινὰς ἐκ τῶν ἱππέων
γράμματα εἰς τὴν Ῥώμην κομίζοντας, δι᾽ ὧν ἠξίου
ταχεῖαν αὐτοῖς ἐλθεῖν ἐπικουρίαν, ὡς κινδυνευούσης
2 ὅλης διαφθαρῆναι τῆς σὺν αὐτῷ στρατιᾶς. ταῦτα
ἐπιλεξάμενος ὁ συνύπατος αὐτοῦ Ποστόμιος (ἦσαν
δὲ μέσαι νύκτες μάλιστα ὅτε οἱ ἱππεῖς ἀφίκοντο)
διὰ κηρύκων πολλῶν τοὺς βουλευτὰς ἐκ τῶν οἰκιῶν
συνεκάλει· καὶ γίνεται δόγμα βουλῆς, πρὶν ἡμέραν
λαμπρὰν γενέσθαι, Τίτον μὲν Κοΐντιον τὸν ὑπα-
τεύσαντα τὸ τρίτον, ἔχοντα τοὺς ἀκμαιοτάτους
τῶν νέων πεζούς τε καὶ ἱππεῖς, ἀρχῇ κοσμηθέντα
ἀνθυπάτῳ χωρεῖν ἐπὶ τοὺς πολεμίους ἐξ ἐφόδου·
Αὖλον δὲ Ποστόμιον τὸν ἕτερον τῶν ὑπάτων τὰς
λοιπὰς δυνάμεις συναγαγόντα, ἃς ἔδει χρονιώτερον
συνελθεῖν, ὡς ἂν αὐτῷ τάχους ἐγγένηται βοηθεῖν.
3 ἡμέρα δ᾽ ἤδη διέφωσκε,[1] καὶ ὁ Κοΐντιος συνήγαγε
τοὺς ἐθελοντὰς[2] πεντακισχιλίους μάλιστ᾽ ἄνδρας·

---

[1] Kiessling : διεπέφωσκε O, ἐπέφωσκε L. Dindorf.

Romans did not come out to fight, they engaged in skirmishes, and without performing any noteworthy exploit retired with great boasting. But the Roman consul on the following day left his entrenchments— for the place was not very safe—and shifted his camp to a more advantageous position, where he dug a deeper trench and threw up a higher rampart. The enemy, seeing this, were greatly emboldened, and still more so when an army came to their assistance from both the Volscian and the Aequian nations ; so that without further delay they led their forces against the camp of the Romans.

LXIII. The consul, realizing that the army under his command would not be strong enough to contend against both these nations, sent some of his horsemen to Rome with letters in which he asked that reinforcements might speedily reach him, as his whole army was in danger of being destroyed. When his colleague Postumius had read the letter—it was about midnight when the horsemen arrived—he sent out numerous heralds to call the senators together from their homes ; and before it was broad daylight a decree was passed by them that Titus Quintius, who had been thrice consul, should take the flower of the young men, both foot and horse, and, invested with proconsular power, should march against the enemy and attack them immediately ; also that Aulus Postumius, the other consul, should get together the rest of the troops, whose assembling would require more time, and go to the assistance of the others as speedily as possible. By the time day began to break Quintius got together the volunteers, about five thousand in

---

² Sylburg : ἐθέλοντας O.

καὶ οὐ πολὺ ἐπισχὼν ἐξῆγεν ἐκ τῆς πόλεως. τοῦτο
ὑποπτεύσαντες ἔμενον οἱ Αἰκανοί, καὶ πρὶν ἐλθεῖν
ἐπικουρίαν τοῖς Ῥωμαίοις προσβάλλειν τῷ χάρακι
αὐτῶν διανοηθέντες[1] ὡς βίᾳ καὶ πλήθει ἁλωσο-
μένων,[2] ἐξῆλθον ἀθρόοι διχῇ νείμαντες αὑτούς.
4 γίνεταί τε μέγας ἀγὼν δι' ὅλης τῆς ἡμέρας ἰταμῶς
αὐτῶν ἐπιβαινόντων τοῖς προτειχίσμασι κατὰ
πολλὰ μέρη καὶ οὔτε παλτῶν οὔτε βελῶν ἀποτοξευτῶν[3] οὔτε χερμάδων ἀπὸ σφενδόνης ἀφιεμένων
ἀδιαλείπτοις βολαῖς ἀνειργομένων. ἔνθα δὴ παρακελευσάμενοι ἀλλήλοις ὅ τε ὕπατος καὶ ὁ πρεσβευτὴς ὑφ' ἕνα καιρὸν ἀναπετάσαντες τὰς πύλας, ἅμα
τοῖς ἀκμαιοτάτοις ἐκτρέχουσιν ἐπὶ τοὺς πολεμίους,
κατ' ἄμφω τε τὰ μέρη τῆς προσβολῆς συρράξαντες
αὐτοῖς ἀποτρέπουσι τοὺς ἐπιβαίνοντας τῷ χάρακι.
5 τροπῆς δὲ γενομένης ὁ μὲν ὕπατος ἐπ' ὀλίγον
διώξας τοὺς καθ' ἑαυτὸν τεταγμένους[4] ἀνέστρεψεν·
ὁ δ' ἀδελφὸς αὐτοῦ καὶ πρεσβευτὴς Πόπλιος Φούριος ὑπὸ λήματός τε καὶ προθυμίας φερόμενος ἄχρι
τῆς παρεμβολῆς τῶν πολεμίων ἤλασε διώκων τε
καὶ κτείνων. ἦσαν δὲ δύο σπεῖραι περὶ αὐτὸν οὐ
πλείους ἀνδρῶν ἔχουσαι χιλίων. τοῦτο μαθόντες
οἱ πολέμιοι, περὶ πεντακισχιλίους μάλιστα γενόμενοι, χωροῦσιν ἐπ' αὐτὸν ἐκ τοῦ χάρακος· καὶ
οὗτοι μὲν ἐξ ἐναντίας προσῄεσαν, ἱππεῖς δ' αὐτῶν
κύκλῳ περιελάσαντες κατὰ νώτου τοῖς Ῥωμαίοις
6 ἐφίστανται. τούτῳ δὴ τῷ τρόπῳ κυκλωθέντες ὑπ'
αὐτῶν οἱ σὺν τῷ Ποπλίῳ καὶ δίχα τῶν σφετέρων

---

[1] διανοηθέντες O : καὶ διανοηθέντες Kiessling, Jacoby.
[2] Post : ἁλωσόμενον O, Jacoby.
[3] βελῶν ἀποτοξευτῶν Post, βελῶν ἀπὸ τόξων Sylburg, βελῶν
ὑπὸ τοξοτῶν Jacoby : βελῶν ἀπὸ τοξοτῶν ACmg, τοξοτῶν
(omitting βελῶν ἀπὸ) BC.

number ; and after waiting only a short time he led them out of the city. The Aequians, suspecting this move, remained where they were ; and having determined, before reinforcements should come to the Romans, to attack their camp, in the belief that it would be taken by main strength and superior numbers, they sallied out in force after dividing themselves into two bodies. There ensued a mighty struggle, lasting throughout the entire day, as the enemy boldly mounted the outworks in many places and were not repulsed, though exposed to a continual shower of javelins, missiles shot from bows, and stones thrown by slings. Then it was that the consul and the legate, after encouraging one another, both opened the gates at the same time, and sallying out against their opponents with the best of their men, engaged them where they were attacking on both sides of the camp, and repulsed those who were mounting the ramparts. When the enemy had been routed, the consul pursued for a short distance those who had been arrayed opposite to him, and then returned. But his brother and legate, Publius Furius, inspired by courage and ardour, drove ahead, pursuing and slaying, till he came to the enemy's camp. He had with him two cohorts, not exceeding a thousand men. Upon learning of this, the enemy, who were about five thousand, advanced against him from their camp. These attacked the Romans in front, while their horse, circling round them, fell upon their rear. The troops of Publius, when thus surrounded and cut off from their own army, though

---

[4] τεταγμένους R : om. B, Jacoby.

ἀποληφθέντες, ἐξὸν αὐτοῖς σώζεσθαι παραδοῦσι τὰ
ὅπλα (προὐκαλοῦντο γὰρ αὐτοὺς εἰς τοῦτο οἱ πολέμιοι καὶ περὶ πολλοῦ ἐποιοῦντο χιλίους Ῥωμαίων
τοὺς ἀρίστους αἰχμαλώτους λαβεῖν, ὡς διὰ τούτων
διαλύσεις εὑρησόμενοι καλὰς τοῦ πολέμου), καταφρονήσαντες αὐτῶν καὶ παρακελευσάμενοι ἀλλήλοις
μηδὲν ἀνάξιον πρᾶξαι τῆς πόλεως, μαχόμενοι καὶ
πολλοὺς ἀποκτείναντες τῶν πολεμίων ἅπαντες ἀπο-
θνήσκουσιν.

LXIV. Διαφθαρέντων δὲ τούτων ἐπαρθέντες οἱ
Αἰκανοὶ τῷ προτερήματι παρῆσαν ἐπὶ τὸν χάρακα
τῶν Ῥωμαίων, τήν τε τοῦ Ποπλίου κεφαλὴν ἐπὶ
δορατίου πεπηγυῖαν ἀνατείνοντες καὶ τῶν ἄλλων
ἀνδρῶν τῶν ἐπιφανῶν, ὡς δὴ τούτῳ καταπληξόμενοι τοὺς ἔνδον καὶ ἀναγκάσοντες παραδοῦναι
σφίσι τὰ ὅπλα. τοῖς δ' ἄρα πρὸς μὲν τὴν συμφορὰν
τῶν ἀπολωλότων ἔλεός τις παρέστη καὶ ἀνεκλάοντο
αὐτῶν τὴν τύχην, πρὸς δὲ τὸν ἀγῶνα θράσος δι-
πλάσιον ἐνέφυ καὶ τοῦ νικᾶν ἢ τὸν αὐτὸν ἐκείνοις
τρόπον ἀποθανεῖν, πρὶν εἰς πολεμίων χεῖρας ἐλθεῖν,
2 καλὸς ἔρως. ἐκείνην μὲν οὖν τὴν νύκτα παρεστρα-
τοπεδευκότων τῷ χάρακι τῶν πολεμίων ἄγρυπνοί
τε οἱ¹ Ῥωμαῖοι καὶ ἐπισκευάζοντες τὰ πεπονηκότα
τοῦ χάρακος διετέλεσαν, τά τ' ἄλλα οἷς ἀπερύκειν
ἔμελλον αὐτούς, εἰ πειραθεῖεν πάλιν τειχομαχεῖν,
πολλὰ καὶ παντοῖα εὐτρεπιζόμενοι. τῇ δ' ἑξῆς αἵ
τε προσβολαὶ πάλιν ἐγίνοντο καὶ ὁ χάραξ διεσπᾶτο
κατὰ πολλὰ μέρη· καὶ πολλάκις μὲν ὑπὸ τῶν ἐξιόν-
των κατὰ συστροφὰς ἐκ τοῦ χάρακος ἐξεκρούσθησαν οἱ Αἰκανοί, πολλάκις δ' ἀνεκόπησαν ὑπ' ἐκείνων
3 οἱ θρασύτεροι ἐπεξιόντες. καὶ τοῦτο δι' ὅλης τῆς
ἡμέρας ἐγίνετο· ἔνθα ὅ τε ὕπατος Ῥωμαίων σαυνίῳ

they had it in their power to save their lives by giving up their arms—for the enemy urged them to do so and were extremely anxious to take prisoner a thousand of the bravest Romans, in order to obtain through them an honourable peace—nevertheless scorned the enemy and exhorting one another to do nothing unworthy of the commonwealth, all died fighting after they had killed many of the enemy.

LXIV. When these men had been slain, the Aequians, elated by their success, advanced to the camp of the Romans, bearing aloft, fixed to their spears, the heads of Publius and the other prominent men, hoping to terrify the troops inside by this spectacle and compel them to surrender to them their arms. But though the Romans were indeed somewhat stirred by compassion at the fate of the slain and lamented their misfortune, yet they were inspired with a double boldness for the struggle and with a noble passion either to conquer or to die like their comrades rather than fall into the enemy's hands. That night, accordingly, while the enemy bivouacked beside their camp, the Romans went without sleep as they repaired the damaged portions of their camp and made ready the other means, of many and various kinds, with which to ward off the enemy if they should attempt again to breach their walls. The next day the assaults were renewed and the rampart was torn apart at many points. Often the Aequians were repulsed by sorties of massed troops from the camp, and often the men who rushed out too recklessly were beaten back by the Aequians. And this kept happening all day long. In these encounters the Roman consul was wounded in the thigh by a javelin

---

[1] οἱ B : om. R.

διὰ τοῦ θυρεοῦ διαπερονηθεὶς τιτρώσκεται τὸν μη-
ρόν, καὶ ἄλλοι συχνοὶ τῶν ἐπιφανῶν ὅσοι περὶ
αὐτὸν ἐμάχοντο· ἤδη δὲ τοῖς Ῥωμαίοις ἀπειρη-
κόσιν ἀπροσδόκητος ἐπιφαίνεται περὶ δείλην ὀψίαν
προσιὼν Κοΐντιος, ἄγων τὴν ἐθελούσιον ἐπικουρίαν
τῶν ἀκμαιοτάτων, οὓς ἰδόντες οἱ πολέμιοι προσιόντας ἀνέστρεφον ἀφέντες τὴν πολιορκίαν ἀτελῆ·
καὶ οἱ Ῥωμαῖοι ἐπεξελθόντες αὐτοῖς ἀπιοῦσι τοὺς
4 ὑστερίζοντας ἐφόνευον. οὐ μέντοι ἐπὶ πολύν γε[1]
χρόνον ἐδίωξαν ἀσθενεῖς ὄντες οἱ πολλοὶ ὑπὸ τραυμάτων, ἀλλὰ διὰ τάχους ἀνέστρεψαν. καὶ μετὰ
ταῦτα διὰ φυλακῆς εἶχον ἑκάτεροι σφᾶς αὐτοὺς
μένοντες[2] ἐν ταῖς παρεμβολαῖς ἄχρι πολλοῦ.

LXV. Ἔπειτα Αἰκανῶν τε καὶ Οὐολούσκων
ἑτέρα δύναμις καλὸν ὑπολαμβάνουσα καιρὸν ἔχειν
προνομεῦσαι τὴν Ῥωμαίων γῆν ἐξεστρατευμένης
αὐτῶν τῆς κρατίστης δυνάμεως, ἐξῆλθε νυκτός·
καὶ ἐμβαλοῦσα εἰς τὴν προσωτάτω χώραν, ἔνθα
τοῖς γεωργοῖς δέος οὐδὲν εἶναι ἐδόκει, πολλῶν γί-
2 νονται χρημάτων καὶ σωμάτων ἐγκρατεῖς. οὐ μὴν
καλάς γε οὐδ' εὐτυχεῖς τὰς ἐσχάτας ἔσχον ἐκεῖθεν
ἀπαλλαγάς.[3] ὁ γὰρ ἕτερος τῶν ὑπάτων Ποστόμιος
ἄγων τὴν συναχθεῖσαν ἐπικουρίαν τοῖς ἐν τῷ χάρακι
πολεμουμένοις, ὡς ἔμαθε τὰ γινόμενα ὑπὸ τῶν
πολεμίων, ἐπιφαίνεται αὐτοῖς ἐκ τοῦ ἀνελπίστου.
3 οἱ δ' οὔτε κατεπλάγησαν οὔτ' ἔδεισαν αὐτοῦ τὴν
ἔφοδον, ἀλλ' ἀποθέμενοι σχολῇ τὰς ἀποσκευὰς καὶ
τὰ λάφυρα εἰς ἓν χωρίον ἐχυρὸν καὶ φυλακὴν τὴν
ἀρκοῦσαν ἐπὶ τούτοις καταλιπόντες οἱ λοιποὶ συν-
τεταγμένοι χωροῦσι τοῖς Ῥωμαίοις ὁμόσε· καὶ
συμπεσόντες ἄξια λόγου ἔργα ἀπεδείκνυντο, ὀλίγοι

───────────

[1] γε B : om. R. [2] Sylburg : μένοντας O.

that pierced his shield ; wounded also were many other persons of distinction who fought at his side. At last, when the Romans had reached exhaustion, Quintius unexpectedly appeared in the late afternoon with his reinforcement of volunteers composed of the choicest troops. When the enemy saw these approaching, they turned back, leaving the siege uncompleted ; and the Romans, sallying out against them as they withdrew, set about slaying the laggards. They did not pursue them for long, however, weakened as most of them were by their wounds, but speedily returned. After this both sides acted upon the defensive, remaining a long time in their camps.

LXV. Later another force of Aequians and Volscians, thinking they now had a fine opportunity to plunder the Romans' country while their best troops were in the field, set out in the night ; and invading the remotest part of the land, where the husbandmen thought there was nothing to fear, they gained possession of much booty and many captives. But in the end their return from there proved neither glorious nor fortunate. For the other consul, Postumius, who was bringing the reinforcements he had got together for the relief of the Romans besieged in their camp, when he learned what the enemy were doing, appeared before them unexpectedly. They were neither astonished nor terrified at his approach, but when they had leisurely deposited their baggage and booty in a single strong place and left a sufficient guard to defend it, the rest marched in good order to meet the Romans. And when they had joined combat, they performed notable deeds, though they

---

³ ἀπαλλαγάς Cmg, Reiske : ἀπαλλαγέντες O.

μὲν πρὸς πολλοὺς ἀγωνιζόμενοι (συνέρρεον γὰρ ἐκ
τῶν ἀγρῶν ἐπ' αὐτοὺς συχνοὶ ἤδη διεσκεδασμένοι[1]),
ψιλῇ δ'[2] ὁπλίσει πρὸς ἄνδρας ὅλα τὰ σώματα
ἔχοντας ἐν φυλακῇ, ἐποίησάν τε πολλοὺς τῶν
Ῥωμαίων νεκροὺς καὶ μικροῦ ἐδέησαν ἐν ἀλλοτρίᾳ
γῇ καταληφθέντες τρόπαια τῶν ἐλθόντων ἐπὶ σφᾶς
4 αὐτοὺς ἀναστῆσαι. ἀλλ' ὅ γε ὕπατος καὶ οἱ σὺν
αὐτῷ Ῥωμαίων ἱππεῖς ἐπίλεκτοι, ἀχαλινώτοις
ἐπελάσαντες[3] τοῖς ἵπποις κατὰ τὸ καρτερώτατόν
τε καὶ ἄριστα μαχόμενον αὐτῶν μέρος,[4] διασπῶσι
τὴν τάξιν καὶ καταβάλλουσι συχνούς. διαφθαρέντων δὲ τῶν προμάχων καὶ ἡ λοιπὴ δύναμις ἀπο-
τραπεῖσα ἐνέκλινεν εἰς φυγήν, οἵ τε φυλάττοντες
τὰς ἀποσκευὰς μεθέμενοι αὐτῶν ἀπιόντες ᾤχοντο
ἀνὰ τὰ πλησίον ὄρη. κατ' αὐτὸν μὲν οὖν τὸν
ἀγῶνα ὀλίγοι τινὲς αὐτῶν διεφθάρησαν, ἐν δὲ τῇ
φυγῇ πάνυ πολλοί, χώρας τε ἄπειροι ὄντες καὶ ὑπὸ
τῆς Ῥωμαίων ἵππου διωκόμενοι.

LXVI. Ἐν ᾧ δὲ ταῦτ' ἐγίνετο χρόνῳ, πεπυσ-
μένος ἅτερος τῶν ὑπάτων Σερούιος ἐπὶ βοήθειαν
αὐτῷ προσιόντα τὸν συνύπατον, δείσας μὴ ὑπαντή-
σωσιν αὐτῷ οἱ πολέμιοι καὶ διακλείσωσι τῆς πρὸς
αὐτὸν ὁδοῦ, περισπᾶν αὐτοὺς διενοεῖτο προσβολὰς
2 ποιούμενος τῷ χάρακι. ἀλλὰ γὰρ φθάσαντες αὐτὸν
οἱ πολέμιοι, ἐπειδὴ ἔγνωσαν τὴν συμφορὰν τῶν
σφετέρων, ἣν ἀπήγγειλαν οἱ περισωθέντες ἐκ τῆς
προνομῆς, λύσαντες τὴν παρεμβολὴν ἐν τῇ πρώτῃ
νυκτὶ μετὰ τὴν μάχην[5] εἰς τὴν πόλιν ἀπῆραν, οὐχ
3 ἅπαντα πεπραχότες ὅσα ἐβούλοντο. χωρὶς γὰρ
τῶν ἀποθανόντων ἔν τε ταῖς μάχαις καὶ κατὰ τὰς

---

[1] ἤδη διεσκεδασμένοι AC : om. B.
[2] δ' Cary : om. O, Jacoby.

fought few against many—for large numbers came
streaming in to oppose them from their farms, to
which they had earlier scattered—and lightly-armed
against men whose bodies were entirely protected.
They killed many of the Romans and, though intercepted in a foreign land, came very near erecting
trophies over those who had come to attack them.
But the consul and the Roman horsemen who were
with him, all chosen men, charging with their horses
unbridled that part of the enemy which was firmest
and fought best, broke their ranks and killed a goodly
number. When those in the front line had been slain,
the rest of the army gave way and fled ; and the men
appointed to guard the baggage abandoned it and
made off by way of the near-by mountains. In the
action itself only a few of them were slain, but very
many in the rout, as they were both unacquainted
with the country and pursued by the Roman horse.

LXVI. While these things were occurring, the
other consul, Servius, being informed that his colleague was coming to his assistance and fearing that
the enemy might go out to meet him and prevent him
from getting through to him, planned to divert them
from this purpose by delivering attacks upon their
camp. But the enemy forestalled him ; for as soon
as they learned of the disaster that had befallen their
forces, the report being brought by those who had
survived the pillaging expedition, they broke camp
the first night after the battle and retired to their
city without having accomplished all that they desired. For, besides those who had lost their lives in
the battles and the pillaging expeditions, they lost

---

³ Hudson : πελάσαντες O.   ⁴ μέρος B : om. R.
      ⁵ μετὰ τὴν μάχην B : om. R.

προνομὰς τοὺς ὑστερήσαντας ἐν τῇ τότε φυγῇ
πολλῷ πλείους τῶν προτέρων ἀπέβαλον. οἱ γὰρ
ὑπὸ καμάτου τε καὶ τραυμάτων βαρυνόμενοι σχολῇ
προβαίνοντες ἐγκαταλιπόντων αὐτοὺς τῶν μελῶν
ἔπιπτον, μάλιστα δὲ περὶ τὰ νάματα καὶ ποταμοὺς
ὑπὸ δίψης φλεγόμενοι· οὓς οἱ Ῥωμαίων ἱππεῖς
4 καταλαμβάνοντες ἐφόνευον. οὐ μὲν δὴ οὐδὲ Ῥωμαῖοι πάντα ἐκ τοῦ τότε ἀγῶνος εὐτυχηκότες ἀν-
έστρεψαν· ἄνδρας μὲν γὰρ[1] ἀγαθοὺς καὶ πολλοὺς ἐν
ταῖς μάχαις ἀπολωλέκεσαν καὶ πρεσβευτὴν ἁπάντων λαμπρότατον γενόμενον ἐν τῷ ἀγῶνι· νίκην δ᾽
οὐδεμιᾶς ἥττονα τῇ πόλει φέροντες ἀνέστρεψαν.
ταῦτ᾽ ἐπ᾽ ἐκείνων τῆς ἀρχῆς ἐπράχθη.

LXVII. Τῷ δὲ κατόπιν ἔτει Λευκίου Αἰβουτίου[2]
καὶ Ποπλίου Σερουϊλίου[3] Πρίσκου παρειληφότων
τὴν ἀρχὴν οὐδὲν οὔτε κατὰ πολέμους ἔργον ἀπεδείξαντο Ῥωμαῖοι λόγου ἄξιον οὔτε πολιτικόν,
ὑπὸ νόσου κακωθέντες ὡς οὔπω πρότερον λοιμικῆς·
ἢ τὸ μὲν πρῶτον ἵππων τε φορβάδων καὶ βοῶν
ἀγέλαις προσῆλθεν, ἀπὸ δὲ τούτων εἴς τε αἰπόλια
καὶ ποίμνας κατέσκηψε, καὶ διέφθειρεν ὀλίγου δεῖν
πάντα τὰ τετράποδα· ἔπειτα τῶν νομέων τε καὶ
γεωργῶν ἥψατο, καὶ διελθοῦσα διὰ πάσης τῆς
2 χώρας εἰς τὴν πόλιν ἐνέπεσε. θεραπόντων μὲν οὖν
καὶ θητῶν καὶ τοῦ πένητος ὄχλου πλῆθος ὅσον
διέφθειρεν οὐ ῥάδιον ἦν εὑρεῖν. κατ᾽ ἀρχὰς μὲν[4]
γὰρ ἐφ᾽ ἁμάξαις σωρηδὸν οἱ θνήσκοντες ἀπεκομί-
ζοντο, τελευτῶντες δ᾽[5] ὧν ἐλάχιστος ἦν λόγος,[6] εἰς
τὸ τοῦ παραρρέοντος ποταμοῦ ῥεῖθρον ὠθοῦντο.

---

[1] γὰρ B : om. R.   [2] Sylburg : φαβίου O.
[3] Sylburg : σερουίου O.   [4] μὲν Reiske : τε O.
[5] δὲ Sylburg : τε O.

many more stragglers in their retreat at this time than on the former occasion. For those who were overcome by fatigue and their wounds marched slowly, and when their limbs failed them, they fell down, particularly at the fountains and rivers, as they were parched with thirst ; and the Roman horse, overtaking them, put them to the sword. Nor did the Romans, either, return home completely successful from this campaign ; for they had lost many brave men in the several actions and a legate who had distinguished himself above all the rest in the combat ; but they did return with a victory second to none for the commonwealth. These were the achievements of that consulship.

LXVII. The next year,[1] when Lucius Aebutius and Publius Servilius Priscus had assumed office, the Romans accomplished nothing worthy of mention either in war or at home, as they were afflicted by a pestilence more severely than ever before. It first attacked the studs of mares and herds of cattle and then seized upon the flocks of goats and sheep and destroyed almost all the live-stock. After that it fell upon the herdsmen and husbandmen, and having spread through the whole country, it invaded the city. It was no easy matter to discover the number of servants, labourers and poor people who were carried off by it. For at first the dead bodies were carried away heaped up in carts and at last the persons of least account were shoved into the river that flows past the city. Of the senate the fourth

---

[1] For chaps. 67 f. *cf.* Livy iii. 6 f.

[6] λόγος Cobet : ὁ λόγος O, Jacoby.

τῶν δ᾽ ἐκ τοῦ βουλευτικοῦ συνεδρίου τὸ τέταρτον
μέρος συνελογίσθη διεφθαρμένον, ἐν οἷς ἦσαν οἵ τε
ὕπατοι ἀμφότεροι καὶ τῶν δημάρχων οἱ πλείους.
3 ἤρξατο μὲν οὖν ἡ νόσος περὶ τὰς καλάνδας τοῦ
Σεπτεμβρίου μηνός, διέμεινε δὲ τὸν ἐνιαυτὸν ἐκεῖνον ὅλον, ἅπασαν ὁμοίως καταλαμβάνουσα καὶ δι-
εργαζομένη φύσιν τε καὶ ἡλικίαν. γενομένης δὲ
τοῖς πλησιοχώροις γνώσεως τῶν κατεχόντων τὴν
Ῥώμην κακῶν, καλὸν ἡγησάμενοι καιρὸν ἔχειν[1]
Αἰκανοί τε καὶ Οὐολοῦσκοι καταλῦσαι τὴν ἀρχὴν
αὐτῆς, συνθήκας τε καὶ ὅρκους ἐποιήσαντο πρὸς
ἀλλήλους περὶ συμμαχίας· καὶ παρασκευασάμενοι
τὰ εἰς πολιορκίαν ἐπιτήδεια, ὡς εἶχον ἀμφότεροι
4 τάχους, ἐξῆγον τὰς δυνάμεις. ἵνα δὲ τὴν ἀπὸ τῶν
συμμάχων ἀφέλοιντο τῆς Ῥώμης ἐπικουρίαν εἰς
τὴν Λατίνων τε καὶ Ἑρνίκων γῆν πρῶτον ἐνέβαλον.
ἀφικομένης δὲ πρεσβείας ἐπὶ τὴν βουλὴν ἀφ᾽ ἑκα-
τέρου τῶν πολεμουμένων ἐθνῶν ἐπὶ συμμαχίας
παράκλησιν ὁ μὲν ἕτερος τῶν ὑπάτων · Λεύκιος
Αἰβούτιος ἐκείνην ἔτυχε τὴν ἡμέραν τεθνηκώς,
Πόπλιος δὲ Σερουΐλιος ἐγγὺς ὢν τοῦ θανάτου· ὃς
5 ἔτι ὀλίγον ἐμπνέων συνεκάλει τὴν βουλήν. τῶν δ᾽
οἱ πλείους ἡμιθνῆτες ἐπὶ κλινιδίων κομισθέντες καὶ
συνεδρεύσαντες ἀπεκρίναντο τοῖς πρέσβεσιν[2] ἀγ-
γέλλειν τοῖς σφετέροις ὅτι διὰ τῆς ἑαυτῶν ἀρετῆς
τοὺς πολεμίους ἀμύνεσθαι ἡ βουλὴ αὐτοῖς ἐπι-
τρέπει μέχρις ἂν ὁ ὕπατος ῥαΐσῃ καὶ ἡ συναγωνιου-
6 μένη δύναμις αὐτοῖς συναχθῇ. ταῦτα Ῥωμαίων
ἀποκριναμένων Λατῖνοι μὲν ὅσα ἠδυνήθησαν ἐκ τῶν
ἀγρῶν εἰς τὰς πόλεις ἀνασκευασάμενοι φυλακὴν

---

[1] ἔχειν added by Cobet, εἶναι by Kiessling, Jacoby.
[2] Naber : παροῦσιν Ο, Jacoby.

part was estimated to have perished, including not only both consuls but also most of the tribunes.[1] The pestilence began about the calends of September and continued all that year, seizing and destroying people without distinction of sex or age. When the neighbouring peoples learned of the evils that were afflicting Rome, the Aequians and the Volscians, thinking they had an excellent opportunity to overthrow her supremacy, concluded a treaty of alliance with each other, confirmed by oaths ; and after making the preparations necessary for a siege, both led out their forces as speedily as possible. In order to deprive Rome of the assistance of her allies, they first invaded the territories of the Latins and the Hernicans. When envoys from the two nations which were attacked came to the senate to beg assistance, it chanced that one of the consuls, Lucius Aebutius, had died that very day, while Publius Servilius was at the point of death. Though he could barely breathe, he convened the senate, of whom the larger part were brought in half dead in litters ; and after deliberating, they instructed the envoys to report to their countrymen that the senate gave them leave to repulse the enemy by their own courage till the consul should recover and the army that was to participate with them in the conflict should be assembled. When the Romans had given this answer, the Latins removed everything they could out of the country into their cities, and keeping their walls under

[1] It was not until the second century B.C. that the tribunes could become senators, and then only after the expiration of their term of office. They had been allowed, however, from an early date to attend meetings of the senate, and this is probably the explanation of the careless form of statement here used.

149

ἐποιοῦντο τῶν τειχῶν, τὰ δ' ἄλλα περιεώρων ἀπ-
ολλύμενα. Ἔρνικες δὲ δυσανασχετοῦντες ἐπὶ τῇ
λύμῃ καὶ διαρπαγῇ τῶν ἀγρῶν, ἀναλαβόντες τὰ
ὅπλα ἐξῆλθον. ἀγωνισάμενοι δὲ λαμπρῶς καὶ
πολλοὺς μὲν[1] ἀποβαλόντες τῶν σφετέρων, πολλῷ
δ' ἔτι πλείους ἀποκτείναντες τῶν πολεμίων, ἐκβιασθέντες εἰς τὰ τείχη κατέφυγον, καὶ οὐκέτι μάχης
ἐπειρῶντο.

LXVIII. Αἰκανοὶ δὲ καὶ Οὐολοῦσκοι προνομεύ-
σαντες αὐτῶν τὴν χώραν ἀδεῶς ἐπὶ τοὺς Τυσκλανῶν ἀγροὺς ἀφίκοντο. διαρπάσαντες δὲ καὶ
τούτους οὐδενὸς ἀμυνομένου παρῆσαν εἰς τοὺς Γα-
βίνων[2] ὅρους. ἐλάσαντες δὲ καὶ διὰ ταύτης ἀδεῶς
2 τῆς γῆς ἐπὶ τὴν Ῥώμην ἀφικνοῦντο. ἐθορύβησαν
μὲν οὖν ἱκανῶς τὴν πόλιν, οὐ μὴν κρατῆσαί γε
αὐτῆς ἠδυνήθησαν· ἀλλὰ καίπερ ἐξασθενοῦντες[3] οἱ
Ῥωμαῖοι τὰ σώματα καὶ τοὺς ὑπάτους ἀπολωλε-
κότες ἀμφοτέρους (καὶ γὰρ ὁ Σερουΐλιος ἐτεθνήκει
νεωστί), καθοπλισάμενοι παρὰ δύναμιν τοῖς τείχε-
σιν ἐπέστησαν, τοῦ περιβόλου τῆς πόλεως ὄντος
ἐν τῷ τότε χρόνῳ ὅσος Ἀθηναίων τοῦ ἄστεος ὁ
κύκλος· καὶ τὰ μὲν ἐπὶ λόφοις κείμενα καὶ πέτραις
ἀποτόμοις ὑπ' αὐτῆς ἐστιν[4] ὠχυρωμένα τῆς φύσεως καὶ ὀλίγης δεόμενα φυλακῆς· τὰ δ' ὑπὸ τοῦ
Τεβέριος[5] τετειχισμένα ποταμοῦ, οὗ τὸ μὲν εὖρός
ἐστι τεττάρων πλέθρων μάλιστα, βάθος δ' οἷόν τε
ναυσὶ πλεῖσθαι μεγάλαις, τὸ δὲ ῥεῦμα εἴπερ[6] τι καὶ
ἄλλο ὀξὺ καὶ δίνας ἐργαζόμενον μεγάλας· ὃν οὐκ
ἔνεστι πεζοῖς διελθεῖν εἰ μὴ κατὰ γέφυραν, ἣ ἦν ἐν
τῷ τότε χρόνῳ μία ξυλόφρακτος, ἣν ἔλυον ἐν τοῖς

---

[1] μὲν B : om. R.　　　　　[2] Kiessling : σαβίνων O.
[3] ἐξασθενοῦντες B : ἀσθενοῦντες R.

guard, permitted everything else to be destroyed.
But the Hernicans, resenting the ruin and desolation
of their lands, took up their arms and marched out.
And though they fought brilliantly and, while losing
many of their own men, slew many more of the
enemy, they were forced to take refuge inside their
walls and no longer risked an engagement.

LXVIII. When the Aequians and Volscians had
laid waste the Hernicans' country, they came un-
opposed to the lands of the Tusculans. And having
plundered these also, none offering to defend them,
they arrived at the borders of the Gabini. Then,
passing through their territory also without opposition, they advanced upon Rome. They caused the
city enough alarm, it is true, yet they could not
make themselves masters of it ; on the contrary,
the Romans, though they were utterly weakened
in body and had lost both consuls—for Servilius
had recently died—armed themselves beyond their
strength and manned the walls, the circuit of which
was at that time of the same extent as that of
Athens. Some sections of the walls, standing on
hills and sheer cliffs, have been fortified by Nature
herself and require but a small garrison ; others are
protected by the river Tiber, the breadth of which
is about four hundred feet and the depth capable of
carrying large ships, while its current is as rapid as
that of any river and forms great eddies. There is
no crossing it on foot except by means of a bridge,
and there was at that time only one bridge, constructed of timber, and this they removed in time

⁴ ἐστιν added by Reiske.
⁵ τεβέριος Ba : τεβέρεως Bb, τιβέρεως A.
⁶ Hertlein : ὥσπερ O, Jacoby.

3 πολέμοις. ἔν δὲ χωρίον, ὃ τῆς πόλεως ἐπιμαχώ-
τατόν ἐστιν, ἀπὸ τῶν Ἰσκυλίνων¹ καλουμένων
πυλῶν μέχρι τῶν Κολλίνων, χειροποιήτως ἐστὶν
ὀχυρόν. τάφρος τε γὰρ ὀρώρυκται πρὸ αὐτοῦ
πλάτος ᾗ βραχυτάτη μείζων ἑκατὸν ποδῶν, καὶ
βάθος ἐστὶν αὐτῆς² τριακοντάπουν· τεῖχος δ' ὑπερ-
ανέστηκε τῆς τάφρου χώματι προσεχόμενον³ ἔν-
δοθεν ὑψηλῷ καὶ πλατεῖ, οἷον μήτε κριοῖς
4 κατασεισθῆναι μήτε ὑπορυττομένων τῶν θεμελίων
ἀνατραπῆναι. τοῦτο τὸ χωρίον ἑπτὰ μέν ἐστι μάλιστα ἐπὶ μῆκος σταδίων, πεντήκοντα δὲ ποδῶν
ἐπὶ πλάτος· ἐν ᾧ τότε οἱ Ῥωμαῖοι τεταγμένοι κατὰ
πλῆθος ἀνεῖρξαν τῶν πολεμίων τὴν ἔφοδον, οὔτε
χελώνας χωστρίδας εἰδότων κατασκευάζειν τῶν
τότε ἀνθρώπων οὔτε τὰς καλουμένας ἑλεπόλεις μη-
χανάς.⁴ οἱ μὲν δὴ πολέμιοι ἀπογνόντες τῆς πόλεως
τὴν ἅλωσιν ἀπῄεσαν ἀπὸ τοῦ τείχους, καὶ δῃώσαντες τὴν χώραν ὅσην διεξῆλθον ἀπῆγον ἐπ' οἴκου
τὰς δυνάμεις.

LXIX. Ῥωμαῖοι δὲ τοὺς καλουμένους ἀντιβασιλεῖς ἑλόμενοι τῶν ἀρχαιρεσίων ἕνεκα, ὃ ποιεῖν
εἰώθασιν ὅταν ἀναρχία κατάσχῃ τὴν πόλιν, ὑπάτους
ἀπέδειξαν Λεύκιον Λοκρήτιον καὶ Τίτον Οὐετούριον Γέμινον.⁵ ἐπὶ τῆς τούτων ἀρχῆς ἥ τε νόσος
ἐπαύσατο καὶ τὰ πολιτικὰ ἐγκλήματα ἀναβολῆς

¹ ἰσκυλίνων Bb : εἰσκυλίνων AC, Αἰσκυλίνων Kiessling,
Jacoby.
² Steph. : αὐτοῦ ABC.
³ προσεχόμενον B : συνεχόμενον R, προσκεχωμένον Reiske.
⁴ μηχανάς deleted by Cobet.
⁵ Sylburg : γεμίνιον AB.

¹ *Testudines.*

of war. One section, which is the most vulnerable
part of the city, extending from the Esquiline gate,
as it is called, to the Colline, is strengthened arti-
ficially. For there is a ditch excavated in front of
it more than one hundred feet in breadth where it
is narrowest, and thirty in depth ; and above this
ditch rises a wall supported on the inside by an
earthen rampart so high and broad that it can
neither be shaken by battering rams nor thrown
down by undermining the foundations. This section
is about seven stades in length and fifty feet in
breadth. Here the Romans were drawn up at that
time in force and checked the enemy's assault ; for
the men of that day were unacquainted with the
building of either sheds [1] to protect the men filling
up ditches or the engines called *helepoleis*.[2] The
enemy, therefore, despairing of taking the city,
retired from the walls, and after laying waste all the
country through which they marched, led their forces
home.

LXIX. The Romans,[3] after choosing *interreges*,[4] as
they are called, to preside at the election of magistrates—a course they are accustomed to take
whenever a state of " anarchy," or lack of a regular
government, occurs—elected Lucius Lucretius and
Titus Veturius Geminus consuls. In their consulship
the pestilence ceased and all civil complaints, both

[2] The *helepolis* (" taker of cities ") was a huge siege tower,
several stories in height and mounted on wheels so that it
could be readily moved up close to the walls of the beleaguered
city. Originally an adjective, the name usually appears as
a noun ; hence Cobet would omit the noun μηχανάς here.

[3] For chaps. 69-71 *cf.* Livy iii. 8, 1–10, 4.

[4] *Cf.* ii. 57. In this single instance Dionysius uses the
term ἀντιβασιλεῖς instead of the usual μεσοβασιλεῖς.

ἔτυχε, τά τε ἴδια καὶ τὰ κοινά, πειραθέντος μὲν
αὖθις τὸ περὶ τῆς κληρουχίας πολίτευμα κινεῖν ἑνὸς
τῶν δημάρχων Σέξτου Τιτίου,[1] κωλύσαντος δὲ τοῦ
δήμου καὶ εἰς ἐπιτηδειοτέρους ὑπερθεμένου και-
2 ρούς. προθυμία τε πολλὴ πᾶσιν ἐνέπεσε τιμωρήσα-
σθαι τοὺς ἐπιστρατεύσαντας τῇ πόλει κατὰ τὸν τῆς
νόσου καιρόν· καὶ αὐτίκα τῆς βουλῆς ψηφισαμένης
καὶ τοῦ δήμου τὸν πόλεμον ἐπικυρώσαντος κατέγραφον[2] τὰς δυνάμεις, οὐδενὸς τῶν ἐχόντων στρα-
τεύσιμον ἡλικίαν, οὐδ᾽ εἴ τινα ὁ νόμος ἀπέλυεν,
ἀξιοῦντος ἐκείνης ἀπολειφθῆναι τῆς στρατείας·
νεμηθείσης δὲ τριχῇ τῆς δυνάμεως μία μὲν ὑπελείφθη φυλάττειν τὴν πόλιν, ἧς ἡγεῖτο Κόιντος
Φούριος ἀνὴρ ὑπατικός· αἱ δὲ δύο σὺν τοῖς ὑπάτοις
3 ἐξῆλθον ἐπί τε Αἰκανοὺς καὶ Οὐολούσκους. τὸ δ᾽
αὐτὸ τοῦτο καὶ ὑπὸ τῶν πολεμίων ἔτυχεν ἤδη
γεγονός. ἡ μὲν γὰρ κρατίστη δύναμις ἀφ᾽ ἑκατέ-
ρου τῶν ἐθνῶν συνελθοῦσα ὑπαίθριος ἦν ὑπὸ δυσὶν
ἡγεμόσι, καὶ ἔμελλεν ἀπὸ τῆς Ἑρνίκων γῆς, ἐν ᾗ
τότε ἦν, ἀρξαμένη πᾶσαν ἐπελεύσεσθαι τὴν Ῥωμαίων ὑπήκοον· ἡ δ᾽ ἧττον ἐκείνης χρησίμη τὰ
οἰκεῖα πολίσματα ὑπελείφθη φυλάττειν, μή τις
4 ἔφοδος αἰφνίδιος πολεμίων ἐπ᾽ αὐτὰ γένηται. πρὸς
ταῦτα βουλευομένοις τοῖς Ῥωμαίων ὑπάτοις ἐδόκει κράτιστον[3] εἶναι ταῖς πόλεσιν αὐτῶν πρῶτον[4]
ἐπιχειρεῖν, κατὰ τοιόνδε τινὰ λογισμόν, ὅτι διαλυ-
θήσεται τὸ κοινὸν αὐτῶν στράτευμα εἰ πύθοιντο
ἕκαστοι τὰ οἰκεῖα ἐν τοῖς ἐσχάτοις ὄντα κινδύνοις,
καὶ πολὺ κρεῖττον ἡγήσεται[5] τὰ σφέτερα σώζειν

---

[1] Gelenius : τίτου O.
[2] Cobet : κατεγράφοντο O, Jacoby.
[3] Cobet : κράτιστα O.   [4] πρῶτον B : om. R.

154

public and private, were postponed. Sextus Titius, one of the tribunes, endeavoured, it is true, to revive the measure for the allotment of land, but the populace would not permit it and deferred the matter to more suitable times. A great eagerness came upon all to take revenge on those who had made expeditions against the city on the occasion of the pestilence. And the senate having straightway voted for war and the people having confirmed the decree, they proceeded to enrol their forces ; and no man who was of military age, not even if the law exempted him, wished to be left out of the expedition. The army having been divided into three bodies, one of them, commanded by Quintus Furius,[1] an ex-consul, was left to defend the city, while the other two marched out with the consuls against the Aequians and the Volscians. This same course had also been taken already by the enemy. For their best army, assembled from both nations, was in the field under two commanders, and intended to begin with the territory of the Hernicans, in which they were then encamped, and to proceed against all the territory that was subject to the Romans ; their less useful forces were left to guard their towns, lest some sudden attack might be made upon them by enemies. In view of this situation the Roman consuls thought it best to attack their foes' cities first; for they reasoned to this effect, that the allied army would fall apart if each of the two nations learned that their own possessions were in the direst peril, and that they would think it much more important to save their own

[1] Livy calls him Q. Fabius.

[5] Kiessling : ἡγήσεσθαι O.

ἢ τὰ τῶν πολεμίων φθείρειν. Λοκρήτιος μὲν οὖν
εἰς τὴν Αἰκανῶν ἐνέβαλεν, Οὐετούριος δ' εἰς τὴν
Οὐολούσκων. Αἰκανοὶ μὲν οὖν τὰ ἔξω πάντα ἀπ-
ολλύμενα περιορῶντες τὴν πόλιν καὶ τὰ φρούρια
εἶχον ἐν φυλακῇ.

LXX. Οὐολοῦσκοι δ' ὑπό τε θράσους καὶ αὐθαδείας προαχθέντες τοῦ τε Ῥωμαϊκοῦ στρατεύματος
ὡς οὐκ ἀξιομάχου ὄντος πρὸς τὸ ἑαυτῶν πλῆθος
συμφέρεσθαι καταφρονήσαντες, ἐξῆλθον ἀγωνιού-
μενοι περὶ τῆς γῆς καὶ πλησίον τοῦ Οὐετουρίου
κατεστρατοπέδευσαν. οἷα δὲ φιλεῖ πάσχειν στρατιὰ
νεοσύλλεκτος ἔκ τε πολιτικοῦ καὶ γεωργικοῦ πρὸς
καιρὸν συνελθόντος ὄχλου συναχθεῖσα, ἐν ᾗ πολὺ
καὶ τὸ ἄνοπλον ἦν καὶ κινδύνων ἄπειρον, οὐδ' εἰς
2 χεῖρας ἐλθεῖν τοῖς πολεμίοις ἐθάρσησεν· ἀλλ' ἅμα
τῇ πρώτῃ τῶν Ῥωμαίων ἐφόδῳ διαταραχθέντες
οἱ πολλοὶ καὶ οὔτε ἀλαλαγμὸν οὔθ' ὅπλων κτύπον
ἀνασχόμενοι, προτροπάδην ἔφευγον εἰς τὰ τείχη·
ὥστε πολλοὺς μὲν ἐν ταῖς στενοχωρίαις τῶν ὁδῶν
καταληφθέντας ἀποθανεῖν, πολλῷ δὲ πλείους παρὰ
ταῖς πύλαις ὠθουμένους τῶν ἱππέων ἐπιδιωκόντων.
3 Οὐολοῦσκοι μὲν οὖν ταύτῃ χρησάμενοι τῇ συμφορᾷ
σφᾶς αὐτοὺς ᾐτιῶντο τῆς ἀφροσύνης, καὶ οὐδὲν ἔτι
παρακινδυνεύειν ἐπειρῶντο. οἱ δὲ τὰς ἐν ὑπαίθρῳ
στρατιὰς Οὐολούσκων τε καὶ Αἰκανῶν ἔχοντες
ἡγεμόνες, πυνθανόμενοι τὰ οἰκεῖα πολεμούμενα,
γενναῖόν τι καὶ οὗτοι δρᾶν ἐβουλεύσαντο, ἀναστάντες ἐκ τῆς Ἑρνίκων τε καὶ Λατίνων γῆς ἐπὶ τὴν
Ῥώμην ἄγειν, ὡς εἶχον ὀργῆς τε καὶ τάχους, τὸν
στρατόν, κατὰ τοιάνδε τινὰ καὶ αὐτοὶ δόξαν, ὅτι

possessions than to destroy those of the enemy. Lucretius accordingly invaded the country of the Aequians and Veturius that of the Volscians. The Aequians, for their part, permitted everything outside their walls to be destroyed, but guarded their city and their fortresses.

LXX. The Volscians, however, inspired by rashness and arrogance and despising the Roman army as inadequate to cope with their own large numbers, came out to fight in defence of their own land and encamped near Veturius. But, as usually happens with an army of fresh levies composed of a crowd of both townsmen and farmers got together for the occasion, of which many are not only unarmed but also unacquainted with danger, the Volscian army dared not so much as encounter the enemy ; but the greater part of them, thrown into confusion at the first onset of the Romans and unable to endure either their warcry or the clash of their arms, fled precipitately inside the walls, with the result that many of them perished when overtaken in the narrow parts of the roads and many more when they were crowding about the gates as the cavalry pursued them. The Volscians, therefore, having met with this disaster, reproached themselves for their folly and were unwilling to hazard another engagement. But the generals who commanded the armies of the Volscians and Aequians in the field, when they heard that their possessions were being attacked, resolved to perform some brave action on their part also, namely, to take their army out of the country of the Hernicans and Latins and lead it against Rome in their present mood of anger and haste. For they too had some such thought as this in mind, that they should succeed in one or

δυεῖν ἔργων καλῶν θάτερον αὐτοῖς κατορθῶσαι
ὑπάρξει, ἢ τὴν 'Ρώμην ἀφύλακτον οὖσαν ἑλεῖν ἢ
τοὺς πολεμίους ἐκ τῆς ἑαυτῶν χώρας ἐκβαλεῖν, ὡς
δὴ τῶν ὑπάτων ἀναγκασθησομένων πολεμουμένῃ
4 τῇ πατρίδι βοηθεῖν. ταῦτα διανοηθέντες ἦγον τὴν
στρατιὰν ἐπιταχύνοντες, ἵν' ἐξ ἀπροσδοκήτου τῇ
πόλει συμμίξαντες εὐθὺς ἔργου ἔχωνται.

LXXI. Ἀφικόμενοί τε μέχρι Τύσκλου πόλεως,
μαθόντες τὸν περίβολον τῆς 'Ρώμης ὅλον πληθύ-
οντα ὅπλων καὶ πρὸ τῶν πυλῶν τέτταρας ἐξεστρα-
τευμένας σπείρας, ἀνδρῶν ἑξακοσίων ἑκάστην, τῆς
μὲν ἐπὶ τὴν 'Ρώμην ὁδοῦ ἀπετράποντο, τὴν δ'
ὑπὸ τῇ πόλει χώραν, ἣν ἐν τῇ προτέρᾳ παρέλιπον
2 εἰσβολῇ, ἐγκαθεζόμενοι ἐδῄουν. ἐπιφανέντος δ'
αὐτοῖς θατέρου τῶν ὑπάτων Λευκίου Λοκρητίου
καὶ θεμένου τὴν παρεμβολὴν οὐ πρόσω, καλὸν
ὑπολαβόντες εἶναι καιρόν, πρὶν ἐλθεῖν τῷ Λοκρη-
τίῳ τὴν ἑτέραν 'Ρωμαίων δύναμιν σύμμαχον, ἧς
Οὐετούριος ἡγεῖτο, συνάψαι μάχην, θέμενοι τὰς
ἀποσκευὰς ἐπὶ λόφου τινὸς καὶ δύο σπείρας ἐπ'
αὐταῖς καταλιπόντες, οἱ λοιποὶ προῆλθον εἰς τὸ πε-
δίον· καὶ συμβαλόντες τοῖς 'Ρωμαίοις ἄνδρες ἀγαθοὶ
3 κατὰ τὸν ἀγῶνα ἐγίνοντο μέχρι πολλοῦ. μαθόντες
δ' ἐκ τῶν κατὰ νώτου φρουρῶν τινες καταβαί-
νουσαν ὑπὲρ ὄχθου στρατιὰν ὑπέλαβον ἥκειν τὸν
ἕτερον τῶν ὑπάτων ἄγοντα τὴν σὺν αὐτῷ δύναμιν,
καὶ δείσαντες μὴ κυκλωθεῖεν ὑπ' ἀμφοῖν, οὐκέτι
διέμειναν, ἀλλ' εἰς φυγὴν τρέπονται. ἐν τούτῳ τῷ
ἀγῶνι οἵ τε ἡγεμόνες αὐτῶν ἀμφότεροι γενναίων ἀνδρῶν ἔργα ἀποδειξάμενοι πίπτουσι καὶ ἄλλοι πολλοὶ μαχόμενοι περὶ αὐτοὺς ἀγαθοί· οἱ δὲ φυγόντες
ἐκ τῆς μάχης εἰς τὰς ἑαυτῶν ἕκαστοι πατρίδας

the other of two glorious achievements—either to
take Rome, if it was unguarded, or to drive the
enemy out of their own territory, since the consuls
would be forced to hasten to the relief of their own
country when it was attacked. Having come to this
decision, they made a forced march, in order that
they might fall upon the city unexpectedly and immediately get to work.

LXXI. Having got as far as the city of Tusculum
and learning that the whole circuit of Rome was lined
with armed men and that four cohorts of six hundred
men each were encamped before the gates, they
abandoned their march on Rome ; and encamping,
they laid waste the district close to the city, which
they had left untouched on their former incursion.
But when one of the consuls, Lucius Lucretius,
appeared and made camp not far from them, they
thought this an excellent opportunity to join battle
before the other army of the Romans, commanded by
Veturius, should come to the assistance of Lucretius ;
and placing their baggage on a certain hill and leaving
two cohorts to defend it, the rest advanced into the
plain. Then they engaged the Romans and acquitted
themselves bravely in the conflict for a long time ;
but some of them, being informed by the guards in
the rear that an army was coming down over a hill,
assumed that the other consul had arrived with the
forces under his command, and fearing to be hemmed
in between the two armies, they no longer stood their
ground, but turned to flight. In this action both
their generals fell after performing the deeds of
valiant men, and likewise many other brave men
fighting at their side. Those who escaped from the
battle scattered and every man retired to his own

DIONYSIUS OF HALICARNASSUS

4 σκεδασθέντες ἀνεχώρησαν. ἐκ δὲ τούτου πολλὴν ἄδειαν λαβὼν ὁ Λοκρήτιος ἔφθειρε τὴν Αἰκανῶν γῆν, καὶ Οὐετούριος τὴν Οὐολούσκων, ἕως ὁ τῶν ἀρχαιρεσίων ἐπέστη καιρός. τότε δ' ἀναστήσαντες τὰς δυνάμεις ἀπῆγον ἐπ' οἴκου καὶ κατήγαγον ἀμφότεροι τοὺς ἐπινικίους θριάμβους, Λοκρήτιος μὲν ἐπὶ τοῦ τεθρίππου παρεμβεβηκώς, Οὐετούριος δὲ πεζὸς εἰσελαύνων. δύο γὰρ οὗτοι θρίαμβοι δίδονται τοῖς ἡγεμόσιν ὑπὸ τῆς βουλῆς, ὥσπερ ἔφην, τὰ μὲν ἄλλα[1] ἔχοντες ἴσα, τῷ δὲ τὸν μὲν ἱππικὸν εἶναι, τὸν δὲ πεζικόν, διαφέροντες.

[1] After ἄλλα the MSS. have ταμεῖα (ταμῖα Ba), deleted by Jacoby ; Kiessling emended to τίμα.

city. As a result of this victory Lucretius laid waste the country of the Aequians in great security, and Veturius that of the Volscians, till the time for the elections was at hand. Then both of them, breaking camp, returned to Rome with their armies and celebrated the triumphs awarded for victories, Lucretius entering the city in a chariot drawn by four horses and Veturius on foot. For these two triumphs are granted to generals by the senate, as I have stated [1] ; they are equal in other respects, but differ in this, that one is celebrated in a chariot and the other on foot.

[1] See v. 47, 3 f.

ΔΙΟΝΥΣΙΟΥ

ΑΛΙΚΑΡΝΑΣΕΩΣ

ΡΩΜΑΙΚΗΣ ΑΡΧΑΙΟΛΟΓΙΑΣ

ΛΟΓΟΣ ΔΕΚΑΤΟΣ

I. Μετὰ δὲ τούτους ὀλυμπιὰς μὲν ἦν ὀγδοηκοστή, ἣν ἐνίκα στάδιον Τορύμβας Θεσσαλός, ἄρχοντος Ἀθήνησι Φρασικλέους· ὕπατοι δὲ ἀπεδείχθησαν ἐν Ῥώμῃ Πόπλιος Οὐολούμνιος καὶ Σερούιος[1] Σολπίκιος Καμερῖνος.[2] οὗτοι στρατιὰν μὲν οὐδεμίαν ἐξήγαγον οὔτε ἐπὶ τιμωρίας ἀναπράξει τῶν ἀδικούντων σφᾶς τε αὐτοὺς καὶ τοὺς συμμάχους οὔθ' ὡς διὰ φυλακῆς τὰ οἰκεῖα ἕξοντες· τῶν δ' ἐντὸς τείχους κακῶν πρόνοιαν ἐποιοῦντο, μή τι δεινὸν ὁ 2 δῆμος ἐπὶ τῇ βουλῇ συστὰς ἐξεργάσηται. ἐταράττετο γὰρ αὖθις ὑπὸ τῶν δημάρχων ἀναδιδασκόμενος ὅτι πολιτειῶν κρατίστη τοῖς ἐλευθέροις ἐστὶν ἡ[3] ἰσηγορία, καὶ κατὰ νόμους ἠξίου διοικεῖσθαι τά

---

[1] Sylburg : σερουίλιος AB.　　　　[2] μακερῖνος B.
[3] ἡ added by Grimm.

---

[1] For chaps. 1-4 cf. Livy iii. 10, 5–11, 5.　The year was 459 B.C.

162

THE ROMAN ANTIQUITIES

OF

DIONYSIUS OF HALICARNASSUS

BOOK X

I. The year after their consulship [1] occurred the eightieth Olympiad (the one at which Torymbas, a Thessalian, won the foot-race), Phrasicles being archon at Athens; and Publius Volumnius and Servius Sulpicius Camerinus were chosen consuls at Rome. These men led no army into the field, either to take revenge on those who had injured the Romans themselves as well as their allies or to keep guard over their possessions, but they devoted their attention to the domestic evils, fearing lest the populace might organize against the senate and work some mischief. For they were being stirred up again by the tribunes and instructed that the best of political institutions for free men is an equality of rights [2]; and they demanded that all business both private

---

[2] Literally ἰσηγορία is "equal freedom of speech"; but it seems to be used by Dionysius in the more general sense of "equal civic rights." Other terms used by him in this Book for the same idea are ἰσονομία (35, 5) and ἰσοτιμία (30, 4).

τε ἰδιωτικὰ καὶ τὰ δημόσια. οὔπω γὰρ τότε ἦν
οὔτ' ἰσονομία παρὰ 'Ρωμαίοις οὔτ' ἰσηγορία, οὐδ'
ἐν γραφαῖς ἅπαντα τὰ δίκαια τεταγμένα· ἀλλὰ τὸ
μὲν ἀρχαῖον οἱ βασιλεῖς αὐτῶν ἔταττον τοῖς δεομένοις τὰς δίκας, καὶ τὸ δικαιωθὲν ὑπ' ἐκείνων
3 τοῦτο νόμος ἦν. ὡς δ' ἐπαύσαντο μοναρχούμενοι,
τοῖς κατ' ἐνιαυτὸν ὑπατεύουσιν ἀνέκειτο τά τε
ἄλλα τῶν βασιλέων ἔργα καὶ ἡ τοῦ δικαίου διά-
γνωσις, καὶ τοῖς ἀμφισβητοῦσι πρὸς ἀλλήλους ὑπὲρ
ὁτουδήτινος ἐκεῖνοι τὰ δίκαια οἱ διαιροῦντες ἦσαν.
4 τούτων δὲ τὰ μὲν πολλὰ τοῖς τρόποις[1] τῶν ἀρχόντων
ἀριστίνδην ἀποδεικνυμένων ἐπὶ τὰς ἀρχὰς ἀκό-
λουθα ἦν· κομιδῇ δ' ὀλίγα τινὰ ἐν ἱεραῖς ἦν βύβλοις
ἀποκείμενα, ἃ νόμων εἶχε δύναμιν, ὧν οἱ πατρίκιοι
τὴν γνῶσιν εἶχον μόνοι διὰ τὰς ἐν ἄστει διατριβάς,
οἱ δὲ πολλοὶ ἐμπορευόμενοί τε καὶ γεωργοῦντες διὰ
πολλῶν ἡμερῶν εἰς ἄστυ καταβαίνοντες ἐπὶ τὰς
5 ἀγορὰς ἄπειροι ἔτι ἦσαν. τὸ δὲ πολίτευμα τοῦτο
πρῶτος μὲν ἐπείρασεν εἰσαγαγεῖν Γάιος Τερέντιος[2]
δημαρχῶν ἐν τῷ παρελθόντι ἔτει, ἀτελὲς δὲ ἠναγκάσθη καταλιπεῖν τοῦ τε πλήθους ὄντος ἐπὶ στρα-
τοπέδων καὶ τῶν ὑπάτων ἐπίτηδες ἐν τῇ πολεμίᾳ
γῇ τὰς δυνάμεις κατασχόντων ἕως ὁ τῆς ἀρχῆς
αὐτοῖς παρέλθῃ χρόνος.

II. Τότε δ' αὐτὸ παραλαβόντες οἱ περὶ Αὖλον
Οὐεργίνιον δήμαρχοι τελειῶσαι ἐβούλοντο· ἵνα δὲ
μὴ τοῦτο γένοιτο μηδὲ κατὰ νόμους ἀναγκασθεῖεν

---

[1] Reiske : ἐπιτρόποις O.
[2] Sigonius : τεργέντιος AB.

---

[1] This, in an aristocratic state, meant inherited virtue.

and public should be carried on according to laws.
For at that time there did not exist as yet among the
Romans an equality either of laws or of rights, nor
were all their principles of justice committed to
writing ; but at first their kings had dispensed justice
to those who sought it, and whatever they decreed
was law.   After they ceased to be governed by kings,
along with the other functions of royalty that of
determining what justice is devolved upon the annual
consuls, and it was they who decided what was just
between litigants in any matter whatsoever.   These
decisions as a rule conformed to the character of the
magistrates, who were appointed to office on the basis
of good birth.[1]   A very few of them, however, were
kept in sacred books and had the force of laws ; but
the patricians alone were acquainted with these, because they spent their time in the capital, while the
masses, who were either merchants or husbandmen
and came down to the capital only for the markets
at intervals of many days, were as yet unfamiliar
with them.   The first attempt to introduce this
measure establishing an equality of rights was made
by Gaius Terentius in the preceding year,[2] while he
was tribune ; but he was forced to leave the business
unfinished because the plebeians were then in the
field and the consuls purposely detained the armies
in the enemy's country till their term of office expired.

II. At the time in question Aulus Verginius and
the other tribunes took up the measure and wished
to carry it through.   But in order to prevent this
from happening and that the magistrates might not
be compelled to conduct the government in accord-

[2] For § 5 cf. Livy iii. 9.   Livy gives the name as C. Teren-
tilius Harsa.

πολιτεύεσθαι, πάντα ἐπιμηχανώμενοι διετέλουν οἵ
τε ὕπατοι καὶ ἡ βουλὴ καὶ τῶν ἄλλων πολιτῶν οἱ
πλεῖστον ἐν τῇ πόλει δυνάμενοι· βουλαί τε πολλαὶ
καὶ ἐκκλησίαι συνεχεῖς ἐγίνοντο πεῖραί τε παντοῖαι
ταῖς ἀρχαῖς κατ᾽ ἀλλήλων, ἐξ ὧν οὐκ ἄδηλον ἅπασιν
ἦν ὅτι μεγάλη τις καὶ ἀνήκεστος ἐξ ἐκείνης τῆς
2 φιλονεικίας ἀναστήσεται τῇ πόλει συμφορά. συν-
ήπτετο δὲ τοῖς ἀνθρωπίνοις λογισμοῖς καὶ τὰ θεῖα
δείματα προσγενόμενα, ὧν ἔνια οὔτ᾽ ἐν δημοσίαις
εὑρίσκετο γραφαῖς οὔτε κατ᾽ ἄλλην φυλαττόμενα
3 μνήμην οὐδεμίαν. ὅσα μὲν γὰρ ἐν οὐρανῷ σέλα
φερόμενα καὶ πυρὸς ἀνάψεις ἐφ᾽ ἑνὸς μένουσαι
τόπου γῆς τε μυκήματα καὶ τρόμοι συνεχεῖς ἐγίνοντο, μορφαί τ᾽ εἰδώλων ἄλλοτ᾽ ἀλλοῖαι δι᾽ ἀέρος
φερόμεναι καὶ φωναὶ ταράττουσαι διάνοιαν ἀνθρώπων, καὶ πάντα ὅσα τούτοις ὅμοια συνέπιπτεν,
εὑρίσκετο καὶ πάλαι ποτὲ γεγονότα ἧττόν τε[1] καὶ
μᾶλλον· οὗ δὲ ἄπειροί τε καὶ ἀνήκοοι ἔτι ἦσαν καὶ
ἐφ᾽ ᾧ δὴ[2] μάλιστα ἐταράχθησαν, τοιόνδ᾽ ἦν· νιφετὸς
ἐξ οὐρανοῦ κατέσκηψεν εἰς γῆν πολὺς οὐ χιόνα
καταφέρων, ἀλλὰ σαρκῶν θραύσματα ἐλάττω τε
4 καὶ μείζω. τούτων τὰ μὲν πολλὰ μετάρσια προσπετόμεναι πτηνῶν[3] ὅσαι εἰσὶν ἀγέλαι τοῖς στόμα-
σιν ἥρπαζον, τὰ δ᾽ ἐπὶ τὴν[4] γῆν ἐνεχθέντα ἐν αὐτῇ
τε τῇ πόλει καὶ κατὰ τοὺς ἀγροὺς μέχρι πολλοῦ
χρόνου κείμενα διέμεινεν[5] οὔτε χρόαν μεταβάλ-
λοντα, οἵαν ἴσχουσι[6] παλαιούμεναι σάρκες, οὔτε

---

[1] Sylburg : δὲ AB.
[2] Naber : δὲ B, om. R, Jacoby.
[3] προσπετόμεναι πτηνῶν B : προσπετόμενα πτερῶν A.
[4] τὴν B : om. R.
[5] διέμεινεν added by Casaubon, ἦν by Jacoby ; Kiessling
would read διέμεινεν in place of κείμενα.

ance with laws, the consuls, the senate and all the rest
of the citizens of greatest influence in the commonwealth kept resorting to all manner of devices. There
were many sessions of the senate and continual
meetings of the assembly, and attempts of all kinds
were made by the magistrates against one another ;
from all of which it was manifest to everyone that
some great and irreparable mischief to the commonwealth would arise out of this contention. To these
human reasonings were added the terrible portents
sent by the gods, some of which were neither found
recorded in the public archives nor was the memory
of them preserved by any other means. As for all the
flashes shooting through the sky and outbursts of fire
continuing in one place, the rumblings of the earth
and its continual tremblings that occurred, the
spectres, now of one shape and now of another, flitting
through the air and voices that disturbed men's
minds, and everything else of that nature which took
place, all these manifestations were found to have
occurred in times past as well, to either a greater or
lesser degree. But a prodigy which they were unfamiliar with as yet and had never heard of, and the
one which caused them the greatest terror was this :
There descended upon the earth from heaven what
appeared to be a heavy snowstorm, only it brought
down, instead of snow, pieces of flesh, some smaller
and some larger. Most of these while still in mid air
were seized by flocks of birds of every kind, which
flew up and snatched them in their beaks ; but those
pieces which fell to the ground, both in the city itself
and in the country, lay there a long time without
either changing to such a colour as pieces of flesh

---

[6] οἶαν ἴσχουσι O : οἶα πάσχουσι Casaubon.

σηπεδόνι διαλυόμενα,[1] ὦζέ τε ἀπ' αὐτῶν οὐδὲν
5 πονηρόν. τοῦτο τὸ τέρας οἱ μὲν ἐπιχώριοι μάντεις
οὐχ οἷοί τ' ἦσαν συμβαλεῖν· ἐν δὲ τοῖς Σιβυλλείοις
εὑρέθη χρησμοῖς ὅτι πολεμίων ἀλλοεθνῶν παρ-
ελθόντων εἰς τὸ τεῖχος ἀγὼν ὑπὲρ ἀνδραποδισμοῦ
καταλήψεται τὴν πόλιν, ἄρξει δὲ τοῦ πρὸς τοὺς
ἀλλοεθνεῖς πολέμου στάσις ἐμφύλιος, ἣν χρῆν ἀρ-
χομένην ἐξελαύνοντας ἐκ τῆς πόλεως καὶ θεοὺς
παραιτουμένους θυσίαις τε καὶ εὐχαῖς ἀποτρέψαι[2]
6 τὰ δεινά· καὶ κρείττους ἔσονται[3] τῶν ἐχθρῶν. ὡς
δ' ἐξηνέχθη ταῦτ' εἰς τὸ πλῆθος, ἱερὰ μὲν πρῶτον
ἔθυσαν, οἷς ἡ τούτων ἐπιμέλεια ἀνέκειτο, θεοῖς
ἐξακεστηρίοις τε καὶ ἀποτροπαίοις, ἔπειτα συν-
αχθέντες εἰς τὸ βουλευτήριον οἱ σύνεδροι παρόντων
καὶ τῶν δημάρχων ὑπὲρ ἀσφαλείας τε καὶ σωτηρίας
τῆς πόλεως ἐσκόπουν.

III. Τὸ μὲν οὖν καταλύσασθαι τὰ πρὸς ἀλλήλους
ἐγκλήματα καὶ μιᾷ χρήσασθαι γνώμῃ περὶ τῶν
κοινῶν, ὡς ὑπετίθεντο οἱ χρησμοί, πάντες ὡμο-
λόγουν· ὅπως δ' ἂν τοῦτο γένοιτο καὶ ἀπὸ τίνων
ἀρξαμένων εἴκειν τοῖς ἑτέροις τὸ διάφορον παύσαιτο[4] τὸ[5] στασιάζον, οὐ μικρὰν αὐτοῖς παρεῖχεν
2 ἀπορίαν. οἱ μὲν γὰρ ὕπατοι καὶ οἱ τῆς βουλῆς
προεστῶτες τοὺς εἰσφέροντας καινὰ πολιτεύματα
δημάρχους καὶ καταλύειν ἀξιοῦντας τὸν πάτριον
τῆς πολιτείας κόσμον αἰτίους ἀπέφαινον τῆς ταραχῆς. οἱ δὲ δήμαρχοι σφᾶς μὲν αὐτοὺς οὐδὲν
ἔλεγον ἀξιοῦν[6] οὔτε ἄδικον οὔτε ἀσύμφορον εὑ-

---

[1] Steph. : διαλυόμεναι O.
[2] ἀποτρέψαι B : ἀποστρέψαι R.
[3] ἔσονται R : ἔσεσθαι A.
[4] παύσαιτο B : καὶ πῶς παύσεται A, καὶ πῶς παύσαιτο R (?).

acquire with lime, or becoming rotten, and no bad
smell was given off by them. The native soothsayers
were unable to conjecture the meaning of this prodigy ; but in the Sibylline books it was found that
the city would be involved in a struggle to prevent the
enslavement of its citizens after foreign enemies had
penetrated inside the walls, and that this war against
the foreigners would begin with civil strife, which
they must banish from the city in its inception, invok-
ing the gods by sacrifices and prayers to avert the
dangers ; then they would gain the victory over their
enemies. When this had been announced to the
multitude, the priests who were in charge of such
matters first sacrificed victims to the gods who remedy
and avert evils ; after which the senate assembled in
the senate-house, the tribunes being also present,
and considered means of safeguarding and preserving
the commonwealth.

III. As for putting an end to their mutual recrimi-
nations and acting with unanimity concerning public
affairs, as the oracles advised, all were in agreement ;
but how this was to be brought about, and which
party should take the first step by yielding to the
other the point at issue and thus put an end to
the dissension, caused them no little embarrassment.
For the consuls and the leaders of the senate declared
that the tribunes who were proposing new measures
and demanding the overthrow of the time-honoured
constitution were to blame for the disturbance. On
the other hand, the tribunes denied that they were
asking for anything that was either unjust or disadvantageous when they wished to introduce a good

---

[5] τὸ A : om. R, Jacoby.
[6] ἀξιοῦν B : ἀνάξιον δρᾶν A, Jacoby.

νομίαν[1] εἰσάγειν βουλομένους καὶ ἰσηγορίαν· τοὺς δὲ
ὑπάτους καὶ τοὺς πατρικίους αἰτίους ἔσεσθαι τῆς
στάσεως ἔλεγον ἀνομίαν αὔξοντας καὶ πλεονεξίαν
3 καὶ ζηλοῦντας τὰ τῶν τυράννων ἔθη. ταῦτα καὶ
πολλὰ τούτοις ὅμοια παρ' ἑκατέρων ἐπὶ πολλὰς
ἡμέρας ἐλέγετο, καὶ προὔβαινε διὰ κενῆς ὁ χρόνος·
ἐν ᾧ τῶν κατὰ τὴν πόλιν οὔτε δημοσίων οὔτε ἰδίων
οὐδὲν ἐτελεῖτο. ὡς δ' οὐδὲν ἐγίνετο τῶν προὔργου,
λόγων μὲν[2] ἐκείνων καὶ κατηγοριῶν ἃς ἐποιοῦντο
κατὰ τῆς βουλῆς οἱ δήμαρχοι ἀπέστησαν· συναγαγόντες δὲ τὸ πλῆθος εἰς τὴν[3] ἐκκλησίαν ὑπέσχοντο
4 τῷ δήμῳ νόμον εἰσοίσειν ὑπὲρ ὧν ἠξίουν. ἐπαινέ-
σαντος δὲ τοῦ πλήθους τὸν λόγον οὐδὲν ἔτι ἀναβαλόμενοι[4] τὸν παρασκευασθέντα νόμον ἀνέγνωσαν·
κεφάλαια δὲ αὐτοῦ τάδε ἦν· ἄνδρας αἱρεθῆναι δέκα
ὑπὸ τοῦ δήμου συναχθείσης ἀγορᾶς ἐννόμου τοὺς
πρεσβυτάτους τε καὶ φρονιμωτάτους,[5] οἷς ἐστι
πλείστη πρόνοια τιμῆς τε καὶ δόξης ἀγαθῆς· τούτους δὲ συγγράψαντας τοὺς ὑπὲρ ἁπάντων νόμους
τῶν τε κοινῶν καὶ τῶν ἰδίων εἰς τὸν δῆμον ἐξενεγ-
κεῖν· τοὺς δὲ συγγραφησομένους ὑπ' αὐτῶν νόμους
ἐκκεῖσθαι[6] ἐν ἀγορᾷ ταῖς καθ' ἕκαστον ἐνιαυτὸν
ἀποδειχθησομέναις ἀρχαῖς καὶ τοῖς ἰδιώταις ὅρους
5 τῶν πρὸς ἀλλήλους δικαίων. τοῦτον προθέντες
τὸν νόμον ἐξουσίαν ἔδοσαν τοῖς βουλομένοις αὐτοῦ
κατηγορεῖν, ἀποδείξαντες τὴν τρίτην ἀγοράν. ἦσαν
δὲ πολλοὶ καὶ οὐχ οἱ φαυλότατοι τῶν ἐκ τοῦ συν-

---

[1] ἰσονομίαν Benzler in his translation, Cobet. *Cf.* chap. 1,
2 ; 15, 7.　　　　　　　　[2] μὲν B : om. R.
[3] τὴν deleted by Kiessling.
[4] ἀναβαλόμενοι B : ἀναβαλλόμενοι R.
[5] Sylburg : φρονίμους O.
[6] Naber : κεῖσθαι O, Jacoby.

system of laws [1] and equality of rights, but declared that the consuls and the patricians would be to blame for the dissension if they increased the spirit of lawlessness and greed and emulated the usual practices of tyrants. These and many like reproaches were uttered by each side for many days and the time passed in vain ; meanwhile no business in the city, either public or private, was being brought to completion. When nothing worth while was being accomplished, the tribunes desisted from the kind of harangues and accusations they were wont to make against the senate ; and calling an assembly of the populace, they promised them to bring in a law embodying their demands. This being approved of by the populace, they read without further delay the law which they had prepared, the chief provisions of which were as follows : That ten men should be chosen by the people meeting in a legitimate assembly, men who were at once the oldest and the most prudent and had the greatest regard for honour and a good reputation ; that these men should draw up the laws concerning all matters both public and private and lay them before the people ; and that the laws to be drawn up by them should be exposed in the Forum for the benefit of the magistrates who should be chosen each year and also of persons in private station, as a code defining the mutual rights of citizens. After the tribunes had proposed this law, they gave leave to all who so desired to speak against it, appointing the third market-day for that purpose. Many in fact—and those not the least important of

---

[1] Cobet proposed to read ἰσονομίαν (" equality of laws ") here in place of εὐνομίαν. But εὐνομίαν is probably justified by ἀνομίαν just below.

εδρίου, πρεσβύτεροι[1] καὶ νέοι, κατήγοροι τοῦ νόμου,
λόγους διεξιόντες ἐκ πολλῆς ἐπιμελείας καὶ παρα-
σκευῆς· καὶ τοῦτ' ἐφ' ἡμέρας ἐγίνετο συχνάς.
6 ἔπειτα οἱ δήμαρχοι δυσχεραίνοντες ἐπὶ τῇ διατριβῇ
τοῦ χρόνου λόγον μὲν οὐδένα ἔτι τοῖς κατηγόροις
τοῦ νόμου προέθεσαν, ἡμέραν δὲ ἀποδείξαντες ἐν ᾗ
κυρώσειν αὐτὸν ἔμελλον, παρεῖναι τοὺς δημότας εἰς
αὐτὴν παρεκάλουν ἀθρόους, ὡς οὐκέτι ταῖς μακραῖς
δημηγορίαις ἐνοχληθησομένους, ἀλλ' ἐποίσοντας
ὑπὲρ αὐτοῦ τὴν ψῆφον κατὰ φυλάς. οἱ μὲν δὴ
ταῦτα ὑποσχόμενοι διέλυσαν τὴν ἐκκλησίαν.
    IV. Μετὰ δὲ ταῦτα οἵ τε ὕπατοι καὶ τῶν πατρι-
κίων οἱ πλεῖστον δυνάμενοι τραχύτερον ἤδη αὐτῶν
προσιόντες καθήπτοντο, λέγοντες ὡς οὐκ ἐπιτρέψουσιν[2] αὐτοῖς νόμους εἰσηγεῖσθαι καὶ τούτους
ἀπροβουλεύτους. συνθήκας γὰρ εἶναι κοινὰς πόλεων τοὺς νόμους, οὐχὶ μέρους τῶν ἐν ταῖς πόλεσιν
οἰκούντων. τοῦ τε πονηροτάτου[3] ὀλέθρου καὶ
ἀνηκέστου[4] καὶ οὐδ'[5] εὐσχήμονος ἀρχὴν ἀπέφαινον
εἶναι πόλεσί τε καὶ οἴκοις ὅταν τὸ κάκιστον τῷ
2 κρατίστῳ νομοθετῇ. "Ποίαν[6] δὲ ὑμεῖς," ἔφασαν,
"ὦ δήμαρχοι, νόμων εἰσφορᾶς ἢ ἀναιρέσεως ἐξουσίαν ἔχετε; οὐκ ἐπὶ ῥητοῖς μὲν δικαίοις ταύτην
τὴν ἀρχὴν παρὰ τῆς βουλῆς ἐλάβετε, τοῖς δ' ἀδι-
κουμένοις ἢ κατισχυομένοις τῶν πενήτων βοηθεῖν
ᾐτήσασθε τοὺς δημάρχους, ἄλλο δὲ μηδὲν πολυπραγμονεῖν; εἰ δ' οὖν καὶ πρότερον ἦν τις ὑμῖν
δύναμις ἣν οὐκ ἐκ τοῦ δικαίου βιασάμενοι ἡμᾶς
ἐλάβετε, ὑποκατακλινομένης ἑκάστῳ πλεονεκτή-

---

[1] πρεσβύτεροι B : πρεσβύτατοι R.
[2] ἐπιτρέψουσιν A : ἐπιτρέπουσιν R.
[3] φανερωτάτου Kiessling.

the senators, both old and young—did speak against the law, delivering speeches that were the result of much thought and preparation ; and this went on for many days. Then the tribunes, chafing at the loss of time, would no longer permit the opponents of the law to speak against it, but appointing a day for ratifying it, urged the plebeians to be present in force, assuring them that they should not be bored by any more long harangues but should give their votes by tribes concerning the law. After making these promises the tribunes dismissed the assembly.

IV. After this the consuls and the most influential of the patricians, going to the tribunes, upbraided them more harshly than before, saying they would not permit them to propose laws, and especially laws not recommended by a preliminary decree of the senate. For laws were compacts of states affecting all alike, and not of a single portion of the residents of states. They further pointed out that it is the first step in the most wicked, irremediable and indecent ruination for both states and households when the worst element prescribes laws for the best. " And what authority," they asked, " have you, tribunes, to introduce or to abrogate laws ? Did you not receive this magistracy from the senate upon explicit terms ? Did you not ask that the tribunes might come to the assistance of those of the poor who were injured and oppressed, but should meddle with nothing else ? But, be that as it may, even if you previously possessed some power which you had wrongfully extorted from us, because the senate

4 καὶ ἀνηκέστου B : om. R.
5 οὐδ' B : οὐκ R.
6 ποίαν Lapus, Sylburg : ποίας AB.

ματι τῆς βουλῆς, οὐχὶ καὶ ταύτην νῦν ἀπολωλέκατε
3 τῇ μεταβολῇ τῶν ἀρχαιρεσίων;[1] οὔτε γὰρ βουλῆς
δόγμα ὑμᾶς οὐκέτι[2] ἀποδείκνυσιν ἐπὶ τὴν ἀρχήν,
οὔτε αἱ φρᾶτραι τὴν ψῆφον ὑπὲρ ὑμῶν ἐπιφέρουσιν,
οὔτε ἱερὰ προθύεται τοῖς θεοῖς πρὸ τῶν ἀρχαιρεσίων,[3] ἃ κατὰ νόμους ἐχρῆν ἐπιτελεῖσθαι, οὔτε ἄλλο
τῶν πρὸς τοὺς θεοὺς εὐσεβῶν ἢ πρὸς ἀνθρώπους
ὁσίων οὐθὲν ἐπὶ τῆς ἀρχῆς τῆς ὑμετέρας γίνεται.
τίνος οὖν ὑμῖν ἔτι μέτεστι τῶν ἱερῶν καὶ σεβασμοῦ
δεομένων, ὧν ἕν τι[4] καὶ ὁ νόμος ἦν, ἐξαρνησαμένοις
4 ἅπαντα τὰ νόμιμα;" ταῦτά τε δὴ τοῖς δημάρχοις
ἔλεγον οἱ πρεσβύτεροι καὶ οἱ νέοι αὐτῶν καθ᾽
ἑταιρίας διεξιόντες ἀνὰ τὴν πόλιν, καὶ τοὺς μὲν
ἐπιεικεστέρους τῶν δημοτῶν[5] ὁμιλίαις ἀνελάμβανον
κεχαρισμέναις, τοὺς δ᾽ ἀπειθεῖς καὶ ταραχώδεις
ἀπειλαῖς κατεπλήττοντο κινδύνων, εἰ μὴ σωφρονήσειαν[6] ἤδη δέ τινας τῶν πάνυ ἀπόρων καὶ ἀπερριμ-
μένων, οἷς οὐθενὸς τῶν κοινῶν παρὰ τὰ ἴδια κέρδη
φροντὶς ἦν, παίοντες ὥσπερ ἀνδράποδα ἀνεῖργον ἐκ
τῆς ἀγορᾶς.

V. Ὁ δὲ πλείστους τε περὶ αὐτὸν[7] ἔχων ἑταίρους
καὶ μέγιστον τῶν τότε νέων δυνάμενος Καίσων
Κοΐντιος ἦν, υἱὸς Λευκίου Κοϊντίου τοῦ καλουμένου
Κικιννάτου, ᾧ γένος τ᾽ ἦν ἐπιφανὲς καὶ βίος οὐθενὸς δεύτερος, ἀνὴρ ὀφθῆναί τε κάλλιστος νέων
καὶ τὰ πολέμια πάντων λαμπρότατος φύσει τε περὶ

---

[1] ἀρχαιρεσίων B : ἀρχαιρεσιῶν R, Jacoby.
[2] οὐκέτι B : om. R.
[3] ἀρχαιρεσίων AB : ἀρχαιρεσιῶν Jacoby.
[4] ἕν τι B : ἔτι R.
[5] δημοτῶν B : πολιτῶν R.
[6] σωφρονήσειαν R : συμφρονήσειαν A, Jacoby.
[7] Kiessling : αὐτὸν O.

weakly gave in to each encroachment of yours, have
you not lost even this power now through the changed
character of your elections ? [1]   For neither a decree
of the senate appoints you any longer to the magistracy, nor do the *curiae* give their votes concerning
you, nor are there offered up to the gods before your
election the sacrifices appointed by the laws, nor is
anything else done in connexion with your magistracy that is holy in the eyes of the gods or right in
the sight of men.   What share have you, then, any
longer in any of the things that are holy and call for
reverence—of which the law was one—now that you
have renounced everything lawful ? "   These were
the arguments that the older and the young patricians, going about the city in organized groups, used
with the tribunes.   The more fair-minded of the
plebeians they sought to win over by friendly intercourse, and the refractory and turbulent they attempted to terrify with threats of dangers which
they would incur unless they came to their senses.
Indeed, in the case of some who were very poor and
abject and cared naught for the public interests in
comparison with their own advantage, they drove
them out of the Forum with blows as if they had
been slaves.

V.   But the person [2] who was attended with the
largest number of followers and had the most influence of all the young men at that time was Caeso
Quintius, the son of Lucius Quintius called Cincinnatus, a man both of illustrious birth and of a fortune
inferior to none, the handsomest of youths to look
upon, distinguished above all others in warfare, and

---

[1] *Cf.* ix. 41, 2 f.; 49, 5.
[2] For chaps. 5–8, 4 *cf.* Livy iii. 11, 6–13, 10.

λόγους κεχρημένος ἀγαθῇ· ὃς ἐν τῷ τότε χρόνῳ
πολὺς ἔρρει κατὰ τῶν δημοτικῶν οὔτε λόγων
φειδόμενος ὧν βαρὺ τοῖς ἐλευθέροις ἀκούειν, οὔτ᾽
ἔργων ἀκολούθων τοῖς λόγοις ἀπεχόμενος. οἱ μὲν
οὖν πατρίκιοι τίμιον αὐτὸν ἐπὶ τούτοις εἶχον[1] καὶ
μένειν παρὰ τὰ δεινὰ ἠξίουν, αὐτοὶ[2] παρασχεῖν[3] τὸ
ἀσφαλὲς ὑπισχνούμενοι· οἱ δ᾽ ἐκ τοῦ δήμου πάν-
2 των δὴ μάλιστα αὐτὸν ἀνθρώπων ἐμίσουν. τοῦτον
τὸν ἄνδρα ἔγνωσαν οἱ δήμαρχοι πρῶτον ἐκποδὼν
ποιήσασθαι, ὡς καταπληξόμενοι τοὺς λοιποὺς τῶν
νέων καὶ προσαναγκάσοντες σωφρονεῖν. γνόντες δὲ
ταῦτα καὶ παρασκευασάμενοι λόγους τε καὶ μάρτυρας πολλοὺς εἰσάγουσιν αὐτὸν ὑπὸ δίκην ἀδικήματος δημοσίου, θανάτου τιμησάμενοι τὴν δίκην.
παραγγείλαντες δ᾽ αὐτῷ παρεῖναι πρὸς τὸν δῆμον,
ἐπειδὴ καθῆκεν ὁ χρόνος ὃν ἔταξαν τῇ δίκῃ, συναγαγόντες ἐκκλησίαν μακροὺς ἐποιήσαντο κατ᾽ αὐτοῦ λόγους, διεξιόντες ὅσα βίᾳ διαπεπραγμένος
ἐτύγχανεν εἰς τοὺς δημότας, ὧν τοὺς πεπονθότας
3 αὐτοὺς παρῆγον μάρτυρας. ὡς δὲ παρέδωκαν τὸν
λόγον, αὐτὸ μὲν τὸ μειράκιον οὐχ ὑπήκουε καλούμενον ἐπὶ τὴν ἀπολογίαν, ἀλλ᾽ ἠξίου τοῖς ἰδιώταις
αὐτοῖς ὑπὲρ ὧν ᾐτιῶντο παθεῖν κατὰ τὸν νόμον
ὑπέχειν δίκας, ἐπὶ τῶν ὑπάτων τῆς κρίσεως γινο-
μένης· ὁ δὲ πατὴρ αὐτοῦ χαλεπῶς φέροντας τὴν
αὐθάδειαν τοῦ μειρακίου τοὺς δημοτικοὺς ὁρῶν
ἀπελογεῖτο τὰ μὲν πολλὰ ψευδῆ τε καὶ ἐξ ἐπιβουλῆς συγκείμενα κατὰ τοῦ παιδὸς ἀποδεικνύς·
4 ὅσα δ᾽ οὐκ ἐνῆν ἀρνήσασθαι μικρὰ καὶ φαῦλα καὶ
οὐκ ἄξια δημοσίας ὀργῆς εἶναι λέγων καὶ οὐδὲ ταῦτα

---

[1] εἶχον O : ἦγον Cobet.
[2] αὐτοὶ B : αὐτὸν R.

176

possessing a natural talent for speaking. This he
freely indulged at that time against the plebeians ;
and he neither spared words hard for free men to
listen to nor refrained from deeds that matched his
words. For these reasons the patricians held him
in great esteem and urged him to continue on his
dangerous course, promising to afford him impunity ;
but the plebeians hated him above all men. This
man the tribunes determined to remove out of the
way first, expecting to terrify the rest of the youths
and compel them to act sensibly. Having come to
this decision and got ready their accusations and
numerous witnesses, they brought him to trial for a
crime against the state, for which they fixed death
as the penalty. When they had summoned him to
appear before the populace and the day they had
appointed for the trial had come, they called an
assembly and delivered lengthy speeches against
him, enumerating all the acts of violence he had
committed against the plebeians and presenting as
witnesses the victims of his acts in person. When
they gave him leave to speak, the youth himself,
being called upon to make his defence, refused, but
asked the right to give satisfaction to the private
persons themselves for the injuries of which they
accused him, the hearing to take place before the
consuls. His father, however, observing that the plebeians were offended by the haughtiness of the
youth, endeavoured to excuse him by showing that
most of the accusations were false and deliberately
invented against his son ; that the instances which he
could not deny were slight and trivial and not de-
serving the resentment of the public, and that not

---

[3] παρέξειν Cobet, παρασχήσειν Hertlein.

ἐξ ἐπιβουλῆς ἢ δι' ὕβριν, ἀλλ' ὑπὸ φιλοτιμίας
μειρακιώδους γεγονότα ἐπιδεικνύμενος, δι' ἣν
πολλὰ μὲν αὐτῷ συμβῆναι δρᾶσαι τῶν ἀβουλήτων
ἐν ἀψιμαχίαις, πολλὰ δ' ἴσως καὶ παθεῖν, οὔτε
ἡλικίας ἐν τῷ κρατίστῳ ὄντι οὔτε φρονήσεως ἐν
5 τῷ καθαρωτάτῳ. ἠξίου τε τοὺς δημοτικοὺς μὴ
μόνον ὀργὴν μὴ ἔχειν ἐφ' οἷς ἥμαρτεν εἰς ὀλίγους,[1]
ἀλλὰ καὶ χάριν εἰδέναι περὶ ὧν ἅπαντας εὖ ποιῶν
ἐν τοῖς πολέμοις διετέλεσε, τοῖς μὲν ἰδιώταις ἐλευθερίαν κτώμενος, τῇ δὲ πατρίδι ἡγεμονίαν, ἑαυτῷ
δὲ εἴ ποτε ἁμάρτοι τι φιλανθρωπίαν παρὰ τῶν πολλῶν[2] καὶ βοήθειαν. καὶ διεξῄει τάς τε στρατείας
πάσας καὶ τοὺς ἀγῶνας ἅπαντας ἐξ ὧν ἀριστεῖα
καὶ στεφάνους παρὰ τῶν στρατηγῶν ἔλαβε, πολιτῶν τε ὁπόσων ἐν ταῖς μάχαις ὑπερήσπισε καὶ
6 τείχεσι πολεμίων ὁσάκις πρῶτος ἐπέβη. τελευτῶν
δ' εἰς οἴκτους κατέβαινε καὶ δεήσεις, ἀντὶ[3] τῆς
ἑαυτοῦ πρὸς ἅπαντας ἐπιεικείας βίου τε, ὃς ἐμαρ-
τυρεῖτο αὐτῷ πάσης καθαρὸς διαβολῆς, μίαν ἀπ-
αιτῶν παρὰ τοῦ δήμου χάριν, φυλάξαι τὸν υἱὸν
αὐτῷ.

VI. Ὁ μὲν οὖν δῆμος ἥδετο πάνυ τοῖς λόγοις καὶ
χαρίζεσθαι τὸ μειράκιον τῷ πατρὶ πρόθυμος ἦν.
ὁ δὲ Οὐεργίνιος ὁρῶν ὅτι μὴ δόντος ἐκείνου δίκην
ἀφόρητον ἔσται τὸ[4] θράσος τῶν αὐθάδων μειρα-
2 κίων, ἀνίσταται καί φησιν· "Σοὶ μέν, ὦ Κοΐντιε,
ἥ τε ἄλλη μαρτυρεῖται πᾶσα ἀρετὴ καὶ ἡ πρὸς τοὺς
δημοτικοὺς εὔνοια, ἀνθ' ὧν τὸ τιμᾶσθαί σοι περί-

---

[1] ὀλίγους Kiessling : λόγους O.
[2] πολλῶν O : πολιτῶν Kiessling.
[3] ἀντὶ B : om. R.
[4] τὸ added by Kiessling.

even these had proceeded from design or insolence, but from a youthful ambition which had led him to do many unpremeditated things in scrimmages—and perhaps to suffer many too—since he was neither at the prime of life nor at the best age for clear judgement. And he asked the plebeians not only to entertain no resentment for the offences which he had committed against a few, but even to feel grateful for the services he had constantly rendered to them all in the wars while trying to secure liberty for his fellow citizens in private life, supremacy for his country, and for himself, if he should be guilty of any offence, friendly consideration and succour from the people generally. He proceeded to enumerate all the campaigns and all the battles in which he had received from his generals rewards of valour and crowns, how many citizens he had shielded in battle, and how often he had been the first man to scale the enemy's walls. And at last he ended with appeals to their compassion and with entreaties ; in consideration of his fairness toward all men and of his life in general, which stood approved as free from all reproach, he asked of the people one single favour —to safeguard his son for him.

VI. The people were exceedingly pleased with this speech and were eager to grant the life of the youth to his father. But Verginius, perceiving that if he were not punished the boldness of the headstrong youths would become intolerable, rose up and said : " As for you, Quintius, not only all your other merits, but also your goodwill toward the plebeians is amply attested, and for these you have received

ἐστιν.[1] ἡ δὲ τοῦ μειρακίου βαρύτης καὶ ἡ πρὸς
ἅπαντας ἡμᾶς ὑπερηφανία παραίτησιν ἢ συγγνώμην
οὐδεμίαν ἐπιδέχεται· ὅστις ὑπὸ τοῖς σοῖς ἤθεσι
τραφεὶς οὕτως οὖσι δημοτικοῖς καὶ μετρίοις, ὡς
ἅπαντες ἴσμεν, τῶν μὲν σῶν ὑπερεῖδεν ἐπιτηδευ-
μάτων, τυραννικὴν δὲ αὐθάδειαν καὶ βαρβάρων
ἀνθρώπων ὕβριν ἠγάπησε, καὶ πονηρῶν ἔργων
3 ζῆλον εἰς τὴν πόλιν ἡμῶν εἰσαγήοχεν. εἰ μὲν οὖν
ἐλάνθανέ σε τοιοῦτος ὤν, νῦν[2] ὅτ᾽ ἔγνωκας ἀγα-
νακτεῖν ὑπὲρ ἡμῶν δίκαιος ἂν εἴης· εἰ δὲ συνῄδεις τε
καὶ συνέπραττες οἷς προεπηλάκιζε τὴν τῶν πενήτων
πολιτῶν τύχην, πονηρὸς ἄρα καὶ αὐτὸς ἦσθα, καὶ
ἡ τῆς καλοκἀγαθίας δόξα οὐκ ἐκ τοῦ δικαίου σοι
περιγέγονεν. ἀλλὰ γὰρ ὅτι[3] ἠγνόεις αὐτὸν οὐκ
ὄντα τῆς σῆς ἀρετῆς ἄξιον, ἐγώ σοι τοῦτ᾽ ἔχω
μαρτυρεῖν. ἀπολύων δέ σε τοῦ τότε συναδικεῖν
ἡμᾶς μέμφομαι τοῦ νῦν ἡμῖν μὴ συναγανακτεῖν.
4 ἵνα δὲ μᾶλλον μάθῃς ἡλίκον ἄρα τῇ πόλει κακὸν
ἐπιτρέφων ἐλάνθανες, ὡς ὠμὸν καὶ τυραννικὸν καὶ
οὐδὲ φόνου πολιτικοῦ καθαρόν, ἄκουσον αὐτοῦ
φιλότιμον ἔργον καὶ ἀντιπαρεξέτασον αὐτῷ τὰς ἐν
τοῖς πολέμοις ἀριστείας· καὶ ὑμῶν ὅσοι συνεπάθεῖτε
ἀρτίως οἰκτιζομένῳ τῷ ἀνδρὶ σκοπεῖτε, εἰ ἄρα
καλῶς ὑμῖν ἔχει τοιούτου φείσασθαι πολίτου.''

VII. Ταῦτ᾽ εἰπὼν ἀνίστησιν ἐκ τῶν συναρχόντων Μάρκον Οὐολούσκιον καὶ λέγειν ἐκέλευσεν ἃ
σύνοιδε τῷ μειρακίῳ. σιωπῆς δὲ γενομένης καὶ
πολλῆς ἐξ ἁπάντων προσδοκίας μικρὸν ἐπισχὼν ὁ
2 Οὐολούσκιος εἶπεν· '' Ἐγὼ μάλιστα ἐβουλόμην ἄν,[4]

[1] Reiske : πάρεστιν O, Jacoby.
[2] νῦν γ᾽ Kiessling.   [3] ὅτι A : om. B.
[4] μάλιστ᾽ ἂν ἐβουλόμην Cobet.

honour. But the offensive behaviour of this youth
and his haughtiness toward us all admit of no pallia-
tion or pardon ; for though nurtured in your principles, which are so democratic and moderate, as we
are all aware, he despised your ways of life and grew
fond of a tyrannical arrogance and a barbarian insolence, and has introduced into our commonwealth
an emulation of base deeds. If, therefore, you were
unaware hitherto of his character, now that you know
it, you ought in justice to be indignant on our account;
but if you were privy to and took part in the foul
abuse he was wont to pour out upon the unhappy lot
of the poor citizens, then you too were base and did
not deserve the reputation for uprightness that has
come to you. But that you did not know him to be
unworthy of your excellence I myself can bear you
witness. Nevertheless, though I acquit you of joining with him in injuring us at that time, I blame you
for not joining with us now in resenting those injuries.
And that you may know better how great a bane you
have reared up unwittingly against the commonwealth, how cruel and tyrannical and not even free
from the murder of his fellow citizens, listen to an
ambitious exploit of his and balance it against the
rewards of valour he received in the wars. And as
many of you plebeians as were just now affected with
the compassion which this man endeavoured to
arouse, consider whether it is after all well for you to
spare such a citizen."

VII. Having spoken thus, he asked Marcus Volscius, one of his colleagues, to rise up and tell what
he knew about the youth. When all had become
silent and full of expectation, Volscius, after a short
pause, said : " I should have preferred, citizens, to

ὦ πολῖται, δίκην ἰδίαν, ἣν ὁ νόμος δίδωσί μοι,
παρὰ τούτου λαβεῖν δεινὰ καὶ πέρα δεινῶν πεπον-
θώς· κωλυθεὶς δὲ τούτου τυχεῖν διὰ πενίαν καὶ
ἀσθένειαν καὶ τὸ τῶν πολλῶν εἷς εἶναι, νῦν γ᾽[1]
ἡνίκα ἔξεστί μοι τὸ τοῦ μάρτυρος σχῆμα, ἐπειδὴ
οὐ τὸ τοῦ κατηγόρου, λήψομαι. ἃ δὲ πέπονθα, ὡς
3 ὠμὰ καὶ ἀνήκεστα, ἀκούσατέ μου. ἀδελφὸς ἦν μοι
Λεύκιος, ὃν ἐγὼ πάντων ἀνθρώπων μᾶλλον[2] ἠγά-
πησα. οὗτός μοι συνεδείπνει παρὰ φίλῳ, καὶ μετὰ
ταῦτ᾽ ἀναστάντες ἐρχομένης τῆς νυκτὸς[3] ᾠχόμεθα.
διεληλυθόσι δ᾽ ἡμῖν τὴν ἀγορὰν περιτυγχάνει Καίσων οὑτοσὶ κωμάζων σὺν ἑτέροις ἀγερώχοις μειρα-
κίοις. καὶ οὗτοι τὸ μὲν πρῶτον ἔσκωπτόν τε καὶ
ὕβριζον εἰς[4] ἡμᾶς, οἷ᾽ ἂν μεθύοντες[5] νέοι καὶ αὐθά-
δεις εἰς[6] ταπεινοὺς καὶ πένητας,[7] ὡς δ᾽ ἠγανακτοῦ-
μεν πρὸς αὐτούς, Λεύκιος ἐλεύθερον ῥῆμα[8] εἰς
τοῦτον[9] εἶπε. δεινὸν δ᾽ ἡγησάμενος οὑτοσὶ Καίσων
ἀκοῦσαί τι ὧν οὐκ ἐβούλετο, προσδραμὼν αὐτῷ
παίων καὶ λακτίζων καὶ πᾶσαν ἄλλην ὠμότητα καὶ[10]
4 ὕβριν ἐνδεικνύμενος ἀποκτείνει. ἐμοῦ δὲ κεκρα-
γότος καὶ ἀμυνομένου τοσαῦτα[11] ὅσα ἐδυνάμην,
ἐκεῖνον ἤδη νεκρὸν κείμενον ἀφεὶς ἐμὲ[12] πάλιν ἔπαιε
καὶ οὐ πρότερον ἐπαύσατο πρὶν ἀκίνητόν τε καὶ
ἄφωνον εἶδεν ἐρριμμένον, δόξας εἶναι νεκρόν. μετὰ

---

[1] γ᾽ B : om. R.
[2] μάλιστα Cobet.
[3] ἐρχομένης τῆς νυκτὸς Portus, ἀρχομένης τῆς νυκτὸς Cobet :
τῆς ἐχομένης νυκτὸς O, Jacoby.
[4] εἰς om. B.
[5] οἷ᾽ ἂν μεθύοντες Cobet : οἷα μεθύοντες ἂν O, Jacoby.
[6] εἰς Hertlein, Cobet : ὡς ἂν εἰς O.
[7] πένητας Hertlein : πένητας ὑβρίσαιεν O.

receive from this man private satisfaction, such as the
law affords me, for the terrible and worse than terrible
wrongs I have suffered ; but having been prevented
from obtaining this by reason of poverty and lack of
influence and because of my being one of the common
crowd, now, when it is possible, I shall take the rôle
of a witness, since I can not take that of an accuser.
Hear from me, then, the things I have suffered, how
cruel, how irreparable they were. I had a brother,
Lucius, whom I loved above all men. He and I
supped with a friend and afterwards, as night came
on,[1] we rose and departed. When we had passed
through the Forum, Caeso here fell in with us as he
was revelling with other insolent youths. At first
they laughed at us and abused us, as young men
when drunk and arrogant are apt to abuse the humble
and poor ; and when we were vexed at them, Lucius [2]
spoke out frankly to this man. But Caeso here,
thinking it outrageous to have anything said to him
that he did not like, ran up to him, and beating and
kicking him and showing every other form of cruelty
and abuse, killed him. And when I cried out and
was doing all I could to defend him, Caeso, leaving
my brother Lucius where he already lay dead, fell to
beating me in turn, and ceased not until he saw me
cast down upon the ground motionless and speechless,
so that he took me to be dead. After that he went

[1] The MSS. give " during the following night."
[2] See the critical note.

[8] Λεύκιος ἐλεύθερον ῥῆμα Smit : ἐλεύθερον ῥῆμα O, Jacoby.
Gelenius added ὁ ἀδελφὸς.
[9] εἰς τοῦτον B : εἰς τούτων A.
[10] ὠμότητα καὶ B : om. R.
[11] τοσαῦτα B : om. R.   [12] ἐμὲ B : om. R.

δὲ ταῦτα οὗτος μὲν ἀπιὼν ᾤχετο χαίρων ὥσπερ
ἐπὶ καλῷ ἔργῳ· ἡμᾶς δὲ οἱ παραγενόμενοι μετὰ
ταῦτα αἵματι πεφυρμένους αἴρουσι καὶ εἰς τὴν
οἰκίαν ἀπεκόμισαν, τὸν μὲν ἀδελφόν μου[1] Λεύκιον[2]
νεκρόν, ὥσπερ ἔφην, ἐμὲ δὲ ἡμιθανῆ καὶ ἐλπί-
5 δας ἔχοντα τοῦ ζῆν ὀλίγας. ταῦτα δ' ἐγένετο
Ποπλίου Σερουιλίου καὶ Λευκίου Αἰβουτίου τὴν
ὑπατείαν ἐχόντων, ὅτε ἡ μεγάλη νόσος κατέλαβε
τὴν πόλιν, ἧς ἀπηλαύσαμεν καὶ ἡμεῖς ἀμφότεροι.
τότε μὲν οὖν δίκην οὐχ οἷόν τ' ἦν μοι παρ' αὐτοῦ
λαβεῖν τεθνηκότων ἀμφοτέρων τῶν ὑπάτων· Λευκίου δὲ[3] Λοκρητίου καὶ Τίτου Οὐετουρίου παραλαβόντων τὴν ἀρχὴν βουλόμενος αὐτὸν ἀγαγεῖν ὑπὸ
δίκην ἐκωλύθην διὰ τὸν πόλεμον, ἐκλελοιπότων
6 ἀμφοτέρων τῶν ὑπάτων τὴν πόλιν. ὡς δὲ ἀνέστρεψαν ἀπὸ τῆς στρατείας, πολλάκις αὐτὸν ἐπὶ
τὴν ἀρχὴν καλῶν, ὁσάκις προσέλθοιμι[4] (καὶ ταῦτα
δὴ πολλοὶ τῶν πολιτῶν ἴσασι), πληγὰς ἐλάμβανον
ὑπ' αὐτοῦ. ταῦτ' ἐστὶν ἃ πέπονθα, ὦ δημόται,
μετὰ πάσης ἀληθείας εἰρημένα πρὸς ὑμᾶς."

VIII. Ταῦτ' εἰπόντος αὐτοῦ κραυγή τε ἐκ τῶν
παρόντων ἐγένετο καὶ ὁρμὴ πολλῶν ἐπὶ τὴν ἐκ
χειρὸς δίκην. ἀλλ' οἵ τε ὕπατοι ἐμποδὼν ἐγένοντο
καὶ τῶν δημάρχων οἱ πλείους πονηρὸν ἔθος οὐκ
ἀξιοῦντες εἰς τὴν πόλιν εἰσάγειν. ἦν δὲ καὶ τοῦ
δήμου τὸ καθαρώτατον οὐ βουλόμενον ἀποστερεῖν
λόγου τοὺς ὑπὲρ τῶν μεγίστων ἀγωνιζομένους.
2 τότε μὲν οὖν ἐπέσχε τὴν τῶν θρασυτέρων ὁρμὴν
ἡ τοῦ δικαίου πρόνοια, καὶ ἀναβολὴν ἔλαβεν ἡ δίκη,
οὐ μικρᾶς ἐμπεσούσης φιλοτιμίας καὶ ζητήσεως
ὑπὲρ τοῦ σώματος, εἴτ' ἐν δεσμοῖς αὐτὸ δεῖ φυλάτ-

---

[1] μου B : om. R.   [2] Λεύκιον deleted by Cobet.

away rejoicing, as if over a noble deed. As for us, some persons who came along later took us up, covered with blood, and carried us home, my brother being dead, as I said, and I half dead and having little hope of living. This happened in the consulship of Publius Servilius and Lucius Aebutius, when the city was attacked by the great pestilence, which both of us caught. At that time, therefore, it was not possible for me to obtain justice against him, since both consuls were dead ; then, when Lucius Lucretius and Titus Veturius had succeeded to the office, I wished to bring him to trial, but was prevented by the war, both consuls having left the city. After they returned from the campaign, I often cited him to appear before those magistrates, but as often as I approached them—as many of the citizens know—I received blows from him. These are the things I have suffered, plebeians, and I have related them to you with complete truthfulness."

VIII. After he had finished speaking, an outcry arose from those who were present and many rushed to take vengeance out of hand ; but they were prevented both by the consuls and also by the majority of the tribunes, who were unwilling to introduce a pernicious custom into the commonwealth. Indeed, the most honourable element among the plebeians too was unwilling to deprive of a defence those who were in jeopardy of their lives. Upon this occasion, therefore, a regard for justice restrained the impulse of the bolder spirits, and the trial was put off ; though no small contest and questioning arose concerning the defendant's person, whether he should be kept in

---

³ λευκίου δὲ B : om. R.
⁴ Reiske : προέλθοιμι O.

DIONYSIUS OF HALICARNASSUS

τεσθαι τέως, εἶτ᾽ ἐγγυητὰς δοῦναι τῆς ἀφίξεως,
ὥσπερ καὶ[1] ὁ πατὴρ ἠξίου· καὶ ἡ βουλὴ συνελθοῦσα[2]
ἐψηφίσατο χρήμασι διεγγυηθὲν ἐλεύθερον εἶναι τὸ
3 σῶμα μέχρι δίκης. τῇ δ᾽ ἑξῆς ἡμέρᾳ συναγαγόντες
οἱ δήμαρχοι τὸ πλῆθος, ἐκλιπόντος τοῦ μειρακίου
τὴν δίκην, ἐκύρωσαν τὴν κατ᾽ αὐτοῦ ψῆφον καὶ
τοὺς ἐγγυητὰς δέκα ὄντας ἐπράξαντο τὰ περὶ τοῦ
σώματος τῆς ἀποκαταστάσεως ὁμολογηθέντα χρή-
4 ματα. Καίσων μὲν οὖν τοιαύτῃ περιπεσὼν ἐπι-
βουλῇ, κατασκευασαμένων ἅπαντα τῶν δημάρχων
καὶ Οὐολουσκίου ψευδῆ[3] μαρτυρήσαντος, ὡς[4] ἐγένετο φανερὸν σὺν χρόνῳ, φεύγων εἰς Τυρρηνίαν
ᾤχετο· ὁ δὲ πατὴρ αὐτοῦ τὰ πλεῖστα τῆς οὐσίας
ἀπεμπολήσας καὶ τὰ ὁμολογηθέντα ὑπὸ τῶν ἐγ-
γυητῶν χρήματα ἀποδούς, ἑαυτῷ χωρίον ἓν μικρὸν
ὑπολειπόμενος πέραν τοῦ Τεβέριος ποταμοῦ, ἐν ᾧ
ταπεινή τις ἦν καλύβη, γεωργῶν αὐτόθι μετὰ
δούλων ὀλίγων ἐπίπονον καὶ ταλαίπωρον ἔζη βίον
ὑπὸ λύπης τε καὶ πενίας, οὔτε πόλιν ὁρῶν οὔτε
φίλους ἀσπαζόμενος οὔθ᾽ ἑορτάζων οὔτ᾽ ἄλλης
5 εὐφροσύνης οὐδεμιᾶς ἑαυτῷ μεταδιδούς. τοῖς μέντοι δημάρχοις πολὺ τὸ παράλογον ἐγένετο τῆς
ἐλπίδος. οὐ γὰρ ὅπως ἐπαύσατο ἡ τῶν νέων φιλοτιμία σωφρονισθεῖσα τῇ Καίσωνος συμφορᾷ, πολὺ
δὲ χαλεπωτέρα καὶ πλείων ἐγένετο ἔργοις τε καὶ
λόγοις καταγωνιζομένη τὸν νόμον· ὥστ᾽ οὐθὲν ἔτι
αὐτοῖς ἐξεγένετο διαπράξασθαι δαπανηθέντος εἰς
ταῦτα τοῦ χρόνου τῆς ἀρχῆς. ὁ μέντοι δῆμος εἰς
τὸν ἐπιόντα πάλιν ἐνιαυτὸν ἄρχοντας ἀπέδειξεν
αὐτούς.[5]

---

[1] καὶ A : om. R.   [2] συνελθοῦσα B : om. R.
[3] ψευδῆ om. B.

chains in the meantime or should give sureties for his appearance, as his father requested. The senate, assembling, ordered that if bail were offered his person should be free till the trial. The next day the tribunes assembled the populace and, the youth not appearing for trial, they caused a vote to be passed for his condemnation and compelled his sureties, ten in number, to pay over the sums agreed upon in case of their failure to produce his person. Caeso, accordingly, having fallen a victim to a plot of this sort—for the tribunes had contrived the whole business and Volscius had borne false witness, as became clear later—went into exile in Tyrrhenia. His father sold the greater part of his estate and repaid the sureties the sums agreed upon, leaving nothing for himself but one small farm lying on the other side of the river Tiber, on which there was an humble cottage ; and there, cultivating the farm with the help of a few slaves, he led a laborious and miserable life because of his grief and poverty, neither visiting the city nor greeting his friends nor taking part in the festivals nor allowing himself any other pleasure. The tribunes,[1] however, were greatly disappointed in their expectations ; for the contentiousness of the young men, far from being chastened by the unhappy fate of Caeso, grew much more vexatious and excessive as they fought the law with both actions and words. The result was that the tribunes were unable to accomplish anything more, the whole time of their magistracy being taken up with these contests. The populace, however, chose them again as their magistrates for the following year.

[1] For § 5 *cf.* Livy iii. 14.

IX. Ποπλίου δὲ Οὐαλερίου Ποπλικόλα καὶ
Γαΐου Κλαυδίου Σαβίνου τὴν ὑπατικὴν ἐξουσίαν
παραλαβόντων κίνδυνος ὅσος οὔπω τὴν Ῥώμην
κατέσχεν ἐξ ἀλλοεθνοῦς πολέμου, ὃν παρήγαγεν
ἐντὸς τείχους ἡ πολιτικὴ στάσις, ὡς οἵ τε Σιβύλ-
λειοι χρησμοὶ προὔλεγον καὶ τὰ ἐκ τοῦ δαιμονίου
φανέντα προεθέσπισε τῷ παρελθόντι ἐνιαυτῷ.
διηγήσομαι δὲ τήν τε αἰτίαν ἀφ᾽ ἧς ὁ πόλεμος
εἰσῆλθε καὶ τὰ πραχθέντα τοῖς ὑπάτοις κατὰ τὸν
2 τότε ἀγῶνα. οἱ παρειληφότες τὸ δεύτερον τὴν
δημαρχίαν ἐπὶ τῇ ἐλπίδι τοῦ κυρώσειν τὸν νόμον,
ὁρῶντες τῶν τε ὑπάτων τὸν ἕτερον, Γάιον Κλαύδιον, ἔμφυτον τὸ πρὸς τοὺς δημοτικοὺς ἔχοντα
μῖσος διὰ προγόνων καὶ παρεσκευασμένον ἁπάσῃ
μηχανῇ κωλύειν τὰ γινόμενα, τῶν τε νέων τοὺς
πλεῖστον δυναμένους εἰς ἀπόνοιαν φανερὰν προελη-
λυθότας, οὓς οὐκ ἐνῆν τῷ βιαίῳ καταγωνίσασθαι,
μάλιστα δὲ τοῦ δήμου τὸ πλεῖον ὑποκατακλινό-
μενον ταῖς θεραπείαις τῶν πατρικίων καὶ προθυμίαν
οὐκέτι περὶ τοῦ νόμου τὴν αὐτὴν παρεχόμενον,
ἰταμωτέραν ὁδὸν ἔγνωσαν ἐπὶ τὰ πράγματα πορεύ-
εσθαι, δι᾽ ἧς καταπλήξονται μὲν τὸν δῆμον, ἀνα-
3 βαλοῦσι δὲ τὸν ὕπατον. πρῶτον μὲν κατεσκεύασαν
φήμας λέγεσθαι κατὰ τὴν πόλιν παντοδαπάς· ἔπειτ᾽
ἐξ ἑωθινοῦ καθεζόμενοι δι᾽ ὅλης ἡμέρας συνήδρευον
ἐν τῷ φανερῷ, μεταδιδόντες οὐθενὶ τῶν ἔξωθεν
οὔτε βουλεύματος οὔτε λόγου. ἐπεὶ δὲ καιρὸς
ἐπιτήδειος ἔδοξεν αὐτοῖς εἶναι πράττειν τὰ βεβου-
λευμένα, πλασάμενοι γράμματα καὶ ταῦτα[1] παρασκευάσαντες ἀναδοθῆναι σφίσιν ὑπ᾽ ἀνδρὸς ἀγνῶτος
καθημένοις ἐν ἀγορᾷ, ὡς διῆλθον αὐτά, παίοντες

---

[1] ταῦτα om. A.

IX. When Publius Valerius Publicola and Gaius Claudius Sabinus [1] had assumed the consular power, a danger greater than ever before came upon Rome from a foreign war [2]; and it was brought upon her by the civil dissension inside the walls, as both the Sibylline oracles and the portents sent by Heaven had foretold the year before.[3] I shall relate not only the cause from which the war arose, but also the action taken by the consuls during that contest. The men who had assumed the tribuneship for the second time in the hope of securing the ratification of the law, observing that one of the consuls, Gaius Claudius, had an inborn hatred of the plebeians, inherited from his ancestors, and was prepared to defeat the plans afoot by every possible means, that the most influential of the youths had reached the point of open desperation, with no possibility of their being subdued by forcible means, and above all, that most of the populace were yielding to the blandishments of the patricians and no longer exhibiting the same zeal for the law, resolved to take a bolder course toward their goal, by which they expected to dumbfound the populace and unseat the consul. First, then, they caused all manner of rumours to be spread throughout the city; afterwards they sat in council publicly throughout the whole day from early morning without admitting any outsiders to their counsels and discussions. Then, when it seemed to them to be the proper time for putting their plans into execution, they forged letters and contrived to have these delivered to them by an unknown person as they sat in the Forum; and as soon as they had perused them, they sprang up,

---

[1] For chaps. 9-13 cf. Livy iii. 15, 1-4.
[2] See chaps. 14 ff.   [3] See chap. 2, 5.

τὰ μέτωπα καὶ κατηφεῖς τὰς ὄψεις ποιήσαντες
4 ἀνίστανται. πολλοῦ δὲ συνδραμόντος ὄχλου καὶ
μέγα τι κακὸν ἐν τοῖς γράμμασιν ἐνεῖναι γεγραμ-
μένον μαντευομένου σιωπὴν προκηρύξαντες εἶπον·
'' Ἐν ἐσχάτοις ἐστὶν ὑμῖν κινδύνοις, ὦ πολῖται,
τὸ δημοτικόν· καὶ εἰ μὴ θεῶν τις εὔνοια προείδετο[1]
τῶν[1] ἄδικα πάσχειν μελλόντων, εἰς δεινὰς ἂν
ἅπαντες ἤλθομεν συμφοράς. αἰτούμεθα δὲ ὑμᾶς
βραχὺν ἐπισχεῖν χρόνον, ἕως ἂν[2] τῇ βουλῇ δηλώσωμεν[3] τὰ προσαγγελθέντα καὶ μετὰ κοινῆς γνώμης
5 πράξωμεν[4] τὰ δέοντα[5].'' ταῦτ' εἰπόντες ᾤχοντο
πρὸς τοὺς ὑπάτους. ἐν ὅσῳ δὲ ἡ βουλὴ συνήγετο
χρόνῳ, πολλοὶ καὶ παντοδαποὶ λόγοι κατὰ τὴν
ἀγορὰν ἐγίνοντο, τῶν μὲν ἐκ παρασκευῆς ἃ παρηγγέλλετο[6] αὐτοῖς ὑπὸ τῶν δημάρχων κατὰ συστροφὰς
λαλούντων, τῶν δέ, ἃ μάλιστα ἐδεδοίκεσαν μὴ
γένηται, ταῦτα ὡς ἀπηγγελμένα τοῖς δημάρχοις
6 λεγόντων. ἔφη δ' ὁ μέν τις Αἰκανοὺς καὶ Οὐολούσκους ὑποδεξαμένους Καίσωνα Κοΐντιον τὸν ὑπὸ
τοῦ δήμου καταδικασθέντα ᾑρῆσθαι στρατηγὸν
αὐτοκράτορα τῶν ἐθνῶν καὶ πολλὰς δυνάμεις ἀγεί-
ραντας[7] μέλλειν ἐπὶ τὴν Ῥώμην ἐλαύνειν· ὁ δέ τις
ἀπὸ κοινῆς γνώμης τῶν πατρικίων τὸν ἄνδρα
κατάγεσθαι ξενικαῖς δυνάμεσιν, ἵνα ἡ φυλακὴ
καταλυθείη[8] νῦν τε καὶ εἰς τὸν λοιπὸν χρόνον τῶν
δημοτικῶν· ὁ δέ τις οὐχ ἅπαντας εἶναι τοὺς πατρικίους ἔφη τοὺς ταῦτα βεβουλευμένους, ἀλλὰ μόνους
7 τοὺς νέους. ἐτόλμων δέ τινες λέγειν ὅτι καὶ ἐντὸς

---

[1] προείδετο τῶν Sylburg : προείδε τούτων AB.
[2] ἂν R : om. B.   [3] δηλώσωμεν R : δηλώσομεν Bb.
[4] πράξωμεν R : πράξομεν Bb.
[5] δέοντα A : δόξαντα B.

190

beating their foreheads and assuming downcast
countenances. And when a large crowd had flocked
together and was conjecturing that some dreadful
intelligence was contained in the letters, they ordered
the heralds to proclaim silence and then said : " Your
plebeians are in the gravest peril, citizens ; and if
some benevolence of the gods had not provided for
those who were on the point of suffering injustice, we
should all have fallen into dire calamities. We ask
you to have a little patience till we acquaint the
senate with the information we have received and
after consulting with them take the necessary measures." Having spoken thus, they went to the consuls. While the senate was assembling, many reports
of all kinds circulated in the Forum, as some persons,
by previous arrangement, talking in groups, retailed
the stories suggested to them by the tribunes, and
others named the things they most dreaded to have
happen as the matters that had been reported to the
tribunes. One said that the Aequians and the Volscians, having received Caeso Quintius, the man condemned by the populace, had chosen him general of
both nations with absolute power, had raised numerous forces, and were upon the point of marching on
Rome ; another said that by the concerted plan of
the patricians he was being brought back by foreign
troops in order that the magistracy which was the
guardian of the plebeians might be abolished now and
forever ; and still another said that not all the
patricians had decided on this course, but only the
young men. Some ventured to state that Caeso was

---

6 παρηγγέλλετο AB : παρήγγελτο R (?).
7 Kiessling : ἀγείραντα O, Jacoby.
8 καταλυθείη B : καταλυθῇ R.

191

τῆς πόλεως ὁ ἀνὴρ εἴη κρυπτόμενος καὶ μέλλοι
καταλαμβάνεσθαι τῶν τόπων τοὺς ἐπικαιροτάτους.
ὅλης δὲ κραδαινομένης ἐπὶ τῇ προσδοκίᾳ τῶν
δεινῶν τῆς πόλεως, καὶ πάντων ἀλλήλους ἐχόντων
δι' ὑποψίας καὶ φυλακῆς, οἱ μὲν ὕπατοι τὴν βουλὴν
ἐκάλουν, οἱ δὲ δήμαρχοι παρελθόντες[1] ἐδείκνυσαν
τὰ προσαγγελλόμενα. ἦν δὲ ὁ τοὺς λόγους ὑπὲρ
αὐτῶν ποιούμενος Αὖλος Οὐεργίνιος καὶ ἔλεξε
τοιάδε·

X. "῞Οσον μὲν χρόνον οὐθὲν ἀκριβὲς ἡμῖν ἐφαίνετο τῶν προσαγγελλομένων δεινῶν, ἀλλὰ φῆμαι
μετέωροι καὶ τὸ βεβαίωσον αὐτὰς οὐθὲν ἦν,
ὠκνοῦμεν, ὦ βουλή, φέρειν τοὺς περὶ αὐτῶν λόγους εἰς μέσον,[2] ταραχάς τε ὑποπτεύοντες ἔσεσθαι
μεγάλας, οἷα εἰκὸς ἐπὶ δεινοῖς ἀκούσμασι, καὶ δι'
εὐλαβείας ἔχοντες μὴ ταχύτερα δόξωμεν ὑμῖν
2 βεβουλεῦσθαι μᾶλλον ἢ φρονιμώτερα. οὐ μὴν
ὀλιγωρίᾳ γ' αὐτὰ παραδόντες ἀφήκαμεν, ἀλλ' ὅση
δύναμις ἡμῖν ἦν ἐπιμελῆ ζήτησιν ἐποιούμεθα τῆς
ἀληθείας. ἐπεὶ δὲ ἡ τοῦ δαιμονίου πρόνοια, ὑφ'
ἧς ἀεὶ σωζόμεθα κοινῇ, καλῶς ποιοῦσα τὰ κεκρυμ-
μένα βουλεύματα καὶ τὰς ἀνοσίους ἐπιχειρήσεις
τῶν θεοῖς ἐχθρῶν εἰς φῶς ἄγει, καὶ γράμματα
πάρεστιν ἡμῖν ἃ δεδέγμεθα νεωστὶ παρὰ ξένων
εὔνοιαν ἡμῖν ἐνδεικνυμένων, οὓς ὕστερον ἀκούσε-
σθε, καὶ συντρέχει τε καὶ συνᾴδει τοῖς ἔξωθεν
ἐπιστελλομένοις τὰ ἐνθένδε μηνυόμενα, καὶ τὰ
πράγματα οὐκέτι μέλλησιν οὐδ' ἀναβολὴν ἐν χερσὶν
ὄντα ἐπιδέχεται, πρὶν εἰς τὸν δῆμον ἐξενεγκεῖν,
ὑμῖν πρώτοις, ὥσπερ ἐστὶ δίκαιον, ἀπαγγεῖλαι
3 διέγνωμεν αὐτά. ἴστε δὴ συνωμοσίαν ἐπὶ τῷ δήμῳ

---

[1] παρελθόντες B : προσελθόντες A.

actually inside the city, in hiding, and was about to seize the most advantageous positions. While the whole city was shaken by expectation of these calamities and all men suspected and were on their guard against one another, the consuls assembled the senate, and the tribunes, going in, acquainted them with the reports that were being received. The one who addressed them on behalf of the others was Aulus Verginius, and he spoke as follows :

X. " As long as there seemed to us to be nothing definite about the dangers that were being reported, but there were only vague rumours and nothing to confirm them, we were reluctant, senators, to lay before you the reports about them, both because we suspected there would be great disturbances, as would be likely in a time of dreadful rumours, and also because we were afraid of appearing to you to have acted with greater precipitancy than prudence. We did not, however, ignore or neglect these reports, but inquired with all possible diligence into the truth of them. And since the divine providence, by which our commonwealth is ever preserved, is rightly bringing to light the hidden plans and wicked attempts of those who are enemies to the gods ; since we have letters, just now received from foreign friends, who thus show their goodwill to us and whose names you shall later hear ; since information given here at home coincides and agrees with the reports sent in from outside ; and since these matters no longer admit of delay or postponement, being at our very doors, we have decided to report them to you, as is proper, before laying them before the populace. Know, then, that a conspiracy has been formed

---

² εἰς μέσον B : εἰς τὸ μέσον R.

γεγενημένην ὑπ' ἀνδρῶν οὐκ ἀφανῶν, ἐν οἷς ἐνεῖναι
μέν τι λέγεται μέρος οὐ πολὺ καὶ τῶν εἰς τόδε
συλλεγομένων τὸ συνέδριον πρεσβυτέρων, τὸ δὲ
πλεῖστον ἐκ τῶν ἔξω τῆς βουλῆς ἱππέων, οὓς οὔπω
4 καιρὸς οἵτινές εἰσιν ὑμῖν λέγειν. μέλλουσι δ' οὖν,
ὡς πυνθανόμεθα, σκοταίαν φυλάξαντες νύκτα κοι-
μωμένοις ἡμῖν ἐπιχειρεῖν, ἡνίκα οὔτε προϊδεῖν τι[1]
τῶν γινομένων οὔτε φυλάξασθαι καθ' ἓν γενόμενοι
δυνάμεθα· ἐπιπεσόντες δὲ ταῖς οἰκίαις τούς τε
δημάρχους ἡμᾶς κατασφάττειν καὶ τῶν δημοτῶν
ἄλλους τοὺς[2] ἐναντιωθέντας ποτὲ αὐτοῖς περὶ ἐλευ-
5 θερίας ἢ τὸ λοιπὸν ἐναντιωσομένους. ὅταν δὲ
ἡμᾶς ἐκποδὼν ποιήσωνται, τότ' ἤδη κατὰ πολλὴν
ἀσφάλειαν ἡγοῦνται διαπράξεσθαι[3] παρ' ὑμῶν[4]
ἀναιρεθῆναι διὰ κοινοῦ ψηφίσματος τὰς γενομένας
ὑμῖν πρὸς τὸν δῆμον ὁμολογίας. ὁρῶντες δὲ ὅτι
ξενικῆς αὐτοῖς χειρὸς εἰς τὰ πράγματα δεῖ κρύφα
παρασκευασθείσης καὶ οὐδὲ ταύτης μετρίας, ἄνδρα
προσειλήφασιν εἰς ταῦτα τῶν ὑμετέρων[5] φυγάδων
Καίσωνα Κοΐντιον ἡγεμόνα, ὃν ἐπὶ φόνοις πολιτῶν
καὶ διαστάσει τῆς πόλεως ἐξελεγχθέντα διεπρά-
ξαντό τινες τῶν ἐνθάδε μὴ δοῦναι δίκην, ἀλλ'
ἀθῷον ἀπελθεῖν ἐκ τῆς πόλεως, κάθοδόν τε πράξειν
ὑπέσχηνται καὶ ἀρχὰς προτείνονται[6] καὶ τιμὰς καὶ
6 ἄλλους μισθοὺς τῆς ὑπουργίας. κἀκεῖνος ὑπέσχηται στρατιὰν[7] αὐτοῖς Αἰκανῶν καὶ Οὐολούσκων

[1] τι B : om. R.

[2] τοὺς deleted by Jacoby ; Reiske preferred to delete
ἄλλους.

[3] Cobet : διαπράξασθαι O, Jacoby.

[4] τὰ λοιπὰ after ὑμῶν deleted by Cary (repeated from
second line above).

[5] ὑμετέρων B : ἡμετέρων A.

against the populace by men of prominence, among
whom, it is said, there is a small number—not many—
even of the older men who meet in this chamber,
though the larger number are knights who are not
members of the senate, whose names it is not yet
the time to tell you.   They intend, now, as we learn,
to take advantage of a dark night and attack us while
we are asleep, when we can neither provide against
anything that is taking place nor get together in a
body to defend ourselves, and, rushing into our
houses, to cut the throats, not only of us tribunes, but
of all the other plebeians also who have ever opposed
them in defence of their liberty or may oppose them
for the future.   And after they have made away with
us, they believe that then at last they will easily
bring about the abrogation, by a unanimous vote on
your part, of the compacts you made with the populace.   But perceiving that they need for their purpose a body of foreign troops secretly got in readiness
—and that no moderate force—they have to this end
adopted as their leader one of your exiles, Caeso
Quintius, a man whom, though convicted of the
murder of his fellow citizens and of raising a sedition
in the state, some of the members of this body contrived to save from paying the penalty, letting him
go out of the city unharmed, and have promised to
restore him to his country and are offering him
magistracies and honours and other rewards for his
help.   And he on his part has promised to bring to
their assistance as large a force of the Aequians

---

⁶ προτείνονται A : προτείνουσι R.

⁷ κἀκεῖνος ὑπέσχηται στρατιὰν B : στρατιὰν δὲ κἀκεῖνος
ὑπέσχηται R.

ἄξειν ἐπίκουρον ὅσης ἂν δεηθῶσιν· ἥξει[1] τε οὐκ εἰς
μακρὰν αὐτὸς μὲν ἐπαγόμενος τοὺς εὐτολμοτάτους
κρύφα κατ' ὀλίγους εἰσάγων καὶ σποράδας, ἡ δ'
ἄλλη δύναμις, ὅταν οἱ τοῦ δήμου προεστηκότες
ἡμεῖς διαφθαρῶμεν, ἐπὶ τὸ ἄλλο πλῆθος τῶν πενήτων χωρήσει,[2] ἐάν τινες ἄρα περιέχωνται τῆς
7 ἐλευθερίας. ταῦτ' ἐστὶν ἃ βεβούλευνται ὑπὸ
σκότους καὶ μέλλουσι δρᾶν, ὦ βουλή, δεινὰ καὶ
ἀνόσια ἔργα, οὔτε θεῖον φοβηθέντες χόλον οὔτε
ἀνθρωπίνην ἐντραπέντες νέμεσιν.

XI. " Ἐν τοσούτῳ δὴ κινδύνῳ σαλεύοντες ἱκέται
γινόμεθα ὑμῶν, ὦ πατέρες, ἐπισκήπτοντες θεούς τε
καὶ δαίμονας οἷς κοινῇ θύομεν, καὶ πολέμων ὑπο-
μιμνήσκοντες οὓς πολλοὺς καὶ μεγάλους σὺν ὑμῖν
ἠράμεθα, μὴ περιιδεῖν ὠμὰ καὶ ἀνόσια ὑπὸ τῶν
ἐχθρῶν παθόντας ἡμᾶς, ἀλλ' ἐπαμῦναί τε καὶ συν-
αγανακτῆσαι τιμωρίας ἡμῖν συνεισπράξαντας παρὰ
τῶν ταῦτα βουλευσαμένων τὰς προσηκούσας, μάλιστα μὲν παρὰ πάντων, εἰ δὲ μή γε, παρὰ
2 τῶν ἀρξάντων τῆς ἀθεμίτου συνωμοσίας. πρῶτον
δὲ πάντων ἀξιοῦμεν ὑμᾶς, ὦ βουλή, ψηφίσασθαι
πρᾶγμα ὅπερ ἐστὶ δικαιότατον, τὴν ὑπὲρ τῶν μηνυομένων ζήτησιν ὑφ' ἡμῶν τῶν δημάρχων γίνεσθαι. χωρὶς γὰρ τοῦ δικαίου καὶ ἀκριβεστάτας
ἀνάγκη γίνεσθαι ζητήσεις ἃς ἂν οἱ κινδυνεύοντες
3 ὑπὲρ αὑτῶν ποιήσωνται. εἰ δέ τινες ὑμῶν εἰσιν
οἷοι μηδὲ καθ' ἓν εὐγνωμονεῖν, ἀλλὰ πρὸς ἅπαντας
τοὺς ὑπὲρ τοῦ δήμου λέγοντας ἀντιτάττεσθαι,
ἡδέως ἂν πυθοίμην παρ' αὐτῶν, ἐπὶ τῷ δυσ-
χεραίνουσι τῶν ἀξιουμένων καὶ τί μέλλουσιν ὑμᾶς[3]

---

[1] ἥξει R : ἥξειν A.   [2] Portus : χωρήσειν A, om. B.
[3] Kiessling : ἡμᾶς AB.

and Volscians as they shall ask for. He himself will
soon appear at the head of the most daring, whom
he will introduce into the city secretly, a few at a
time and in small bodies ; the rest of the force, as
soon as we who are the leaders of the populace are
destroyed, will fall next upon the rest of the poor,
if any of them cling to their liberty. These are
the dreadful and wicked plans, senators, which they
have concocted under cover of darkness and intend
to carry out without either fearing the anger of the
gods or heeding the indignation of men.

XI. " Being tossed about on such a rough sea of
perils, fathers, we come to you as suppliants, calling
to witness the gods and lesser divinities to whom we
sacrifice in common ; and reminding you of the many
great wars we have waged side by side with you, we
implore you not to allow us to suffer this cruel and
wicked fate at the hands of our enemies, but to assist
us and share our indignation, joining with us in exacting suitable punishment from those who have formed
these designs—from all of them preferably, but if that
may not be, then at least from the authors of this
nefarious conspiracy. First of all we ask, senators,
that you will pass a measure that is in every respect
just, to the effect that the investigation of the matters
of which we have been informed shall be conducted
by us, the tribunes. For, apart from the justice of
this request, those investigations are bound to be
strictest which are made by those whose own lives
are in danger. If there are any among you who are
not disposed to show a conciliatory spirit at all, but
oppose every man who speaks in favour of the populace, I should like to inquire of them what there is
in our demands that displeases them and what course

πείθειν· πότερα μηδεμίαν ποιεῖσθαι ζήτησιν, ἀλλ'
ὑπεριδεῖν ἔργον οὕτω μέγα καὶ μιαρὸν ἐπὶ τῷ δήμῳ
συνιστάμενον; καὶ τίς ἂν τοὺς ταῦτα λέγοντας
ὑγιαίνειν φήσειεν, ἀλλ' οὐχὶ συνδιεφθάρθαι καὶ
κοινωνεῖν τῆς συνωμοσίας, ἔπειτα ὑπὲρ αὐτῶν
δεδιότας, ἵνα μὴ γένωνται καταφανεῖς, ἀποσπεύδειν
τὴν τῆς ἀληθείας ἐξέτασιν; οἷς οὐκ ἂν δικαίως
4 προσέχοιτε δήπου τὸν νοῦν. ἢ¹ τῆς διαγνώσεως
τῶν μηνυομένων οὐχ ἡμᾶς εἶναι κυρίους ἀξιώσου-
σιν, ἀλλὰ τὴν βουλὴν καὶ τοὺς ὑπάτους; τί οὖν τὸ
κωλῦον ἔσται τὸ αὐτὸ τοῦτο καὶ τοὺς προεστηκότας
τοῦ δήμου λέγειν, ἐάν τινες ἐκ τῶν δημοτικῶν ἐπὶ
τοῖς ὑπάτοις καὶ τῇ βουλῇ συστάντες πράττωσι
τὴν τοῦ συνεδρίου κατάλυσιν, ὅτι τὴν περὶ τῶν
δημοτῶν ἐξέτασιν αὐτοὺς δίκαιόν ἐστι ποιεῖσθαι
τοὺς ἀνειληφότας τὴν τοῦ δήμου φυλακήν; τί οὖν
ἐκ τούτου συμβήσεται; μηδεμίαν πώποτε² γενέσθαι ζήτησιν περὶ μηδενὸς πράγματος ἀπορρήτου.
5 ἀλλ' οὔθ' ἡμεῖς ἂν ταῦτα ἀξιώσαιμεν (ὕποπτος
γὰρ ἡ φιλοτιμία) ὑμεῖς τ' οὐκ ἂν ὀρθῶς ποιοῖτε
τοῖς τὰ ὅμοια ἀξιοῦσι³ καθ' ἡμῶν προσέχοντες τὸν
νοῦν, ἀλλὰ κοινοὺς ἡγούμενοι τῆς πόλεως ἐχθρούς.
οὐδενὸς μέντοιγε, ὦ βουλή, τοῖς πράγμασιν ὡς
τάχους δεῖ. ὁ γὰρ κίνδυνος ὀξύς, καὶ ἡ μέλλη-
σις τῆς ἀσφαλείας ἄωρος ἐν οὐ⁴ μέλλουσι δεινοῖς.
ὥστ' ἀφέντες τὸ φιλονεικεῖν καὶ λόγους διεξιέναι
μακροὺς ψηφίσασθε ὅ τι ἂν δοκῇ κοινῇ συμφέρειν
ἤδη.''

XII. Ταῦτα εἰπόντος αὐτοῦ πολλή τις ἔκπληξις

---

¹ ἢ B : εἰ δὲ μή που A. ² πώποτε B : om. R.
³ ἀξιοῦσι B : οὐκ ἀξιοῦσι R.
⁴ οὐ Ba : οἷς ABb.

they intend to recommend to you. Will it be to make no investigation whatever, but to ignore so awful and abominable a plot that is forming against the populace ? Yet who would say that those who take that line are honest, and are not rather tainted with the same corruption and sharers in the conspiracy, and then, because they are afraid they will be discovered, vigorously oppose the inquiry into the truth ? To such, surely, you would not rightly pay any heed. Or will they demand that those who are to have authority to determine the truth of these reports shall be, not we, the tribunes, but the senate and the consuls ? What, then, is to prevent the leaders of the populace also from saying the same thing in case some plebeians, conspiring against the consuls and the senate, should plot the abolition of the latter—that, namely, the investigation of the plebeians would justly be made by the very men who have assumed the protection of the populace ? What, then, will be the consequence of this procedure ? Why, that no inquiry will ever be made into any secret matter. But, just as we would never make this demand—for partisan zeal arouses suspicion—so you would not be doing right in paying heed to those who insist upon the same course against us ; on the contrary, you should look upon them as the common enemies of the state. However, senators, nothing is so necessary in the present juncture as haste ; for the danger is acute, and delay in providing for our security is unseasonable in the presence of dangers that delay not. Do you, therefore, putting aside your rivalry and your long harangues, pass at once whatever decree seems conducive to the public good."

XII. When he had thus spoken, great consterna-

κατέσχε τὸ συνέδριον καὶ ἀμηχανία· διελογίζοντό
τε καὶ συνελάλουν ἀλλήλοις ὡς χαλεπὸν ἑκάτερον
ἦν, καὶ τὸ συγχωρεῖν τοῖς δημάρχοις ζητήσεις ἐφ'
ἑαυτῶν ποιεῖσθαι περὶ κοινοῦ καὶ μεγάλου πράγματος καὶ τὸ μὴ συγχωρεῖν.[1] ὑποπτεύσας δ' αὐτῶν
τὴν γνώμην ἀνέστη τῶν ὑπάτων ἅτερος,[2] Γάιος
Κλαύδιος, καὶ ἔλεξε τοιάδε·

2 "Οὐ δέδοικα, Οὐεργίνιε, μή με ὑπολάβωσιν οὗτοι
κοινωνὸν εἶναι τῆς συνωμοσίας ἣν ἐφ' ὑμῖν καὶ
τῷ δήμῳ πράττεσθαι λέγετε, εἶτα[3] ὑπὲρ ἐμαυτοῦ
δεδιότα ἢ τῶν ἐμῶν τινος ἐνόχου[4] ταῖς αἰτίαις
ὄντος[5] ἀνεστάναι τἀναντία ὑμῖν ἐροῦντα· ὁ γὰρ βίος
ἀπολύει με πάσης ὑποψίας τοιαύτης. ἃ δὲ νομίζω
τῇ τε βουλῇ καὶ τῷ δήμῳ συμφέρειν, ἀπὸ τοῦ
3 κρατίστου καὶ δίχα πάσης εὐλαβείας ἐρῶ. πολλοῦ,
μᾶλλον δὲ τοῦ παντός, ἁμαρτάνειν δοκεῖ μοι Οὐεργίνιος, εἴ τινα ὑπείληφεν ἡμῶν ἐρεῖν ἢ ὡς ἀνεξ-
έταστον ἀφεῖσθαι δεῖ πρᾶγμα οὑτωσὶ[6] μέγα καὶ
ἀναγκαῖον, ἢ ὡς οὐ δεῖ κοινωνεῖν οὐδὲ παρεῖναι
τῇ ζητήσει τοὺς ἀνειληφότας τὴν τοῦ δήμου ἀρχήν.
οὐθεὶς οὔτε ἠλίθιός ἐστιν οὕτως οὔτε τῷ δήμῳ
4 κακόνους ὥστε ταῦτα λέγειν. τί οὖν, εἴ τις ἔροιτό
με,[7] παθών, ἃ συγχωρῶ καί φημι δίκαια εἶναι,
τούτοις ἀντιλέξων ἀνέστην, καὶ τί βούλεταί μου ὁ
λόγος, ἐγὼ νὴ Δία φράσω πρὸς ὑμᾶς. παντὸς
οἶμαι δεῖν πράγματος, ὦ βουλή, τὰς ἀρχὰς καὶ
τὰς πρώτας ὑποθέσεις τοὺς εὖ φρονοῦντας ἀκριβῶς
σκοπεῖν· οἷαι γὰρ ἂν αὗται τύχωσιν οὖσαι, τοιούτους ἀνάγκη γίνεσθαι καὶ τοὺς περὶ αὐτῶν λόγους.

---

[1] συγχωρεῖν A : om. B.   [2] ἅτερος B : ἕτερος R.
[3] εἶτα Post : ἢ τὰ O, ἤτοι Cobet, ἢ Jacoby.
[4] ἐνόχου B : ὡς ἐνόχου R.   [5] ὄντος B : οὕτως A.

tion and embarrassment came upon the senate. They
discussed and talked over with one another the difficulty of either course—either to grant or to refuse
the tribunes permission to make investigations by
themselves of a matter of general concern and great
importance. And one of the consuls, Gaius Claudius,
suspecting their intentions, rose up and spoke as
follows :

" I am not afraid, Verginius, that these men here
will imagine that I am an accomplice in the conspiracy which you say is being formed against you
and the populace, and that then, out of fear for myself
or for some relation of mine who is guilty of this
charge, I have risen to oppose you ; for the whole
course of my life clears me of any suspicion of the
sort. But what I consider to be advantageous for
both the senate and the people I will say in all good
faith and without reservation. Verginius seems to
me to be greatly, or rather totally, mistaken if he
imagines that any of us will say either that a matter
of so great importance and necessity ought to be left
uninvestigated or that the magistrates of the populace
ought not to take part in or be present at the inquiry.
No man is so foolish or so ill-disposed toward the
populace as to say that. If, then, anyone should ask
me what possessed me to rise up to oppose those
measures which I agree to and admit to be just, and
what my purpose is in speaking, by Heaven I will tell
you. I believe, senators, that sensible men ought
to examine minutely the beginnings and basic principles of every measure ; for of whatever nature
these may be, such also must be all discussion about

---

⁶ οὕτωσὶ B : οὕτως ἂν A, Jacoby.
⁷ εἴ τις ἔροιτό με deleted by Cobet.

5 φέρε δή, τίς ἡ τοῦδε τοῦ πράγματος ὑπόθεσίς ἐστι
καὶ τί τὸ βούλευμα[1] τῶν δημάρχων, ἀκούσατέ μου.
οὐκ ἐνῆν τούτοις οὐδὲν ὧν ἐν τῷ παρελθόντι ἐνιαυτῷ πράττειν ἐπιβαλλόμενοι διεκωλύθησαν, ἐπιτελέσασθαι νῦν ὑμῶν τε ἐναντιουμένων αὐτοῖς ὡς
πρότερον καὶ τοῦ δήμου μηκέθ' ὁμοίως συναγωνιζομένου. συνιδόντες δὴ τοῦτο ἐσκόπουν ὅπως ἂν
ὑμεῖς τ' ἀναγκασθείητε παρὰ γνώμην αὐτοῖς εἶξαι
καὶ ὁ δῆμος ἅπαντα ὅσ' ἂν ἀξιῶσι[2] συμπράττειν.
6 ἀληθῆ μὲν οὖν καὶ δικαίαν ὑπόθεσιν οὐδεμίαν εὕ-
ρισκον δι' ἧς ἑκάτερον τούτων[3] ἔσται, πολλὰ δὲ
βουλεύματα πειράζοντες καὶ στρέφοντες ἄνω καὶ
κάτω τὸ πρᾶγμα τελευτῶντες ἐπὶ τοιοῦτον δή τινα
λογισμὸν ἦλθον· ' αἰτιασώμεθα συνίστασθαί τινας
ἐκ τῶν ἐπιφανῶν ἐπὶ καταλύσει τοῦ δήμου καὶ
σφάττειν διεγνωκέναι τοὺς παρέχοντας[4] αὐτῷ τὸ
7 ἀσφαλές. καὶ ταῦτα ἐκ πολλοῦ παρασκευάσαντες
λέγεσθαι κατὰ τὴν πόλιν, ὅταν ἤδη πιστὰ εἶναι τοῖς
πολλοῖς δόξῃ[5]—δόξει δὲ διὰ τὸ δέος—ἐπιστολὰς
μηχανησώμεθα πολλῶν παρόντων ἡμῖν ὑπ' ἀνδρὸς
ἀγνῶτος ἀναδοθῆναι· ἔπειτ' ἐλθόντες ἐπὶ τὸ συνέδριον ἀγανακτῶμέν τε καὶ σχετλιάζωμεν καὶ τοῦ
ζητεῖν τὰ προσηγγελμένα αἰτῶμεν[6] τὴν[7] ἐξουσίαν.
8 ἐάν τε[8] γὰρ ἀντιλέγωσιν ἡμῖν οἱ πατρίκιοι, ταύτην
ληψόμεθα τοῦ διαβαλεῖν αὐτοὺς πρὸς τὸν δῆμον
ἀφορμήν, καὶ οὕτως ἅπαν τὸ δημοτικὸν ἠγριωμένον
αὐτοῖς ἕτοιμον ἡμῖν εἰς ἃ βουλόμεθα ὑπάρξει· ἐάν
τε συγχωρῶσι, τοὺς γενναιοτάτους ἐξ αὐτῶν καὶ

---

[1] Sylburg : βούλημα O.
[2] ἀξιῶσι Ba : ἀξιώσῃ ABb.
[3] τούτων, (or αὐτοῖς) Cary : τούτοις O, Jacoby.
[4] τοὺς παρέχοντας Ba : τοὺς μὴ παρέχοντας R.
[5] δόξῃ A : δοκῇ B. [6] αἰτῶμεν B : δῶμεν R.

them. Well then, learn from me what the basic principle of this measure is and what the purpose of the tribunes is. These men would not be able to carry out now any of the undertakings they were prevented from accomplishing last year if both you were to oppose them as before and the populace were no longer to espouse their quarrel with the same zeal. Since they were aware of these difficulties, they considered by what means not only you might be compelled to yield to them contrary to your judgement, but the populace also might be forced to assist them in everything they should desire. But finding no true or just basis for gaining both these ends, after trying various plans and turning the matter this way and that, they at last hit upon some such reasoning as this : ' Let us accuse some prominent men of a conspiracy to overthrow the power of the populace and of having decided to cut the throats of those who assure the safety of the populace. And after we have contrived to have these reports talked about for a long time throughout the city and when the multitude at last believe them to be trustworthy—and they will do so because of their fear—let us devise a way to have letters delivered to us in the presence of many by an unknown person. Then let us go to the senate, express our indignation, make angry complaints and demand authority to investigate the reports. For if the patricians oppose our demand, we will seize this opportunity to malign them before the populace, and by this means the whole body of the plebeians will become enraged against them and will be ready to support us in everything we desire ; and, on the other hand, if they grant it, let us banish those

---

⁷ τὴν B : om. R.　　　　　⁸ τε B : om. R.

πλεῖστα ἡμῖν ἐναντιωθέντας πρεσβυτέρους τε καὶ
νέους ἐλαύνωμεν, ὡς εὑρηκότες ταῖς αἰτίαις ἐνόχους.
9 ἐκεῖνοι δὲ ἄρα τὰς καταγνώσεις δεδιότες ἢ συμβή-
σονται πρὸς ἡμᾶς ἐπὶ τῷ μηθὲν ἔτι ἀντιπράττειν
ἢ καταλιπεῖν ἀναγκασθήσονται τὴν πόλιν. ἐκ δὲ
τούτου πολλὴν ποιήσομεν ἐρημίαν τοῦ ἀντιπάλου.'

XIII. '' Ταῦτα τὰ βουλεύματα ἦν αὐτῶν, ὦ βουλή, καὶ τὸν μεταξὺ χρόνον ὃν ἑωρᾶτε συνεδρεύοντας[1] αὐτοὺς οὗτος ὁ δόλος ὑπ' αὐτῶν ὑφαίνετο
ἐπὶ τοῖς ἀρίστοις ὑμῶν, καὶ τοῦτο τὸ δίκτυον κατὰ
τῶν εὐγενεστάτων[2] ἱππέων ἐπλέκετο. καὶ ὅτι
ἀληθῆ ταῦτ' ἐστὶ βραχέος μοι πάνυ δεῖ λόγου.
2 φέρε γὰρ εἴπατέ μοι, Οὐεργίνιε, οἱ τὰ δεινὰ πεισό-
μενοι, παρὰ τίνων ἐδέξασθε τὰ γράμματα ξένων;
τῶν ποῦ κατοικούντων, ἢ πόθεν ὑμᾶς εἰδότων, ἢ
πῶς τἀνθάδε συνεδρευόμενα ἐπισταμένων; τί ἀνα-
βάλλεσθε καὶ μετὰ ταῦτ' ἐρεῖν αὐτοὺς ὑπισχνεῖσθε,
ἀλλ' οὐ πάλαι λέγετε; τίς δ' ὁ τὰ γράμματα
κομίσας ὑμῖν ἀνήρ ἐστι; τί οὐ κατάγετε αὐτὸν εἰς
μέσον, ἵν' ἀπ' ἐκείνου πρῶτον ἀρξώμεθα ζητεῖν εἴτε
ἀληθῆ ταῦτ' ἐστίν, εἴτε, ὡς ἐγώ φημι, πλάσματα
3 ὑμέτερα; αἱ δὲ δὴ συνάδουσαι τοῖς ξενικοῖς γράμ-
μασι μηνύσεις παρὰ τῶν ἐνθάδε τίνες τ' εἰσὶ καὶ
ὑπὸ τίνων γενόμεναι; τί κρύπτετε τὰς πίστεις,
ἀλλ' οὐκ εἰς τὸ ἐμφανὲς ἄγετε; ἀλλ' οἶμαι τῶν
μήτε γενομένων μήτε ἐσομένων ἀδύνατον εὑρεθῆ-
4 ναι πίστιν. ταῦτ' ἐστίν, ὦ βουλή, μηνύματα, οὐ
κατὰ τούτων συνωμοσίας, ἀλλὰ καθ' ὑμῶν[3] δόλου

---

[1] συνεδρεύοντας B : συμβουλεύοντας καὶ συνεδρεύοντας R.
[2] εὐγενεστάτων B : εὐαγεστάτων R.   [3] ὑμῶν A : ἡμῶν B.

of them who are of the most noble birth and have
opposed us the most, both older men and young, as
persons we have discovered to be guilty of the charge.
These men, then, in their fear of being condemned,
will either come to terms with us to make no further
opposition or else will be compelled to leave the city.
By this means we shall thoroughly devastate the
opposition.'

XIII. " These were their plans, senators, and
during the time you saw them holding sessions this
plot was being spun by them against the best of
your members and this net was being woven against
the noblest of the knights. To prove that this is true
requires very few words on my part. For come, tell
me, Verginius and you others who are to suffer these
dreadful evils, who are the foreign friends from whom
you received the letters ? Where do they live ?
How did they become acquainted with you ? Or by
what means do they know what is being discussed
here ? Why do you defer naming these men and
keep promising to do it later on, instead of having
named them long since ? And who is the man who
brought the letters to you ? Why do you not bring
him before us, that we may begin first of all with him
to pursue the inquiry whether these reports are true
or, as I maintain, your own fictions ? And the in-
formations that come from persons here, which you
say agree with the foreign letters, what are they and
by whom given ? Why do you conceal the proofs
and not bring them to light ? But I suspect it is
impossible to find proof of such things as neither have
happened nor will happen. These are indications,
senators, not of a conspiracy against the tribunes here,
but of treachery and an evil purpose against you

καὶ πονηρᾶς γνώμης, ἧ κέχρηνται κρύψαντες οὗτοι·
τὰ γὰρ πράγματα αὐτὰ βοᾷ. αἴτιοι δ' ὑμεῖς οἱ
τὰ πρῶτα ἐπιτρέψαντες αὐτοῖς καὶ τὸ ἀνόητον τῆς
ἀρχῆς μεγάλῃ καθοπλίσαντες ἐξουσίᾳ, ὅτε Κοΐντιον
Καίσωνα τῷ παρελθόντι ἐνιαυτῷ κρίνειν ἐπ' αἰτίαις
ψευδέσιν εἰάσατε, καὶ τοσοῦτον φύλακα τῆς ἀριστοκρατίας ἀναρπαζόμενον[1] ὑπ' αὐτῶν περιείδετε.
5 τοιγαροῦν οὐκέτι μετριάζουσιν οὐδὲ καθ' ἕνα τῶν
εὐγενῶν περικόπτουσιν, ἀλλ' ἀθρόους[2] ἤδη περι-
βαλόντες τοὺς ἀγαθοὺς ἐλαύνουσιν[3] ἐκ τῆς πόλεως·
καὶ πρὸς τοῖς ἄλλοις κακοῖς οὐδ' ἀντειπεῖν αὐτοῖς
ἀξιοῦσιν οὐθένα ὑμῶν, ἀλλ' εἰς ὑποψίας καὶ δια-
βολὰς ἄγοντες ὡς κοινωνοῦντα τῶν ἀπορρήτων
δεδίττονται καὶ μισόδημον εὐθὺς εἶναί φασι, καὶ
προλέγουσιν ἥκειν ἐπὶ τὸν δῆμον ὑφέξοντα τῶν
6 ἐνθάδε ῥηθέντων δίκας. ἀλλ' ὑπὲρ μὲν τούτων
ἕτερος ἔσται καιρὸς ἐπιτηδειότερος τοῖς λόγοις,
νυνὶ δὲ συντεμῶ[4] τὸν λόγον καὶ παύσομαι τὰ πλείω
διατεινόμενος, φυλάττεσθαι ὑμῖν παραινῶν[5] τούσδε
τοὺς ἄνδρας ὡς συνταράττοντας τὴν πόλιν καὶ μεγάλων ἐκφέροντας[6] ἀρχὰς κακῶν· καὶ οὐκ ἐνθάδε
μὲν ταῦτα λέγω, πρὸς δὲ τὸν δῆμον ἀποκρύψομαι,
ἀλλὰ κἀκεῖ παρρησίᾳ δικαίᾳ χρήσομαι, διδάσκων
ὡς οὐδὲν αὐτοῖς ἐπικρέμαται δεινὸν ὅτι μὴ κακοὶ
καὶ δόλιοι προστάται πολεμίων ἔργα ἐν προσποιή-
ματι φίλων διαπραττόμενοι."
7 Ταῦτ' εἰπόντος τοῦ ὑπάτου κραυγή τε καὶ πολὺς
ἔπαινος ἐκ τῶν παρόντων ἐγένετο,[7] καὶ οὐδὲ λόγου

---

[1] Hertlein, Cobet : ἀρπαζόμενον O.
[2] Kiessling : ἀθρόως O.   [3] Cobet : ἕλκουσιν O.
[4] συντεμῶ Steph. : συντέμω AB.
[5] Kiessling : παραινῶ O.

which these men have been secretly cherishing. For the facts themselves cry aloud. But you senators are to blame for this, since you made the first concessions to them and armed their senseless magistracy with great power when you permitted Caeso Quintius to be tried by them last year on false charges and permitted so great a defender of the aristocracy to be destroyed by them. For this reason they no longer show any moderation nor do they lop off the men of birth one by one, but are already rounding up the good men *en masse* and expelling them from the city. And, in addition to all the other evils, they demand that no one of you even speak in opposition to them, but by exposing him to suspicions and accusations as an accomplice in those secret plots they try to terrify him and promptly call him an enemy of the populace and cite him to appear before their assembly to stand trial for what he has said here. But another occasion will be more suitable for discussing this matter. For the present I will curtail my remarks and will cease running on at greater length, merely advising you to guard against these men as disturbers of the commonwealth and as publishing [1] the germs of great evils. And not here alone do I say these things, while intending to conceal them from the populace ; on the contrary, I shall there also employ a frankness that is merited, showing them that no mischief hangs over their heads unless it be wicked and deceitful leaders who under the guise of friendship are doing the deeds of enemies.''

When the consul had thus spoken, there was shouting and much applause by all present ; and without

[1] Or, following Kiessling's emendation, '' introducing.''

⁶ εἰσφέροντας Kiessling.   ⁷ ἐγίνετο ABb.

τοῖς δημάρχοις ἔτι μεταδόντες διέλυσαν τὸν σύλ-
λογον. ἔπειθ' ὁ μὲν Οὐεργίνιος ἐκκλησίαν συναγαγὼν κατηγόρει τῆς τε βουλῆς καὶ τῶν ὑπάτων,
ὁ δὲ Κλαύδιος ἀπελογεῖτο τοὺς αὐτοὺς λόγους
διεξιὼν οὓς εἶπεν ἐπὶ τῆς βουλῆς. οἱ μὲν οὖν
ἐπιεικέστεροι τῶν δημοτικῶν κενὸν ὑπώπτευον
εἶναι τὸν φόβον, οἱ δ' εὐηθέστεροι πιστεύοντες ταῖς
φήμαις ἀληθῆ· ὅσοι δὲ κακοήθεις ἦσαν ἐν αὐτοῖς
καὶ μεταβολῆς ἀεὶ δεόμενοι, τοῦ μὲν ἐξετάζειν
τἀληθὲς ἢ τὸ ψεῦδος[1] οὐκ εἶχον πρόνοιαν, ἀφορμὴν
δὲ διχοστασίας ἐζήτουν καὶ θορύβου.

XIV. Ἐν τοιαύτῃ δὲ ταραχῇ τῆς πόλεως οὔσης
ἀνήρ τις ἐκ τοῦ Σαβίνων ἔθνους πατέρων τε οὐκ
ἀφανῶν καὶ χρήμασι δυνατός, Ἄππιος Ἑρδώνιος
ὄνομα, καταλῦσαι τὴν Ῥωμαίων ἡγεμονίαν ἐπεβά-
λετο εἴθ' ἑαυτῷ τυραννίδα κατασκευαζόμενος εἴτε
τῷ Σαβίνων ἔθνει πράττων ἀρχὴν καὶ κράτος εἴτ'
ὀνόματος ἀξιωθῆναι βουλόμενος μεγάλου. κοινωσάμενος δὲ πολλοῖς τῶν φίλων ἣν εἶχε διάνοιαν καὶ
τὸν τρόπον τῆς ἐπιχειρήσεως ἀφηγησάμενος, ἐπειδὴ
κἀκείνοις ἐδόκει, συνήθροιζε τοὺς πελάτας καὶ τῶν
θεραπόντων οὓς εἶχε τοὺς[2] εὐτολμοτάτους· καὶ δι'
ὀλίγου χρόνου συγκροτήσας δύναμιν ἀνδρῶν τε-
τρακισχιλίων μάλιστα, ὅπλα τε καὶ τροφὰς καὶ
τἆλλα ὅσων δεῖ πολέμῳ πάντα εὐτρεπισάμενος, εἰς
2 σκάφας ποταμηγοὺς ἐνεβάλετο. πλεύσας δὲ διὰ
τοῦ Τεβέριος ποταμοῦ προσέσχε τῆς Ῥώμης κατὰ
τοῦτο τὸ χωρίον ἔνθα τὸ Καπιτώλιόν ἐστιν οὐδ'
ὅλον στάδιον ἀπέχον τοῦ ποταμοῦ. ἦσαν δὲ μέσαι
τηνικαῦτα νύκτες, καὶ πολλὴ καθ' ὅλην τὴν πόλιν

---

[1] ἢ τὸ ψεῦδος Cary : ἢ ψεῦδος O, Jacoby, om. Cobet.
[2] τοὺς Reiske : om. O, Jacoby.

even permitting the tribunes to reply, they dismissed the session. Then Verginius, calling an assembly of the populace, inveighed against both the senate and the consuls, and Claudius defended them, repeating the same things he had said in the senate. The more fair-minded among the plebeians suspected that their fear was unwarranted, while the more simple-minded, giving credence to the reports, thought it real; but all among them who were ill-disposed and were forever craving a change did not have the foresight to examine into the truth or falsehood of the reports, but sought an occasion for sedition and tumult.

XIV. While the city was in such turmoil,[1] a man of the Sabine race, of no obscure birth and powerful because of his wealth, Appius Herdonius by name, attempted to overthrow the supremacy of the Romans, with a view either of making himself tyrant or of winning dominion and power for the Sabine nation or else of gaining a great name for himself. Having revealed his purpose to many of his friends and explained to them his plan for executing it, and having received their approval, he assembled his clients and the most daring of his servants and in a short time got together a force of about four thousand men. Then, after supplying them with arms, provisions and everything else that is needed for war, he embarked them on river-boats and, sailing down the river Tiber, landed at that part of Rome where the Capitol stands, not a full stade distant from the river. It was then midnight and there was profound quiet throughout

---

[1] For chaps. 14-16 *cf.* Livy iii. 15, 5–18, 11.

DIONYSIUS OF HALICARNASSUS

ἡσυχία, ἣν συνεργὸν λαβὼν ἐξεβίβασε τοὺς ἄνδρας
κατὰ σπουδὴν καὶ διὰ τῶν ἀκλείστων πυλῶν (εἰσὶ
γάρ τινες ἱεραὶ πύλαι τοῦ Καπιτωλίου κατά τι
θέσφατον ἀνειμέναι, Καρμεντίδας[1] αὐτὰς καλοῦσιν)
ἀναβιβάσας τὴν δύναμιν εἷλε[2] τὸ φρούριον. ἐκεῖθεν
δ᾽ ἐπὶ τὴν ἄκραν ὠσάμενος—ἔστι δὲ τῷ Καπιτωλίῳ
3 προσεχής—κἀκείνης ἐγεγόνει κύριος. ἦν δὲ αὐτοῦ
γνώμη μετὰ τὸ κρατῆσαι τῶν ἐπικαιροτάτων τόπων τούς τε φυγάδας εἰσδέχεσθαι καὶ τοὺς δούλους
εἰς ἐλευθερίαν καλεῖν καὶ χρεῶν ἄφεσιν ὑπισχνεῖσθαι τοῖς ἀπόροις τούς τε ἄλλους πολίτας, οἳ τα-
πεινὰ πράττοντες διὰ φθόνου καὶ μίσους εἶχον τὰς
ὑπεροχὰς καὶ μεταβολῆς ἄσμενοι ἂν ἐλάβοντο,
κοινωνοὺς ποιεῖσθαι τῶν ὠφελειῶν. ἡ δὲ θαρρεῖν
τε αὐτὸν ἐπαγομένη καὶ πλανῶσα ἐλπίς, ὡς οὐθενὸς
ἀτυχήσοντα τῶν προσδοκωμένων, ἡ πολιτικὴ στάσις ἦν, δι᾽ ἣν οὔτε φιλίαν οὔτε κοινωνίαν οὐδεμίαν[3]
ὑπελάμβανε τῷ δήμῳ πρὸς τοὺς πατρικίους ἔτι
4 γενήσεσθαι. ἐὰν δὲ ἄρα μηθὲν αὐτῷ τούτων κατὰ
νοῦν χωρῇ, τηνικαῦτα Σαβίνους τε πανστρατιᾷ
καλεῖν ἐδέδοκτο καὶ Οὐολούσκους καὶ τῶν ἄλλων
πλησιοχώρων ὅσοις ἂν ᾖ βουλομένοις ἀπηλλάχθαι
τῆς Ῥωμαίων ἐπιφθόνου ἀρχῆς.

XV. Συνέβη δὲ αὐτῷ πάντων διαμαρτεῖν ὧν
ἤλπισεν οὔτε δούλων αὐτομολησάντων πρὸς αὐτὸν
οὔτε φυγάδων κατελθόντων οὔτε ἀτίμων καὶ κατα-
χρέων τὸ ἴδιον κέρδος ἀντὶ τοῦ κοινῇ συμφέροντος
ἀλλαξαμένων, τῆς τε ἔξωθεν ἐπικουρίας οὐ λαβούσης χρόνον ἱκανὸν εἰς παρασκευὴν τοῦ πολέμου·

---

[1] Kiessling (cf. Plut. Cam. 25, 2) : καρμεντίνας O.
[2] Kiessling : εἶχε O, Jacoby.
[3] οὐδεμίαν om. B.

the entire city ; with this to help him he disembarked
his men in haste, and passing through the gate which
was open (for there is a certain sacred gate of
the Capitol, called the porta Carmentalis, which by
the direction of some oracle is always left open), he
ascended the hill with his troops and captured the
fortress. From there he pushed on to the citadel,
which adjoins the Capitol, and took possession of that
also. It was his intention, after seizing the most
advantageous positions, to receive the exiles, to
summon the slaves to liberty, to promise the needy
an abolition of debts, and to share the spoils with any
other citizens who, being themselves of low condition, envied and hated those of lofty station and
would have welcomed a change. The hope that
both inspired him with confidence and deceived him,
by leading him to believe that he should fail of none
of his expectations, was based on the civil dissension,
because of which he imagined that neither any friendship nor any intercourse would any longer exist
between the populace and the patricians. And if
none of these expectations should turn out according
to his wish, he had resolved in that event to call in
not only the Sabines with all their forces, but also the
Volscians and as many from the other neighbouring
peoples as desired to be delivered from the hated
domination of the Romans.

XV. It so happened, however, that all his hopes
were disappointed ; for neither the slaves deserted to
him nor did the exiles return nor did the unenfran-
chised and the debtors seek their private advantage
at the expense of the public good, and the reinforcements from outside did not have time enough to pre-

τρισὶ γὰρ ἢ τέτταρσι ταῖς πάσαις[1] ἡμέραις τέλος
εἰλήφει τὰ πράγματα μέγα δέος καὶ πολλὴν ταρα-
2 χὴν Ῥωμαίοις παρασχόντα. ἐπεὶ γὰρ ἑάλω τὰ
φρούρια, κραυγῆς ἄφνω γενομένης καὶ φυγῆς τῶν
περὶ ἐκείνους οἰκούντων τοὺς τόπους ὅσοι μὴ
παραχρῆμα ἐσφάγησαν, ἀγνοοῦντες οἱ πολλοὶ τὸ
δεινὸν ὅ τι ποτ᾽ ἦν, ἁρπάσαντες τὰ ὅπλα συνέτρε-
χον, οἱ μὲν ἐπὶ τὰ μετέωρα χωρία τῆς πόλεως, οἱ
δ᾽ εἰς τοὺς ἀναπεπταμένους αὐτῆς τόπους πολλοὺς
σφόδρα ὄντας, οἱ δ᾽ εἰς τὰ παρακείμενα πεδία·
ὅσοι δ᾽ ἡλικίας ἐν τῷ παρηκμακότι ἦσαν καὶ ῥώμης σώματος ἐν τῷ ἀδυνάτῳ τὰ τέγη τῶν οἰκιῶν
κατεῖχον ἅμα γυναιξὶν ὡς ἀπὸ τούτων ἀγωνιού-
μενοι πρὸς τοὺς εἰσεληλυθότας· ἅπαντα γὰρ αὐτοῖς
3 ἐδόκει μεστὰ εἶναι πολέμου. ἡμέρας δὲ γενομένης
ὡς ἐγνώσθη τὰ κεκρατημένα τῆς πόλεως φρούρια
καὶ ὅστις ἦν ὁ κατέχων ἀνὴρ τοὺς τόπους, οἱ μὲν
ὕπατοι προελθόντες εἰς τὴν ἀγορὰν ἐκάλουν τοὺς
πολίτας ἐπὶ τὰ ὅπλα, οἱ δὲ δήμαρχοι προσκαλεσά-
μενοι τὸν δῆμον εἰς ἐκκλησίαν ἔλεγον ὅτι τῷ μὲν
συμφέροντι τῆς πόλεως οὐδὲν ἀξιοῦσι πράττειν ἐναντίον, δίκαιον δὲ ὑπολαμβάνουσιν εἶναι τηλικοῦ-
τον ἀγῶνα μέλλοντα τὸν δῆμον ὑπομένειν ἐπὶ ῥητοῖς
τισι καὶ διωρισμένοις ἐπὶ τὸ κινδύνευμα χωρεῖν.
4 " Εἰ μὲν οὖν," ἔφασαν λέγοντες, " ὑπισχνοῦνταί
τε ὑμῖν οἱ πατρίκιοι καὶ πίστεις βούλονται δοῦναι
τὰς ἐπὶ θεῶν ὅτι καταλυθέντος τοῦδε τοῦ πολέμου
συγχωρήσουσιν ὑμῖν ἀποδεῖξαι νομοθέτας καὶ τὸν
λοιπὸν χρόνον ἐν ἰσηγορίᾳ πολιτεύεσθαι, συνελευ-
θερῶμεν αὐτοῖς τὴν πατρίδα· εἰ δὲ οὐθὲν ἀξιοῦσι
ποιεῖν τῶν μετρίων, τί κινδυνεύομεν καὶ τὰς ψυχὰς
ὑπὲρ αὐτῶν προϊέμεθα μηθενὸς ἀγαθοῦ μέλλοντες

pare for war, since within three or four days all told
the affair was at an end, after causing the Romans
great fear and turmoil. For upon the capture of the
fortresses, followed by a sudden outcry and flight of all
those living near those places—save those who were
slain at once—the mass of the citizens, not know-
ing what the peril was, seized their arms and rushed
together, some hastening to the heights of the city,
others to the open places, which were very numerous,
and still others to the plains near by. Those who
were past the prime of life and were incapacitated in
bodily strength occupied the roofs of the houses
together with the women, thinking to fight from
there against the invaders ; for they imagined that
every part of the city was full of fighting. But when
it was day and it came to be known what fortresses
of the city were taken and who the person was who
had possession of them, the consuls, going into the
Forum, called the citizens to arms. The tribunes,
however, summoned the populace to an assembly and
declared that, while they did not care to do anything
opposed to the advantage of the commonwealth, they
thought it just, when the populace were going to
undertake so great a struggle, that they should go to
meet the danger upon fixed and definite terms. " If,
therefore," they went on to say, " the patricians will
promise you, and are willing to give pledges, confirmed by oaths, that as soon as this war is over they
will allow you to appoint lawgivers and for the future
to enjoy equal rights in the government, let us assist
them in freeing the fatherland. But if they consent
to no reasonable conditions, why do we incur danger
and give up our lives for them, when we are to reap

---

[1] πάσαις Naber : πρώταις O, Jacoby.

5 ἀπολαύσεσθαι;" ταῦτα λεγόντων αὐτῶν καὶ τοῦ
δήμου πειθομένου καὶ μηδὲ φωνὴν ὑπομένοντος
ἀκούειν τῶν ἄλλο τι παραινούντων ὁ μὲν Κλαύδιος
οὐθὲν ἠξίου δεῖσθαι τοιαύτης[1] συμμαχίας, ἥτις οὐχ
ἑκούσιος ἀλλ' ἐπὶ μισθῷ καὶ οὐδὲ τούτῳ μετρίῳ
βοηθεῖν βούλεται τῇ πατρίδι, ἀλλ' αὐτοὺς ἔφη τοὺς
πατρικίους ἑαυτῶν σώμασι καὶ τῶν συνόντων αὐτοῖς πελατῶν ὁπλισαμένους, καὶ εἴ τι ἄλλο πλῆθος
ἐθελούσιον αὐτοῖς συναρεῖται[2] τοῦ πολέμου, μετὰ
τούτων πολιορκεῖν τὰ φρούρια· ἐὰν δὲ μηδ' οὕτως
ἀξιόχρεως ἡ δύναμις αὐτοῖς εἶναι δοκῇ, Λατίνους
τε καὶ Ἕρνικας παρακαλεῖν, ἐὰν δ' ἀνάγκη, καὶ
δούλοις ἐλευθερίαν ὑπισχνεῖσθαι καὶ πάντας μᾶλλον
ἢ τοὺς ἐπὶ τοιούτων καιρῶν μνησικακοῦντας σφίσι
6 παρακαλεῖν. ὁ δ' ἕτερος τῶν ὑπάτων Οὐαλέριος
ἀντέλεγε πρὸς ταῦτα οὐκ οἰόμενος δεῖν ἠρεθισμένον
τὸ δημοτικὸν ἐκπολεμῶσαι τελέως τοῖς πατρικίοις,
εἶξαί τε συνεβούλευε τῷ καιρῷ καὶ πρὸς μὲν τοὺς
ἔξωθεν πολεμίους[3] τά γε δίκαια ἀντιτάττειν, πρὸς
δὲ τὰς πολιτικὰς διατριβὰς[4] τὰ μέτρια καὶ εὐγνώ-
7 μονα. ἐπειδὴ δὲ τοῖς πλείοσι τῶν ἐν τῷ συνεδρίῳ
τὰ κράτιστα ἐδόκει λέγειν, προελθὼν[5] εἰς τὴν ἐκκλησίαν καὶ λόγον εὐπρεπῆ διεξελθὼν τελευτῶν
τῆς δημηγορίας ὤμοσεν, ἐὰν ὁ δῆμος συνάρηται
μετὰ προθυμίας τοῦ πολέμου καὶ καταστῇ τὰ πράγματα τῆς πόλεως, συγχωρήσειν τοῖς δημάρχοις
προθεῖναι[6] τῷ πλήθει τὴν περὶ τοῦ νόμου διάγνωσιν

---

[1] τοιαύτης B : τῆς τοιαύτης R.
[2] συναρεῖται Ba (?) : συνάρηται ABb.
[3] πολέμους Kiessling.
[4] διαφορὰς or παρατριβὰς Reiske, ἔριδας Cobet.
[5] προελθὼν B : παρελθὼν R.
[6] προθεῖναι Ba : προσθεῖναι R.

214

no advantage ? '' While they were speaking thus and
the people were persuaded and would not listen to
even a word from those who offered any other advice,
Claudius declared that he had no use for such allies,
who were not willing to come to the aid of the fatherland voluntarily, but only for a reward, and that no
moderate one ; but the patricians by themselves, he
said, taking up arms in their own persons and in the
persons of the clients who adhered to them, joined
also by any of the plebeians who would voluntarily
assist them in the war, must with these besiege the
fortresses. And if even so their force should seem to
them inadequate, they must call on the Latins and
the Hernicans, and, if necessary, must promise liberty
to the slaves and invite all sorts of people rather than
those who harboured a grudge against them in times
like these. But the other consul, Valerius, opposed
this, believing that they ought not to render the
plebeians, who were already exasperated, absolutely
implacable against the patricians ; and he advised
them to yield to the situation, and while arraying
against their foreign foes the demands of strict justice,
to combat the long-winded discourses of their fellow
citizens with terms of moderation and reasonableness.
When the majority of the senators decided that his
advice was the best, he appeared before the popular
assembly and made a decorous speech, at the end
of which he swore that if the people would assist in
this war with alacrity and conditions in the city
should become settled, he would permit the tribunes
to lay before the populace for decision the law which
they were trying to introduce concerning an equality

ὃν εἰσέφερον ὑπὲρ τῆς ἰσονομίας, καὶ σπουδάσειν
ὅπως ἐπὶ τῆς ἑαυτοῦ ἀρχῆς ἐπὶ τέλος ἀχθῇ τὰ
δόξαντα τῷ δήμῳ. ἦν δὲ ἄρα οὐθὲν αὐτῷ πε-
πρωμένον ἐπιτελέσαι τῶν ὁμολογηθέντων πλησίον
οὔσης τῆς τοῦ θανάτου μοίρας.

XVI. Λυθείσης δὲ τῆς ἐκκλησίας περὶ δείλην
ὀψίαν συνέρρεον ἐπὶ τοὺς ἀποδειχθέντας ἕκαστοι
τόπους, ἀπογραφόμενοί τε πρὸς τοὺς ἡγεμόνας τὰ
ὀνόματα καὶ τὸν στρατιωτικὸν ὀμνύντες ὅρκον.
ἐκείνην μὲν οὖν τὴν ἡμέραν καὶ τὴν ἐπιοῦσαν νύκτα
ὅλην ἀμφὶ ταῦτα ἦσαν, τῇ δ' ἑξῆς ἡμέρᾳ λοχαγοί
τε προσενέμοντο ὑπὸ τῶν ὑπάτων καὶ ἐπὶ[1] τὰς
ἱερὰς ἐτάττοντο σημείας, συνεπιρρέοντος καὶ τοῦ
2 κατ' ἀγροὺς διατρίβοντος ὄχλου. γενομένων δὲ διὰ
τάχους ἁπάντων[2] εὐτρεπῶν μερισάμενοι τὰς δυνάμεις οἱ ὕπατοι κλήρῳ διείλοντο τὰς ἀρχάς. Κλαυδίῳ μὲν οὖν ὁ κλῆρος ἀπέδωκε τὰ πρὸ τῶν τειχῶν
διὰ φυλακῆς ἔχειν, μή τις ἔξωθεν ἐπέλθῃ στρατιὰ
τοῖς ἔνδον ἐπίκουρος· ὑποψία γὰρ ἅπαντας κατεῖχε
μεγάλης σφόδρα κινήσεως, καὶ τὸ ἀντίπαλον ἅπαν
ὡς ὁμοῦ συνεπιθησόμενον σφίσιν ἐφοβοῦντο· Οὐαλερίῳ δὲ τὰ φρούρια πολιορκεῖν ὁ δαίμων ἐφῆκεν.
3 ἐτάχθησαν δὲ καὶ ἐπὶ τοῖς ἄλλοις ἐρύμασιν ἡγεμόνες ὅσα τῆς πόλεως ἐντὸς ἦν καθέξοντες, καὶ
κατὰ τὰς ἐπὶ τὸ Καπιτώλιον ἀγούσας ὁδοὺς ἕτεροι
κωλύσεως ἕνεκεν τῶν ἀποστησομένων πρὸς τοὺς
πολεμίους δούλων τε καὶ ἀπόρων, ὅ γε[3] παντὸς
μάλιστα ἐφοβοῦντο. ἐπικουρικὸν δὲ αὐτοῖς οὐδὲν
ἔφθασε παρὰ τῶν συμμάχων ἀφικόμενον ὅτι μὴ
παρὰ Τυσκλανῶν μόνον ἐν μιᾷ νυκτὶ ἀκουσάντων
τε καὶ παρασκευασαμένων, οὓς ἦγε Λεύκιος Μαμί-

---

[1] ὑπὸ Sylburg. [2] Kiessling : πάντων O, Jacoby.

of laws, and would use his utmost endeavours that their vote should be carried into effect during his consulship. But it was fated, it seems, that he should perform none of these promises, the doom of death being near at hand for him.

XVI. After the assembly had been dismissed in the late afternoon, they all flocked to their appointed places, giving in their names to the generals and taking the military oath. During that day, then, and all the following night they were thus employed. The next day the centurions were assigned by the consuls to their commands and to the sacred standards; and the crowd which lived in the country also in great numbers flocked in. Everything being soon made ready, the consuls divided the forces and drew lots for their commands. It fell to the lot of Claudius to keep guard before the walls, lest some army from outside should come to the relief of the enemy in the city; for everybody suspected that there would be a very serious turmoil, and they feared that all their foes would fall upon them at the same time with united forces. To Valerius Fortune assigned the siege of the fortresses. Commanders were appointed to occupy the other strong places also that lay within the city, and others were posted in the streets leading to the Capitol, to prevent the slaves and the poor from going over to the enemy—the thing of which they were most afraid. No assistance reached them in time from any of their allies save only from the Tusculans,[1] who, the same night they heard of the invasion, had made ready to march, their com-

---

[1] For the part played by the Tusculans cf. Livy iii. 18, 1-7, 10.

---

[3] ὅ γε Capps, ὁ Gelenius : οὓς O, Jacoby.

λιος, ἀνὴρ δραστήριος, ἔχων τὴν μεγίστην ἐν τῇ
πόλει τότε ἀρχήν· καὶ συνεκινδύνευον οὗτοι τῷ
Οὐαλερίῳ μόνοι καὶ συνεξεῖλον τὰ φρούρια πᾶσαν
4 εὔνοιαν καὶ προθυμίαν ἀποδειξάμενοι. ἐγένετο[1] δ’
ἡ προσβολὴ τοῖς φρουρίοις πανταχόθεν· οἱ μὲν γὰρ
ἀπὸ τῶν πλησίον οἰκιῶν ἀσφάλτου καὶ πίσσης
πεπυρωμένης ἀγγεῖα σφενδόναις ἐναρμόττοντες
ἐπέβαλλον ὑπὲρ τῶν λόφων[2]· οἱ δὲ συμφοροῦντες[3]
αὔων[4] φακέλλους φρυγάνων καὶ παρὰ τοῖς ἀποτόμοις τῆς πέτρας θωμοὺς[5] ἐγείροντες ὑψηλοὺς
ὑφῆπτον ἀνέμῳ παραδιδόντες τὰς φλόγας ἐπιφόρῳ.
ὅσοι δ’ ἦσαν ἀνδρειότατοι, πυκνώσαντες τοὺς λόχους ἐχώρουν ἄνω κατὰ τὰς χειροποιήτους ὁδούς.
5 ἦν δ’ αὐτοῖς οὔτε τοῦ πλήθους, ᾧ παρὰ πολὺ τῶν
ἀντιπάλων προεῖχον, ὄφελος οὐθὲν διὰ στενῆς
ἀνιοῦσιν ὁδοῦ καὶ πληθούσης προβόλων ἄνωθεν
ἐπικαταραττομένων, ἔνθα συνεξισωθήσεσθαι ἔμελλε
τῷ πολλῷ τὸ ὀλίγον· οὔτε τῆς παρὰ τὰ δεινὰ ὑπο-
μονῆς, ἣν πολλοῖς κατασκήσαντες[6] πολέμοις εἶχον,
οὐδεμία ὄνησις πρὸς ὀρθίους βιαζομένοις σκοπάς.
οὐ γὰρ συστάδην μαχομένους ἔδει τὸ εὔτολμον καὶ
καρτερικὸν ἀποδείξασθαι, ἀλλ’ ἐκηβόλοις χρῆσθαι
6 μάχαις. ἦσαν δὲ τῶν μὲν κάτωθεν ἐπὶ τὰ μετέωρα βαλλομένων βραδεῖαί τε καὶ ἀσθενεῖς, εἰ καὶ
τύχοιεν, ὥσπερ εἰκός, αἱ πληγαί· τῶν δ’ ἀφ’
ὕψους κάτω ῥιπτουμένων ὀξεῖαι καὶ καρτεραὶ συν-

---

[1] ἐγένετο A : ἐγίνετο B.
[2] ὑπὲρ τῶν λόφων B : ὑπὲρ τὸν λόφον R (?), Jacoby, ἐπὶ τὸν
λόφον Reiske.　　[3] συμφοροῦντες A : συμφέροντες B.
[4] αὔων Kiessling : αὐτῶν A, om. B.
[5] θωμοὺς Capps : βωμοὺς O, Jacoby.

mander being Lucius Mamilius, a man of action, who
held the chief magistracy in their city at that time.
These alone shared the danger with Valerius and
aided him in capturing the fortresses, displaying all
goodwill and alacrity. The fortresses were attacked
from all sides ; some of the attackers, fitting vessels
of bitumen and burning pitch to their slings, hurled
them over the hills from the roofs of neighbouring
houses, and others, gathering bundles of dry faggots,
raised lofty heaps of them against the steep parts of
the cliff and set them on fire when they could commit
the flames to a favourable wind. All the bravest of the
troops, closing their ranks, went up by the roads that
had been built to the summits. But neither their
numbers, in which they were greatly superior to the
enemy, were of any service to them when they were
ascending by a narrow road, full of broken fragments
of rock that came crashing down upon them from
above, where a small body of men would be a match
for a large one ; nor was their constancy in dangers,
which they had acquired by their training in many
wars, of any advantage to them when forcing their
way up steep heights. For it was not a situation that
called for the display of the daring and perseverance
of hand-to-hand fighting, but rather for the tactics of
fighting with missiles. Moreover, the blows made by
missiles shot from below up to lofty targets were
slow on arrival and ineffective, naturally, even if they
hit their mark, while the blows of missiles hurled
down from above came with high speed and violence,
the very weight of the weapons contributing to the

---

[6] κατασκήσαντες Post, ἀσκήσαντες Kiessling : καταστήσαντες
O, Jacoby.

ἐργούντων τοῖς βλήμασι καὶ τῶν ἰδίων βαρῶν.[1]
οὐ μὴν ἔκαμνόν γε οἱ προσβάλλοντες τοῖς ἐρύμασιν, ἀλλὰ διεκαρτέρουν ἀναγκοφαγοῦντες[2] τὰ δεινὰ
οὔτε ἡμέρας οὔτε νυκτὸς ἀναπαυόμενοι τῶν πόνων.
τέλος δ᾽ οὖν ὑπολιπόντων τοὺς πολιορκουμένους τῶν
βελῶν καὶ τῶν σωμάτων ἐξαδυνατούντων τρίτῃ
7 τὰ φρούρια ἐξεπολιόρκησαν ἡμέρᾳ. ἐν ταύτῃ τῇ
μάχῃ πολλοὺς Ῥωμαῖοι καὶ ἀγαθοὺς ἄνδρας ἀπέβαλον, κράτιστον δέ, ὥσπερ πρὸς ἁπάντων ὡμο-
λόγητο,[3] τὸν ὕπατον· ὃς οὐκ ὀλίγα τραύματα λαβὼν
οὐδ᾽ ὡς ἀφίστατο τῶν δεινῶν ἕως ἐπικαταραγεὶς[4]
αὐτῷ πέτρος ὑπερμεγέθης ἐπιβαίνοντι τοῦ περι-
τειχίσματος ἅμα τήν τε νίκην αὐτὸν ἀφείλετο καὶ
τὴν ψυχήν. ἁλισκομένων δὲ τῶν φρουρίων ὁ μὲν
Ἐρδώνιος, ἦν γὰρ καὶ ῥώμῃ σώματος διάφορος
καὶ κατὰ χεῖρα γενναῖος, ἄπιστόν τι χρῆμα περὶ
αὐτὸν ποιήσας νεκρῶν ὑπὸ πλήθους βελῶν ἀποθνήσκει, τῶν δὲ σὺν αὐτῷ τὰ φρούρια καταλαβο-
μένων ὀλίγοι μέν τινες ζῶντες ἑάλωσαν, οἱ δὲ
πλείους σφάττοντες ἑαυτοὺς ἢ κατὰ τῶν κρημνῶν
ὠθοῦντες διεφθάρησαν.

XVII. Τοῦτο τὸ τέλος λαβόντος τοῦ ληστρικοῦ
πολέμου τὴν πολιτικὴν πάλιν ἀνερρίπιζον[5] οἱ δήμαρχοι στάσιν ἀξιοῦντες ἀπολαβεῖν παρὰ τοῦ περι-
όντος ὑπάτου τὰς ὑποσχέσεις ἃς ἐποιήσατο πρὸς
αὐτοὺς ὁ τεθνηκὼς ἐν τῇ μάχῃ Οὐαλέριος ὑπὲρ τῆς
εἰσφορᾶς τοῦ νόμου. ὁ δὲ Κλαύδιος μέχρι μέν
τινος παρεῖλκε τὸν χρόνον, τοτὲ μὲν καθαρμοὺς τῆς
πόλεως ἐπιτελῶν, τοτὲ δὲ θυσίας τοῖς θεοῖς χα-

---

[1] βαρῶν B : βαρημάτων R.
[2] Cobet : ἀναγκοφοροῦντες O.
[3] ὡμολογεῖτο Naber.

force with which they were thrown. Nevertheless, the men attacking the ramparts were not discouraged, but bravely endured the hard rations of unavoidable dangers, ceasing not from their toils either by day or by night. At last, when the missiles of the besieged gave out and their strength failed them, the Romans reduced the fortresses on the third day. In this action they lost many brave men, among them the consul, who was universally acknowledged to have been the best of them all ; he, even after he had received many wounds, did not retire from danger until a huge rock, crashing down upon him as he was mounting the outer wall, snatched from him at once the victory and his life. As the fortresses were being taken, Herdonius, who was remarkable for his physical strength and brave in action, after piling up an incredible heap of dead bodies about him, perished under a multitude of missiles. Of those who had aided him in seizing the fortresses some few were taken alive, but the greater part either killed themselves with their swords or hurled themselves down the cliffs.

XVII. The war [1] with the brigands being thus ended, the tribunes rekindled the civil strife once more by demanding of the surviving consul the fulfilment of the promises made to them by Valerius, who perished in the fighting, with regard to the introduction of the law. But Claudius for a time kept procrastinating, now by performing lustrations for the city, now by offering sacrifices of thanksgiving to the

---

[1] *Cf.* Livy iii. 19, 1-3.

---

4 Cobet : ἐπικαταρραγεὶς O.
Sylburg : ἀνερίπτουν Ba, ἀνερρίπτουν R.

ριστηρίους ἀποδιδούς, τοτὲ δ' ἀγῶσι καὶ θέαις
2 ἀναλαμβάνων τὸ πλῆθος εἰς εὐπαθείας. ὡς δ' αἱ
σκήψεις αὐτῷ πᾶσαι κατανάλωντο, τελευτῶν ἔφη
δεῖν εἰς τὸν τοῦ τεθνηκότος ὑπάτου τόπον ἕτερον
ἀποδειχθῆναι. τὰ μὲν γὰρ ὑφ' ἑαυτοῦ μόνου πραχθέντα οὔτε νόμιμα οὔτε βέβαια ἔσεσθαι, τὰ δ' ὑπ'
ἀμφοῖν ἔννομά τε καὶ κύρια. ταύτῃ διακρουσάμενος
αὐτοὺς τῇ προφάσει προεῖπεν ἀρχαιρεσίων ἡμέραν
ἐν ᾗ τὸν συνάρχοντα ἔμελλεν ἀποδείξειν. ἐν δὲ
τῷ μεταξὺ χρόνῳ δι' ἀπορρήτων βουλευμάτων οἱ
προεστηκότες τοῦ συνεδρίου συνέθεντο κατὰ σφᾶς
3 αὐτοὺς ὅτῳ παραδώσουσι τὴν ἀρχήν. καὶ ἐπειδὴ[1] ὁ τῶν ἀρχαιρεσίων ἐνέστη χρόνος καὶ ὁ κῆρυξ
τὴν πρώτην τάξιν ἐκάλεσεν, εἰσελθόντες εἰς τὸν
ἀποδειχθέντα τόπον οἵ τ' ὀκτωκαίδεκα λόχοι τῶν
ἱππέων καὶ οἱ τῶν πεζῶν ὀγδοήκοντα τῶν τὸ μέγιστον τίμημα ἐχόντων Λεύκιον Κοΐντιον Κικιν-
νᾶτον ἀποδεικνύουσιν ὕπατον, οὗ τὸν υἱὸν Καίσωνα
Κοΐντιον εἰς ἀγῶνα θανάτου καταστήσαντες οἱ
δήμαρχοι τὴν πόλιν ἠνάγκασαν ἐκλιπεῖν· καὶ οὐδεμιᾶς ἔτι κληθείσης ἐπὶ τὴν ψηφοφορίαν τάξεως
(τρισὶ γὰρ ἦσαν λόχοις πλείους οἱ διενέγκαντες τὴν
ψῆφον λόχοι τῶν ὑπολειπομένων[2]) ὁ μὲν δῆμος
ἀπῄει συμφορὰν βαρεῖαν ἡγούμενος ὅτι μισῶν αὐτοὺς ἀνὴρ ἐξουσίας ὑπατικῆς ἔσται κύριος, ἡ βουλὴ
δὲ ἔπεμπε τοὺς παραληψομένους τὸν ὕπατον[3] καὶ
4 ἄξοντας ἐπὶ τὴν ἀρχήν. ἔτυχε δὲ τηνικαῦτα ὁ Κοΐντιος ἄρουράν τινα ὑπεργαζόμενος εἰς σπόραν, αὐτὸς
ἀκολουθῶν τοῖς σχίζουσι τὴν νειὸν βοιδίοις ἀχίτων,

---

[1] καὶ ἐπειδὴ B : ἐπειδὴ δὲ R.
[2] Kiessling : ἀπολειπομένων O.
[3] ὕπατον O : ἄνδρα Kiessling.

gods, and again by entertaining the multitude with
games and shows. When all his excuses had been
exhausted, he finally declared that another consul
must be chosen in place of the deceased ; for he said
that the acts performed by him alone would be neither
legal nor lasting, whereas those performed by two
of them would be legitimate and valid. Having put
them off with this pretence, he appointed a day for
the election, when he would nominate his colleague.
In the meantime the leading men of the senate, consulting together in private, agreed among themselves
upon the person to whom they would entrust the
magistracy. And when the day appointed for the
election had come and the herald had called the first
class, the eighteen centuries of knights together
with the eighty centuries of foot, consisting of the
wealthiest citizens, entering the appointed place,
chose as consul Lucius Quintius Cincinnatus, whose
son Caeso Quintius the tribunes had brought to trial
for his life and compelled to leave the city. And no
other class being called to vote—for the centuries
which had voted were three more in number than the
remaining centuries—the populace departed, regarding it as a grievous misfortune that a man who hated
them was to be possessed of the consular power.
Meanwhile the senate sent men to invite the consul
and to conduct him to the city to assume his magistracy. It chanced that Quintius was just then
ploughing a piece of land for sowing,[1] he himself
following the gaunt oxen that were breaking up the
fallow ; he had no tunic on, wore a small loin-cloth

[1] Compare Livy's description (iii. 26, 8 ff.) of Cincinnatus'
humble activities at the time of his appointment to the dic-
tatorship ; see also *inf.* chaps. 23, 5–24, 2.

περιζωμάτιον ἔχων καὶ ἐπὶ τῇ κεφαλῇ πῖλον. ἰδὼν
δὲ πλῆθος ἀνθρώπων εἰς τὸ χωρίον εἰσιόντων τό
τε ἄροτρον ἐπέσχε καὶ πολὺν ἠπόρει χρόνον οἵτινές τε[1] εἶεν καὶ τίνος δεόμενοι πρὸς αὐτὸν ἥκοιεν·
ἔπειτα προσδραμόντος τινὸς καὶ κελεύσαντος κοσμι-
ώτερον ἑαυτὸν ποιῆσαι παρελθὼν εἰς τὴν καλύβην
5 καὶ ἀμφιεσάμενος προῆλθεν. οἱ δ' ἐπὶ τὴν παρά-
ληψιν αὐτοῦ παρόντες ἠσπάσαντό τε ἅπαντες οὐκ
ἐκ τοῦ ὀνόματος, ἀλλ' ὕπατον, καὶ τὴν περιπόρφυ-
ρον ἐσθῆτα περιέθεσαν τούς τε πελέκεις καὶ τἆλλα
παράσημα τῆς ἀρχῆς παραστήσαντες ἀκολουθεῖν
εἰς τὴν πόλιν ἠξίουν. κἀκεῖνος μικρὸν ἐπισχὼν καὶ
δακρύσας[2] τοσοῦτον εἶπεν· " Ἄσπορον ἄρα μοι τὸ
χωρίον ἔσται τοῦτον τὸν ἐνιαυτόν, καὶ κινδυνεύσο-
μεν οὐχ ἕξειν πόθεν διατραφῶμεν." ἔπειτα ἀσπα-
σάμενος τὴν γυναῖκα καὶ τῶν ἔνδον ἐπιμελεῖσθαι
6 παραγγείλας ᾤχετο εἰς τὴν πόλιν. ταῦτα δὲ οὐχ
ἑτέρου τινὸς χάριν εἰπεῖν προήχθην, ἀλλ' ἵνα φανερὸν γένηται πᾶσιν οἷοι τότε ἦσαν οἱ τῆς Ῥωμαίων
πόλεως προεστηκότες, ὡς αὐτουργοὶ καὶ σώφρονες
καὶ πενίαν δικαίαν οὐ βαρυνόμενοι καὶ βασιλικὰς
οὐ διώκοντες ἐξουσίας, ἀλλὰ καὶ διδομένας ἀναινό-
μενοι· φανήσονται γὰρ οὐδὲ κατὰ μικρὸν ἐοικότες
ἐκείνοις οἱ νῦν, ἀλλὰ τἀναντία πάντα ἐπιτηδεύοντες,
πλὴν πάνυ ὀλίγων, δι' οὓς ἕστηκεν ἔτι τὸ τῆς
πόλεως ἀξίωμα καὶ τὸ σώζειν τὴν πρὸς ἐκείνους
τοὺς ἄνδρας ὁμοιότητα. ἀλλὰ περὶ μὲν τούτων
ἅλις.

XVIII. Ὁ δὲ Κοΐντιος παραλαβὼν τὴν ὑπατείαν
πρῶτον μὲν ἔπαυσε τοὺς δημάρχους τῶν καινῶν
πολιτευμάτων καὶ τῆς ἐπὶ τῷ νόμῳ σπουδῆς, προ-

---

[1] τε B : om. R.   [2] Cobet : διαδακρύσας O.

and had a cap upon his head. Upon seeing a crowd of people come into the field he stopped his plough and for a long time was at a loss to know who they were or what they wanted of him ; then, when some one ran up to him and bade him make himself more presentable, he went into the cottage and after putting on his clothes came out to them. Thereupon the men who were sent to escort him all greeted him, not by his name, but as consul ; and clothing him with the purple-bordered robe and placing before him the axes and the other insignia of his magistracy, they asked him to follow them to the city. And he, pausing for a moment and shedding tears, said only this : " So my field will go unsown this year, and we shall be in danger of not having enough to live on." Then he kissed his wife, and charging her to take care of things at home, went to the city. I am led to relate these particulars for no other reason than to let all the world see what kind of men the leaders of Rome were at that time, that they worked with their own hands, led frugal lives, did not chafe under honourable poverty, and, far from aiming at positions of royal power, actually refused them when offered. For it will be seen that the Romans of to-day do not bear the least resemblance to them, but follow the very opposite practices in everything—with the exception of a very few by whom the dignity of the commonwealth is still maintained and a resemblance to those men preserved. But enough on this subject.

XVIII. Quintius,[1] having succeeded to the consulship, caused the tribunes to desist from their new measures and from their insistence upon the proposed

---

[1] For chaps. 18 f. *cf.* Livy iii. 19, 4–21, 8.

εἰπὼν ὡς εἰ μὴ παύσονται ταράττοντες τὴν πόλιν
ἀπάξει Ῥωμαίους ἅπαντας ἐκ τῆς πόλεως στρα-
2 τείαν κατὰ Οὐολούσκων παραγγείλας. ἐπεὶ δὲ
κωλύσειν αὐτὸν ἔλεγον οἱ δήμαρχοι στρατοῦ ποιεῖσθαι καταγραφήν, συναγαγὼν τὸ πλῆθος εἰς
ἐκκλησίαν εἶπεν ὅτι πάντες ὀμωμόκασι τὸν στρατιωτικὸν ὅρκον ἀκολουθήσειν τοῖς ὑπάτοις ἐφ᾽ οὓς
ἂν καλῶνται πολέμους καὶ μήτε ἀπολείψειν τὰ
σημεῖα μήτε ἄλλο πράξειν μηθὲν ἐναντίον τῷ νόμῳ·
παραλαβὼν δὲ τὴν ὑπατικὴν ἐξουσίαν αὐτὸς ἔχειν
3 ἔφη κρατουμένους ἅπαντας τοῖς ὅρκοις. εἰπὼν δὲ
ταῦτα καὶ διομοσάμενος χρήσεσθαι[1] τῷ νόμῳ κατὰ
τῶν ἀπειθούντων ἐκέλευσεν ἐκ τῶν ἱερῶν τὰ σημεῖα
καταφέρειν· " Καὶ ἵνα," ἔφη, " πᾶσαν ἀπογνῶτε
δημαγωγίαν ἐπὶ τῆς ἐμῆς ὑπατείας, οὐ πρότερον
ἀναστήσω τὸν στρατὸν ἐκ τῆς πολεμίας πρὶν ἢ πᾶς
ὁ τῆς ἀρχῆς μοι διέλθῃ χρόνος. ὡς οὖν ἐν ὑπαίθρῳ
χειμάσοντες παρασκευάσασθε τὰ εἰς ἐκεῖνον τὸν
4 καιρὸν ἐπιτήδεια." τούτοις καταπληξάμενος αὐτοὺς τοῖς λόγοις, ἐπειδὴ κοσμιωτέρους εἶδε γεγονότας καὶ δεομένους ἀφεθῆναι τῆς στρατείας, ἐπὶ
τούτοις ἔφη χαριεῖσθαι τὰς ἀναπαύλας τῶν πολέμων, ἐφ᾽ ᾧ τε μηθὲν ἔτι παρακινεῖν αὐτούς, ἀλλ᾽
ἐᾶν αὐτὸν ὡς βούλεται τὴν ἀρχὴν τελεῖσθαι,[2] καὶ
ἐπὶ τῷ τὰ δίκαια διδόναι τε καὶ λαμβάνειν παρ᾽
ἀλλήλων.

XIX. Καταστάντος δὲ τοῦ θορύβου δικαστήριά
τε ἀπεδίδου τοῖς δεομένοις ἐκ πολλῶν παρειλκυσμένα χρόνων, καὶ τὰ πλεῖστα τῶν ἐγκλημάτων
αὐτὸς ἴσως καὶ δικαίως διέκρινε δι᾽ ὅλης[3] ἡμέρας

---

[1] Steph.[2] : χρήσασθαι O.
[2] τελέσαι Reiske.

law by announcing that if they did not cease disturbing the commonwealth he would give notice of an expedition against the Volscians and would lead all the Romans out of the city. When the tribunes said they would not permit him to enrol an army, he called an assembly of the populace and declared that since they had all taken the military oath, swearing that they would follow the consuls in any wars to which they should be called and would neither desert the standards nor do anything else contrary to law, and since he had assumed the consular power, he held them all bound to him by their oaths. Having said this and sworn that he would invoke the law against those who disobeyed, he ordered the standards to be brought out of the temples. " And to the end," he added, " that you may renounce all agitation by demagogues during my consulship, I will not withdraw the army from the enemy's country until my whole term of office has expired. Expect therefore, to pass the winter in the field and prepare everything necessary against that time." Having terrified them with these threats, when he saw that they had become more orderly and begged to be let off from the campaign, he said he would grant them a respite from war upon these conditions, that they create no more disturbances but allow him to administer his office as he wished to the end, and that in their dealings with one another they give as well as receive strict justice.

XIX. The tumult having been appeased, he restored to all plaintiffs recourse to courts of law, a matter for a long time delayed ; and he himself decided most suits, with fairness and justice, sitting

---

³ ὅλης B : ὅλης τῆς R.

ἐπὶ τοῦ βήματος καθεζόμενος, εὐπρόσοδόν τε καὶ
πρᾷον καὶ φιλάνθρωπον τοῖς ἐπὶ τὴν δικαιοδοσίαν
ἀφικνουμένοις ἑαυτὸν παρεῖχε καὶ παρεσκεύασεν
ἀριστοκρατικὴν οὕτως φανῆναι τὴν πολιτείαν ὥστε
μήτε δημάρχων δεηθῆναι τοὺς διὰ πενίαν ἢ δυσγένειαν ἢ ἄλλην τινὰ ταπεινότητα ὑπὸ τῶν κρειττόνων κατισχυομένους μήτε καινῆς νομοθεσίας
πόθον ἔχειν ἔτι τοὺς ἐν ἰσηγορίᾳ πολιτεύεσθαι βουλομένους,¹ ἀλλ' ἀγαπᾶν τε καὶ χαίρειν ἅπαντας ἐπὶ
2 τῇ τότε κατασχούσῃ τὴν πόλιν εὐνομίᾳ. ταῦτά τε
δὴ τὰ ἔργα τοῦ ἀνδρὸς ἐπῃνεῖτο² ὑπὸ τοῦ δήμου,
καὶ ἐπεὶ τὸν ὡρισμένον ἐτέλεσε τῆς ἀρχῆς χρόνον
τὸ μὴ δέξασθαι τὴν ὑπατείαν διδομένην τὸ δεύτερον μηδὲ ἀγαπῆσαι τηλικαύτην λαμβάνοντα τιμήν.
3 κατεῖχε γὰρ αὐτὸν ἐπὶ τῆς ὑπατικῆς ἐξουσίας ἡ
βουλὴ πολλὰς προσφέρουσα δεήσεις, ἐπεὶ τὸ τρίτον
οἱ δήμαρχοι διεπράξαντο μὴ ἀποθέσθαι τὴν ἀρχήν,
ὡς ἐναντιωσόμενον αὐτοῖς καὶ παύσοντα τῶν καινῶν πολιτευμάτων, τὰ μὲν αἰδοῖ, τὰ δὲ φόβῳ, τὸν
δὲ δῆμον ὁρῶσα οὐκ ἀναινόμενον ὑπ' ἀνδρὸς ἀγαθοῦ
ἄρχεσθαι. ὁ δ' οὔτε τῶν δημάρχων ἐπαινεῖν ἔφη
τὸ ἀπαραχώρητον τῆς ἐξουσίας οὔτε αὐτὸς εἰς
4 ὁμοίαν ἐκείνοις ἥξειν διαβολήν. συναγαγὼν δὲ τὸν
δῆμον εἰς ἐκκλησίαν καὶ πολλὴν κατηγορίαν τῶν
οὐκ ἀποτιθεμένων τὰς ἀρχὰς διαθέμενος ὅρκους τε
διομοσάμενος ἰσχυροὺς περὶ τοῦ μὴ λήψεσθαι πάλιν
τὴν ὑπατείαν πρὶν ἀποθέσθαι τὴν προτέραν ἀρχήν,
προεῖπεν ἀρχαιρεσίων ἡμέραν· ἐν ᾗ καταστήσας

---

¹ πολιτεύεσθαι βουλομένους B : πολιτευομένους R.
² ἐπῃνεῖτο B : ἐπηνεῖτο δ' R.

---

¹ " Aristocracy " is here used in its literal meaning of
" government by the best (citizens)."

on the tribunal the whole day and showing himself
easy of access, mild and humane to all who came to
him for judgement. By this means he made the
government seem so truly an aristocracy [1] that neither
tribunes were needed by those who through poverty, humble birth or any other point of inferiority
were oppressed by their superiors, nor was any desire
for new legislation longer felt by those who wished for
a government based on equal rights ; but all were
contented and pleased with the law and order which
then came to prevail in the commonwealth. Not
only for these actions was Quintius praised by the
populace, but also for refusing the consulship when,
upon his completion of the appointed term of office,
it was offered to him a second time, and for not even
being pleased when that great honour was tendered
him. For the senate attempted to retain him in the
consulship, using many entreaties, because the tribunes for the third time had so managed that they
did not have to lay down their office ; for they were
confident that he would oppose the tribunes and
make them drop their new measures, partly out of
respect and partly out of fear, and they also saw that
the populace did not refuse to be governed by a good
man. But Quintius answered that he not only did
not approve of this unwillingness on the part of the
tribunes to give up their power, but he would not
himself incur the same censure as they had. Then
he called an assembly of the populace, and having
inveighed in a long speech against those who would
not resign their magistracies, and taken solemn oaths
with reference to his refusal to take the consulship
again before he had retired from his first term, he
announced a day for the election ; then on the ap-

ὑπάτους ἀπήει πάλιν εἰς τὸ μικρὸν ἐκεῖνο καλύβιον καὶ τὸν αὐτουργὸν ἔζη βίον ὡς πρότερον.

XX. Κοΐντου δὲ Φαβίου Οὐιβολανοῦ παρειλη-φότος τὴν ὑπατείαν τὸ τρίτον καὶ Λευκίου Κορ-νηλίου καὶ τελούντων πατρίους ἀγῶνας Αἰκανῶν ἄνδρες ἐπίλεκτοι πλῆθος ἀμφὶ τοὺς ἑξακισχιλίους ὁπλισμῷ τ' εὐζώνῳ συνεσταλμένοι καὶ ἐν νυκτὶ ποιησάμενοι τὴν ἔξοδον σκότους ἔτι ὄντος ἐπὶ πόλιν ἀφικνοῦνται Τυσκλανῶν, ἥ ἐστι μὲν τοῦ Λατίνων ἔθνους, ἀφέστηκε δὲ τῆς Ῥώμης οὐκ ἔλαττον 2 σταδίων ἑκατόν. εὑρόντες δὲ ὡς ἐν εἰρήνῃ πύλας τε ἀκλείστους καὶ τεῖχος ἀφύλακτον αἱροῦσι τὴν πόλιν ἐξ ἐφόδου μνησικακοῦντες τοῖς Τυσκλανοῖς ὅτι τῇ Ῥωμαίων πόλει τά τε ἄλλα μετὰ προθυμίας συμπράττοντες διετέλουν καὶ ἐν τῇ πολιορκίᾳ τοῦ 3 Καπιτωλίου μόνοι συνήραντο τοῦ πολέμου. ἄνδρας μὲν[1] οὖν οὐ[2] πολλούς τινας ἐν τῇ καταλήψει διέφθει-ραν, ἀλλ' ἔφθασαν ἤδη αὐτοὺς ὑπὸ τὴν ἅλωσιν τῆς πόλεως ὠσάμενοι δι' ἄλλων πυλῶν[3] οἱ ἔνδον, χωρὶς ἢ ὅσοι ὑπὸ νόσων ἢ γήρως φυγεῖν ἀδύνατοι ἦσαν, γύναια δὲ καὶ παιδία καὶ θεράποντας αὐτῶν ἠν-4 δραποδίσαντο καὶ τὰ χρήματα διήρπασαν. ὡς δ' ἀπηγγέλθη τὸ δεινὸν εἰς τὴν Ῥώμην ἐκ τῶν δια-φυγόντων ἐκ τῆς ἁλώσεως, οἱ μὲν ὕπατοι βοηθεῖν ᾤοντο δεῖν τοῖς φυγάσι κατὰ τάχος καὶ τὴν πόλιν αὐτοῖς ἀποδιδόναι, ἀντέπραττον δὲ οἱ δήμαρχοι στρατιὰν οὐκ ἐῶντες καταγράφειν ἕως ἂν ἡ περὶ τοὺς νόμους διενεχθῇ ψῆφος. ἀγανακτούσης δὲ τῆς

---

[1] ἄνδρας μὲν B : καὶ ἄνδρας A.
[2] οὖν οὐ Cary, οὐ Reiske : οὖν B, om. A.
[3] δι' ἄλλων πυλῶν Cobet, διὰ τῶν ἐναντίων πυλῶν Reiske διὰ τῶν πυλῶν O, Jacoby.

pointed day having named the consuls, he returned to that little cottage of his and lived, as before, the life of a farmer working his own land.

XX. Quintus Fabius Vibulanus [1] (for the third time) and Lucius Cornelius having succeeded to the consulship and being employed in exhibiting the traditional games, a chosen body of the Aequians, amounting to about six thousand men and lightly equipped, set out from their confines by night and came, while it was still dark, to the city of Tusculum, which belongs to the Latin race and is not less than a hundred stades distant from Rome. And finding the gates not locked and the walls unguarded, it being a time of peace, they took the town by assault, to gratify their resentment against the Tusculans because these were always zealously assisting the Romans and particularly because they alone had aided them in their struggle when they were besieging the Capitol.[2] The Aequians did not kill very many men in taking the city, since those inside, except such as were unable to flee because of illness or age, had forestalled them by crowding out through other gates just before the capture of the place; but they made slaves of their wives, children and domestics, and plundered their effects. As soon as news of the disaster was brought to Rome by those who had escaped capture, the consuls thought they ought to assist the fugitives promptly and restore their city to them; but the tribunes opposed them and would not permit an army to be enrolled until a vote should be taken concerning the law. While the senators were expressing their

[1] For chaps. 20 f. cf. Livy iii. 22-24.
[2] See chap. 16, 3.

231

βουλῆς καὶ διατριβὴν λαμβανούσης τῆς στρατείας
ἕτεροι παρῆσαν ἀπὸ τοῦ Λατίνων ἔθνους ἀποσταλέντες, οἳ τὴν Ἀντιατῶν πόλιν ἤγγελλον ἐκ τοῦ
φανεροῦ ἀφεστηκέναι, μιᾷ χρησαμένων γνώμη Οὐολούσκων τε τῶν ἀρχαίων οἰκητόρων τῆς πόλεως καὶ
Ῥωμαίων τῶν ἀφικομένων ὡς αὐτοὺς ἐποίκων καὶ
μερισαμένων τὴν γῆν. Ἑρνίκων τε ἄγγελοι κατὰ
τοὺς αὐτοὺς παρῆσαν χρόνους δηλοῦντες ὅτι Οὐολούσκων τε καὶ Αἰκανῶν δύναμις πολλὴ ἐξελήλυθε
5 καί ἐστιν ἐν τῇ αὐτῶν ἤδη γῇ. τούτων ἅμα προσαγγελλομένων οὐδεμίαν ἀναστροφὴν ἔτι ποιεῖσθαι
τοῖς ἐκ τοῦ συνεδρίου ἐδόκει, ἀλλὰ πανστρατιᾷ βοηθεῖν καὶ τοὺς ὑπάτους ἀμφοτέρους ἐξιέναι· ἐὰν δέ
τινες ἀπολειφθῶσι τῆς στρατείας Ῥωμαίων ἢ τῶν
6 συμμάχων, ὡς πολεμίοις αὐτοῖς χρῆσθαι. εἰξάν-
των δὲ καὶ τῶν δημάρχων καταγράψαντες τοὺς
ἐν ἡλικίᾳ πάντας οἱ ὕπατοι καὶ τὰς παρὰ τῶν
συμμάχων δυνάμεις μεταπεμψάμενοι κατὰ σπουδὴν
ἐξῄεσαν ὑπολιπόμενοι[1] φυλακὴν τῇ πόλει τρίτην
μοῖραν τῆς ἐπιχωρίου στρατιᾶς. Φάβιος μὲν οὖν
ἐπὶ τοὺς ἐν τῇ Τυσκλανῶν[2] ὄντας Αἰκανοὺς τὴν
7 στρατιὰν ἦγε διὰ τάχους.[3] τῶν δ᾽ οἱ μὲν πλείους
ἀπεληλύθεσαν ἤδη διηρπακότες τὴν πόλιν, ὀλίγοι
δέ τινες ὑπέμενον φυλάττοντες τὴν ἄκραν· ἔστι δὲ
σφόδρα ἐχυρὰ καὶ οὐ πολλῆς δεομένη φυλακῆς.
τινὲς μὲν οὖν φασι τοὺς φρουροὺς τῆς ἄκρας ἰδόντας
ἐξιοῦσαν ἐκ τῆς Ῥώμης τὴν στρατιὰν (εὐσύνοπτα
γάρ ἐστιν ἐκ μετεώρου τὰ μεταξὺ χωρία πάντα)
ἑκόντας ἐξελθεῖν, ἕτεροι δὲ ἐκπολιορκηθέντας ὑπὸ
τοῦ Φαβίου καθ᾽ ὁμολογίαν παραδοῦναι τὸ φρού-

---

[1] ὑπολιπόμενοι Ba : ὑπολειπόμενοι R.

indignation and the expedition was being delayed,
other messengers arrived, from the Latin nation,
reporting that Antium had openly revolted by the
joint action of the Volscians, who were the original
inhabitants of the place, and of the Romans who
had come to them as colonists and had received a
portion of the land. Messengers from the Hernicans
also arrived during these same days, informing
them that a large force of Volscians and Aequians
had marched forth and was already in the country
of the Hernicans. All these things being reported
at the same time, the senators resolved to make
no further delay, but to go to the rescue with all
their forces, and that both consuls should take the
field ; and if any of the Romans or the allies should
decline to serve, to treat them as enemies. When
the tribunes also yielded, the consuls, having enrolled
all who were of military age and sent for the forces
of the allies, hastily marched out, leaving a third part
of their own army to guard the city. Fabius, accordingly, marched in haste against the Aequians who
were in the Tusculans' territory. Most of these had
already left the city after plundering it, but a few
remained to guard the citadel, which is very strong
and does not require a large garrison. Some state
that the garrison of the citadel, seeing the army
marching from Rome—for all the region lying between may be easily seen from a height—came out
of their own accord ; others say that after being
reduced by Fabius to the necessity of surrendering
they handed over the fortress by capitulation, stipu-

---

[2] ἐν τῇ Τυσκλανῶν Cary, ἐν τῷ Τυσκλάνων (or ἐν τῷ Τύσκλῳ)
Sylburg, Jacoby : ἐν τῷ τυσκλάνῳ AB.
[3] διὰ τάχους B : διὰ τάχους ἐλαύνων R.

ριον, τοῖς σώμασιν αὐτοῖς ἄδειαν αἰτησαμένους καὶ
ζυγὸν ὑποστάντας.

XXI. Ἀποδοὺς δὲ τοῖς Τυσκλανοῖς τὴν πόλιν
Φάβιος περὶ δείλην ὀψίαν ἀνίστησι τὴν στρατιάν,
καὶ ὡς εἶχε τάχους ἤλαυνεν ἐπὶ τοὺς πολεμίους,
ἀκούων περὶ πόλιν Ἀλγιδὸν[1] ἀθρόας εἶναι τάς τε
Οὐολούσκων καὶ τὰς Αἰκανῶν δυνάμεις. ποιησάμενος δὲ δι' ὅλης νυκτὸς σύντονον ὁδὸν ὑπ' αὐτὸν
τὸν ὄρθρον ἐπιφαίνεται τοῖς πολεμίοις ἐστρατοπε-
δευκόσιν ἐν πεδίῳ καὶ οὔτε τάφρον περιβεβλημένοις
οὔτε χάρακα, ὡς ἐν οἰκείᾳ τε γῇ καὶ καταφρονήσει
2 τοῦ ἀντιπάλου. παρακελευσάμενος δὲ τοῖς ἀμφ'
αὐτὸν ἀγαθοῖς ἀνδράσι γίνεσθαι πρῶτος εἰσελαύνει
μετὰ τῶν ἱππέων εἰς τὴν τῶν πολεμίων παρεμβο-
λήν, καὶ οἱ πεζοὶ συναλαλάξαντες[2] εἵποντο· τῶν δ'
οἱ μὲν ἔτι κοιμώμενοι ἐφονεύοντο, οἱ δ' ἀρτίως
ἀνεστηκότες καὶ πρὸς ἀλκὴν ἐπιχειροῦντες τραπέ-
3 σθαι, οἱ δὲ πλείους φεύγοντες ἐσκεδάννυντο.[3] ἁλόντος δὲ τοῦ στρατοπέδου κατὰ πολλὴν εὐπέτειαν
ἐπιτρέψας τοῖς στρατιώταις τὰ χρήματα ὠφελεῖσθαι
καὶ τὰ σώματα πλὴν ὅσα Τυσκλανῶν ἦν, οὐ πολὺν
ἐνταῦθα διατρίψας χρόνον ἐπὶ τὴν Ἐχετρανῶν
πόλιν ἦγε τὴν δύναμιν, ἣ τότε ἦν τοῦ Οὐολούσκων
ἔθνους ἐπιφανεστάτη τε κἂν[4] τῷ κρατίστῳ μάλιστα
4 τόπῳ κειμένη. στρατοπεδεύσας δὲ πλησίον τῆς πόλεως ἐπὶ πολλὰς ἡμέρας κατ' ἐλπίδα τοῦ προελεύ-
σεσθαι τοὺς ἔνδον εἰς μάχην, ὡς οὐδεμία ἐξῄει
στρατιά, τὴν γῆν αὐτῶν ἐδῄου ἀνθρώπων μεστὴν
οὖσαν καὶ βοσκημάτων. οὐ γὰρ ἔφθασαν ἀνασκευασάμενοι τὰ ἐκ τῶν ἀγρῶν αἰφνιδίου γενηθείσης

---

[1] ἀλγιδὸν Ba : ἀλγηδόνα ABb.
[2] Reiske : οὖν ἀλαλάξαντες B, ἀλαλάξαντες A.

lating that their lives should be spared and submitting to pass under the yoke.

XXI. After Fabius had restored the city to the Tusculans, he broke camp in the late afternoon and marched with all possible speed against the enemy, upon hearing that the combined forces of the Volscians and the Aequians lay near the town of Algidum. And having made a forced march all that night, he appeared before the enemy at early dawn, as they lay encamped in a plain without either a ditch or a palisade to defend them, inasmuch as they were in their own country and were contemptuous of their foe. Then, exhorting his troops to acquit themselves as brave men should, he was the first to charge into the enemy's camp at the head of the horse, and the foot, uttering their war-cry, followed. Some of the enemy were slain while they were still asleep and others just as they had got up and were attempting to defend themselves ; but most of them scattered in flight. The camp having been taken with great ease, Fabius permitted the soldiers to keep for themselves the booty and the prisoners, except those who were Tusculans. Then, after a short stay there, he led them to Ecetra, which was at that time the most prominent city of the Volscian nation and the most strongly situated. When he had encamped near this city for many days in hopes that those inside would come out to fight, and no army issued forth, he laid waste their land, which was full of men and cattle ; for the Volscians, surprised by the suddenness of the attack upon them, had not had time to remove their

---

³ φεύγοντες ἐσκεδάννυντο A : ἔφευγον B.
⁴ Jacoby : καὶ AB.

αὐτοῖς τῆς ἐφόδου. ἐφεὶς δὲ καὶ ταῦτα τοῖς στρατιώταις διαρπάζειν ὁ Φάβιος καὶ πολλὰς ἐν τῇ προ-
νομῇ διατρίψας ἡμέρας ἀπῆγεν ἐπ' οἴκου τὴν δύναμιν.
5 ῾Ο δ' ἕτερος τῶν ὑπάτων Κορνήλιος ἐπὶ τοὺς ἐν
᾿Αντίῳ ῾Ρωμαίους τε καὶ Οὐολούσκους ἐλαύνων ἐπι-
τυγχάνει στρατιᾷ πρὸ τῶν ὁρίων αὐτὸν ὑποδεχο-
μένῃ. παραταξάμενος δὲ αὐτοῖς καὶ πολλοὺς μὲν
φονεύσας, τοὺς δὲ λοιποὺς τρεψάμενος, ἀγχοῦ τῆς
πόλεως κατεστρατοπέδευσεν. οὐ τολμώντων δὲ τῶν
ἐκ τῆς πόλεως οὐκέτι χωρεῖν εἰς μάχην πρῶτον μὲν
τὴν γῆν αὐτῶν ἔκειρεν, ἔπειτα τὴν πόλιν[1] ἀπετά-
φρευε καὶ περιεχαράκου. τότε δὴ πάλιν ἀναγκασ-
θέντες ἐξῆλθον ἐκ τῆς πόλεως πανστρατιᾷ, πολὺς
καὶ ἀσύντακτος ὄχλος, καὶ συμβαλόντες εἰς μάχην
ἔτι κάκιον ἀγωνισάμενοι κατακλείονται τὸ δεύτερον
εἰς τὴν πόλιν, αἰσχρῶς καὶ ἀνάνδρως φεύγοντες.
6 ὁ δ' ὕπατος οὐδεμίαν αὐτοῖς ἀναστροφὴν ἔτι δοὺς
κλίμακας προσέφερε τοῖς τείχεσι καὶ κριοῖς ἐξ-
έκοπτε τὰς πύλας. ἐπιπόνως δὲ καὶ ταλαιπώρως
τῶν ἔνδον ἀπομαχομένων οὐ πολλὰ πραγματευθεὶς
κατὰ κράτος αἱρεῖ τὴν πόλιν. χρήματα μὲν οὖν αὐτῶν, ὅσα χρυσὸς καὶ ἄργυρος καὶ χαλκὸς ἐνῆν, εἰς
τὸ δημόσιον ἐκέλευσεν ἀναφέρειν, ἀνδράποδα δὲ
τοὺς ταμίας παραλαμβάνοντας καὶ τὰ λοιπὰ λάφυρα
πωλεῖν· τοῖς δὲ στρατιώταις ἐσθῆτα καὶ τροφὰς καὶ
ὅσα ἄλλα τοιαῦτα ἐδύναντο ὠφελεῖσθαι ἐπέτρεψεν.
7 ἔπειτα διακρίνας τῶν τε κληρούχων καὶ τῶν ἀρχαίων ᾿Αντιατῶν τοὺς ἐπιφανεστάτους τε καὶ τῆς
ἀποστάσεως αἰτίους—ἦσαν δὲ πολλοί[2]—ῥάβδοις τε
ᾐκίσατο μέχρι πολλοῦ καὶ τοὺς αὐχένας αὐτῶν

---

[1] πόλιν B : πόλιν αὐτῶν R, πόλιν αὐτὴν Reiske.
[2] ἦσαν δὲ οὐ πολλοί Kiessling.

possessions out of the fields. These things also Fabius permitted his soldiers to plunder ; and after spending many days in ravaging the country, he led the army home.

The other consul, Cornelius, marching against the Romans and Volscians in Antium, found an army awaiting him before their borders ; and arraying his forces against them, he killed many, and after putting the rest to flight, encamped near the city. But when the inhabitants no longer ventured to come out for battle, he first laid waste their land and then surrounded the city with a ditch and palisades. Then indeed the enemy were compelled to come out again from the city with all their forces, a numerous and disorderly multitude ; and engaging in battle and fighting with less bravery than before, they were shut up inside the city a second time, after a shameful and unmanly flight. But the consul, giving them no longer any rest, planted scaling-ladders against the walls and broke down the gates with battering-rams ; then, as the besieged with difficulty and painfully tried to fight them off, he with little trouble took the town by storm. He ordered that such of their effects as consisted of gold, silver and copper should be turned in to the treasury, and that the slaves and the rest of the spoils should be taken over and sold by the quaestors ; but to the soldiers he granted the apparel and provisions and everything else of the sort that they could use for booty. Then, selecting both from the colonists and from the original inhabitants of Antium those who were the most prominent and had been the authors of the revolt—and there were many of these [1]—he ordered them to be scourged

---

[1] Kiessling would read, " there were not many of these."

ἐκέλευσεν ἀποτεμεῖν. ταῦτα διαπραξάμενος ἀπῆγε
8 καὶ αὐτὸς ἐπ' οἴκου τὴν δύναμιν. τούτοις ἡ βουλὴ
τοῖς ὑπάτοις προσιοῦσί τε ἀπήντησε καὶ θριάμβους
ἀμφοτέροις καταγαγεῖν ἐψηφίσατο· καὶ πρὸς Αἰκανοὺς πρεσβευσαμένους ὑπὲρ εἰρήνης ἐποιήσατο
συνθήκας περὶ καταλύσεως τοῦ πολέμου, ἐν αἷς
ἐγράφη πόλεις τε καὶ χώραν[1] ἔχοντας Αἰκανοὺς
ὧν ἐκράτουν ὅτε αἱ σπονδαὶ ἐγίνοντο Ῥωμαίοις
εἶναι ὑπηκόους, ἄλλο μὲν ὑποτελοῦντας μηθέν, ἐν
δὲ τοῖς πολέμοις συμμαχίαν ἀποστέλλοντας ὁσην-
δήποτε, ὥσπερ καὶ οἱ ἄλλοι σύμμαχοι. καὶ τὸ ἔτος
τοῦτο ἐτελεύτα.

XXII. Τῷ δ' ἑξῆς ἐνιαυτῷ Γάιος Ναύτιος τὸ
δεύτερον αἱρεθεὶς καὶ Λεύκιος Μηνύκιος παραλαβόντες[2] τὴν ὕπατον ἀρχὴν τέως μὲν ὑπὲρ τῶν
πολιτικῶν δικαίων πόλεμον ἐντὸς τείχους ἐπολέ-
μουν πρὸς τοὺς ἅμα Οὐεργινίῳ δημάρχους τοὺς
τέταρτον ἔτος ἤδη τὴν αὐτὴν κατασχόντας ἀρχήν.
2 ἐπεὶ δ' ἀπὸ τῶν πλησιοχώρων ἐθνῶν πόλεμος ἐπ-
εγένετο τῇ πόλει καὶ δέος ἦν μὴ τὴν ἀρχὴν ἀφ-
αιρεθῶσιν, ἀσμένως δεξάμενοι τὸ συμβὰν ἀπὸ τῆς
τύχης τὸν στρατιωτικὸν ἐποιοῦντο κατάλογον καὶ
μερισάμενοι τριχῇ τάς τε οἰκείας καὶ τὰς παρὰ τῶν
συμμάχων δυνάμεις μίαν μὲν ἐν τῇ πόλει μοῖραν
κατέλιπον, ἧς ἡγεῖτο Κόιντος Φάβιος Οὐιβολανός,
τὰς δὲ λοιπὰς αὐτοὶ παραλαβόντες ἐξῇεσαν διὰ
ταχέων, ἐπὶ μὲν Σαβίνους Ναύτιος, ἐπὶ δ' Αἰκανοὺς
3 Μηνύκιος. ἀμφότερα γὰρ ταῦτα τὰ ἔθνη κατὰ τὸν
αὐτὸν χρόνον ἀφειστήκει τῆς Ῥωμαίων ἀρχῆς,
Σαβῖνοι μὲν ἐκ τοῦ[3] φανεροῦ, καὶ μέχρι Φιδήνης

---

[1] Kiessling : χώρας O, Jacoby.
[2] Sylburg : παραλαβὸν Ba, παραλαβὼν ABb.

with rods for a long time and then beheaded. After accomplishing these things he too led his army home. The senate went to meet these consuls as they approached the city and decreed that they both should celebrate a triumph. And when the Aequians sent heralds to sue for peace, they concluded with them a treaty for the termination of the war, in which it was stipulated that the Aequians should retain the cities and land which they possessed at the time of the treaty and be subject to the Romans without paying any tribute, but sending to their assistance in time of war a certain number of troops, like the rest of the allies. Thus ended that year.

XXII. The following year[1] Gaius Nautius (chosen for the second time) and Lucius Minucius succeeded to the consulship, and were for a time waging a war inside the walls, concerning the rights of citizens, against Verginius and the other tribunes, who had obtained the same magistracy now for the fourth year. But when war was brought upon the commonwealth by the neighbouring peoples and there was fear that they might be deprived of their empire, the consuls gladly accepted the opportunity presented to them by Fortune ; and having held the military levy, and divided both their own forces and those of the allies into three bodies, they left one of them in the city, commanded by Quintus Fabius Vibulanus, and themselves taking the other two, they marched out in haste, Nautius against the Sabines and Minucius against the Aequians. For both these nations had revolted from the Roman rule at the same time. The Sabines had done so openly, and had advanced as far

---

[1] For chaps. 22 f. cf. Livy iii. 25-26, 6.

[3] τοῦ added by Kiessling.

DIONYSIUS OF HALICARNASSUS

πόλεως ἤλασαν, ἧς ἐκράτουν Ῥωμαῖοι (τετταράκοντα δ᾽ εἰσὶν οἱ διὰ μέσου τῶν πόλεων στάδιοι),
Αἰκανοὶ δὲ λόγῳ μὲν φυλάττοντες τὰ τῆς νεωστὶ
γενομένης συμμαχίας δίκαια, ἔργῳ δὲ καὶ οὗτοι
4 πράττοντες τὰ τῶν πολεμίων. ἐπὶ γὰρ τοὺς συμμάχους αὐτῶν Λατίνους ἐστράτευσαν, ὡς οὐ γενομένων αὐτοῖς πρὸς ἐκείνους ὁμολογιῶν περὶ φιλίας.
ἡγεῖτο δὲ τῆς στρατιᾶς[1] Γράκχος Κλοίλιος,[2] ἀνὴρ
δραστήριος ἀρχῇ κοσμηθεὶς αὐτοκράτορι, ἣν ἐπὶ τὸ
βασιλικώτερον ἐξήγαγεν. ἐλάσας δὲ μέχρι Τύσκλου πόλεως, ἣν Αἰκανοὶ τῷ πρόσθεν ἐνιαυτῷ
καταλαβόμενοι καὶ διαρπάσαντες ὑπὸ Ῥωμαίων
ἐξεκρούσθησαν, ἀνθρώπους τε πολλοὺς ἐκ τῶν
ἀγρῶν συνήρπασε καὶ βοσκήματα ὅσα κατέλαβε καὶ
5 τοὺς καρποὺς τῆς γῆς ἐν ἀκμῇ ὄντας ἔφθειρεν. ἀφικομένης δὲ πρεσβείας, ἣν ἀπέστειλεν ἡ Ῥωμαίων
βουλὴ μαθεῖν ἀξιοῦσα τί παθόντες Αἰκανοὶ πολε-
μοῦσι τοῖς Ῥωμαίων συμμάχοις, φιλίας τ᾽ αὐτοῖς
ὀμωμοσμένης νεωστὶ καὶ οὐδενὸς ἐν τῷ μεταξὺ
χρόνῳ γενομένου προσκρούσματος τοῖς ἔθνεσι, καὶ
παραινούσης τῷ Κλοιλίῳ τούς τ᾽ αἰχμαλώτους αὐτῶν οὓς εἶχεν ἀφιέναι καὶ τὴν στρατιὰν ἀπάγειν καὶ
περὶ ὧν ἠδίκησεν ἢ κατέβλαψε Τυσκλανοὺς δίκην
ὑποσχεῖν, πολὺν μὲν χρόνον διέτριψεν ὁ Γράκχος οὐδ᾽ εἰς λόγους τοῖς πρεσβευταῖς ἐρχόμενος,
6 ὡς ἐν ἀσχολίαις δή τισι γεγονώς. ἐπεὶ δ᾽ οὖν
ἔδοξεν αὐτῷ προσάγειν τοὺς πρέσβεις, κἀκεῖνοι
τοὺς ἐπισταλέντας ὑπὸ τῆς βουλῆς λόγους διεξ-

---

[1] στρατιᾶς B : στρατείας R.
[2] Γράκχος Κλοίλιος Sylburg : γράγχος κοίλιος AB, Jacoby
(and so throughout the following chapters). Both names
are similarly corrupted in some other places (e.g., γράγχος

as Fidenae, which was in the possession of the
Romans ; the two cities are forty stades apart. As
for the Aequians, though nominally they were observing the terms of the alliance they had recently made,
in reality they too were acting like enemies ; for they
had made war upon the Latins, the allies of the
Romans, claiming that they had made no compact
of friendship with that nation. Their army was commanded by Cloelius Gracchus,[1] a man of action who
had been invested with absolute authority, which he
increased to more nearly royal power. This leader,
marching as far as the city of Tusculum, which the
Aequians had taken and plundered the year before,
only to be driven out of it by the Romans, seized a
great number of men and all the cattle he found in
the fields, and destroyed the crops, which were then
ripe. When an embassy arrived, sent by the Roman
senate, which demanded to know what provocation
had induced the Aequians to make war upon the
allies of the Romans, though they had recently sworn
to a treaty of peace with them and no cause of offence
had since arisen between the two nations, and the
envoys advised Cloelius to release the Tusculan
prisoners whom he held, to withdraw his forces and
to stand trial for the injuries and damage he had
done to the Tusculans, he delayed a long time without
even giving audience to them, pretending that he
was occupied with some business or other. And
when he did see fit to have them introduced and they
had delivered the senate's message, he said : " I

---

[1] See the critical note.

A in ii. 11, 3, κοιλίου A in x. 42, 3 ; see also the note on
iii. 2, 1).

ἦλθον· "Θαυμάζω," φησίν, "ὑμῶν, ὦ Ῥωμαῖοι,
τί δή ποτ' αὐτοὶ μὲν ἅπαντας ἀνθρώπους ἡγεῖσθε
πολεμίους, καὶ ὑφ' ὧν οὐδὲν κακὸν πεπόνθατε,
ἀρχῆς καὶ τυραννίδος ἕνεκα, Αἰκανοῖς δ' οὐ συγ-
χωρεῖτε παρὰ τουτωνὶ Τυσκλανῶν ἐχθρῶν ὄντων
ἀναπράττεσθαι δίκας, οὐθενὸς ἡμῖν διομολογημένου
περὶ αὐτῶν ὅτε τὰς πρὸς ὑμᾶς ἐποιούμεθα συνθήκας. εἰ μὲν οὖν τῶν ὑμετέρων ἰδίων ἀδικεῖσθαί τι
7 ἢ βλάπτεσθαι λέγετε ὑφ' ἡμῶν, τὰ δίκαια ὑφέξομεν
ὑμῖν κατὰ τὰς ὁμολογίας· εἰ δὲ περὶ Τυσκλανῶν
ἀναπραξόμενοι δίκας ἥκετε, οὐθείς ἐστιν ὑμῖν πρὸς
ἐμὲ περὶ τούτων λόγος, ἀλλὰ πρὸς ταύτην λαλεῖτε
τὴν φηγόν"—δείξας αὐτοῖς τινα πλησίον πεφυκυῖαν.

XXIII. Ῥωμαῖοι δὲ τοιαῦτα ὑβρισθέντες ὑπὸ
τοῦ ἀνδρὸς οὐκ εὐθὺς ὀργῇ ἐπιτρέψαντες ἐξήγαγον
τὴν στρατιάν, ἀλλὰ καὶ δευτέραν ὡς αὐτὸν ἀπέστειλαν πρεσβείαν καὶ τοὺς φητιάλεις[1] καλουμένους
ἄνδρας ἱερεῖς[2] ἔπεμψαν ἐπιμαρτυρόμενοι[3] θεούς τε
καὶ δαίμονας ὅτι μὴ δυνηθέντες τῶν δικαίων τυχεῖν
ὅσιον ἀναγκασθήσονται πόλεμον ἐκφέρειν· καὶ μετὰ
ταῦτα τὸν ὕπατον ἀπέστειλαν. ὁ δὲ Γράκχος,
2 ἐπειδὴ τοὺς Ῥωμαίους προσιόντας ἔμαθεν, ἀναστήσας τὴν δύναμιν ἀπῆγε προσωτέρω, τῶν πολεμίων ἐκ ποδὸς ἑπομένων, βουλόμενος αὐτοὺς εἰς
τοιαῦτα προαγαγέσθαι[4] χωρία ἐν οἷς πλεονεκτήσειν
ἔμελλεν· ὅπερ καὶ συνέβη. φυλάξας γὰρ αὐλῶνα
περικλειόμενον ὄρεσιν, ὡς ἐνέβαλον εἰς τοῦτον οἱ
Ῥωμαῖοι διώκοντες αὐτόν, ὑποστρέφει τε καὶ
στρατοπεδεύεται κατὰ τὴν ἐκ τοῦ αὐλῶνος ἔξω

---

[1] Sylburg : φιτιάλεις B, φιτιαλεῖς R.
[2] ἱερεῖς A : ἱερούς R.
[3] ἐπιμαρτυρόμενοι A : ἐπιμαρτυρούμενοι B.

wonder at you, Romans, why in the world, when you yourselves regard all men as enemies, even those from whom you have received no injury, because of your lust for dominion and tyranny, you do not concede to the Aequians the right to take vengeance on these Tusculans here, who are our enemies, inasmuch as we made no agreement with regard to them at the time we concluded the treaty with you. Now if you claim that any interest of your own is suffering injustice or injury at our hands, we will afford you proper indemnity in accordance with the treaty; but if you have come to exact satisfaction on behalf of the Tusculans, you have no reckoning with me on that subject, but go talk to yonder oak "— pointing to one that grew near by.

XXIII. The Romans, though thus insulted by the man, did not immediately give way to their resentment and lead their army forth, but sent a second embassy to him and likewise the priests called *fetiales*, calling the gods and lesser divinities to witness that if they were unable to obtain satisfaction they should be obliged to wage a holy war ; and after that they sent out the consul. When Gracchus learned that the Romans were approaching, he broke camp and retired with his forces to a greater distance, the enemy following close at his heels. His purpose was to lead them on into a region where he would have an advantage over them ; and that is what in fact happened. For waiting until he found a valley surrounded by hills, he then, as soon as the Romans had entered it in pursuit of him, faced about and encamped astride the road that led out of the valley.

---

⁴ Hertlein : προσαγαγέσθαι O.

3 φέρουσαν ὁδόν. ἐκ δὲ τούτου συνεβεβήκει τοῖς
Ῥωμαίοις οὐχ ὃν ἐβούλοντο ἐκλέξασθαι τόπον εἰς
στρατοπεδείαν, ἀλλ' ὃν ἔδωκεν αὐτοῖς ὁ καιρός,
ἔνθα οὔθ' ἵπποις χιλὸν εὔπορον ἦν λαμβάνειν, ὄρεσι
περικλειομένου τοῦ τόπου ψιλοῖς καὶ δυσβάτοις,
οὔθ' ἑαυτοῖς τροφὰς ἐκ τῆς πολεμίας συγκομίζειν,
ἐπειδὴ κατηνάλωντο ἃς οἴκοθεν ἔφερον, οὔτε μετα-
στρατοπεδεύσασθαι τῶν πολεμίων ἀντικαθημένων
καὶ κωλυόντων τὰς ἐξόδους. βιάσασθαί τε προελό-
μενοι καὶ προελθόντες εἰς μάχην ἀνεκρούσθησαν καὶ
πολλὰς πληγὰς λαβόντες εἰς τὸν αὐτὸν[1] κατεκλείσ-
θησαν χάρακα. ὁ δὲ Κλοίλιος ἐπαρθεὶς τῷ προτερήματι τούτῳ περιετάφρευέ τε αὐτοὺς καὶ περιεχαράκου καὶ πολλὰς ἐλπίδας εἶχε λιμῷ πιεσθέντας
4 παραδώσειν αὐτῷ τὰ ὅπλα. ἀφικομένης δ' εἰς
Ῥώμην περὶ τούτων ἀγγελίας Κόιντος Φάβιος ὁ
καταλειφθεὶς ἐπὶ τῆς πόλεως ἔπαρχος ἀπὸ τῆς σὺν
αὐτῷ στρατιᾶς ὅσον ἦν ἀκμαιότατόν[2] τε καὶ κράτιστον ἐπιλέξας μέρος ἐπὶ συμμαχίαν ἔπεμψε τῷ
ὑπάτῳ. ἡγεῖτο δὲ τῆς δυνάμεως ταύτης Τίτος
5 Κοΐντιος ὁ ταμίας ἀνὴρ ὑπατικός. πρὸς δὲ τὸν
ἕτερον τῶν ὑπάτων Ναύτιον ἐπὶ τῆς ἐν Σαβίνοις
στρατιᾶς ὄντα γράμματα διαπέμψας τά τε συμβάντα
τῷ Μηνυκίῳ διεσάφησε καὶ αὐτὸν ἥκειν ἠξίου διὰ
ταχέων. κἀκεῖνος ἐπιτρέψας τοῖς πρεσβευταῖς τὸν
χάρακα φυλάττειν αὐτὸς σὺν ὀλίγοις[3] ἱππεῦσιν εἰς
τὴν Ῥώμην ἐλαύνει συντόνῳ χρησάμενος ἱππασίᾳ·
εἰσελθὼν δ' εἰς τὴν πόλιν ἔτι πολλῆς νυκτὸς οὔσης
ἐβουλεύετο σὺν τῷ Φαβίῳ καὶ τῶν ἄλλων πολιτῶν[4]
τοῖς πρεσβυτάτοις ὅ τι χρὴ ποιεῖν. ἐπεὶ δὲ πᾶσιν

---

[1] αὐτὸν O : αὐτῶν Gelenius.
[2] Sylburg : ἀναγκαιότατον O.

As a consequence the Romans were unable to choose
for their camp the place they preferred, but had to
take the one the situation offered, where it was not
easy either to get forage for the horses, the place
being surrounded by hills that were bare and difficult
of access, or to bring in provisions for themselves out
of the enemy's country, since what they had brought
from home had been consumed, nor yet easy to shift
their camp while the enemy lay before them and
blocked the exits. Choosing, therefore, to force their
way out, they engaged in battle and were repulsed,
and after receiving many wounds were shut up again
in the same camp. Cloelius, elated by this success,
began to surround the place with a ditch and palisades and had great hopes of forcing them by famine
to deliver up their arms to him. The news of this
disaster being brought to Rome, Quintus Fabius,
who had been left as prefect in charge of the city,
chose out of his own army a body of the fittest and
strongest men and sent them to the assistance of the
consul; they were commanded by Titus Quintius,
who was quaestor and an ex-consul. And sending a
letter to Nautius, the other consul, who commanded
the army in the country of the Sabines, he informed
him of what had happened to Minucius and asked
him to come in haste. Nautius committed the guarding of the camp to the legates and he himself with
a small squadron of cavalry made a forced ride to
Rome; and arriving in the city while it was still
deep night, he took counsel with Fabius and the
oldest of the other citizens concerning the measures
that should be taken. When all were of the opinion

---

³ ὀλίγοις B : τοῖς ἄλλοις R.
⁴ πολιτῶν O : βουλευτῶν Kiessling.

245

ἐδόκει δικτάτορος δεῖσθαι ὁ καιρός, ἀποδείκνυσιν
ἐπὶ τὴν ἀρχὴν ταύτην Λεύκιον Κοΐντιον[1] Κικιννᾶ-
τον. καὶ αὐτὸς μὲν ταῦτα διαπραξάμενος ᾤχετο
πάλιν ἐπὶ τὸ στρατόπεδον.

XXIV. Ὁ δὲ τῆς πόλεως ἔπαρχος Φάβιος
ἔπεμπε τοὺς παραληψομένους τὸν Κοΐντιον ἐπὶ τὴν
ἀρχήν. ἔτυχε δὲ καὶ τότε ὁ ἀνὴρ τῶν κατ' ἀγρὸν
ἔργων τι διαπραττόμενος· ἰδὼν δὲ τὸν προσιόντα
ὄχλον καὶ ὑποπτεύσας ἐπ' αὐτὸν ἥκειν ἐσθῆτά τ'
ἐλάμβανεν εὐπρεπεστέραν καὶ ὑπαντήσων αὐτοῖς
2 ἐπορεύετο. ὡς δ' ἐγγὺς ἦν, ἵππους τ' αὐτῷ φαλάροις κεκοσμημένους ἐκπρεπέσι προσῆγον καὶ πελέκεις ἅμα ταῖς ῥάβδοις εἰκοσιτέτταρας παρέστησαν
ἐσθῆτά τε ἁλουργῆ καὶ τἆλλα παράσημα οἷς πρότερον ἡ τῶν βασιλέων ἐκεκόσμητο ἀρχὴ προσήνεγκαν.
ὁ δὲ μαθὼν ὅτι δικτάτωρ ἀποδέδεικται τῆς πόλεως,
οὐχ ὅπως ἠγάπησε τηλικαύτης τιμῆς τυχών, ἀλλὰ
προσαγανακτήσας εἶπεν· "'Απολεῖται ἄρα καὶ τούτου τοῦ ἐνιαυτοῦ ὁ καρπὸς διὰ τὰς ἐμὰς ἀσχολίας,
3 καὶ πεινήσομεν ἅπαντες κακῶς." μετὰ ταῦτα
παραγενόμενος εἰς τὴν πόλιν πρῶτον μὲν ἐθάρρυνε
τοὺς πολίτας λόγον ἐν τῷ πλήθει διεξελθὼν ἐξεγεῖ-
ραι τὰς ψυχὰς δυνάμενον ἐλπίσιν ἀγαθαῖς· ἔπειτα
συναγαγὼν ἅπαντας τοὺς ἐν ἀκμῇ, τούς τε κατὰ
πόλιν[2] καὶ τοὺς ἐκ τῶν ἀγρῶν, καὶ τὰς παρὰ τῶν
συμμάχων ἐπικουρίας μεταπεμψάμενος ἱππάρχην
τ' ἀποδείξας Λεύκιον Ταρκύνιον, ἄνδρα τῶν ἠμελη-
μένων μὲν διὰ πενίαν, τὰ δὲ πολέμια γενναῖον,
ἐξῆγε[3] συγκεκροτημένην ἔχων δύναμιν, καὶ καταλαβὼν τὸν ταμίαν Τίτον Κοΐντιον ἀναδεχόμενον

---

[1] Κοΐντιον added by Kiessling.
[2] πόλιν O : τὴν πόλιν Ambrosch, Jacoby.

that the situation required a dictator, he named Lucius Quintius Cincinnatus to that magistracy. Then, having attended to this business, he himself returned to the camp.

XXIV. Fabius,[1] the prefect of the city, sent men to invite Quintius to come and assume his magistracy. It chanced that Quintius was on this occasion also engaged in some work of husbandry ; and seeing the approaching throng and suspecting that they were coming after him, he put on more becoming apparel and went to meet them. When he drew near, they brought to him horses decked with magnificent trappings, placed beside him twenty-four axes with the rods and presented to him the purple robe and the other insignia with which aforetime the kingly office had been adorned. Quintius, when he learned that he had been appointed dictator, far from being pleased at receiving so great an honour, was actually vexed, and said : " This year's crop too will be ruined, then, because of my official duties, and we shall all go dreadfully hungry." After that he went into the city and first encouraged the citizens by delivering a speech before the populace calculated to raise their spirits with good hopes ; then, after assembling all the men in their prime, both of the city and of the country, and sending for the forces of the allies, he appointed as his Master of Horse Lucius Tarquinius, a man who because of his poverty had been overlooked, but valiant in war. After which he led out his forces, now that he had them assembled, and joined Titus Quintius, the quaestor, who was awaiting

---

[1] For chaps. 24 f. *cf.* Livy iii. 26, 7–29, 9.

[3] ἐξῆγε B : om. R.

αὐτοῦ τὴν παρουσίαν, λαβὼν καὶ τὴν σὺν ἐκείνῳ
4 δύναμιν ἦγεν[1] ἐπὶ τοὺς πολεμίους. ὡς δὲ κατ-
ώπτευσε τὴν τῶν χωρίων φύσιν ἐν οἷς ἦν τὰ
στρατόπεδα, μέρος μέν τι τῆς στρατιᾶς ἐπὶ τοῖς
μετεώροις ἔταξεν, ὡς μήτε βοήθεια παραγένοιτο τοῖς
Αἰκανοῖς ἑτέρα μήτε τροφαί, τὴν δὲ λοιπὴν δύναμιν
αὐτὸς ἔχων προῆγεν ἐκτεταγμένην ὡς εἰς μάχην.
καὶ ὁ Κλοίλιος οὐθὲν ὑποδείσας (ἥ τε γὰρ δύναμις ἡ
περὶ αὐτὸν ἦν οὐκ ὀλίγη καὶ αὐτὸς ἐδόκει ψυχὴν
οὐ κακὸς εἶναι κατὰ[2] τὰ πολέμια) δέχεται αὐτὸν
5 ἐπιόντα, καὶ γίνεται μάχη καρτερά. χρόνου δὲ
πολλοῦ διελθόντος καὶ τῶν Ῥωμαίων διὰ τοὺς
συνεχεῖς πολέμους ἀναφερόντων τὸν πόνον τῶν τε
ἱππέων κατὰ τὸ κάμνον μέρος ἀεὶ ἐπιβοηθούντων
τοῖς πεζοῖς ἡσσηθεὶς ὁ Γράκχος κατακλείεται πάλιν[3]
εἰς τὸν ἑαυτοῦ[4] χάρακα. καὶ μετὰ τοῦθ᾽ ὁ[5] Κόιντος
περιταφρεύσας αὐτὸν ὑψηλῷ χάρακι καὶ πύργοις
πυκνοῖς περιλαβών, ἐπεὶ κάμνοντα ἔμαθε τῶν
ἀναγκαίων τῇ σπάνει, αὐτός τε προσβολὰς ἐποιεῖτο
συνεχεῖς πρὸς τὸν χάρακα τῶν Αἰκανῶν καὶ τῷ
Μηνυκίῳ προσέταξεν ἀπὸ τῶν ἑτέρων ἐξιέναι[6]
6 μερῶν. ὥστε ἠναγκάσθησαν οἱ Αἰκανοὶ τροφῆς τε
ἀπορούμενοι καὶ συμμάχων βοήθειαν ἀπεγνωκότες
πολιορκούμενοί τε πολλαχόθεν[7] ἱκετηρίας ἀναλαβόντες ἐπιπρεσβεύεσθαι πρὸς τὸν Κόιντον περὶ
φιλίας.[8] ὁ δὲ τοῖς μὲν ἄλλοις Αἰκανοῖς ἔφη σπένδεσθαι καὶ διδόναι τοῖς σώμασι[9] τὴν ἄδειαν τά τε

---

[1] Reiske : ἧκεε O, Jacoby.
[2] κατὰ added by Jacoby. Kiessling preferred to delete τὰ
πολέμια or else to read καὶ τὰ πολέμια δεινός.
[3] πάλιν B : om. R.   [4] ἑαυτοῦ R (?) : αὐτοῦ B.
[5] τοῦθ᾽ ὁ Jacoby, τοῦτο ὁ Kiessling : τοῦτο O.
[6] ἐπιέναι Kiessling.   [7] πανταχόθεν Kiessling.

his arrival ; and taking with him Quintius' forces
also, he led them against the enemy. After observing the nature of the places in which the camps lay,
he posted a part of his army on the heights, in order
that neither another relief force nor any provisions
might reach the Aequians, and he himself marched
forward with the remainder arrayed as for battle.
Cloelius, unmoved by fear—for the force he had was
no small one and he himself was looked upon as no
craven in spirit when it came to fighting—awaited
his attack, and a severe battle ensued. After this
had continued for a long time, and the Romans
because of their continuous wars endured the toil,
and the horse kept relieving the foot wherever the
latter were hard pressed, Gracchus was beaten and
shut up once more in his camp. After that Quintius
surrounded it with a high palisade, fortified with
many towers ; and when he learned that Gracchus
was in distress for want of provisions, he not only
himself made continual attacks upon the camp of the
Aequians, but also ordered Minucius to make a sortie
on the other side.[1] Consequently the Aequians,
lacking provisions, despairing of aid from any allies,
and besieged on many sides,[2] were compelled to send
envoys to Quintius with the tokens of suppliants to
treat for peace. Quintius said he was ready to make
peace with the rest of the Aequians and grant them
immunity for their persons if they would lay down

---

[1] Kiessling would read, " make an attack from the other
side."

[2] Kiessling suggests " on all sides."

---

[8] διαλεγόμενοι after φιλίας deleted by Garrer ; Sylburg
read διαλεξόμενοι.

[9] σώμασιν B. Kiessling would read σώμασιν ἄδειαν.

ὅπλα ἀποθεμένοις καὶ καθ᾽ ἕνα διεξιοῦσιν ὑπὸ
ζυγόν, Γράκχῳ δὲ τῷ ἡγεμόνι τῶν πολεμίων καὶ
τοῖς σὺν ἐκείνῳ βουλεύσασι τὴν ἀπόστασιν ὡς
πολεμίοις χρήσεσθαι,[1] ἐκέλευσέ τε αὐτοῖς ἄγειν
7 τοὺς ἄνδρας δεδεμένους. ὑπομενόντων δὲ ταῦτα
τῶν Αἰκανῶν τελευταῖον αὐτοῖς ἐκεῖνο προσέταξεν·
ἐπειδὴ Τύσκλον πόλιν Ῥωμαίων σύμμαχον ἐξην-
δραποδίσαντο καὶ διήρπασαν οὐδὲν ὑπὸ Τυσκλανῶν
παθόντες κακόν, ἀντιπαρασχεῖν ἑαυτῷ πόλιν τῶν
8 σφετέρων Κορβιῶνα τὰ ὅμοια διαθεῖναι. ταύτας
λαβόντες τὰς ἀποκρίσεις οἱ πρέσβεις[2] ἀπῇεσαν[3] καὶ
μετ᾽ οὐ πολὺ παρῆσαν ἄγοντες τὸν Γράκχον καὶ
τοὺς σὺν αὐτῷ δεδεμένους· αὐτοὶ δὲ τὰ ὅπλα θέντες
ἐξέλιπον τὴν παρεμβολὴν διαπορευόμενοι, καθάπερ
ὁ στρατηγὸς ἐκέλευσε, διὰ τοῦ Ῥωμαίων χάρακος
καθ᾽ ἕνα ὑπὸ ζυγόν, καὶ τὴν Κορβιῶνα κατὰ τὰς
ὁμολογίας παρέδοσαν, τὰ ἐλεύθερα σώματα μόνον
ἐξελθεῖν αἰτησάμενοι, περὶ ὧν διήλλαξαν τοὺς
Τυσκλανῶν αἰχμαλώτους.

XXV. Παραλαβὼν δὲ ὁ Κόιντιος τὴν πόλιν τὰ
μὲν ἐπιφανέστατα τῶν λαφύρων εἰς Ῥώμην ἐκέλευσε φέρειν, τὰ δ᾽ ἄλλα πάντα διελέσθαι κατὰ
λόχους ἐπέτρεψε τοῖς τε σὺν αὐτῷ[4] παραγενομένοις
στρατιώταις καὶ τοῖς ἅμα Κοϊντίῳ τῷ ταμίᾳ προ-
αποσταλεῖσι. τοῖς δὲ μετὰ Μηνυκίου τοῦ ὑπάτου
κατακλεισθεῖσιν ἐν τῷ χάρακι μεγάλην ἔφη δεδω-
κέναι δωρεὰν τὰ σώματα αὐτῶν ἐκ θανάτου ῥυσά-
2 μενος. ταῦτα πράξας καὶ τὸν Μηνύκιον ἀποθέσθαι
τὴν ἀρχὴν ἀναγκάσας ἀνέστρεψεν εἰς τὴν Ῥώμην

---

[1] Sylburg : χρήσασθαι O, Jacoby.
[2] οἱ πρέσβεις R : οἱ πρέσβεις τῶν αἰκανῶν B, Jacoby.
[3] Sylburg : προῄεσαν O, Jacoby.

their arms and pass under the yoke one at a time ; but as for Gracchus, their commander, and those who had planned the revolt with him, he would treat them as enemies, and he ordered them to bring these men to him in chains. When the Aequians consented to do so, the last demand he made of them was this— that, inasmuch as they had enslaved the inhabitants of Tusculum, a city in alliance with the Romans, and plundered it, though they had received no injury from the Tusculans, they should in turn put at his disposal one of their own cities, Corbio, to be treated in like manner. The envoys, having received this answer, departed, and not long afterward returned, bringing with them in chains Gracchus and his associates. They themselves, laying down their arms, left their camp and, pursuant to the general's orders, marched through the Roman camp one by one under the yoke ; and they delivered up Corbio according to their agreement, merely asking that the inhabitants of free condition might leave the city, in exchange for whom they released the Tusculan captives.

XXV. Quintius, having taken possession of Corbio, ordered the choicest of the spoils to be carried to Rome and permitted all the rest to be distributed by centuries both to the troops that had been with him and to those that had been sent ahead with Quintius the quaestor. As for the forces which had been shut up in their camp with Minucius the consul, he said that he had already bestowed a great gift upon them in delivering them from death. After doing these things and forcing Minucius to resign his magistracy, he returned to Rome and celebrated a triumph more

---

⁴ αὐτῷ Bb : ἑαυτῷ ABa.

καὶ κατήγαγε λαμπρότατον ἁπάντων ἡγεμόνων
θρίαμβον, ἐν ἡμέραις ἑκκαίδεκα ταῖς πάσαις, ἀφ'
ἧς παρέλαβε τὴν ἀρχήν, στρατόπεδόν τε σώσας
φίλιον καὶ πολεμίων δύναμιν ἀκμάζουσαν καθελὼν
πόλιν τε αὐτῶν πορθήσας καὶ φρουρὰν αὐτῆς
ὑπολιπὼν τόν τε ἡγεμόνα τοῦ πολέμου καὶ τοὺς
ἄλλους ἐπιφανεῖς ἄνδρας ἁλύσει δεδεμένους ἀγα-
3 γών.[1] καί, ὃ μάλιστα πάντων αὐτοῦ θαυμάζειν
ἄξιον,[2] τὴν τοσαύτην ἀρχὴν εἰς ἑξάμηνον εἰληφὼς
οὐκ ἐχρήσατο παντὶ τῷ νόμῳ, ἀλλὰ συναγαγὼν
τὸν δῆμον εἰς ἐκκλησίαν καὶ περὶ τῶν πεπραγμένων
λόγον ἀποδοὺς ἐξωμόσατο τὴν ἀρχήν, τῆς τε βουλῆς δεομένης γῆν τε ὅσην ἐβούλετο λαβεῖν ἐκ τῆς
δορικτήτου καὶ ἀνδράποδα καὶ χρήματα ἐκ τῶν λαφύρων ἐπανορθῶσαί τε[3] τὴν πενίαν πλούτῳ δικαίῳ,
ὃν ἀπὸ πολεμίων κάλλιστον ἐκτήσατο τοῖς ἰδίοις
πόνοις, οὐκ ἠξίωσε, φίλων τε καὶ συγγενῶν δωρεὰς
προσφερόντων μεγάλας καὶ ἀντὶ παντὸς ἀγαθοῦ
τιθεμένων ἐκεῖνον τὸν ἄνδρα εὖ ποιεῖν, ἐπαινέσας
αὐτοὺς τῆς προθυμίας οὐθὲν τῶν διδομένων ἔλαβεν,
ἀλλ' ἀπῆλθε πάλιν εἰς τὸ μικρὸν ἐκεῖνο χωρίον, καὶ
τὸν αὐτουργὸν αὐτοῦ[4] ἀντὶ τοῦ βασιλικοῦ μετειλήφει[5] βίον, μεῖζον φρονῶν ἐπὶ πενίᾳ ἢ ἄλλοι ἐπὶ
4 πλούτῳ. μετ' οὐ πολὺν δὲ χρόνον καὶ Ναύτιος,
ἅτερος τῶν ὑπάτων, νικήσας Σαβίνους ἐκ παρατάξεως καὶ τῆς χώρας αὐτῶν πολλὴν καταδραμὼν
ἀπῆγεν ἐπ' οἴκου τὰς δυνάμεις.

XXVI. Μετὰ δὲ τούτους ὀλυμπιὰς μὲν ἦν ὀγδοη-
κοστὴ καὶ πρώτη, ἣν ἐνίκα στάδιον Πολύμναστος

---

[1] ἀγαγών A : om. B, ἄγων R.
[2] ὅτι after ἄξιον deleted by Vassis.
[3] τε B : om. R, Jacoby.   [4] αὐτοῦ O : αὖθις Cobet.

brilliant than that of any other general, having in the
space of sixteen days in all from that on which he had
received the magistracy saved an army of his fellow
citizens, defeated a first-rate force of the enemy,
plundered one of their cities and left a garrison in it,
and brought back the leader of the war and the other
prominent men bound in chains. But—what most
of all was worthy of admiration about him—though
he had received so great power for six months, he
did not take full advantage of the law, but having
called the people together in assembly and given
them an account of his achievements, he abdicated
his magistracy. And when the senate wanted him
to accept as much of the conquered land as he wished,
together with slaves and money out of the spoils, and
to relieve his poverty with deserved riches which he
had acquired most honourably from the enemy by
his own toils, he refused to do so. Also when his
friends and relations offered him magnificent gifts
and placed their greatest happiness in assisting such
a man, he thanked them for their zeal, but would
accept none of their presents. Instead, he retired
again to that small farm of his and resumed his life of
a farmer working his own land in preference to the life
of a king, glorying more in his poverty than others in
their riches. Not long afterwards Nautius also, the
other consul, returned to Rome with his forces, after
defeating the Sabines in a pitched battle and overrunning a large part of their country.

XXVI. After these consuls [1] came the eighty-first
Olympiad [2] (the one at which Polymnastus of Cyrenê

[1] For chaps. 26-30 cf. Livy iii. 30.
[2] 455 B.C.

5 μετειλήφει AB : μετείληφε R.

Κυρηναῖος, Ἀθήνησι δὲ ἄρχων Καλλίας, ἐφ' οὗ τὴν
ὕπατον ἀρχὴν ἐν Ῥώμῃ παρέλαβον[1] Γάιος Ὁράτιος καὶ Κόιντος Μηνύκιος. ἐπὶ τούτων Σαβῖνοι
πάλιν στρατεύσαντες ἐπὶ Ῥωμαίους πολλὴν τῆς
χώρας αὐτῶν ἐδῄωσαν, καὶ ἧκον οἱ φυγόντες ἐκ
τῶν ἀγρῶν ἀθρόοι κρατεῖσθαι πάντα ὑπ' αὐτῶν τὰ
μεταξὺ Κρουστομερίας τε καὶ Φιδήνης λέγοντες.
2 Αἰκανοί τε οἱ νεωστὶ καταπολεμηθέντες ἐν τοῖς
ὅπλοις αὖθις ἦσαν· καὶ οἱ μὲν ἀκμαιότατοι αὐτῶν
νυκτὸς ἐλάσαντες ἐπὶ Κορβιῶνα πόλιν, ἣν τῷ[2]
παρελθόντι ἐνιαυτῷ Ῥωμαίοις παρέδοσαν, τήν τε
φρουρὰν τὴν ἐν αὐτῇ κοιμωμένην εὑρόντες κατ-
έσφαξαν πλὴν ὀλίγων, οἳ ἔτυχον ἀφυστεροῦντες, οἱ
δὲ λοιποὶ μεγάλῃ χειρὶ στρατεύσαντες ἐπὶ πόλιν
Ὀρτῶνα[3] τοῦ Λατίνων ἔθνους ἐξ ἐφόδου κατα-
λαμβάνονται, καὶ ὅσα Ῥωμαίους οὐχ οἷοί τε ἦσαν
ἐργάσασθαι, ταῦτα δι' ὀργὴν τοὺς συμμάχους αὐ-
3 τῶν διέθεσαν. τοὺς μὲν γὰρ ἐν ἥβῃ πάντας, πλὴν
εἴ τινες διέφυγον εὐθὺς ἁλισκομένης τῆς πόλεως,
ἀπέκτειναν, γυναῖκας δὲ καὶ παῖδας αὐτῶν καὶ τὰ
γηραιὰ τῶν σωμάτων ἠνδραποδίσαντο, καὶ τῶν
χρημάτων ὅσα δύναμις ἦν αὐτοῖς φέρειν συσκευα-
σάμενοι κατὰ σπουδήν, πρὶν ἅπαντας ἐπιβοηθῆσαι
4 Λατίνους, ἀνέστρεψαν.[4] τούτων δὲ ἅμα προσαγγελλομένων ὑπό τε Λατίνων καὶ τῶν ἐκ τῆς φρουρᾶς διασωθέντων ἡ μὲν βουλὴ στρατιὰν ἐκπέμπειν
ἐψηφίσατο καὶ τοὺς ὑπάτους ἀμφοτέρους πορεύε-
σθαι· οἱ δὲ περὶ τὸν Οὐεργίνιον δήμαρχοι πέμπτον

---

[1] Kiessling : παρέλαβε O.
[2] ἦν τῷ B : ἦν ἐν τῷ R.
[3] πόλιν Ὀρτῶνα Kiessling : πόλιν . . ρτῶνα Ba, πόλιν . .
βοτῶνα Bb, πόλιν βιρτῶνα A.

won the foot-race), the archon at Athens being
Callias, in whose term of office Gaius Horatius [1] and
Quintus Minucius succeeded to the consulship at
Rome. During their term of office the Sabines made
another expedition against the Romans and laid
waste much of their territory; and the country
people who had fled from their fields arrived in great
numbers, reporting that all the country between
Crustumerium and Fidenae was in possession of the
enemy. The Aequians also, who had been recently
conquered, were once more in arms. The flower of
their army, marching by night to the city of Corbio,
which they had handed over to the Romans the year
before, and finding the garrison there asleep, put all to
the sword except a few who chanced to be late to bed.
The rest of the Aequians marched in great force to
Ortona, a city of the Latin nation, and took it by
storm; and the injuries they were unable to inflict
on the Romans they inflicted in their resentment on
the Romans' allies. For they put to death all the
men who were in the prime of life except those who
had escaped at once while the city was being taken,
and enslaved their wives and children together with
the aged; then, hastily gathering together all the
possessions they could carry off, they returned home
before all the Latins could come to the rescue. As
news of these disasters was brought simultaneously
both by the Latins and by those of the garrison who
had escaped, the senate voted to send out an army
and that both consuls should take the field. But
Verginius and his fellow tribunes, who held the same

---

[1] Livy gives the name as M. Horatius Pulvillus.

---

[4] ἀνέστρεψαν Bb : om. ABa.

ἔτος ἐπὶ τῆς αὐτῆς ὄντες ἐξουσίας ἐκώλυον, ὥσπερ
καὶ ἐν τοῖς πρότερον ἐποίουν ἔτεσιν, ἐνιστάμενοι
ταῖς στρατολογίαις τῶν ὑπάτων, τὸν ἐντὸς τείχους
πρῶτον ἀξιοῦντες καταλυθῆναι πόλεμον ἀποδοθεί-
σης τῷ δήμῳ τῆς περὶ τοῦ νόμου διαγνώσεως ὃν
ὑπὲρ τῆς ἰσηγορίας εἰσέφερον, ὅ τε δῆμος αὐτοῖς
συνελάμβανε πολλοὺς κατὰ τῆς βουλῆς καὶ ἐπι-
5 φθόνους διεξιοῦσι λόγους. ἑλκομένου δὲ τοῦ χρόνου
καὶ οὔτε τῶν ὑπάτων ὑπομενόντων προβουλεῦσαί
τε καὶ εἰς τὸν δῆμον ἐξενεγκεῖν τὸν νόμον, οὔτε
τῶν δημάρχων συγχωρῆσαι βουλομένων τὴν κατα-
γραφὴν καὶ τὴν ἔξοδον τῆς στρατιᾶς γενέσθαι, λόγων τε πολλῶν καὶ κατηγοριῶν ἃς ἐποιοῦντο κατ'
ἀλλήλων ἔν τε ταῖς ἐκκλησίαις καὶ ἐπὶ τῆς βουλῆς
μάτην ἀναλισκομένων, ἑτέρα τις εἰσαχθεῖσα ὑπὸ
τῶν δημάρχων ἐπὶ τῇ βουλῇ πολιτεία καὶ παρα-
κρουσαμένη τὸ συνέδριον τὴν μὲν τότε κατέχουσαν
στάσιν ἐπράυνεν, ἑτέρων δὲ πολλῶν καὶ μεγάλων
ἐγένετο πλεονεκτημάτων αἰτία τῷ δήμῳ. διηγήσομαι δὲ καὶ ταύτην τὴν δυναστείαν ὃν τρόπον ὁ
δῆμος ἔλαβε.

XXVII. Φθειρομένης[1] καὶ διαρπαζομένης τῆς τε
Ῥωμαίων καὶ τῶν συμμάχων γῆς, καὶ τῶν πολεμίων ὡς δι' ἐρημίας ἐλαυνόντων κατ' ἐλπίδα τοῦ
μηδεμίαν ἐπ' αὐτοὺς ἐξελεύσεσθαι δύναμιν διὰ τὴν
κατέχουσαν ἐν τῇ πόλει στάσιν, οἱ μὲν ὕπατοι τὴν
βουλὴν συνήγαγον, ὡς περὶ τῶν ὅλων ἔσχατον
2 τοῦτο βουλευσόμενοι.[2] ῥηθέντων δὲ πολλῶν λόγων
πρῶτος ἐρωτηθεὶς γνώμην Λεύκιος Κοΐντιος, ὁ τῷ
παρελθόντι γενόμενος ἔτει δικτάτωρ, ἀνὴρ οὐ μόνον

---

[1] φθειρομένης B : φερομένης A.
[2] βουλευσόμενοι R : βουλευόμενοι AB.

power for the fifth year, sought to prevent this, as
they had also done in the preceding years, opposing
the levies announced by the consuls and demanding
that the war inside the walls should first be termin-
ated by allowing the populace to decide about the
law which the tribunes were trying to introduce
regarding an equality of rights ; and the populace
joined with them in uttering many invidious charges
against the senate. But as the time dragged on and
neither the consuls would consent to a preliminary
vote by the senate or to the laying of the law before
the populace, nor the tribunes to allow the levies to
be made and the army to take the field, and many
speeches were made and charges hurled back and
forth both in the meetings of the assembly and in the
senate, all in vain, another measure that was introduced against the senate and misled its members did
indeed appease the dissension then raging, but
proved the source of many other great gains to the
populace. I shall now give an account of the manner
in which the populace secured this power.

XXVII. While the territory of both the Romans
and their allies was being laid waste and plundered
and the enemy marched through it as through a
solitude, in the confidence that no army would come
out against them by reason of the dissension then
raging in the city, the consuls assembled the senate
with the intention of deliberating finally this time
about the whole situation. After many speeches had
been made, the person who was first asked his opinion
was Lucius Quintius, who had been dictator the year
before, a man who had the reputation of being not

τὰ πολέμια δεινότατος τῶν καθ' ἑαυτόν, ἀλλὰ καὶ
τὰ πολιτικὰ δοκῶν εἶναι φρονιμώτατος, γνώμην
ἀπεφήνατο τήνδε[1]· μάλιστα μὲν πείθειν[2] τούς τε
δημάρχους καὶ τοὺς ἄλλους πολίτας τὴν μὲν ὑπὲρ
τοῦ νόμου διάγνωσιν οὐθὲν ἐν τῷ παρόντι κατ-
επείγουσαν εἰς ἑτέρους ἀναβαλέσθαι καιροὺς ἐπιτηδειοτέρους, τὸν δ' ἐν χερσὶν ὄντα καὶ ὅσον οὔπω
τῇ πόλει πλησιάζοντα πόλεμον ἄρασθαι πάσῃ προθυμίᾳ, καὶ μὴ περιιδεῖν τὴν μετὰ πολλῶν κτηθεῖσαν
ἡγεμονίαν πόνων αἰσχρῶς καὶ ἀνάνδρως ἀπολο-
3 μένην. ἐὰν δὲ μὴ πείθηται ὁ δῆμος, τοὺς πατρικίους
ἅμα τοῖς πελάταις καθοπλισαμένους τῶν τ' ἄλλων
πολιτῶν παραλαβόντας ὅσοις[3] ἦν ἑκοῦσι συνάρασθαι
τοῦ καλλίστου περὶ[4] τῆς πατρίδος ἀγῶνος, χωρεῖν
προθύμως ἐπὶ τὸν πόλεμον θεοὺς ὅσοι φυλάττουσι
τὴν Ῥωμαίων πόλιν ἡγεμόνας τῆς ἐξόδου ποιησα-
4 μένους. συμβήσεσθαι γὰρ αὐτοῖς δυεῖν καλῶν
ἔργων καὶ δικαίων θάτερον, ἢ νίκην ἐξενέγκασθαι
πασῶν ὧν αὐτοί ποτε ἢ οἱ πατέρες ἐξηνέγκαντο
λαμπροτάτην, ἢ περὶ τῶν ἐν αὐτῇ καλῶν εὐψύχως
ἀγωνιζομένοις ἀποθανεῖν. ταύτης μέντοι τῆς καλῆς
πείρας οὔτ' αὐτὸς ἀπολείψεσθαι ἔφη, ἀλλ' ἐν ἴσῳ
τοῖς κράτιστα ἐρρωμένοις παρὼν ἀγωνιεῖσθαι, οὔτε
τῶν ἄλλων τινὰ πρεσβυτέρων οἷς ἐστιν ἐλευθερίας
τε καὶ δόξης ἀγαθῆς λόγος.

XXVIII. Ὡς δὲ καὶ τοῖς ἄλλοις ἅπασι ταῦτ'
ἐδόκει καὶ οὐθεὶς ἦν ὁ τἀναντία ἐρῶν, οἱ μὲν ὕπατοι
τὸν δῆμον εἰς ἐκκλησίαν συνεκάλουν. συνελθόντος
δ' ὡς ἐπὶ καινοῖς ἀκούσμασι παντὸς τοῦ κατὰ τὴν
πόλιν ὄχλου παρελθὼν ἅτερος τῶν ὑπάτων Γάιος

---

[1] τήνδε Jacoby : ἐν ᾗ Bb, om. R.
[2] πείθειν ΑBa : πείθει Bb.

only the ablest general but also the wisest statesman
of his time. The opinion he expressed was as follows :
That they should preferably persuade both the tribunes and the rest of the citizens to postpone to more
suitable times their decision regarding the law, which
was not at all pressing at the moment, and to undertake with all alacrity the war that was at hand and
all but at their gates, and not to allow their empire,
which they had acquired with many toils, to be lost
in a shameful and pusillanimous fashion. But if the
populace would not be persuaded, he advised that the
patricians should arm themselves together with their
clients, and associating with themselves such of the
other citizens as were willing to take part in this most
glorious struggle for the fatherland, to engage in the
war with alacrity, taking as leaders of the expedition
all the gods who protect the Roman state. For one
or the other of two honourable and just destinies
would be theirs : they would either win a victory
more brilliant than all which they or their ancestors
had ever won, or die fighting bravely for the noble
prizes that victory brings with it. He added that
neither he himself would be wanting in this glorious
enterprise, but would be present and fight with a
spirit equal to that of the most robust, nor would any
others of the older men be wanting who had any
regard for liberty and a good name.

XXVIII. All the others approving of this advice
and there being no one to speak in opposition, the
consuls called an assembly of the populace ; and
when all the people of the city had come together
in expectation of hearing something new, Gaius

---

³ Post : οἷς O, Jacoby.
⁴ περὶ added by Post, ὑπὲρ by Reiske.

Ὁράτιος ἐπειρᾶτο πείθειν τοὺς δημοτικοὺς ἑκόντας
ὑπομεῖναι καὶ ταύτην τὴν στρατείαν. ἀντιλεγόντων δὲ τῶν δημάρχων καὶ τοῦ δήμου προσέχοντος
αὐτοῖς τὸν νοῦν παρελθὼν πάλιν ὁ ὕπατος εἶπε·

2 "Καλόν γ',[1] ὦ[2] Οὐεργίνιε, καὶ θαυμαστὸν ἔργον
ἐξειργάσασθε διασπάσαντες ἀπὸ τῆς βουλῆς τὸν
δῆμον· καὶ τὸ μὲν ἐφ' ὑμῖν εἶναι μέρος πάντ' ἀπ-
ολωλέκαμεν ὅσα παρὰ τῶν προγόνων παραλαβόντες
ἢ τοῖς ἑαυτῶν πόνοις κτησάμενοι κατέσχομεν

3 ἀγαθά.[3] οὐ μὴν ἡμεῖς γ' ἀκονιτὶ μεθησόμεθα
αὐτῶν, ἀλλ' ἀναλαβόντες τὰ ὅπλα μετὰ τῶν βουλομένων σῴζεσθαι τὴν πατρίδα χωρήσομεν ἐπὶ τὸν
ἀγῶνα τὰς ἀγαθὰς προβαλλόμενοι τῶν ἔργων
ἐλπίδας· καὶ εἴ τις ἄρα θεὸς ἐπισκοπεῖ τοὺς καλοὺς
καὶ δικαίους ἀγῶνας, καὶ ἡ τὴν πόλιν τήνδε αὔ-
ξουσα ἐκ πολλοῦ[4] τύχη μήπω[5] προλέλοιπεν αὐτήν,
κρείττους τῶν ἐχθρῶν ἐσόμεθα· εἰ δέ τις ἄρα
ἐνέστηκε δαίμων καὶ ἐναντιοῦται τῇ σωτηρίᾳ τῆς
πόλεως, οὗτοι τό γ' ἐν ἡμῖν εὔνουν καὶ πρόθυμον
ἀπολεῖται, ἀλλὰ τὸν ἁπάντων κράτιστον θάνατον

4 αἱρησόμεθα περὶ τῆς πατρίδος. ὑμεῖς δὲ αὐτοῦ
μένοντες οἰκουρεῖτε ἅμα ταῖς γυναιξίν, ὦ καλοὶ καὶ
γενναῖοι προστάται τῆς πόλεως, ἐγκαταλιπόντες,
μᾶλλον δὲ προδόντες, ἡμᾶς, οἷς οὔτ' ἂν νικήσωμεν
ἡμεῖς[6] ὁ[7] βίος[8] ἔσται καλός, οὔτ' ἂν ἄλλως χωρήσῃ

5 τὰ καθ' ἡμᾶς ἀσφαλής· εἰ μὴ ἄρα ἐκείνῃ τῇ ψυχρᾷ
ἐλπίδι ἐπαίρεσθε, ὡς διαφθαρέντων τῶν πατρικίων
ὑμᾶς ἐάσουσιν οἱ πολέμιοι ταύτην ὑπολογιζόμενοι

---

[1] γ' added by Cobet.   [2] ὦ B : om. R.
[3] ἀγαθά R : τἀγαθά B, om. Garrer.
[4] πολλοῦ B : πολλοῦ χρόνου R.
[5] μήπω ABa : εἰ μήπω Bb.

Horatius, one of the consuls, came forward and attempted to persuade the plebeians to submit willingly to this campaign also. But as the tribunes opposed this and the populace gave heed to them, the consul again came forward and said : " A fine and wonderful thing, indeed, have you tribunes accomplished, Verginius, in dividing the populace from the senate ; and, so far as it rests with you, we have lost all the advantages which we possessed, whether inherited from our ancestors or acquired by our own toils. As for us, however, we shall not part with them without a struggle, but shall take up arms along with all who desire the preservation of the fatherland and shall enter the struggle holding before our deeds the buckler of fair hopes.[1] And if any god watches over noble and just struggles, and if Fortune, which long has been exalting this commonwealth, has not yet abandoned it, we shall have the victory over our enemies ; or, if any divinity is opposed to and stands in the way of the preservation of the commonwealth, at any rate our affection and zeal for it will not perish, but we shall choose the best of all deaths—to die for the fatherland. As for you, stay here and keep house with the women, O fine and noble protectors of the commonwealth, after abandoning, or rather betraying, us ; but life for you will be neither honourable, if we conquer, nor safe, if things go otherwise with us. Unless, indeed, you are buoying yourselves up with the bleak hope that when the patricians are all destroyed the enemy will spare you in consideration of

---

[1] The figure is borrowed from Demosthenes, *De Cor.* 97.

[6] ἡμεῖς B : om. R.

[7] ὁ A : om. B. [8] βίος B : βίος ἡμῶν A.

261

τὴν εὐεργεσίαν, καὶ συγχωρήσουσιν ὑμῖν τὴν πατρίδα καὶ τὴν ἐλευθερίαν καὶ τὴν ἡγεμονίαν καὶ
πάντα τἄλλα ἀγαθὰ ὅσα νῦν ἔχετε καρποῦσθαι, ὧν
ὑμεῖς ὅτε τὰ ἄριστα ἐφρονεῖτε πολλὴν μὲν γῆν
ἀπετέμεσθε, πολλὰς δὲ πόλεις ἐξανδραποδισάμενοι
κατεσκάψατε, πολλὰ δὲ καὶ μεγάλα καὶ οὐδ' ὑπὸ
τοῦ παντὸς αἰῶνος ἀφανισθησόμενα τρόπαια καὶ
6 μνημεῖα τῆς ἔχθρας ἀνεστήσατε. ἀλλὰ τί τῷ δήμῳ
ταῦτ' ἐπιτιμῶ, ὃς οὐδέποτε πονηρὸς ἑκὼν ἐγένετο,
μᾶλλον ἢ οὐχ ὑμῖν, ὦ Οὐεργίνιε, τοῖς τὰ καλὰ ταῦτα πολιτευομένοις; ἡμῖν μὲν οὖν, οἷς ἀνάγκη μηδὲν
ταπεινὸν φρονεῖν, δέδοκταί τε καὶ οὐθὲν ἔσται τὸ
κωλῦσον ἄρασθαι τὸν ὑπὲρ τῆς πατρίδος ἀγῶνα,
ὑμῖν δὲ τοῖς ἐγκαταλείπουσι[1] καὶ προδιδοῦσι[2] τὸ
κοινὸν ἥξει δίκη τιμωρὸς οὐ μεμπτὴ παρὰ θεῶν,
ἐὰν ἄρα διαφύγητε τὴν παρ' ἀνθρώπων κόλασιν.
7 ἀλλ' οὐδὲ ταύτην[3] διαφεύξεσθε· καὶ μή με δεδίτ-
τεσθαι ὑπολάβητε, ἀλλ' εὖ ἴστε ὅτι οἱ καταλει-
φθέντες ἡμῶν ἐνθάδε φύλακες τῆς πόλεως, ἐὰν
κρείττω τὰ τῶν ἐχθρῶν γένηται, φρονήσουσιν ἃ
προσῆκεν αὐτοῖς φρονεῖν. οὐ γὰρ ἤδη βαρβάροις
μέν τισιν ἁλισκομένοις ὑπὸ τῶν πολεμίων εἰς νοῦν
ἦλθε μήτε γυναικῶν αὐτοῖς παραχωρῆσαι μήτε
παίδων μήτε πόλεων, ἀλλὰ τὰς μὲν ἐμπρῆσαι, τὰς[4]
8 δὲ κατασφάξαι, Ῥωμαίοις δ' ἄρα, οἷς ἑτέρων ἄρχειν
πάτριόν ἐστιν, οὐ παραστήσεται ταῦτα περὶ ἑαυτῶν
φρονεῖν; οὐχ οὕτως ἀγεννεῖς ἔσονται, ἀλλ' ἀφ'
ὑμῶν τῶν ἐχθίστων ἀρξάμενοι τότε χωρήσουσι

---

[1] ἐγκαταλείπουσι R : ἐγκαταλιποῦσι Bb, Jacoby.
[2] προδιδοῦσι O : προδοῦσι Cobet, Jacoby.
[3] ταύτην γε A.
[4] τὰς A : τὰ B, τοὺς Sylburg.

this service and will allow you to enjoy your country,
your liberty, your empire and all the other blessings
you now have, notwithstanding that you, when you
displayed the noblest spirit, deprived these very
enemies of much land, razed many of their cities and
enslaved their inhabitants, and erected many great
trophies and monuments of your enmity against them
which not even all time to come will ever blot out.
But why do I charge this against the populace, which
never became cowardly of its own accord, and not
rather against you tribunes, Verginius, who are the
authors of these fine measures ?   We, then, who must
needs show no ignoble spirit, have taken our resolution and nothing shall hinder us from undertaking the
struggle in defence of the fatherland ; but upon you,
who abandon and betray the commonwealth, will
come a punishment not to be scorned, as vengeance
from the gods, if so be that you escape the punishment of men ; yet you will not escape that either.
And do not imagine that I am trying to terrify you,
but be assured that those of us who will be left behind
here to guard the city shall, in case the enemy should
prove victorious, show that spirit which it befits
them to show.   Have there not indeed been instances
already of barbarians who, when they were on the
point of being captured by the enemy, resolved not
to yield to them either their wives, their children or
their cities, but to burn the cities and slay their dear
ones ?   And will it fail, then, to occur to the Romans,
to whom it is a heritage from their fathers to rule over
others, to show this same spirit in their own case ?
They will never be so degenerate, but will begin with
you who are their worst enemies and only afterwards

πρὸς τὰ φίλια. πρὸς ταῦτα ὁρῶντες ἐκκλησιάζετε
καὶ νόμους εἰσφέρετε καινούς.''

XXIX. Ταῦτα καὶ πολλὰ τούτοις ὅμοια εἰπὼν
παρεστήσατο τοὺς πρεσβυτάτους τῶν πατρικίων
κλαίοντας, οὓς ἰδόντες πολλοὶ τῶν δημοτικῶν οὐδ'
αὐτοὶ κατέχειν τὰ δάκρυα ἐδύναντο. γενομένης δὲ
πολλῆς συμπαθείας πρός τε τὰς ἡλικίας τῶν ἀνδρῶν καὶ πρὸς τὰς ἀξίας μικρὸν ἐπισχὼν ὁ ὕπα-
2 τος, ''Οὐκ αἰσχύνεσθε,'' ἔφησεν, ''ὦ πολῖται, οὐδὲ
κατὰ γῆς δύεσθε, εἰ οἵδε οἱ γέροντες ὑπὲρ ὑμῶν
τῶν νέων τὰ ὅπλα ἀναλήψονται, ἀλλ' ὑπομενεῖτε
ἀπολειφθῆναι τούτων ἡγουμένων, οὓς ἀεὶ πατέρας
ἐκαλεῖτε; ὦ σχέτλιοι ὑμεῖς καὶ οὐδὲ πολῖται ταύτης ἄξιοι λέγεσθαι[1] τῆς γῆς, ἣν ἔκτισαν οἱ τοὺς
πατέρας ἐπὶ τῶν ὤμων ἐνέγκαντες, οἷς καὶ δι'
ὅπλων καὶ διὰ πυρὸς ὁδοὺς ἀσφαλεῖς θεοὶ παρ-
3 έσχον.'' ὡς δὲ κατέμαθεν ὁ[2] Οὐεργίνιος ἀγόμενον
τὸν δῆμον ὑπὸ τῶν λόγων, δεδοικὼς μὴ παρὰ τὴν
ἑαυτοῦ γνώμην κοινωνεῖν ὑπομείνῃ τοῦ πολέμου,
παρελθὼν εἶπεν· '' Ἡμεῖς οὔτ' ἐγκαταλείπομεν οὔτε προδίδομεν ὑμᾶς, ὦ πατέρες, οὐδ' ἂν ἀπο-
λειφθείημεν ὑμῶν, ὥσπερ οὐδὲ πρότερον ἠξιώσαμεν
οὐδεμιᾶς ἀπολειφθῆναι στρατείας, ἀλλὰ καὶ ζῆν
αἱρούμεθα σὺν ὑμῖν καὶ πάσχειν ὅ τι ἂν τῷ
4 δαίμονι δοκῇ μεθ' ὑμῶν. πρόθυμοι δ' ἐν παντὶ καιρῷ περὶ ὑμᾶς γεγονότες ἀξιοῦμεν[3] μετρίας παρ'
ὑμῶν τυχεῖν χάριτος, ὥσπερ τῶν κοινῶν κινδύνων
ἰσομοιρούμεν ὑμῖν, οὕτως καὶ τῶν δικαίων τὸ ἴσον

---

[1] λέγεσθαι B : om. R.   [2] ὁ Steph. : om. AB.
[3] ἀξιοῦμεν A : ἠξιοῦμεν B.

turn to their loved ones. Consider these matters
before you hold your assemblies and introduce new
laws."

XXIX. After he had said this and many things to
the same purport, he brought before them the oldest
patricians in tears, at sight of whom many of the
plebeians could not even themselves refrain from
weeping. When great compassion had been aroused
both by the age and the dignity of these men, the
consul, after a short pause, said : " Are you not
ashamed, citizens, and ready to sink beneath the
earth, when these old men are going to take up arms
in defence of you who are young ? Will you bear
to abandon these leaders whom you always called
fathers ? Wretched men that you are, and unworthy
even to be called citizens of this land settled by men
who carried their fathers on their shoulders,[1] men to
whom the gods granted a safe passage through arms
and through fire ! " When Verginius perceived that
the people were moved by these words, he was afraid
lest, contrary to his desire, they might consent to
join in the war ; and coming forward, he said : " As
for us, we are neither abandoning nor betraying you,
fathers, nor would we desert you, even as we have
hitherto never declined taking part in any expedition ; on the contrary, we choose both to live with
you and to suffer with you whatever Heaven shall
decree. But since we have at all times been zealous
in your service, we desire to receive from you a
moderate favour—that, even as we share the common
dangers with you, so we may also enjoy an equality

---

[1] Dionysius generalizes the well-known legend concerning
Aeneas and his father Anchises in their flight from burning
Troy.

ἔχειν, νόμους καταστησάμενοι φύλακας[1] τῆς ἐλευ-
5 θερίας, οἷς ἅπαντες ἀεὶ χρησόμεθα. εἰ δὲ προσ-
ίσταται τοῦθ᾽ ὑμῖν, καὶ οὐκ ἀξιοῦτε τοῖς ἑαυτῶν
πολίταις ταύτην συγχωρῆσαι τὴν χάριν, ἀλλὰ θανάτου τιμᾶσθε τὸ μεταδοῦναι τῷ δήμῳ τῆς ἰσηγορίας, οὐκέτι φιλονεικοῦμεν ὑμῖν· αἰτησόμεθα δ᾽
ἑτέραν παρ᾽ ὑμῶν χάριν, ἧς τυχόντες ἴσως ἂν οὐδὲ
καινῶν ἔτι δεηθείημεν νόμων. εἰσέρχεται δ᾽ ἡμᾶς
εὐλάβεια, μή ποτε οὐδὲ ταύτης τύχωμεν, ἐξ ἧς
τῇ βουλῇ μὲν οὐδὲν ἔσται βλάβος, τῷ δὲ δήμῳ τιμή
τις ὑπάρξει καὶ φιλανθρωπία.''

XXX. Εἰπόντος δὲ τοῦ ὑπάτου ὅτι τοῦτο τὸ
πολίτευμα τῇ βουλῇ συγχωροῦντες οὐθενὸς ἄλλου
ἁμαρτήσονται τῶν μετρίων, καὶ κελεύοντος λέγειν
ὅτου δέονται, ὀλίγα διαλεχθεὶς τοῖς συνάρχουσιν ὁ
2 Οὐεργίνιος ἐπὶ τῆς βουλῆς ἔφησεν ἐρεῖν. καὶ μετὰ
ταῦτα συναγαγόντων τὸ συνέδριον τῶν ὑπάτων παρελθὼν καὶ τὰ δίκαια τοῦ δήμου πρὸς τὴν βουλὴν
ἅπαντα εἰσενεγκάμενος[2] ᾐτήσατο διπλασιασθῆναι
τὴν ἀρχὴν τὴν προϊσταμένην τοῦ δήμου, καὶ ἀντὶ
τῶν πέντε δημάρχων δέκα εἰς ἕκαστον ἐνιαυτὸν
ἀποδείκνυσθαι. τοῦτο οἱ μὲν ἄλλοι βλάβην οὐδεμίαν ᾤοντο τῷ κοινῷ φέρειν, ἀλλὰ διδόναι καὶ μὴ
ἀντιπράττειν παρῄνουν, ἄρχοντος τῆς γνώμης Λευκίου Κοϊντίου, τοῦ τότε μέγιστον ἔχοντος ἐν τῇ
3 βουλῇ κράτος. εἷς δὲ μόνος ἀντέλεγε Γάιος Κλαύδιος, υἱὸς Ἀππίου Κλαυδίου, τοῦ παρὰ πάντα τὸν
χρόνον τοῖς εἰσηγήμασι τῶν δημοτικῶν, εἴ τινα μὴ
νόμιμα ἦν, ἐναντιωθέντος, διαδεδεγμένος τὰ πολι-

---

[1] φύλακας om. A.
[2] εἰσενεγκάμενος A : ἐνεγκάμενος B, εἰς ἓν συνενεγκάμενος
Reiske.

of rights, by instituting as safeguards of our liberty laws which we shall all alike use always. However, if this proposal offends you and you do not deign to grant this favour to your fellow citizens, but regard it as a capital crime to give the populace an equal share of rights, we shall no longer contend with you ; but we shall ask another favour of you, upon obtaining which we may possibly no longer stand in need of new laws. We have a shrewd suspicion, however, that we shall not obtain even this favour—one which, while doing no injury to the senate, will bring to the populace a kind of honour and general goodwill."

XXX. When the consul replied that if the tribunes would yield on this measure to the senate they would be denied nothing else that was reasonable, and ordered him to state what they desired, Verginius, after a short conference with his colleagues, said he would announce it in the senate. Thereupon, when the consuls had convened the senate, Verginius came forward, and after presenting to that body all the just demands of the populace, asked that the magistracy which protected the populace should be doubled and that instead of five tribunes ten should be chosen every year. Most of the senators thought this would cause no harm to the commonwealth and advised granting it without offering any opposition ; this opinion was first offered by Lucius Quintius, who at that time had the greatest authority in the senate. Only one person, Gaius Claudius, spoke against it. He was the son of Appius Claudius, who had on every occasion opposed the measures of the plebeians when any of them were contrary to law ; he had inherited

τεύματα τοῦ πατρός, καὶ ὅτ᾽ αὐτὸς εἶχε τὴν ὕπατον
ἀρχὴν κωλύσας δοθῆναι τοῖς δημάρχοις τὴν κατὰ
τῶν ἱππέων τῶν ἐπὶ[1] τῇ συνωμοσίᾳ διαβαλλομένων
ἐξέτασιν, καὶ μακρὸν διεξελθὼν λόγον ἐδίδασκεν
ὅτι μετριώτερος μὲν ὁ δῆμος οὐδὲν οὐδὲ χρηστό-
τερος ἔσται διπλασιασθείσης αὐτῷ τῆς ἀρχῆς,
4 ἀνοητότερος δὲ καὶ βαρύτερος. οὐ γὰρ ἐπὶ ῥητοῖς
τισι παραλήψεσθαι τὴν ἀρχὴν τοὺς ὕστερον ἀπο-
δειχθησομένους, ὥστε μένειν ἐπὶ τοῖς καθεστη-
κόσιν, ἀλλὰ καὶ τὸν περὶ τῆς κληρουχίας αὖθις
προθήσειν[2] λόγον[3] καὶ τὸν ὑπὲρ τῆς ἰσοτιμίας,[4] καὶ
πάντας ἑξῆς ζητήσειν ὅ τι λέγοντες ἢ πράττοντες
τὸ μὲν τοῦ δήμου κράτος αὐξήσουσι, τὰς δὲ τῆς
βουλῆς τιμὰς καταλύσουσι. καὶ σφόδρα ἐκίνησε
5 τοὺς πολλοὺς ὁ λόγος. ἔπειτα μετήγαγεν αὐτοὺς
ὁ Κόιντιος διδάσκων ὅτι πρὸς τῆς βουλῆς ἐστι τὸ
πολλοὺς εἶναι τοῦ δήμου προστάτας. ἧττον γὰρ
ὁμονοήσειν τοὺς πλείους[5] τῶν ἐλαττόνων, μίαν δὲ
βοήθειαν εἶναι τοῖς κοινοῖς, ἣν Ἄππιον Κλαύδιον
τὸν Γαΐου πατέρα πρῶτον ἰδεῖν, ἐὰν στασιάζῃ τὸ
6 ἀρχεῖον[6] καὶ μὴ πᾶσι τὸ αὐτὸ δοκῇ. ἐδόκει τε δὴ
ταῦτα καὶ γίνεται δόγμα βουλῆς· ἐξεῖναι τῷ δήμῳ
δέκα δημάρχους καθ᾽ ἕκαστον ἐνιαυτὸν ἀποδεικνύναι, τῶν δὲ τότε ὄντων ἐν ἀρχῇ μηθένα. τοῦτο τὸ
προβούλευμα οἱ περὶ τὸν Οὐεργίνιον λαβόντες
ἐξήνεγκαν καὶ κυρώσαντες τὸν ἐπ᾽ αὐτῷ γραφέντα

---

[1] ἐπὶ Sylburg : ἐν O.
[2] προθήσειν B : προσθήσειν R.
[3] νόμον Cobet.   [4] ἰσονομίας Spelman, Cobet.
[5] Sylburg : πλείστους O.   [6] Sylburg : ἄρχον O.

the political principles of his father, and when
he himself was consul, had prevented the inquiry
concerning the knights accused of conspiracy from
being committed to the tribunes. This man made
a long speech, pointing out that the populace,
if their magistracy were doubled, would not be
any more moderate or worthy, but more stupid
and more troublesome. For the tribunes to be
chosen thereafter, he said, would not receive the
magistracy upon certain definite terms, so as to
adhere to the established customs, but would again
bring up the question of the allotment of lands
and that of an equality of privileges,[1] and all of them
in turn would seek both by their words and by
their actions to increase the power of the populace
and abolish the privileges of the senate. This speech
had a great effect upon most of the senators. Then
Quintius brought them over again by showing that
it was to the interest of the senate that there should
be many champions of the populace. For there would
be less harmony among many than among a few, and
there was just one way of relieving the commonwealth, a way that Appius Claudius, the father of
Gaius, had been the first to perceive—namely, if
there should be dissension and lack of unanimity
in the college of tribunes. This opinion prevailed,
and the senate passed a decree that the populace
should be permitted to appoint ten tribunes each
year, but that no one of the men then in office should
be eligible. Verginius and his colleagues, having got
this preliminary decree from the senate, laid it before
the populace ; and when they had secured the rati-

---

[1] Or " honours," in the sense of " offices."   Spelman and
Cobet would read " equality of laws."

νόμον δέκα δημάρχους εἰς τὸν ἐπιόντα ἐνιαυτὸν
ἀπέδειξαν.

7 Παυσαμένης δὲ τῆς στάσεως καταγράψαντες τὰς
δυνάμεις οἱ ὕπατοι διεκληρώσαντο τὰς ἐξόδους·
Μηνυκίῳ μὲν οὖν ὁ κατὰ Σαβίνων πόλεμος ἐδόθη,
Ὁρατίῳ δὲ ὁ κατ' Αἰκανῶν, καὶ κατὰ σπουδὴν
ἐξῄεσαν ἀμφότεροι. Σαβῖνοι μὲν οὖν τὰς πόλεις
διὰ φυλακῆς ἔχοντες ὑπερεῖδον ἀγομένων τε καὶ
φερομένων ἁπάντων τῶν κατὰ τοὺς ἀγρούς, Αἰκανοὶ δὲ τὴν ἐναντιωσομένην Ῥωμαίοις δύναμιν
8 ἀπέστειλαν. ἀγωνισάμενοι δὲ λαμπρῶς οὐχ οἷοί
τε ἐγένοντο τὴν Ῥωμαίων ὑπερβαλέσθαι δύναμιν,
ἀλλ' ἠναγκάσθησαν εἰς τὰς πόλεις ἀπελθεῖν ἀποβαλόντες τὸ πολίχνιον ὑπὲρ οὗ τὸν ἀγῶνα ἐποιοῦντο. Ὁράτιος δὲ τρεψάμενος τοὺς πολεμίους καὶ
πολλὰ τῆς χώρας αὐτῶν κακώσας τοῦ τε Κορβι-
ῶνος τὰ τείχη κατασπάσας καὶ τὰς οἰκήσεις ἐκ
θεμελίων ἀνελὼν ἀπῆγε τὴν δύναμιν ἐπ' οἴκου.

XXXI. Τῷ δ' ἑξῆς ἔτει Μάρκου Οὐαλερίου καὶ
Σπορίου Οὐεργινίου τὴν ὑπατείαν ἐχόντων στρατιὰ
μὲν ὑπερόριος οὐδεμία ἐξῆλθε Ῥωμαίων, πολιτικὰ
δέ τινα[1] προσκρούσματα[2] τοῖς δημάρχοις πρὸς τοὺς
ὑπάτους συνέστη πάλιν, ἐξ ὧν ἔσχον οἱ δήμαρχοι
παρασπάσαντές τι τῆς ὑπατικῆς δυναστείας. τὸν
μὲν γὰρ ἔμπροσθεν χρόνον ἐκκλησίας μόνον ἦσαν
οἱ δήμαρχοι κύριοι, βουλὴν δὲ συνάγειν ἢ γνώμην
ἀγορεύειν οὐκ ἐξῆν αὐτοῖς, ἀλλ' ἦν τῶν ὑπάτων
2 τοῦτο τὸ γέρας. οἱ δὲ τότε δήμαρχοι πρῶτοι
συγκαλεῖν ἐπεβάλοντο τὴν βουλὴν Ἰκιλλίου τὴν
πεῖραν εἰσηγησαμένου, ὃς ἡγεῖτο μὲν τοῦ ἀρχείου,
δραστήριος δέ τις ἦν ἀνὴρ καὶ ὡς Ῥωμαῖος εἰπεῖν

---

[1] τινα B : om. R.

fication of the law embodying the measure, they chose ten tribunes for the following year.

After the sedition was appeased the consuls enrolled their forces and drew lots for their commands. To Minucius fell the war against the Sabines and to Horatius that against the Aequians ; and both set out in haste. The Sabines garrisoned their cities and permitted everything in the country districts to be pillaged ; but the Aequians sent an army to oppose the Romans. Though they fought brilliantly, they were unable to overcome the Roman army, but were compelled to retire to their cities after the loss of the small town in defence of which they were fighting. Horatius, after putting the enemy to flight, ravaged a large part of their country, razed the walls of Corbio and demolished the houses to their foundations, then led his army home.

XXXI. The following year,[1] when Marcus Valerius and Spurius Verginius were consuls, no army of the Romans went out of their borders, but there were fresh outbreaks of civil strife between the tribunes and the consuls, as a result of which the former wrested away some part of the consular power. Before this time the power of the tribunes was limited to the popular assembly and they had no authority either to convene the senate or to express an opinion there, that being a prerogative of the consuls. The tribunes of the year in question were the first who undertook to convene the senate, the experiment being made by Icilius, the head of their college, a man of action and, for a Roman, not lacking in elo-

---

[1] For chaps. 31 f. cf. Livy iii. 31, 1.

[2] προσκρούσματα B : προσκρούματα R.

οὐκ ἀδύνατος. εἰσέφερε γάρ τι καὶ οὗτος πολίτευμα
καινὸν ἀξιῶν ἀπομερισθῆναι τοῖς δημόταις τόπον
εἰς οἰκιῶν κατασκευὰς τὸν καλούμενον Αὐεντῖνον.
ἔστι δὲ λόφος ὑψηλὸς ἐπιεικῶς, οὐκ ἐλάττων ἢ
δώδεκα σταδίων τὴν περίμετρον, ἐμπεριεχόμενος
τῇ πόλει, ὃς οὐχ ἅπας τότε ᾠκεῖτο,[1] ἀλλ' ἦν δη-
3 μόσιός τε καὶ ὕλης ἀνάπλεως. τοῦτο τὸ πολίτευμα
εἰσάγων ὁ δήμαρχος τοῖς τότε ὑπάτοις καὶ τῇ
βουλῇ προσῄει δεόμενος τὸν ἐπ'[2] αὐτῷ γραφέντα
νόμον προβουλεῦσαί τε καὶ εἰς τὸν δῆμον ἐξενεγκεῖν. ἀναβαλλομένων δὲ καὶ παρελκόντων τῶν
ὑπάτων τὸν χρόνον πέμψας τὸν ὑπηρέτην ὡς αὐτοὺς ἐκέλευσεν ἐπὶ τὴν ἀρχὴν ἀκολουθεῖν καὶ τὴν
βουλὴν συγκαλεῖν. ἐπεὶ δὲ τῶν ῥαβδούχων τις
ἀπήλασε τὸν ὑπηρέτην κελευσθεὶς ὑπὸ τῶν ὑπάτων,[3]
ἀγανακτήσας ὁ Ἰκίλλιος καὶ οἱ συνάρχοντες αὐτοῦ,
συνέλαβον τὸν ῥαβδοῦχον καὶ ἀπῆγον ὡς ῥίψοντες
4 κατὰ τῆς πέτρας. οἱ δὲ ὕπατοι βιάσασθαι μὲν ἢ
τὸν ἀγόμενον ἀφελέσθαι, καίτοι δεινὰ δοκοῦντες
ὑβρίσθαι, ἀδύνατοι ἦσαν, ἐπεκαλοῦντο δὲ τὴν ἐκ
τῶν ἄλλων δημάρχων βοήθειαν. οὐθὲν γὰρ τῶν
πραττομένων ὑπὸ τῆς ἀρχῆς ἐκείνης ἐπισχεῖν ἢ
κωλῦσαι τῶν ἄλλων τινὶ ἔξεστιν, ἀλλ' ἑτέρου δημ-
5 άρχου τοῦτ' ἐστὶ τὸ κράτος. τοῖς δ' ἄρα πᾶσιν ἦν
ταῦτα κατ' ἀρχὰς δεδογμένα μήτ' εἰσηγήσασθαί
τινα καινὸν πολίτευμα μηθὲν ἐφ' ἑαυτοῦ[4] βαλόμενον,[5] ἐὰν μὴ πᾶσι τὸ αὐτὸ δοκῇ, μήτε ἐναντιω-
θῆναί τινα τοῖς πραττομένοις ὅσ' ἂν[6] αἱ πλείους

---

[1] ᾠκεῖτο B : ᾤκητο R.   [2] ἐπ' B : ἐν R.
[3] ὑπὸ τῶν ὑπάτων B : om. R.

272

quence. For he too was at that time proposing a new
measure, asking that the region called the Aventine
be divided among the plebeians for the building of
houses. This is a hill of moderate height, not less
than twelve stades in circuit, and is included within
the city ; not all of it was then inhabited, but it was
public land and thickly wooded. In order to get this
measure introduced, the tribune went to the consuls
of the year and to the senate, asking them to pass the
preliminary vote for the law embodying the measure
and to submit it to the populace. But when the
consuls kept putting it off and protracting the time,
he sent his attendant to them with orders that they
should follow him to the office of the tribunes and call
together the senate. And when one of the lictors at
the orders of the consuls drove away the attendant,
Icilius and his colleagues in their resentment seized
the lictor and led him away with the intention of
hurling him down from the rock.[1] The consuls,
though they looked upon this as a great insult, were
unable to use force or to rescue the man who was
being led away, but invoked the assistance of the
other tribunes ; for no one but another tribune has
a right to stop or hinder any of the actions of those
magistrates. Now the tribunes had all come to this
decision at the outset, that no one of their number
should either introduce any new measure on his own
initiative, unless they all concurred in it, or oppose
any proceedings which met with the approval of the

---

[1] The Tarpeian Rock.

---

[4] Kayser : ἑαυτῷ O.
[5] βαλόμενον B : βουλόμενον A.
[6] ὅσ’ ἄν Jacoby, ὅπερ ἄν Kiessling, ἅπερ ἄν Kayser : ὃ γὰρ
ἄν B, ἀλλ’ ὃ ἄν A.

DIONYSIUS OF HALICARNASSUS

γνῶμαι δοκιμάσωσι[1]· καὶ περὶ τούτων εὐθὺς ἅμα
τῷ παραλαβεῖν τὴν ἀρχὴν ἱερὰ θύσαντες ὅρκους
ἔδοσαν ἀλλήλοις, οὕτως οἰόμενοι μάλιστα τὸ τῆς
δημαρχίας ἀκατάλυτον ἔσεσθαι κράτος, ἐὰν τὸ
6 στασιάζον ἐξ αὐτῆς ἀναιρεθῇ. τοῦτο δὴ φυλάττοντες τὸ συνωμόσιον εἶπον ἀπάγεσθαι τὸν φύλακα
τῆς ἀρχῆς τῶν ὑπάτων, κοινὴν ἁπάντων εἶναι
λέγοντες τὴν γνώμην· οὐ μὴν διέμεινάν γ᾽ ἐπὶ τῆς
ὀργῆς, ἀλλὰ τοῖς πρεσβυτάτοις τῶν ἐκ τοῦ συνεδρίου παραιτουμένοις τὸν ἄνδρα ἀφῆκαν,[2] τόν τε
φθόνον ὑφορώμενοι τοῦ πράγματος, ὅτι πρῶτοι
ἔμελλον θανάτῳ ζημιῶσαι ἄνδρα[3] τὸ κελευσθὲν ὑπὸ
τῶν ἀρχόντων ποιήσαντα, καὶ δεδοικότες μὴ ἀπὸ
ταύτης τῆς προφάσεως εἰς ἀπόνοιαν ἀναγκασθῶσιν
οἱ πατρίκιοι τραπέσθαι.

XXXII. Μετὰ τοῦτο τὸ ἔργον συναχθείσης τῆς
βουλῆς οἱ μὲν ὕπατοι κατηγορίαν πολλὴν τῶν δημάρχων ἐποιήσαντο· παραλαβὼν δὲ τὸν λόγον
Ἰκίλλιος[4] περί τε τῆς εἰς τὸν ὑπηρέτην ὀργῆς ἀπελογεῖτο τοὺς ἱεροὺς προφερόμενος νόμους, καθ᾽ οὓς
οὔτε ἄρχοντι οὔτ᾽ ἰδιώτῃ συνεχωρεῖτο πράττειν
οὐδὲν ἐναντίον δημάρχῳ, καὶ περὶ τοῦ συγκαλεῖν
τὴν βουλὴν ἐδίδασκεν ὡς οὐθὲν εἴη πεποιηκὼς
ἄτοπον, πολλοὺς καὶ παντοδαποὺς εἰς τοῦτο παρα-
2 σκευασάμενος λόγους. ὡς δ᾽ ἀπελύσατο ταύτας
τὰς κατηγορίας, τὸν ὑπὲρ τοῦ λόφου νόμον[5] εἰσ-
έφερεν. ἦν δὲ τοιόσδε· ὅσα μὲν ἰδιῶταί τινες εἶχον
ἐκ τοῦ[6] δικαίου κτησάμενοι, ταῦτα τοὺς κυρίους

---

[1] δοκιμάσωσι AB : δοκιμάσωσι τοῦτ᾽ εἶναι κύριον R.
[2] Sylburg : ἐφῆκαν O.
[3] ἄνδρα Reiske : τὸν ἄνδρα O, Jacoby.
[4] ἰκίλλιος AB : ὁ Ἰκίλλιος Steph., Jacoby.

majority ; and just as soon as they had assumed their magistracy they had confirmed this agreement by sacrifices and mutual oaths, believing that the power of the tribuneship would be most effectively rendered impregnable if dissension were banished from it. It was in pursuance, then, of this sworn compact that they ordered the consuls' guardian [1] to be led away, declaring this to be the unanimous decision of their body. Nevertheless, they did not persist in their resentment, but released the man at the intercession of the oldest senators ; for they were not only concerned about the odium that would attend such a procedure, if they should be the first to punish a man by death for obeying an order of the magistrates, but also feared that with this provocation the patricians might be driven to take desperate measures.

XXXII. After this action the senate was assembled and the consuls indulged in many accusations against the tribunes. Then Icilius took the floor and attempted to justify the tribunes' resentment against the lictor, citing the sacred laws which did not permit either a magistrate or a private citizen to offer any opposition to a tribune ; and as for his attempt to convene the senate, he showed them that he had done nothing out of the way, using for this purpose many arguments of every sort, which he had prepared beforehand. After answering these accusations, he proceeded to introduce his law concerning the hill. It was to this effect : All the parcels of land held by private citizens, if justly acquired, should remain

[1] Literally, "the guardian of the consuls' office," *i.e.* the lictor.

---

5 λόφου νόμον A : νόμου λόγον B.
6 τοῦ added by Kiessling.

κατέχειν· ὅσα δὲ βιασάμενοί τινες ἢ κλοπῇ λαβόντες ᾠκοδομήσαντο, κομισαμένους τὰς δαπάνας,
ἃς ἂν οἱ διαιτηταὶ γνῶσι, τῷ δήμῳ παραδιδόναι· τὰ
δὲ ἄλλα, ὅσα ἦν[1] δημόσια, χωρὶς ὠνῆς τὸν δῆ-
3 μον παραλαβόντα διελέσθαι. ἐδίδασκέ τε ὅτι τοῦτο
τὸ πολίτευμα εἰς πολλὰ μὲν καὶ ἄλλα συνοίσει τῇ
πόλει, μάλιστα δὲ εἰς τὸ μὴ στασιάζειν ἔτι περὶ
τῆς δημοσίας χώρας τοὺς πένητας ἣν οἱ πατρίκιοι
κατεῖχον. ἀγαπήσειν γὰρ αὐτοὺς τῆς πόλεως λα-
χόντας μέρος, ἐπειδὴ τῆς χώρας οὐκ ἔξεστι διὰ
τοὺς ἐσφετερισμένους αὐτὴν πολλοὺς ὄντας καὶ
4 δυνατούς. τοιούτων ῥηθέντων ὑπ' αὐτοῦ λόγων ὁ
μὲν ἀντιλέγων Γάιος Κλαύδιος ἦν μόνος, οἱ δὲ
συγκατανεύοντες[2] πολλοί, καὶ ἔδοξε διδόναι τῷ
δήμῳ τὸν τόπον. μετὰ τοῦτο ἱεροφαντῶν τε παρόντων καὶ οἰωνοσκόπων καὶ ἱεροποιῶν δυεῖν καὶ
ποιησαμένων τὰς νομίμους εὐχάς τε καὶ ἀρὰς ἐν
τῇ λοχίτιδι ἐκκλησίᾳ συναχθείσῃ ὑπὸ τῶν ὑπάτων
ὁ νόμος ἐκυρώθη, ὅς ἐστιν ἐν στήλῃ χαλκῇ γεγραμ-
μένος, ἣν ἀνέθεσαν ἐν τῷ Ἀυεντίνῳ κομίσαντες εἰς
5 τὸ τῆς Ἀρτέμιδος ἱερόν. κυρωθέντος δὲ τοῦ νόμου συνελθόντες οἱ δημοτικοὶ τά τε οἰκόπεδα δι-
ελάγχανον καὶ κατῳκοδόμουν ὅσον ἕκαστοι τόπον
δυνηθεῖεν ἀπολαμβάνοντες. εἰσὶ δ' οἳ σύνδυο καὶ
σύντρεις[3] καὶ ἔτι πλείους συνιόντες οἰκίαν κατ-
εσκευάζοντο μίαν, ἑτέρων μὲν τὰ κατάγεια λαγχα-
νόντων, ἑτέρων δὲ τὰ ὑπερῷα. ὁ μὲν οὖν ἐνιαυτὸς
ἐκεῖνος εἰς τὰς κατασκευὰς τῶν οἰκήσεων ἐδαπανήθη.

[1] ὅσα ἦν B : ὅσα ἂν ᾖ R.
[2] συγκατανεύοντες L. Dindorf, συναγορεύοντες Reiske, συγ-
καταινοῦντες Jacoby : συγκαταλέγοντες O.

in the possession of the owners, but such parcels as had been taken by force or fraud by any persons and built upon should be turned over to the populace and the present occupants reimbursed for their expenditures according to the appraisal of the arbitrators ; all the remainder, belonging to the public, the populace should receive free of cost and divide up among themselves. He also pointed out that this measure would be advantageous to the commonwealth, not only in many other ways, but particularly in this, that it would put an end to the disturbances raised by the poor concerning the public land that was held by the patricians. For he said they would be contented with receiving a portion of the city, inasmuch as they could have no part of the land lying in the country because of the number and power of those who had appropriated it. After he had spoken thus, Gaius Claudius was the only person who opposed the law, while many gave their assent ; and it was voted to give the district to the populace. Later, at a centuriate assembly called by the consuls, the pontiffs being present together with the augurs and two sacrificers and offering the customary vows and imprecations, the law was ratified. It is inscribed on a column of bronze, which they set up on the Aventine after taking it into the sanctuary of Diana. When the law had been ratified, the plebeians assembled, and after drawing lots for the plots of ground, began to build, each man taking as large an area as he could ; and sometimes two, three, or even more joined together to build one house, and drawing lots, some had the lower and others the upper stories. That year, then, was employed in building houses.

---

³ σύντρεις Sylburg : τρεῖς O.

XXXIII. Ὁ δὲ μετὰ τοῦτον, ἐν ᾧ τὴν ὕπατον
ἀρχὴν παρειλήφεσαν Τίτος Ῥωμίλιος καὶ Γάιος
Οὐετούριος, δήμαρχοι δ' ἦσαν οἱ περὶ Λεύκιον
Ἰκίλλιον τὸ δεύτερον ἄρχειν ἑξῆς αἱρεθέντες, οὐχ
ἁπλοῦς, ἀλλὰ ποικίλος τις ἐγένετο καὶ μεγάλων
μεστὸς πραγμάτων. ἥ τε γὰρ πολιτικὴ στάσις,
ἤδη μεμαρᾶνθαι δοκοῦσα, ὑπὸ τῶν δημάρχων πάλιν
ἀνεκινεῖτο, καὶ πόλεμοί τινες ἐκ τῶν ἀλλοεθνῶν
ἀνέστησαν, οἳ κακὸν μὲν οὐθὲν διαθεῖναι τὴν πόλιν
ἠδυνήθησαν, οὐ μικρὰν δὲ ὠφέλειαν, τὸ στασιάζον
2 ἀνελόντες ἐξ αὐτῆς. ἐγκύκλιον γὰρ δὴ τοῦτο καὶ
ἐν ἔθει ἦν ἤδη τῇ πόλει πολεμουμένῃ μὲν ὁμονοεῖν,
εἰρήνην δὲ ἀγούσῃ στασιάζειν. τοῦτο συνιδόντες
ἅπαντες οἱ τὰς ὑπάτους ἀρχὰς παραλαβόντες κατ'
εὐχὰς μὲν εἴ τις ἔξωθεν ἀνασταίη[1] πόλεμος ἐλάμβα-
νον· ἡσυχαζόντων δὲ τῶν ἀντιπάλων αὐτοὶ κατ-
εσκεύαζον ἐγκλήματα καὶ προφάσεις πολέμων, ἅτε
ὁρῶντες διὰ μὲν τοὺς πολέμους μεγάλην καὶ εὐ-
δαίμονα γινομένην τὴν πόλιν, διὰ δὲ τὰς στάσεις
3 ταπεινὴν καὶ ἀσθενῆ. οἷς ὅμοια γνόντες οἱ τότε
ὕπατοι στρατιὰν ἐξάγειν ἔκριναν ἐπὶ τοὺς πολεμίους, δεδοικότες μή τι διὰ τὴν εἰρήνην ἄρξωνται
ταράττειν ἀργοὶ καὶ πένητες ἄνθρωποι, τοῦτο μὲν
ὀρθῶς ἰδόντες,[2] ὅτι δεῖ περισπᾶσαι τὸν ὄχλον ἐπὶ
τοὺς ἔξω πολέμους, τὸ δὲ μετὰ τοῦτο οὐκ ὀρθῶς.
δέον γὰρ αὐτοὺς ὡς ἐν νοσούσῃ πόλει μετρίαις
χρῆσθαι ταῖς στρατολογίαις, ἐπὶ τὸ βίᾳ προσ-
αναγκάζειν τοὺς ἀπειθοῦντας ἐτράποντο, οὔτε παραίτησιν οὔτε συγγνώμην οὐδενὶ διδόντες οὐδεμίαν,
ἀλλὰ ταῖς ἐκ τῶν νόμων τιμωρίαις εἴς τε τὰ σώμα-

---

[1] Cobet : ἐπαναασταίη O, Jacoby.
[2] ἰδόντες Ba : εἰδότες R.

XXXIII. The following year,[1] when Titus Romilius and Gaius Veturius had succeeded to the consulship and Lucius Icilius and his colleagues were tribunes, chosen to hold the office for the second time in succession, was not all of one tenor, but varied and fraught with great events. For the civil strife, which seemed to have died down at last, was again stirred up by the tribunes, and some foreign wars arose which, without being able to do the commonwealth any harm, did her a great service by banishing the dissension. For it had by now become the regular and customary thing for the commonwealth to be harmonious in time of war and to be at odds in time of peace. All who assumed the consulship, being well aware of this, regarded it as an answer to prayer if a foreign war arose ; and when their enemies were quiet, they themselves contrived grievances and excuses for wars, since they perceived that through its wars the commonwealth became great and flourishing, but through seditions humiliated and weak. The consuls of that year, having come to this same conclusion, decided to make an expedition against the enemy, fearing that idle and poor men might because of the prevailing peace begin to raise disturbances ; but though they were right in perceiving that the multitude ought to be kept employed in foreign wars, they erred in what they subsequently did. For, whereas they ought, in view of the sickly condition of the commonwealth, to have made the levies with moderation, they resorted instead to violence and compulsion in dealing with the disobedient, granting neither excuse nor pardon to anyone, but harshly imposing the penalties ordained by the laws upon both their

[1] For chaps. 33-47 cf. Livy iii. 31, 2-4.

4 τα καὶ τὰς οὐσίας αὐτῶν πικρῶς χρώμενοι. ταῦτα
ποιούντων αὐτῶν ἀφορμὴν αὖθις εἰλήφεσαν οἱ
δήμαρχοι τοῦ δημαγωγεῖν τὰ πλήθη· καὶ συναγαγόντες ἐκκλησίαν[1] τά τ' ἄλλα τῶν ὑπάτων κατεβόων, καὶ ὅτι πολλοὺς τῶν πολιτῶν ἐκέλευσαν εἰς
τὸ δεσμωτήριον ἀπάγειν τὴν δημαρχικὴν ἐξουσίαν
ἐπικαλεσαμένους, τῆς τε στρατολογίας ἀπολύειν
ἔφασαν αὐτοὶ δὴ μόνοι, ἐξουσίαν ἐκ τῶν νόμων
5 ἔχοντες.[2] ὡς δ' οὐθὲν ἐπέραινον, ἀλλ' ἐπιστρεφε-
στέρας ἔτι τὰς καταγραφὰς ἑώρων γινομένας,
ἔργοις κωλύειν ἐπεβάλλοντο. ἀμυνομένων δὲ τῶν
ὑπάτων καὶ τῷ κράτει τῆς ἀρχῆς ἐρεθισμοί τέ
τινες ἐγίνοντο καὶ χειρῶν ἐπιβολαί. συνηγωνίζετο
δὲ τοῖς μὲν ὑπάτοις ἡ τῶν πατρικίων νεότης, τοῖς
6 δὲ δημάρχοις ὁ πένης καὶ ἀργὸς ὄχλος. ἐκείνην
μὲν οὖν τὴν ἡμέραν παρὰ πολὺ κρείττους ἐγένοντο
τῶν δημάρχων οἱ ὕπατοι, ταῖς δ' ἑξῆς ἡμέραις
πλείονος ὄχλου συρρέοντος εἰς τὴν πόλιν ἐκ τῶν
ἀγρῶν, δόξαντες οἱ δήμαρχοι προσειληφέναι χεῖρα
ἀξιόμαχον ἐκκλησίας τε συνεχεῖς ἐποιοῦντο καὶ
τοὺς ὑπηρέτας κακῶς διακειμένους ἐκ τῶν πληγῶν
ἐπεδείκνυσαν καὶ τὴν ἀρχὴν ἔλεγον ἀποθήσεσθαι εἰ
μή τις αὐτοῖς ἔσται παρὰ τοῦ δήμου βοήθεια.

XXXIV. Συναγανακτοῦντος δ' αὐτοῖς τοῦ πλήθους ἐκάλουν τοὺς ὑπάτους ἐπὶ[3] τὸν δῆμον ὡς τῶν
πεπραγμένων ὑφέξοντας λόγον. ὡς δ' οὐ προσεῖχον
αὐτοῖς ἐκεῖνοι τὸν νοῦν, ἐπὶ τὴν βουλὴν παρῆσαν
(ἔτυχον γὰρ ὑπὲρ αὐτῶν τούτων συνεδρεύοντες)
καὶ παρελθόντες ἐδέοντο μήθ' αὐτοὺς τὰ ἔσχατα[4]

---

[1] ἐκκλησίαν R : εἰς ἐκκλησίαν B, Jacoby.
[2] ἔφασαν αὐτοὶ δὴ μόνοι ἐξουσίαν ἐκ τῶν νόμων ἔχοντες B :
ἔφασαν οἱ ἐκ τῶν νόμων ἐξουσίαν ἔχοντες A.

persons and their property. While they were doing
this, the tribunes took occasion to stir up the
masses again with their harangues ; and calling an
assembly, they denounced the consuls on various
scores, but particularly for having ordered many
citizens to be haled to prison even though they had
invoked the protection of the tribunes ; and they said
that they themselves on their own responsibility released the people from the levy, having as they did
authority to do so under the laws. When this had
no effect and they saw the levies being carried
out with still greater strictness, they undertook to
obstruct them by deeds ; and when the consuls re-
sisted with the power of their magistracy also, there
were sundry provocations and acts of violence. The
consuls were supported by the young patricians, and
the tribunes by the poor and idle multitude. That
day the consuls proved much superior to the tribunes ;
but in the course of the following days, as increasing
numbers flocked into the city from the country, the
tribunes thought they had now acquired an adequate
force, and holding one assembly after another, they
exhibited their assistants, who were in a bad condition from the blows they had received, and said
they would resign their magistracy if they did not
get some assistance from the populace.

XXXIV. The multitude sharing in their resentment, the tribunes summoned the consuls to appear
before their assembly in order to render an account
of their actions. But as these paid no heed to them,
they went to the senate, which happened to be
deliberating about this very matter, and coming
forward, asked the members not to permit either

<hr>

³ ἐπὶ B : εἰς R.   ⁴ Cobet : αἴσχιστα O, Jacoby.

πεπονθότας ὑπεριδεῖν μήτε τὸν δῆμον ἀφαιρεθέντα
τὴν ἐξ αὐτῶν[1] βοήθειαν, διεξιόντες ὅσα ἦσαν πε-
πονθότες ὑπὸ τῶν ὑπάτων καὶ τῆς[2] περὶ αὐτοὺς
συνωμοσίας, οὐ μόνον εἰς τὴν ἐξουσίαν, ἀλλὰ καὶ
2 εἰς τὰ σώματα προπηλακισθέντες. ἠξίουν τε δυεῖν
θάτερον ποιεῖν τοὺς ὑπάτους· εἰ μὲν ἀρνοῦνται μηδὲν ὧν οἱ νόμοι κεκωλύκασιν εἰς τὰ τῶν δημάρχων
πλημμελῆσαι σώματα, παραγενομένους εἰς τὴν ἐκκλησίαν ἀπομόσαι, εἰ δ' οὐχ ὑπομένουσι τὸν ὅρκον,
ἥκειν ἐπὶ τοὺς δημότας λόγον ὑφέξοντας· ἀναδώσειν
3 γὰρ ὑπὲρ αὐτῶν ταῖς φυλαῖς τὴν ψῆφον. οἱ δ' ὕπατοι πρὸς ταῦτ' ἀπελογοῦντο, διδάσκοντες ὅτι τῆς[3]
ὕβρεως οἱ δήμαρχοι ἄρξειαν αὐθαδείᾳ χρησάμενοι
καὶ τολμήσαντες εἰς ὑπάτων σώματα παρανομεῖν,
τὸ μὲν πρῶτον ὑπηρέταις τε καὶ ἀγορανόμοις
ἐπιτάττοντες ἄγειν εἰς τὸ δεσμωτήριον ἄρχοντας
οἷς τὸ πάντων ἀποδέδοται κράτος, ἔπειτ' αὐτοὶ
τολμήσαντες ὁμόσε χωρεῖν σὺν τοῖς ἰταμωτάτοις
4 τῶν δημοτικῶν· τάς τε ἀρχὰς διδάσκοντες ὅσον
ἀλλήλων διαφέρουσιν, ἡ μὲν ὑπατικὴ τὸ τῶν βασιλέων ἔχουσα κράτος, ἡ δὲ δημαρχικὴ τῆς βοηθείας
ἕνεκα παρεληλυθυῖα τῶν κατισχυομένων, ᾗ τοσούτου δεῖν ἐξεῖναι κατὰ τῶν ὑπάτων τινὸς ψῆφον
ἀναδιδόναι τοῖς ὄχλοις, ὥστε μηδὲ κατὰ τῶν ἄλλων
πατρικίων τοῦ φαυλοτάτου[4] ταύτην ἀποδεδόσθαι
τὴν ἐξουσίαν, ἂν μὴ ἡ[5] βουλὴ ψηφίσηται. ἠπείλουν
τε, ὅταν ἐκεῖνοι ψῆφον ἀναδῶσι τοῖς δημόταις,
5 αὐτοὶ τὰ ὅπλα περιθήσειν τοῖς πατρικίοις. τοιού-

---

[1] αὐτῶν Ba : ἑαυτῶν Bb, αὐτοῦ A.　　　　[2] ἀπὸ τῆς A.
[3] τῆς R : τῆς τε B, τῆς γε Kiessling.
[4] τοῦ φαυλοτάτου B : τῶ φαυλοτέρω A, τῶν φαυλοτέρων R.
[5] ἡ Bb : om. ABa.

the tribunes themselves to be treated in a most outrageous manner or the populace to be deprived of their assistance. They enumerated all the injuries they had received at the hands of the consuls and their faction, who had insulted not only their authority but also their persons ; and they asked that the consuls do one of two things—either, in case they denied that they had done any wrong against the persons of the tribunes contrary to the laws, that they go before the popular assembly and make their denial under oath, or, if they could not bring themselves to take that oath, that they appear before the plebeians to render an account of their conduct ; and they (the tribunes) would take the vote of the tribes concerning them. The consuls defended themselves against these charges by saying that the tribunes had begun the violence by their arrogant behaviour and by daring to commit lawless acts against the persons of the consuls, first by ordering their attendants and the aediles to hale to prison magistrates in whom the whole power of the commonwealth is vested, and later by entering the struggle themselves together with the boldest of the plebeians. They pointed out how great a difference there is between the two magistracies—between the consulship, in which the royal power resides, and the tribuneship, which was introduced for the relief of the oppressed and, far from having the right to take the vote of the masses against one of the consuls, has not been given authority to do so against even the meanest of the other patricians, unless the senate shall so vote. And they threatened that they themselves would arm the patricians when the tribunes should take the votes of the plebeians. After such recrimina-

τῶν δὴ ῥηθέντων λόγων δι᾽ ὅλης ἡμέρας οὐδὲν
ἐξήνεγκεν ἡ βουλὴ τέλος, ἵνα μήτε τὴν τῶν ὑπάτων
ἀρχὴν μειώσειε μήτε τὴν τῶν δημάρχων, ἑκάτερον
ὁρῶσα μεγάλων κινδύνων αἴτιον ἐσόμενον.

XXXV. Ἐπεὶ δὲ κἀκεῖθεν ἀπηλάθησαν οἱ δήμαρχοι βοήθειαν οὐδεμίαν εὑρόμενοι, ἐσκόπουν αὖθις ὅ τι χρὴ ποιεῖν εἰς τὸν δῆμον ἀφικόμενοι.
ἐνίοις μὲν οὖν ἐδόκει καὶ μάλιστα τοῖς ταραχωδεσ-
τάτοις ἀπιέναι πάλιν ἐκ τῆς πόλεως τοὺς δημοτικοὺς τὰ ὅπλα ἀναλαμβάνοντας εἰς τὸ ἱερὸν ὄρος,
ἔνθα καὶ τὸ πρῶτον ἐστρατοπεδεύσαντο, καὶ τὸν
πόλεμον ἐκεῖθεν ὁρμωμένους ποιεῖν πρὸς τοὺς πατρικίους, ἐπειδὴ τὰς συνθήκας ἔλυσαν ἐκεῖνοι τὰς
γενομένας αὐτοῖς πρὸς τὸν δῆμον, καταλύοντες τὴν
2 δημαρχικὴν ἐξουσίαν ἐκ τοῦ φανεροῦ. τοῖς δὲ
πλείοσιν ἐδόκει μὴ παραχωρεῖν τῆς πόλεως μηδὲ
κοινὰ πάντων[1] ἐγκλήματα ποιεῖν ὑπὲρ ὧν ἰδίᾳ
τινὲς εἰς τοὺς δημάρχους παρενόμησαν, ἐὰν[2] τὰ
συγκεχωρημένα τοῖς νόμοις[3] λαμβάνωσιν,[4] οἳ κελεύουσι νηποινὶ τεθνάναι[5] τοὺς ὑβρίσαντας τὰ[6] τῶν
δημάρχων σώματα. τοῖς δὲ χαριεστέροις οὐδέτερον
τούτων ἐφαίνετο καλῶς ἔχειν, οὔτε τὴν πόλιν ἐκ-
λιπεῖν οὔτε φόνον ἄκριτον ἐπιτελεῖν, καὶ ταῦτα ὑπάτων, οἷς ἡ μεγίστη ὑπέκειτο ἀρχή, ἀλλ᾽ εἰς τοὺς
συναγωνιζομένους αὐτοῖς μεταφέρειν τὴν ὀργὴν καὶ
τὰς ἐκ τῶν νόμων τιμωρίας παρ᾽ ἐκείνων λαμβάνειν.
3 εἰ μὲν οὖν ἐκείνην τὴν ἡμέραν θυμῷ φερόμενοι
δρᾶσαί τι οἱ δήμαρχοι κατὰ τῶν ὑπάτων ἢ τῆς

[1] μηδὲ κοινὰ πάντων Reiske : μηδὲ τὰ κοινὰ πάντων A, μηδὲ
κοινὰ πάντα τὰ B.　　[2] ἐὰν Bb : ἀλλὰ R.
[3] τοῖς νόμοις Bb : om. ABa.
[4] λαμβάνωσιν B : λαμβάνουσιν R.

tions had lasted the whole day, the senate came
to no decision, being unwilling to lessen the power
of either the consuls or the tribunes, since they saw
that either course would be attended with great
dangers.

XXXV. When the tribunes were repulsed there
also, failing to get any help, they went again to the
popular assembly and considered what they ought to
do. Some, particularly the most turbulent, thought
the plebeians should take arms and again withdraw
from the city to the Sacred Mount, where they had
encamped on the first occasion,[1] and from there make
war upon the patricians, since these had violated
the compact they had made with the populace by
openly overthrowing the tribunician power.[2] But the
majority thought they ought not to leave the city
nor to bring charges against all the patricians as a
body for the lawless acts committed by some particular persons against the tribunes, provided they
could obtain the relief offered by the laws, which
ordain that those who have insulted the persons of
the tribunes may be put to death with impunity.[3]
The more intelligent did not regard either course as
fitting, either to leave the city or to put persons to
death without a trial, and particularly consuls, who
held the chief magistracy, but they advised them to
transfer their resentment to those who were assisting
the consuls and to exact from these the punishment
ordained by the laws. Now if the tribunes had been
carried away by their passion that day to do anything

---

[1] vi. 45, 2.   [2] vi. 87, 3; 88, 3.   [3] vi. 89, 3.

---

[5] κελεύουσι νηποινὶ τεθνάναι Casaubon : κελεύουσιν ἢ ποιεῖν
ἢ τεθνάναι O, κελεύουσιν ἢ ποι⟨νὴν τίν⟩ειν ἢ τεθνάναι Jacoby.
[6] τὰ O : εἰς τὰ Cobet.

βουλῆς προήχθησαν, οὐθὲν ἂν ἦν τὸ κωλῦσον αὐτὴν
ὑφ᾽ αὑτῆς ἀπολωλέναι τὴν πόλιν· οὕτως ἕτοιμοι
πάντες ἦσαν ἐπὶ τὰ ὅπλα καὶ τὸν κατ᾽ ἀλλήλων
πόλεμον. νῦν δ᾽ ἀναβαλόμενοι τὰ πράγματα καὶ
δόντες ἑαυτοῖς χρόνον εἰς ἀμείνω λογισμὸν αὐτοί
τε μετριώτεροι ἐγένοντο καὶ τὰς τῶν πολλῶν ὀρ-
4 γὰς ἐπράυναν. ἔπειτα ταῖς ἑξῆς ἡμέραις τὴν τρίτην
ἀπ᾽ ἐκείνης ἐσομένην ἀγορὰν προειπόντες ἐν ᾗ
τὸν δῆμον συνάξουσι καὶ ζημίαν ἐπιβαλοῦσι τοῖς
ὑπάτοις ἀργυρικήν, διέλυσαν τὴν ἐκκλησίαν. ἐπεὶ
δὲ πλησίον ἦν ὁ χρόνος, ἀπέστησαν καὶ ταύτης τῆς
ἐπιβολῆς τῇ δεήσει τῶν πρεσβυτάτων τε¹ καὶ ἐντι-
5 μοτάτων τὴν χάριν ἀνατιθέναι λέγοντες. καὶ μετὰ
ταῦτα συναγαγόντες τὸν δῆμον ἔλεγον ὅτι τὰς μὲν
εἰς ἑαυτοὺς ὕβρεις ἀφείκασι χαρισάμενοι πολλοῖς
καὶ ἀγαθοῖς ἀνδράσι δεομένοις, οἷς οὐκ ἦν ὅσιον
ἀντιλέγειν, ὧν δὲ ὁ δῆμος ἠδικεῖτο κωλυταί τε καὶ
τιμωροὶ ἔσεσθαι. προθήσειν γὰρ αὖθις τόν τε περὶ
τῆς κληρουχίας νόμον ἔτη τριάκοντα παρειλκυσ-
μένον καὶ τὸν περὶ τῆς ἰσονομίας, ὃν οἱ πρὸ αὐτῶν
δήμαρχοι προθέντες οὐκ ἐπεψήφισαν.

XXXVI. Ταῦθ᾽ ὑποσχόμενοι καὶ ὀμόσαντες ἀπέδειξαν ἡμέρας ἐν αἷς ἀγορὰν ποιήσονται τοῦ δήμου
καὶ τὰς ψήφους ἀναδώσουσι περὶ τῶν νόμων· ἐπι-
στάντος δὲ τοῦ χρόνου πρῶτον εἰσέφερον τὸν
χωρονομικὸν νόμον καὶ πολλοὺς διελθόντες λόγους
ἐκάλουν, εἴ τις τῷ νόμῳ συναγορεύειν βούλεται τῶν
2 δημοτικῶν. πολλῶν δὲ παριόντων καὶ τὰς ἑαυ-

¹ τε B : om. R.

---

¹ Or, perhaps, " second " by our reckoning. See vii. 58, 3
and the note on that passage. Normally in such a con-
struction as this Dionysius reckons inclusively.

against the consuls or the senate, nothing would have prevented the commonwealth from being destroyed by its own hands, so ready were all to rush to arms and engage in civil war. But as it was, by deferring matters and giving themselves time for better reasoning, they not only themselves grew more moderate, but also appeased the resentment of the multitude. Then, during the following days, they announced the third[1] market-day from that one as the day when they would assemble the populace and impose a monetary fine upon the consuls ; after which they dismissed the assembly. But when the time drew near, they refrained from imposing even this fine, alleging that they granted the favour at the intercession of men who were the oldest and most honoured. After that they assembled the populace and told them that they had pardoned the insults to themselves, doing this at the request of many worthy men whom it was not right to refuse, but that as for the wrongs done to the populace, they would both avenge them and prevent their recurrence. For they would again propose not only the law concerning the allotment of land, the enactment of which had been postponed for thirty years, but also the one concerning an equality of laws, which their predecessors had proposed but had not put to vote.

XXXVI. Having made these promises and confirmed them by oaths, they appointed days on which they would hold an assembly of the populace and take their votes concerning the laws. When the time came, they first proposed the agrarian law, and after discussing it at great length, called upon any of the plebeians who so desired to speak in favour of the law. Many came forward, and enumerating the

τῶν πράξεις, ἃς ἐν τοῖς πολέμοις ἀπεδείξαντο,
προφερομένων καὶ ἀγανακτούντων ὅτι πολλὴν ἀφ-
ελόμενοι γῆν τοὺς πολεμίους αὐτοὶ μὲν οὐδεμίαν
εἰλήφασι μοῖραν, τοὺς δὲ χρήμασι καὶ φίλοις δυνα-
τοὺς ἐσφετερισμένους ὁρῶσι τὰ κοινὰ καὶ καρπου-
μένους ἐκ τοῦ βιαιοτάτου, ἀξιούντων τε μὴ μόνον
τοὺς κινδύνους εἶναι τῷ δήμῳ τοὺς ὑπὲρ τῶν
κοινῶν ἀγαθῶν κοινούς, ἀλλὰ καὶ τὰς ἀπ' αὐτῶν
ἡδονάς τε καὶ ὠφελείας, καὶ τοῦ πλήθους ἀσμένως
ἀκούοντος τοὺς λόγους, ὁ μάλιστα ἐπιρρώσας τὸν
δῆμον καὶ μηδὲ φωνὴν ὑπομένειν τῶν ἀντιλεγόντων διαπραξάμενος ἦν Λεύκιος Σίκκιος, Δεντᾶτος
ἐπικαλούμενος, πολλὰς πάνυ καὶ μεγάλας ἑαυτοῦ
3 πράξεις διεξελθών. ἦν δ' ὀφθῆναί τε θαυμαστὸς
ὁ ἀνὴρ καὶ ἡλικίας ἐν τῷ κρατίστῳ δυεῖν δέοντα
ἑξήκοντα γεγονὼς ἔτη καὶ φρονῆσαι τὰ δέοντα ἱκα-
νὸς εἰπεῖν τε ὡς στρατιώτης οὐκ ἀδύνατος. ἔφη
δ' οὖν παρελθών·

" Ἐγὼ δ',[1] ὦ δημόται, καθ' ἕκαστον ἔργον τῶν
ἐμοὶ πεπραγμένων εἰ βουλοίμην λέγειν, ἐπιλίποι ἄν
με ὁ τῆς ἡμέρας χρόνος. αὐτὰ δὲ τὰ κεφάλαια δι'
4 ἐλαχίστων ὡς ἐμὴ δύναμις ἐρῶ. τετταρακοστὸν
μὲν[2] ἔτος ἐστί μοι τοῦτο ἐξ οὗ στρατεύομαι περὶ
τῆς πατρίδος, τριακοστὸν δ' ἐξ οὗ στρατιωτικῆς ἀεί
τινος ἡγεμονίας τυγχάνω, τοτὲ μὲν σπείρας ἡγούμενος, τοτὲ δ' ὅλου τάγματος, ἀρξάμενος ἀπὸ ὑπάτων[3] Γαΐου Ἀκυλλίου καὶ Τίτου Σικκίου, οἷς

---

[1] ἐγὼ δὲ ABmg : ἐγώ Steph., Jacoby, ἔγωγε Post.
[2] μὲν B : om. R.   [3] ἀπὸ τῶν ὑπάτων Jacoby.

exploits they had performed in the wars, expressed
their indignation that they who had taken so much
land from their enemies had received no part of it
themselves, while they saw that those who were
powerful by reason of their riches and their friends
had appropriated and now enjoyed, by the most
violent means, the possessions that belonged to all ;
and they demanded that the populace should share,
not only in the dangers that were undertaken for the
common good, but also in the pleasures and profits
that resulted from those dangers. And the multitude listened to them with pleasure. But the one
who encouraged them the most and caused them to
refuse to tolerate even a word from the opponents of
the law was Lucius Siccius, surnamed Dentatus, who
related very many great exploits of his own. He was
a man of remarkable appearance, was in the very
prime of life, being fifty-eight years old, capable of
conceiving practical measures and also, for a soldier,
eloquent in expressing them. This man, then, came
forward and said :

" If I, plebeians, should choose to relate my exploits
one by one, a day's time would not suffice me ; hence
I shall give a mere summary, in the fewest words I
can. This is the fortieth year that I have been making campaigns for my country, and the thirtieth that
I have continued to hold some military command,
sometimes over a cohort and sometimes over a whole
legion, beginning with the consulship of Gaius Aquil-
ius and Titus Siccius,[1] to whom the senate committed

---

[1] Strictly speaking, it was the second of these consuls only
who conducted the war against the Volscians (see viii. 64, 3 ;
67), and according to Dionysius' own chronology the date
of the present speech (453 B.C.) was a little more than the
thirtieth year after their consulship (485).

ἐψηφίσατο ἡ βουλὴ τὸν κατὰ Οὐολούσκων πόλεμον.
ἤμην γὰρ τότε ἑπτακαιεικοσέτης,[1] ἐταττόμην δ'
5 ἔτι ὑπὸ λοχαγῷ. γενομένης δὲ μάχης καρτερᾶς
καὶ τροπῆς, καὶ τοῦ μὲν ἡγεμόνος τῆς σπείρας πε-
πτωκότος, τῶν δὲ σημείων κρατουμένων ὑπὸ τῶν
ἐχθρῶν, μόνος ἐγὼ τὸν ὑπὲρ ἁπάντων κίνδυνον
ἀράμενος τά τε σημεῖα διέσωσα τῇ σπείρᾳ[2] καὶ
τοὺς πολεμίους ἀνέστειλα καὶ τοῦ μὴ περιπεσεῖν
αἰσχύνῃ[3] τοὺς λοχαγοὺς αἰωνίῳ, δι' ἣν θανάτου
κακίων ὁ λοιπὸς ἂν αὐτοῖς βίος ἦν, αἴτιος ἐγενόμην
φανερῶς, ὡς αὐτοί τε[4] ὡμολόγουν χρυσῷ με ἀνα-
δήσαντες στεφάνῳ καὶ ὁ ὕπατος Σίκκιος ἐμαρτύ-
6 ρησεν ἡγεμόνα τῆς σπείρας ἀποδείξας. ἑτέρου τε
πάλιν ἡμῖν ἀγῶνος ἐνστάντος, ἐν ᾧ τόν τε στρατοπεδάρχην τοῦ τάγματος ἡμῶν συνέβη πεσεῖν καὶ
τὸν ἀετὸν ὑπὸ[5] τοῖς πολεμίοις γενέσθαι, τὸν αὐτὸν
τρόπον ὑπὲρ ὅλου τοῦ τάγματος[6] ἀγωνισάμενος τόν
τ' ἀετὸν ἀνεκομισάμην[7] καὶ τὸν στρατοπεδάρχην
ἔσωσα· ὃς ἐμοὶ τῆς τότε βοηθείας χάριν ἀπο-
διδοὺς τῆς ἡγεμονίας τοῦ τάγματος ἀφίστατό μοι
καὶ τὸν ἀετὸν ἐδίδου, ἐγὼ δ' οὐκ ἔλαβον, οὐκ ἀξιῶν
ᾧ τὸν βίον ἐχαρισάμην τούτου παρελέσθαι τὰς τιμὰς
ἃς εἶχε καὶ τὰς ἐπὶ ταύταις εὐφροσύνας. ἐφ' οἷς
ἀγασθείς με ὁ ὕπατος τοῦ πρώτου τάγματος ἀπέδωκε τὴν στρατοπεδαρχίαν ἀπολωλεκότος ἐν τῇ
μάχῃ τὸν ἡγεμόνα.

XXXVII. '' Ταῦτ' ἐστίν, ὦ δημόται, τὰ φανερώ-

---

[1] Kiessling : ἑπτακαιεικοσαέτης O.
[2] τῇ σπείρᾳ B : τῆς σπείρας R.
[3] ἐν before αἰσχύνῃ deleted by Reiske.
[4] τε Kiessling : γε B, om. R.
[5] ἐπὶ Cobet.　　　　　[6] Reiske : συντάγματος O.
[7] ἀνεκομισάμην B : ἀνεσωσάμην R.

the conduct of the war against the Volscians. I was then twenty-seven years of age and in rank I was still under a centurion.[1] When a severe battle occurred and a rout, the commander of the cohort had fallen, and the standards were in the hands of the enemy, I alone, exposing myself in behalf of all, recovered the standards for the cohort, repulsed the enemy, and was clearly the one who saved the centurions from incurring everlasting disgrace—which would have rendered the rest of their lives more bitter than death—as both they themselves acknowledged, by crowning me with a golden crown, and Siccius the consul bore witness, by appointing me commander of the cohort. And in another battle that we had, in which it happened that the *primipilus* [2] of the legion was thrown to the ground and the eagle fell into the enemy's hands, I fought in the same manner in defence of the whole legion, recovered the eagle and saved the *primipilus*. In return for the assistance I then gave him he wished to resign his command of the legion in my favour and to give me the eagle ; but I refused both, being unwilling to deprive the man whose life I had saved of the honours he enjoyed and of the satisfaction resulting from them. The consul was pleased with my behaviour and gave me the post of *primipilus* in the first legion, which had lost its commander in the battle.

XXXVII. " These, plebeians, are the noble actions

---

[1] *i.e.* he was still a common soldier.

[2] The ranking centurion of a legion, who carried the eagle and, in the absence of the tribune, took command. See ix. 10, 2.

σαντά με καὶ εἰς ἡγεμονίας προαγαγόντα γενναῖα
ἔργα. ἐπεὶ δ' ὀνόματος ἤδη λαμπροῦ τυγχάνων
φανερὸς ἤμην, ἅπαντας ὑπέμενον τοὺς λοιποὺς
ἀγῶνας αἰδούμενος τὰς ἐπὶ τοῖς προτέροις ἔργοις
τιμὰς καὶ χάριτας ἀφανίσαι. καὶ διετέλεσα πάντα
τὸν μεταξὺ χρόνον στρατευόμενος καὶ ταλαιπωρῶν
καὶ οὐδένα κίνδυνον δεδιὼς οὐδὲ ὑπολογιζόμενος·
ἐξ ὧν ἁπάντων ἀριστεῖα καὶ σκῦλα καὶ στεφάνους
2 καὶ τὰς ἄλλας τιμὰς παρὰ τῶν ὑπάτων ἔλαβον· ἵνα
δὲ συνελὼν εἴπω, μάχας μὲν ἐν τοῖς τετταράκοντα
ἔτεσιν ἐν οἷς διατελῶ στρατευόμενος ἀμφὶ τὰς
ἑκατὸν εἴκοσι μεμάχημαι, τραύματα δὲ πέντε καὶ
τετταράκοντα εἴληφα καὶ πάντα ἐμπρόσθια, κατὰ
νώτου δ' οὐθέν· καὶ τούτων δώδεκά ἐστιν ἃ συνέβη
μοι λαβεῖν ἐν ἡμέρᾳ μιᾷ, ὅτε Σαβῖνος Ἐρδώνιος
3 τὴν ἄκραν καὶ τὸ Καπιτώλιον κατελάβετο. ἀριστεῖα
δ' ἐκ τῶν ἀγώνων ἐξενήνεγμαι τεσσαρεσκαίδεκα
μὲν στεφάνους πολιτικούς, οἷς ἀνέδησάν με οἱ
σωθέντες ἐν ταῖς μάχαις ὑπ' ἐμοῦ, τρεῖς δὲ πολι-
ορκητικοὺς πρῶτος ἐπιβὰς πολεμίων τείχεσι καὶ
κατασχών, ὀκτὼ δὲ τοὺς ἐκ παρατάξεως, οἷς ὑπὸ
τῶν αὐτοκρατόρων ἐτιμήθην· πρὸς δὲ τούτοις ὀγδοήκοντα μὲν καὶ τρεῖς χρυσοῦς στρεπτοὺς περιαυ-
χενίους, ἑξήκοντα δὲ καὶ ἑκατὸν[1] περιβραχιόνια
χρύσεα, δόρατα δ' ὀκτωκαίδεκα, φάλαρα δ' ἐπίσημα
πέντε πρὸς τοῖς εἴκοσιν, . . .[2] ὧν ἐννέα ἦσαν οὓς
μονομαχῆσαί τινα ἡμῶν προκαλεσαμένους ἑκούσιος
4 ὑποστὰς ἐνίκησα. οὗτος μέντοι Σίκκιος, ὦ πολῖται,

---

[1] καὶ ἑκατὸν B : om. R.
[2] Lacuna recognized after εἴκοσιν by Enthoven, who
supplied: λάφυρα δὲ πολεμίων ἡττηθέντων εἴκοσιν (cf. chap.
45, 3).

which brought me distinction and preferment. After I had already gained an illustrious name and was famous, I submitted to the hardships of all the other engagements, being ashamed to blot out the memory of the honours and favours I had received for my former actions. And all the time since then I have continued to take part in campaigns and undergo their hardships without fearing or even considering any danger. From all these campaigns I received prizes for valour, spoils, crowns, and the other honours from the consuls. In a word, during the forty years I have continued to serve I have fought about one hundred and twenty battles and received forty-five wounds, all in front and not one behind; twelve of these I happened to receive in one day, when Herdonius the Sabine seized the citadel and the Capitol. As to rewards for valour, I have brought out of those contests fourteen civic crowns, bestowed upon me by those I saved in battle, three mural crowns for having been the first to mount the enemy's walls and hold them, and eight others for my exploits on the battlefield, with which I was honoured by the generals; and, in addition to these, eighty-three gold collars, one hundred and sixty gold bracelets, eighteen spears, twenty-five splendid decorations, . . .[1] nine of whom I voluntarily encountered and overcame when they challenged someone of our men to fight in single combat. Nevertheless, citizens, this Siccius,

---

[1] The next clause shows that there is something amiss with the text here. When we compare the words in chap. 45, 3, where Romilius tauntingly reminds Siccius of all these boasted trophies, we naturally look for mention here of the spoils taken from enemy champions slain in single combat. Enthoven, accordingly, would supply at this point the words "and the spoils of twenty conquered enemies."

ὁ τοσαῦτα μὲν ἔτη στρατευσάμενος ὑπὲρ ὑμῶν,
τοσαύτας δὲ μάχας ἀγωνισάμενος, τοσούτοις δὲ
τετιμημένος ἀριστείοις, ὁ μηδένα κίνδυνον ὀκνήσας
πώποτε μηδ' ἀπειπάμενος, ἀλλ' . . .[1] ἐν παρατάξεσι καὶ ἐν τειχομαχίαις καὶ ἐν πεζοῖς καὶ ἐν
ἱππεῦσι καὶ μετὰ πάντων καὶ σὺν ὀλίγοις καὶ μόνος,
καὶ κατατετρωμένος ὅλον τὸ σῶμα, ὁ συγκατακτη-
σάμενος τῇ πατρίδι πολλὴν καὶ ἀγαθὴν γῆν, τοῦτο
μὲν ἦν Τυρρηνούς τε καὶ Σαβίνους ἀφείλεσθε, τοῦτο
δὲ ἦν Αἰκανῶν καὶ Οὐολούσκων καὶ Πωμεντίνων
κρατήσαντες ἔχετε,[2] οὐδὲ τὴν ἐλαχίστην ἔχω μοῖραν
ἐξ αὐτῆς λαβών, οὐδ' ὑμῶν, ὦ δημόται, τῶν τὰ
ὅμοια ταλαιπωρησάντων οὐδείς· οἱ δὲ βιαιότατοι
τῶν ἐν τῇ πόλει καὶ ἀναιδέστατοι τὴν καλλίστην
κατέχουσιν ἐξ αὐτῆς καὶ πολλὰ ἔτη κεκάρπωνται
οὔτε δωρεὰν παρ' ὑμῶν λαβόντες οὔτε χρημάτων
πριάμενοι οὔτε ἄλλην δικαίαν κτῆσιν οὐδεμίαν αὐ-
5 τῆς ἀποδεῖξαι δυνάμενοι. καὶ εἰ μὲν ἴσα τοῖς ἄλλοις ἡμῖν ταλαιπωρήσαντες ὅτ' αὐτὴν ἐκτώμεθα
πλεῖον ἠξίουν ἡμῶν ἔχειν, ἦν μὲν οὐδ' οὕτω δίκαιον
οὐδὲ πολιτικὸν ὀλίγους σφετερίσασθαι τὰ κοινά, οὐ
μὴν ἀλλ' εἶχέ γέ τινα λόγον ἡ πλεονεξία τῶν ἀν-
θρώπων· ὁπότε δ' οὐθὲν ἔχοντες ἐπιδείξασθαι μέγα
καὶ νεανικὸν ἔργον ἀνθ' οὗ τὰ ἡμέτερα[3] βίᾳ κατέσχον, ἀναισχυντοῦσι καὶ οὐδ' ἐξελεγχόμενοι μεθ-
ίενται αὐτῶν, τίς ἂν ἀνάσχοιτο;

---

[1] Lacuna recognized by Reiske. The MSS. give ἀλλ' ἦν ἐν
παρατάξεσι. Kiessling proposed : ἀλλὰ πάντας ὑποστὰς καὶ
ἐν π., Smit ἀλλὰ πάντας ἀράμενος καὶ ἐν π. Jacoby simply
substituted ἄλλη for ἀλλ' ἦν. Post would read μάχην for
ἀλλ' ἦν.

[2] ἔχετε R : ἔσχετε A.

[3] Steph. : ὑμέτερα AB.

who has served so many years in your defence, fought
so many battles, been honoured with so many prizes
for valour, who never shirked or declined any danger,
but . . .[1] in pitched battles and assaults upon walled
towns, among the foot and among the horse, with all,
with a few, and alone, whose body is covered with
wounds, and who has had a share in winning for his
country much fertile land, both that which you have
taken from the Tyrrhenians and the Sabines and that
which you possess after conquering the Aequians,
the Volscians and the Pometini—this Siccius, I say,
has not received even the least portion of this land
as his to possess, nor has any one of you plebeians
who have shared in the same hardships. But the
most violent and shameless men of the city hold the
finest part of it and have had the enjoyment of it for
many years, without having either received it from
you as a gift or purchased it or being able to show
any other just title to it. If, indeed, they had borne
an equal share of the hardships with the rest of us
when we were acquiring this land and had then
demanded to have a larger share of it than we, while
it would not, even so, have been either just or democratic that a few should appropriate what belongs
to all in common, yet there would at least be some
excuse for the greed of these men ; but when, though
they cannot point to any great or daring deed of
theirs in payment for which they seized by force the
possessions that belong to us, they act in this shameless manner and even when convicted do not give
them up, who can bear it ?

[1] The text is corrupt at this point. According to the
conjectures of Kiessling and Smit we should have " but
undertook them all, both in pitched battles," etc,

XXXVIII. " Ἐπεὶ φέρε πρὸς Διός, εἴ τι τούτων
ἐγὼ ψεύδομαι, δειξάτω τις ὑμῖν τῶν σεμνῶν τούτων
παρελθών, τίνας ἐπιφανεῖς καὶ καλὰς πράξεις προ-
εχόμενος ἐμοῦ πλέον ἔχειν ἀξιοῖ· πότερον ἔτη πλείω
στρατευσάμενος ἢ μάχας πλείους ἀγωνισάμενος ἢ
τραύματα πλείω λαβὼν ἢ στεφάνοις καὶ φαλάροις
καὶ σκύλοις καὶ τοῖς ἄλλοις ἐπινικίοις κόσμοις
ὑπερβαλόμενος, δι' ὃν ἀσθενέστεροι μὲν οἱ πολέμιοι
γεγόνασιν ἐπιφανεστέρα δὲ καὶ μείζων ἡ πατρίς;
μᾶλλον δὲ τὸ δέκατον ἐπιδειξάτω μέρος ὧν ὑμῖν
2 ὑπέδειξα ἐγώ. ἀλλὰ τούτων γ' οἱ πλείους οὐδ' ἂν
πολλοστὴν ἔχοιεν προενέγκασθαι μοῖραν τῶν ἐμῶν·
ἔνιοι δὲ οὐδ' ἂν τῷ φαυλοτάτῳ τῶν ἐκ τοῦ δήμου
φανεῖεν τὰ ἴσα κακοπαθήσαντες. οὐ γάρ ἐστιν
αὐτῶν ἐν τοῖς ὅπλοις ἡ λαμπρότης, ἀλλ' ἐν τοῖς
λόγοις, οὐδὲ κατὰ τῶν ἐχθρῶν τὸ δυνάμενον, ἀλλὰ
κατὰ τῶν φίλων· οὐδ' ἡγοῦνται κοινὴν οἰκεῖν πόλιν,
σφῶν δ' αὐτῶν ἰδίαν, ὥσπερ οὐ συνελευθερωθέντες
ἀπὸ τῆς τυραννίδος ὑφ' ἡμῶν, ἀλλὰ κατὰ κληρονο-
μίαν παρὰ τῶν τυράννων παραλαβόντες ἡμᾶς· οἵ
γε—τὰ μὲν ἄλλα, ὅσα ὑβρίζοντες ἡμᾶς μικρὰ καὶ
μείζω διατελοῦσιν, ὡς ἅπαντες ἐπίστασθε, σιωπῶ
3 —ἀλλ' εἰς τοῦτο προεληλύθασιν[1] ὑπερηφανίας ὥστ'
οὐδὲ φωνὴν ἀξιοῦσί τινα ἡμῶν ἀφιέναι περὶ τῆς
πατρίδος ἐλευθέραν οὐδὲ διᾶραι τὸ στόμα, ἀλλὰ
τὸν μὲν πρῶτον[2] εἰπόντα περὶ τῆς κληρουχίας
Σπόριον Κάσσιον, τρισὶ μὲν ὑπατείαις κεκοσμη-
μένον, δυσὶ δὲ θριάμβοις λαμπροτάτοις, τοσαύτην
δὲ δεινότητα περί τε τὰς στρατηγικὰς πράξεις καὶ
περὶ τὰ πολιτικὰ βουλεύματα ἀποδειξάμενον ὅσην

[1] προεληλύθασιν Bb : προσεληλύθασιν Ba, παρεληλύθασιν A.
[2] πρῶτον Steph. : om. AB, Jacoby.

XXXVIII. " Come now, if aught of what I have
said is false, in Heaven's name let one of these grand
men come forward and show what illustrious and
noble achievements he relies on to claim a larger
share of the land than I. Has he served more years,
fought more battles, received more wounds, or ex-
celled me in the number of crowns, decorations, spoils,
and the other ornaments of victory—in fact, shown
himself a man by whom our enemies have been
weakened and our country rendered more illustrious
and powerful ? Nay, let him show the tenth part
of what I have cited to you. But of these men the
majority could not produce even the smallest fraction
of my exploits ; and some would be found not to
have undergone as many hardships as even the
meanest plebeian. For their brilliancy does not lie
in arms, but in words, nor is their power exerted
against their enemies, but against their friends ; and
they do not regard the commonwealth in which they
dwell as belonging to all alike, but as their own
private property—as if they had not been aided by
us in gaining their freedom from tyranny, but had
received us as an inheritance from the tyrants. I say
nothing of the other insults, small and great, which
they continue to heap upon us, as you all know ; but
they have gone so far in their arrogance that they
forbid any one of us even to utter a free word in
behalf of our country or even to open our mouths.
Nay, they accused Spurius Cassius, who first proposed
the allotment of land, a man who had been honoured
with three consulships and two most brilliant triumphs
and had shown greater ability in both military undertakings and political counsels than anyone of that age

οὐδεὶς τῶν τότε γενομένων, τοῦτον τὸν ἄνδρα αἰτιασάμενοι τυραννίδι ἐπιχειρεῖν καὶ ψευδέσι κατ-
αγωνισάμενοι μαρτυρίαις δι᾽ οὐδὲν ἕτερον, ἀλλ᾽ ὅτι
φιλόπολις ἦν καὶ φιλόδημος, ὥσαντες ἀπὸ[1] τοῦ
4 κρημνοῦ διέφθειραν. Γναῖον δὲ Γενύκιον δήμαρχον
ὄντα ἡμέτερον, ἐπεὶ τὸ αὐτὸ τοῦτο πολίτευμα μετὰ
ἔτος[2] ἑνδέκατον ἀνενεοῦτο, καὶ τοὺς ὑπατεύσαντας
ἐν τῷ πρότερον ἐνιαυτῷ κατέστησεν ὑπὸ δίκην
ἀμελήσαντας τῶν ψηφισμάτων τῆς βουλῆς ἃ περὶ
τῶν γεωμόρων ἐψηφίσατο, ἐπεὶ φανερῶς οὐχ οἷοί
τ᾽ ἦσαν ἀνελεῖν, μιᾷ πρότερον ἡμέρᾳ τῆς δίκης
5 ἀφανῶς ἀνήρπασαν. τοιγάρτοι πολὺς ἐνέπεσε τοῖς
μετὰ ταῦτα φόβος, καὶ οὐδεὶς ἔτι τὸ κινδύνευμα
τοῦτο ὑπέδυ, ἀλλὰ τριακοστὸν ἔτος τοῦτο ἀνεχό-
μεθα ὥσπερ ἐν τυραννίδι τὴν ἐξουσίαν ἀπολωλε-
κότες.

XXXIX. '' Ἐῶ τἆλλα· ἀλλ᾽ οἱ νῦν ἄρχοντες
ὑμῶν, ὅτι τοῖς κατισχυομένοις τῶν δημοτικῶν ἠξίουν βοηθεῖν, οὓς ὑμεῖς ἱεροὺς καὶ ἀσύλους ἐποιή-
σατε τῷ νόμῳ, τί οὐ πεπόνθασι τῶν δεινῶν; οὐχὶ
τυπτόμενοι καὶ λακτιζόμενοι καὶ πᾶσαν αἰκίαν
ὑπομείναντες ἀπηλάθησαν ἐκ τῆς ἀγορᾶς; καὶ
ὑμεῖς ταῦτα πάσχοντες ἀνέχεσθε καὶ οὐ ζητεῖτε
ὅπως παρ᾽ αὐτῶν λήψεσθε δίκας ταῖς γοῦν ψήφοις, ἐν αἷς μόναις ἔξεστιν ὑμῖν ἀποδείξασθαι τὴν
2 ἐλευθερίαν;[3] ἀλλ᾽ ἔτι καὶ νῦν, ὦ δημόται, φρόνημα λαβόντες ἐλεύθερον καὶ[4] τὸν γεωμορικὸν νόμον

---

[1] ἀπὸ O : κατὰ Naber.
[2] ἔτος O : τὸ ἔτος Jacoby.
[3] The (;) is due to Capps.   Editors have all treated this as
a declarative sentence.
[4] καὶ deleted by Kiessling, Jacoby.   Kiessling proposed as
an alternative λάβετε ἐλεύθερον καὶ.

—this man, I say, they accused of aiming at tyranny and defeated him by means of false testimony, for no other reason than because he was a lover of his country and a lover of the people, and they destroyed him by shoving him over the cliff.[1] And again, when Gnaeus Genucius, one of our tribunes, revived this same measure after the lapse of eleven years [2] and summoned the consuls of the preceding year to trial for having neglected to carry out the decree which the senate had passed respecting the appointment of the commissioners to divide the land, since they could not destroy him openly, they made away with him secretly the day before the trial. In consequence, great fear came upon the succeeding tribunes, and not one of them would thereafter expose himself to this danger, but for now the thirtieth year we endure this treatment, as if we had lost our power under a tyranny.

XXXIX. " The other things I pass over ; but your present magistrates, because they thought it their duty to help those of the plebeians who were oppressed, though by law you had made these magistrates sacred and inviolable, what dreadful treatment have they not suffered ? Were they not driven out of the Forum with blows, kicks and every form of outrage ? And you, do you endure to suffer such treatment and not seek means of taking revenge on the perpetrators, at least by your votes, in which alone you can show your freedom ? But even now, plebeians, pluck up the courage of free men and, now that the

---

[1] The Tarpeian Rock.
[2] The interval was twelve years (483–471) according to Dionysius' own account. See viii. 77 and ix. 37 f.

εἰσφερόντων τῶν δημάρχων ἐπικυρώσατε μηδὲ φω-
3 νὴν ἀνασχόμενοι τῶν τἀναντία ἀξιούντων. ὑμεῖς
δ᾽, ὦ δήμαρχοι, παρακλήσεως μὲν εἰς τοῦτο τὸ
ἔργον οὐ δεῖσθε· καὶ γὰρ ἤρξατε αὐτοῦ καὶ οὐχ
ὑποκατακλίνεσθε, καλῶς ποιοῦντες· ἐὰν δ᾽ ἐκ τῶν
νέων αὐθάδεια καὶ ἀναίδεια ὑμῖν ἐμποδὼν γένηται
τοὺς καδίσκους ἀνατρεπόντων ἢ τὰς ψήφους ἁρ-
παζόντων ἢ ἄλλο τι περὶ τὴν ψηφοφορίαν ἀκοσ-
μούντων, δείξατε αὐτοῖς ἣν ἔχει τὸ ἀρχεῖον ἰσχύν.
4 καὶ ἐπειδὴ οὐ τοὺς ὑπάτους ἔξεστι παῦσαι τῆς ἐξουσίας, τοὺς ἰδιώτας οἷς πρὸς τὰ βίαια ὑπηρέταις
ἐκεῖνοι χρῶνται καταστήσαντες ὑπὸ δίκην, ἀνάδοτε
τῷ δήμῳ τὰς περὶ αὐτῶν ψήφους, αἰτιασάμενοι
παρὰ τοὺς ἱεροὺς νόμους βιάζεσθαι καὶ καταλύειν
ὑμῶν τὴν ἀρχήν.''

XL. Τοιαῦτ᾽ εἰπόντος αὐτοῦ τὸ μὲν πλῆθος οὕτως οἰκείως διετέθη πρὸς τοὺς λόγους καὶ τοσαύτην ἀπεδείξατο ἀγανάκτησιν πρὸς τὸ ἀντίπαλον,
ὥσθ᾽, ὅπερ ἔφην καὶ κατ᾽ ἀρχάς, μηδὲ λόγον ἔτι
2 βούλεσθαι τῶν ἀντιλεξόντων ὑπομένειν. ὁ μέντοι
δήμαρχος Ἰκίλλιος ἀναστὰς τὰ μὲν ἄλλα ἔφη πάντα ὀρθῶς εἰπεῖν Σίκκιον καὶ μακρὸν ἔπαινον τοῦ
ἀνδρὸς διεξῆλθε· τὸ δὲ μὴ μεταδιδόναι λόγον τοῖς
ἀντιλέξαι βουλομένοις οὔτε δίκαιον ἀπέφαινεν οὔτε
πολιτικόν, ἄλλως τε καὶ περὶ νόμου τῆς ζητήσεως
γινομένης ὃς ἔμελλε κρείττονα ποιήσειν τὴν δίκην
τῆς βίας. ταύτῃ γὰρ ἀφορμῇ χρήσεσθαι[1] τοὺς
μηδὲν ἴσως καὶ δικαίως[2] τοῖς πολλοῖς φρονοῦντας
τοῦ ταράττειν πάλιν καὶ διστάναι τὰ συμφέροντα
3 τῆς πόλεως. ταῦτ᾽ εἰπὼν καὶ τὴν ἐπιοῦσαν ἀπο-

---

[1] Hudson : χρήσασθαι AB.
[2] ἴσον καὶ δίκαιον Cobet.

tribunes propose it, ratify the agrarian law, not
tolerating even a word from those of the opposite
opinion. As for you, tribunes, you need no exhorta-
tion to this task, since you began it and in not yielding
do well. And if the self-willed and shameless young
men obstruct you by overturning the voting-urns,
snatching away the ballots or committing any other
disorders in connexion with the voting, show them
what power your college possesses. And since you
cannot depose the consuls from power, bring to trial
the private persons whom they use as the agents of
their violence and take the votes of the populace
concerning them, after charging them with attempting to violate and overthrow your magistracy contrary to the sacred laws."

XL. When he had spoken to this effect, the
plebeians were so won over by his words and showed
so great indignation against their adversaries that,
as I said at the outset, they were unwilling to tolerate
even another word from those who were intending to
speak against the law. Icilius the tribune, however,
rose and said that everything else Siccius had said
was excellent, and he praised the man at length ;
but as to not permitting those who wished to oppose
the measure to speak, that, he declared, was neither
just nor democratic, especially as the debate was
about a law which would make justice superior to
violence. For such an opportunity would be used
by those who entertained no sentiments of equality
and justice toward the masses to disturb them again
and cause factious divisions about the interests of the
commonwealth. Having spoken thus and assigned

δείξας ἡμέραν τοῖς κατηγόροις τοῦ νόμου διέλυσε
τὴν ἐκκλησίαν. οἱ δὲ ὕπατοι συναγαγόντες ἰδιωτι-
κὸν συνέδριον πατρικίων τῶν ἀνδρειοτάτων τε καὶ
μάλιστα ἐν τῇ πόλει τότ' ἀνθούντων ἐδίδασκον
αὐτοὺς ὡς κωλυτέος εἴη σφίσιν ὁ νόμος, λόγοις
μὲν πρῶτον, ἐὰν δὲ μὴ πείθωσι τὸν δῆμον, ἔργοις.
ἐκέλευόν τε ἅπασιν ἥκειν ἕωθεν εἰς τὴν ἀγορὰν ἅμα
τοῖς ἑταίροις τε καὶ πελάταις, ὅσοις ἂν ἕκαστοι
4 πλείστοις δύνωνται· ἔπειτα τοὺς μὲν περὶ αὐτὸ τὸ
βῆμα καὶ τὸ ἐκκλησιαστήριον ἑστῶτας ὑπομένειν,
τοὺς δὲ κατὰ πολλὰ τῆς ἀγορᾶς μέρη συστρέψαντας
ἑαυτοὺς διαστῆναι, ὥστε διειλῆφθαι τὸ δημοτικὸν
διεσπασμένον καὶ κωλύεσθαι πρὸς αὐτῶν εἰς ἓν
συνελθεῖν. ἐδόκει ταῦτα κράτιστα εἶναι, καὶ πρὶν
ἡμέραν λαμπρὰν γενέσθαι τὰ πολλὰ τῆς ἀγορᾶς
κατείχετο ὑπὸ τῶν πατρικίων.

XLI. Μετὰ ταῦτα οἵ τε δήμαρχοι καὶ οἱ ὕπατοι
παρῆσαν καὶ λέγειν ὁ κῆρυξ ἐκέλευσε τὸν βουλόμενον τοῦ νόμου κατηγορεῖν. πολλῶν δὲ καὶ
ἀγαθῶν ἀνδρῶν παριόντων οὐθενὸς ἐξάκουστος ἦν
ὁ λόγος ὑπὸ τοῦ θορύβου τε καὶ τῆς[1] ἀκοσμίας
τῶν ἐκκλησιαζόντων. οἱ μὲν γὰρ ἐπεκέλευόν τε καὶ
ἐπεθάρρυνον τοὺς λέγοντας, οἱ δ' ἐξέβαλλόν τε καὶ
κατεβόων. ἐκράτει δὲ οὔτε ὁ τῶν συλλαμβανόν-
των ἔπαινος οὔτε ὁ τῶν ἀντιπραττόντων θόρυβος.
2 ἀγανακτούντων δὲ τῶν ὑπάτων καὶ μαρτυρομένων
ὅτι τῆς βίας ὁ δῆμος ἄρχει λόγον οὐκ ἀξιῶν ὑπομένειν, ἀπελογοῦντο οἱ δήμαρχοι πρὸς ταῦτα ὅτι ἤδη
πέμπτον ἔτος τῶν αὐτῶν ἀκούοντες λόγων[2] οὐθὲν
ποιοῦσι θαυμαστὸν εἰ μὴ ἀξιοῦσιν ὑπομένειν ἑώλους

---

[1] τῆς Bb : om. R.
[2] τῶν αὐτῶν ἀ. λόγων AB : τὸν αὐτὸν ἀ. λόγον R.

the following day to the opponents of the law, he dismissed the assembly. The consuls, on their side, called a private meeting of those patricians who were the bravest and in the highest repute in the city at the time, and showed them that they must hinder the law from passing, first by their words, and if they could not persuade the populace, then by their deeds. They bade them all come early in the morning to the Forum with as many friends and clients as each of them could get together ; then some of them should take their stand round the tribunal itself and the comitium and remain there, while others, forming in groups, took up positions in many different parts of the Forum, in order to keep the plebeians divided and hinder them from uniting in one body. This seemed to be the best plan, and before it was broad daylight the greater part of the Forum was occupied by the patricians.

XLI. After that the tribunes and the consuls appeared and the herald bade anyone who so desired to speak against the law. But though many good men came forward, the words of none of them could be heard by reason of the tumult and disorderly behaviour of the assembly. For some cheered and encouraged the speakers, while others were for throwing them out or for shouting them down ; but neither the applause of the supporters nor the clamour of the opponents prevailed. When the consuls were incensed at this and protested that the populace had begun the violence by refusing to tolerate a word, the tribunes attempted to justify them by saying that, inasmuch as the plebeians kept hearing the same arguments for now the fifth year, they were doing nothing remarkable if they did not care to put

3 καὶ κατημαξευμένας ἀντιλογίας. ὡς δὲ τὸ πλεῖον
τῆς ἡμέρας εἰς ταῦτα ἐδαπανήθη καὶ ὁ δῆμος
ἀπῄτει τὰς ψήφους, οὐκέτι ἀνασχετὸν ἡγησάμενοι
τὸ πρᾶγμα οἱ νεώτατοι τῶν πατρικίων διίστασθαί
τε βουλομένοις κατὰ φυλὰς τοῖς δημόταις ἐμποδὼν
ἐγίνοντο καὶ τὰ ἀγγεῖα τῶν ψήφων τοὺς ἔχοντας
ἀφῃροῦντο καὶ τῶν ὑπηρετούντων τοὺς μὴ βουλομένους ταῦτα ἀφιέναι τύπτοντές τε καὶ ὠθοῦντες
4 ἐξέβαλλον. κεκραγότων δὲ τῶν δημάρχων καὶ εἰς
μέσους αὐτοὺς ὠθουμένων ἐκείνοις μὲν ὑπεχώρουν
καὶ παρεῖχον ὅποι βούλοιντο[1] χωρεῖν ἀδεῶς, τοῦ δ᾽
ἄλλου δήμου τό τε ἑπόμενον[2] αὐτοῖς καὶ τὸ κατ᾽
ἄλλα καὶ ἄλλα μέρη τῆς ἀγορᾶς ὑπὸ θορύβου καὶ
ἀταξίας κινούμενον ἐπ᾽ αὐτοὺς[3] οὐ παρίεσαν,[4] ὥστ᾽
5 ἀνωφελὲς ἦν ἡ τῶν ἀρχόντων βοήθεια. τέλος δ᾽
οὖν ἐπεκράτησαν οἱ πατρίκιοι καὶ οὐκ εἴασαν ἐπικυρωθῆναι τὸν νόμον. οἱ δὲ προθυμότατα συλ-
λαβέσθαι δόξαντες τοῖς ὑπάτοις ἐκ τριῶν οἰκιῶν
ἦσαν, Ποστόμιοι καὶ Σεμπρώνιοι καὶ τρίτοι Κλοί-
λιοι, γένους τε ἀξιώσει λαμπρότατοι καὶ ἑταιρίαις
μεγάλα δυνάμενοι πλούτῳ τε καὶ δόξῃ καὶ τοῖς
κατὰ πόλεμον ἔργοις ἐπιφανεῖς· καὶ τοῦ μὴ κυρωθῆναι τὸν νόμον οὗτοι ὡμολογοῦντο αἰτιώτατοι
γενέσθαι.

XLII. Τῇ δ᾽ ἑξῆς ἡμέρᾳ παραλαβόντες οἱ δήμαρχοι τοὺς ἐπιφανεστάτους τῶν δημοτικῶν ἐσκόπουν ὅ τι χρήσονται τοῖς πράγμασι, κοινὸν μὲν

---

[1] βούλοιντο R : βούλονται B.

[2] τό τε ἑπόμενον Sylburg, τὸ ἑπόμενον Jacoby : τότε ἑπομένου A, τοῦ ἑπομένου Bb, τοὺς ἑπομένους Kiessling.

[3] καὶ τὸ κατ᾽ ἄλλα . . . ἐπ᾽ αὐτοὺς Sylburg, from his Co-
dex Romanus : om. AB, Jacoby.

[4] παρίεσαν A : παρεῖσαν (?) Ba, παρῆσαν Bb.

up with stale and trite objections. When most of the day had been spent in these contests and the populace insisted upon giving their votes, the youngest of the patricians, regarding the situation as no longer endurable, hindered the plebeians when they wished to divide themselves by tribes, took away the voting-urns from those who were in charge of them, and beating and pushing such of the attendants as would not part with them, sought to drive them from the comitium. But when the tribunes cried out and rushed into their midst, the youths made way for those magistrates and permitted them to go in safety wherever they wished, but of the rest of the populace they did not let pass either those who were in the tribunes' train or those who in various parts of the Forum were endeavouring amid the uproar and disorder to move toward them[1]; hence the assistance of the tribunes was of no avail. In the end, at any rate, the patricians prevailed and would not permit the law to be ratified. Those who were reputed to have assisted the consuls with the greatest zeal on this occasion were of three families, the Postumii, the Sempronii, and third, the Cloelii, all of them men most illustrious for the dignity of their birth, very powerful because of their bands of followers, and distinguished for their wealth, their reputation and their exploits in war. These, it was agreed, were the chief agents in preventing the law from being ratified.

XLII. The next day the tribunes, having associated with themselves the most prominent plebeians, considered how they should deal with the situation,

---

[1] The clause "or those who in various parts . . . move toward them" is reported only from a MS. now lost. Recent editors have bracketed these words.

τοῦτο καὶ[1] παρὰ πάντων ὁμολογούμενον εἰληφότες,
τὸ μὴ τοὺς ὑπάτους ἄγειν ὑπὸ[2] τὴν[3] δίκην, ἀλλὰ
τοὺς ὑπηρετοῦντας αὐτοῖς ἰδιώτας, ὧν κολαζο-
μένων ἔμελλε τοῖς πολλοῖς τῶν πολιτῶν ἐλάττων
ἔσεσθαι λόγος, ὥσπερ ὁ Σίκκιος ὑπετίθετο· περὶ δὲ
τοῦ πλήθους τῶν ὑπὸ τὰς αἰτίας ἀχθησομένων ὅσον
εἶναι χρή, καὶ περὶ τοῦ ὀνόματος ὃ θήσονται τῇ δίκῃ, καὶ μάλιστα περὶ τοῦ τιμήματος πηλίκον ἔσται
2 τὸ μέγεθος, ἐπιμελῆ ποιούμενοι ζήτησιν. οἱ μὲν
οὖν χαλεπώτεροι τὰς φύσεις ἐπὶ τὸ μεῖζόν τε καὶ
φοβερώτερον[4] ἅπαντα ταῦτα προάγειν παρῄνουν,
οἱ δ' ἐπιεικέστεροι τοὐναντίον ἐπὶ τὸ μετριώτε-
ρον καὶ φιλανθρωπότερον, ὁ δὲ ταύτης ἡγούμενος
τῆς γνώμης καὶ πείσας αὐτοὺς ἦν Σίκκιος, ὁ τοὺς
ἐν τῷ δήμῳ περὶ τῆς κληρουχίας[5] διελθὼν λόγους.
3 ἔδοξε δ' οὖν αὐτοῖς τὸ μὲν ἄλλο πλῆθος τῶν πατρικίων ἐᾶσαι, Κλοιλίους δὲ καὶ Ποστομίους καὶ
Σεμπρωνίους ἐπὶ τὸν δῆμον ἄγειν ὧν ἔπραξαν
ὑφέξοντας δίκας[6]· ἐγκαλεῖν δ' αὐτοῖς ὅτι τῶν ἱερῶν
νόμων, οὓς περὶ τῶν δημάρχων ἐκύρωσεν ἡ βουλὴ
καὶ ὁ δῆμος, οὐθενὶ δεδωκότων ἐξουσίαν ἀναγκά-
ζειν τοὺς δημάρχους ὑπομένειν τι τῶν ἀβουλήτων
ὥσπερ τοὺς ἄλλους πολίτας, ἐκεῖνοι κατασχόντες
αὐτοὺς ἐκώλυσαν ἐπὶ τέλος ἄγειν τὴν περὶ τοῦ
4 νόμου διάγνωσιν. τίμημα δ' ἐφάνη ταῖς δίκαις ὁρί-
σαι μήτε θάνατον μήτε φυγὴν μήτ' ἄλλο ἐπίφθονον
μηδέν, ἵνα μὴ τοῦτ' αὐτοῖς γένηται σωτηρίας αἴτιον, ἀλλὰ τὰς οὐσίας αὐτῶν ἱερὰς εἶναι Δήμητρος,
τὸ μετριώτατον ἐκλεξαμένοις τοῦ νόμου μέρος.

---

[1] καὶ τοῦτο καὶ AB.　　　　　　[2] ἐπὶ A.
[3] τὴν deleted by Garrer.　　　[4] Steph. : φοβερώτατον AB.
[5] περὶ τῆς κληρουχίας om. A.　　[6] δίκας B : δίκην A.

after adopting the general principle, accepted by all,
not to bring the consuls themselves to trial, but only
their attendants who held no office, since their punishment would be a matter of less concern to most
citizens, as Siccius suggested. But the number of
the persons to be indicted, the name that should be
given to the offence, and the amount of the fine were
matters to which they gave careful consideration.
Now while those who were naturally more truculent
advised going in all these matters to a greater and
more terrifying length, and the more reasonable, on
the contrary, to a more moderate and humane extent,
the man who took the lead for the latter opinion and
won the assent of the others was Siccius, who had
made the speech in the popular assembly in favour
of the land-allotment. They resolved, then, to let
the rest of the patricians alone, but to bring the
Cloelii, the Postumii and the Sempronii before the
popular assembly to stand trial for their acts ; and
to make the charge against them that, whereas the
sacred laws, which the senate and the assembly had
enacted concerning the tribunes, had given no one
authority to compel the tribunes to submit, like the
other citizens, to anything against their will, these
men had restrained them and prevented them from
carrying through the deliberation concerning the law.
As for the penalty in these trials, they decided
to fix neither death, banishment, nor any other
invidious punishment, lest that very thing should
become the cause of their salvation,[1] but that their
estates should be consecrated to Ceres—thus choosing the mildest punishment provided by the law.

---

[1] *Cf.* vii. 64, 6.

5 ἐγίνετο ταῦτα καὶ παρῆν ὁ χρόνος ἐν ᾧ τὰς κατὰ
τῶν ἀνδρῶν ἔδει συντελεῖσθαι δίκας. τοῖς δ᾽ ὑπάτοις καὶ τῶν ἄλλων πατρικίων τοῖς παραληφθεῖσιν
εἰς τὸ συνέδριον (ἔτυχον δ᾽ οἱ κράτιστοι παρα-
κληθέντες) ἐδόκει συγχωρεῖν τοῖς δημάρχοις ἐπιτελέσαι[1] τὰς δίκας, ἵνα μή τι μεῖζον κωλυθέντες
ἐξεργάσωνται κακόν, καὶ τοῖς δημόταις ἐπιτρέπειν ἀγριαινομένοις εἰς τὰ χρήματα τῶν ἀνδρῶν
ἐκχέαι τὴν χολήν, ἵνα τιθασώτεροι γένωνται τὸ
λοιπόν, λαβόντες ὁποσηνοῦν[2] παρὰ τῶν ἐχθρῶν δίκην, ἄλλως τε καὶ τῆς εἰς χρήματα ζημίας εὐδιόρθω-
τον ἐχούσης τοῖς πεπονθόσι τὴν συμφοράν· ὅπερ
6 καὶ συνέβη. ἁλόντων γὰρ τῶν ἀνδρῶν ἐρήμους τὰς
δίκας ὅ τε δῆμος ἀγριαινόμενος ἐπαύσατο καὶ
τοῖς δημάρχοις ἐδόκει τις ἀποδεδόσθαι μετρία καὶ
πολιτικὴ βοήθεια,[3] τοῖς τε ἀνδράσι τὰς οὐσίας οἱ
πατρίκιοι παρὰ τῶν ὠνησαμένων ἐκ τοῦ δημοσίου
τῆς ἴσης λυσάμενοι τιμῆς ἀπέδοσαν. καὶ τὰ μὲν
κατεπείγοντα δεινὰ τοῦτον τὸν τρόπον χρησαμένων
τοῖς πράγμασιν αὐτῶν διελέλυτο.

XLIII. Μετ᾽ οὐ πολὺ δὲ πάλιν τῶν δημάρχων
τὸν ὑπὲρ τοῦ νόμου εἰσφερόντων λόγον αἰφνιδίως
τις ἀπαγγελθεῖσα[4] πολεμίων ἔφοδος ἐπὶ τὴν τῶν
Τυσκλανῶν πόλιν αἰτία κωλύσεως ἀποχρῶσα ἐγένετο. τῶν γὰρ Τυσκλανῶν κατὰ πλῆθος[5] εἰς τὴν
Ῥώμην ἀφικομένων καὶ λεγόντων ὅτι δυνάμει
πολλῇ πάρεισιν ἐπ᾽ αὐτοὺς Αἰκανοὶ καὶ τὴν μὲν

---

[1] ἐπιτελέσαι R : ἐπιτελέσασθαι B.
[2] ὁποσηνοῦν (ὁπόσην οὖν) G. Krüger, Kiessling : ὁπόσην
γοῦν O.

While this was going on the time arrived when the
trials of the men were to take place. The consuls
and the other patricians who had been invited to the
senate-house—the most influential had been summoned—decided to let the tribunes carry out the
trials, lest, if they were hindered, they might do
some greater mischief, and to allow the enraged
plebeians to spend their fury upon the goods of these
men, to the end that they might be milder for the
future, after taking some revenge, however slight,
upon their enemies, particularly since a monetary
fine was a misfortune that could easily be made up
to the sufferers. And so in fact it turned out. For
when the men had been condemned by default, the
populace ceased from its anger, and also it seemed that
a moderate and statesmanlike power of rendering
assistance had been restored to the tribunes, while
as for the convicted men, their estates were ransomed
by the patricians from those who had purchased them
from the treasury for the same price they had paid
for them and were restored to the owners. As a
result of their handling the matter in this fashion
the pressing dangers were dispelled.

XLIII. Not long afterwards, when the tribunes
again introduced the subject of the law, the sudden
announcement that enemies had made an attack
upon Tusculum furnished a sufficient reason for preventing such action. For the Tusculans, coming to
Rome in great numbers, said that the Aequians had
come against them with a large army, that they had

---

³ μετρία καὶ πολιτικὴ βοήθεια AB : μετρία γοῦν καὶ πολιτικὴ
δύναμις καὶ βοήθεια R.

⁴ ἀπαγγελθεῖσα Bb, ἀπαγγελεῖσα Jacoby : ἀγγελία A, ἀγ-
γελθεῖσα R.   ⁵ πλῆθος B : πλήθη R.

χώραν αὐτῶν ἤδη διηρπάκασι, τὴν δὲ πόλιν, ἐὰν
μή τις γένηται ταχεῖα ἐπικουρία, φθάσουσιν ἐντὸς
ὀλίγων ἡμερῶν ἀράμενοι, ἡ μὲν[1] βουλὴ τοὺς ὑπάτους αὐτοῖς ἐψηφίσατο βοηθεῖν ἀμφοτέρους, οἱ δ'
ὕπατοι στρατολογίαν προθέντες ἐκάλουν τοὺς πο-
2 λίτας ἅπαντας ἐπὶ τὰ ὅπλα. ἐγένετο μὲν οὖν τις[2]
καὶ τότε στάσις ἐναντιουμένων τῇ καταγραφῇ τῶν
δημάρχων καὶ τὰς ἐκ τῶν νόμων τιμωρίας οὐ
συγχωρούντων ποιεῖσθαι κατὰ τῶν ἀπειθούντων·
ἔπραξαν[3] δ' οὐθέν. συνελθοῦσα γὰρ ἡ βουλὴ γνώμην ἀπεδείξατο τοὺς πατρικίους ἐπὶ τὸν πόλεμον
ἐξιέναι σὺν τοῖς ἑαυτῶν πελάταις, τῶν δ' ἄλλων
πολιτῶν τοῖς μὲν βουλομένοις μετέχειν τῆς στρατείας ἐπὶ σωτηρίᾳ τῆς πατρίδος γινομένης ὅσια
εἶναι τὰ πρὸς θεούς, τοῖς δ' ἐγκαταλείπουσι τοὺς
3 ὑπάτους τἀναντία. ὡς δ' ἀνεγνώσθη τὸ δόγμα τῆς
βουλῆς ἐν τῇ[4] ἐκκλησίᾳ, πολλοὶ καὶ τοῦ δήμου τὸν
ἀγῶνα ἑκόντες ὑπέμειναν· οἱ μὲν ἐπιεικέστατοι δι'
αἰσχύνην εἰ μηδὲν ἐπικουρήσουσι πόλει συμμάχῳ
διὰ τὴν πρὸς αὐτοὺς εὔνοιαν ἀεί τι πρὸς τῶν ἐχθρῶν βλαπτομένῃ· ἐν οἷς ἦν καὶ ὁ Σίκκιος ἐκεῖνος
ὁ κατηγορήσας ἐν τῷ δήμῳ τῶν σφετερισαμένων
τὴν δημοσίαν γῆν, σπεῖραν ἐπαγόμενος ὀκτακοσίων ἀνδρῶν, οἳ στρατεύεσθαι μὲν οὐκέτι ὥραν εἶχον,
ὥσπερ οὐδ' ἐκεῖνος, οὐδ' ἔπιπτον ὑπὸ τὰς ἀνάγκας
τῶν νόμων, τιμῶντες δὲ τὸν ἄνδρα διὰ πολλὰς καὶ
μεγάλας εὐεργεσίας, ἐξιόντος ἐπὶ τὸν πόλεμον οὐκ
4 ἐδικαίωσαν ἀπολείπεσθαι. καὶ ἦν τοῦτο τὸ μέρος
τῆς ἐξελθούσης τότε δυνάμεως ἐμπειρίᾳ τε ἀγώνων

---

[1] μὲν A : μὲν οὖν R.   [2] τις B : om. R.
[3] Reiske : ἔπραξεν O.
[4] τῇ added by Reiske.

already plundered their country, and unless some assistance were speedily sent, they would be masters of the city within a few days. Upon this the senate ordered that both consuls should go to the rescue ; and the consuls, having announced a levy, summoned all the citizens to arms. On this occasion also there was something of a sedition, as the tribunes opposed the levy and would not permit the punishments ordained by law to be inflicted on the disobedient. But they accomplished nothing. For the senate met and passed a resolution ordering that the patricians should take the field with their clients, and declaring that to such of the other citizens as were willing to take part in this expedition undertaken for the preservation of the fatherland the gods were propitious, but to those who deserted the consuls they were unpropitious. When the decree of the senate was read in the assembly, many also of the populace voluntarily consented to enter the struggle, the more respectable moved by shame if they should not succour an allied city which because of its attachment to the Romans was always suffering some injury at the hands of its foes. Among these was Siccius, who in the popular assembly had inveighed against those who had appropriated the public land, and he brought with him a cohort of eight hundred men [1] ; these were, like himself, past the military age and not subject to the compulsion of the laws, but as they honoured him because of his many great services, they did not think it right to desert him when he was setting out to war. Indeed, this contingent of the force which set out at that time was far superior to

---

[1] Livy (iii. 31, 2-4) knows nothing of the story of Siccius related in this and the following chapters.

καὶ τῇ παρὰ τὰ δεινὰ εὐτολμίᾳ μακρῷ τοῦ ἄλλου
ἄμεινον. οἱ δὲ πολλοὶ χάριτι καὶ παρακλήσει τῶν
πρεσβυτάτων ὑπαχθέντες εἵποντο. ἦν δέ τι[1] μέρος
ὃ τῶν ὠφελειῶν ἕνεκα τῶν ἐν ταῖς στρατείαις γινομένων πάντα κίνδυνον ἕτοιμον ἦν ὑπομένειν. καὶ
δι' ὀλίγου χρόνου δύναμις ἐξῆλθε πλήθει τε ἀποχρῶσα καὶ παρασκευαῖς κεχρημένη[2] λαμπροτάταις.
5 οἱ μὲν οὖν πολέμιοι προακούσαντες ὅτι μέλλουσιν
ἐπ' αὐτοὺς ἐξάγειν Ῥωμαῖοι στρατιάν, ἀπῆγον ἐπ'
οἴκου τὰς δυνάμεις. οἱ δ' ὕπατοι κατὰ σπουδὴν
ἐλαύνοντες καταλαμβάνουσιν ἐστρατοπεδευκότας
αὐτοὺς πόλεως Ἀντίου πλησίον ἐν ὑψηλῷ καὶ
ἀποτόμῳ χωρίῳ καὶ τίθενται τὴν παρεμβολὴν τῆς
6 ἐκείνων οὐ πρόσω. τέως μὲν οὖν ἐν ταῖς ἑαυτῶν ἐπέμενον[3] ἀμφότεροι παρεμβολαῖς, ἔπειτα
καταφρονήσαντες τῶν Ῥωμαίων Αἰκανοὶ τῆς οὐ
προεπιχειρήσεως καὶ πλῆθος οὐχ ἱκανοὺς εἶναι νομίσαντες, ἀγοράς τ' αὐτῶν περιέκοπτον ἐξιόντες
καὶ τοὺς ἐπὶ προνομὴν[4] ἀποστελλομένους ἢ χόρτον
ἵπποις[5] ἀνεκρούοντο καὶ τοῖς[6] πρὸς ὑδρείαν κατα-
βαίνουσιν αἰφνιδίως ἐπετίθεντο, προὐκαλοῦντό τ'
αὐτοὺς πολλάκις εἰς μάχην.

XLIV. Ταῦθ' ὁρῶσι τοῖς ὑπάτοις ἐδόκει μηκέτι
διατρίβειν τὸν πόλεμον. ἦν δ' ἐν ἐκείναις ταῖς
ἡμέραις ἡ τοῦ πολεμεῖν ἐξουσία Ῥωμιλίῳ προσήκουσα, καὶ ὁ τὸ σύνθημα διδοὺς καὶ εἰς τάξιν
καθιστὰς ἄρχειν[7] τε καὶ παύεσθαι μάχης τὸν καιρὸν
ταμιεύων ἐκεῖνος ἦν· ὃς ἐπειδὴ τὰ σημεῖα ἐκέλευσεν

---

[1] ἦν δὲ καί τι Cobet.
[2] κεκοσμημένη Garrer, κεχορηγημένη Schenkl.
[3] ἐπέμενον AB : ὑπέμενον R.
[4] προνομὴν B : νομὴν R.   [5] ἱππεῖς Vassis.

the rest of the army in point both of experience in action and of courage in the face of dangers. The majority of those who followed along were led to do so out of goodwill toward the oldest citizens and because of their exhortations. And there was a certain element which was ready to undergo any peril for the sake of the booty that is acquired in campaigns. Thus in a short time an army took the field that was sufficient in numbers and most splendidly equipped. The enemy, who had learned in advance that the Romans intended to lead out an army against them, were returning homeward with their forces. But the consuls, making a forced march, came up with them while they lay encamped on a high and steep hill near the city of Antium and placed their camp not far from that of the foe. For some time both armies remained in their camps; then the Aequians, despising the Romans for not having taken the initiative in attacking, and judging their army to be insufficient in numbers, sallied out and cut off their provisions, drove back those who were sent out for provender or fodder for their horses, fell suddenly upon those who went for water, and challenged them repeatedly to battle.

XLIV. The consuls, seeing this, resolved to put off the fighting no longer. During those days it was Romilius' turn to decide whether to fight or not, and it was he who gave the watchword, drew up the army and determined the proper moment both for beginning and for ending battle. He, having ordered

---

[6] τοῖς added by Kiessling.   [7] τοῦ ἄρχειν Reiske.

ἀρθῆναι τῆς[1] μάχης καὶ προῆγεν[2] ἐκ τοῦ χάρακος
τὸν στρατόν, τοὺς μὲν ἄλλους ἔτασσεν ἱππεῖς τε
καὶ τοὺς πεζοὺς κατὰ σπείρας ἐν τοῖς ἐπιτηδείοις
ἑκάστους τόποις, τὸν δὲ Σίκκιον καλέσας λέγει·
2 "' Ἡμεῖς μέν, ὦ Σίκκιε, μαχούμεθα τοῖς πολεμίοις
ἐνθάδε, σὺ δ', ἐν ὅσῳ μέλλομεν ἔτι καὶ παρασκευα-
ζόμεθα τὰ πρὸς τὸν ἀγῶνα ἀμφότεροι, χώρει τὴν
πλαγίαν ἐκείνην ὁδὸν ἐπὶ τὸ ὄρος ἔνθα ἡ τῶν
πολεμίων ἐστὶ παρεμβολὴ καὶ μάχην τίθεσο πρὸς
τοὺς ἐν τῷ χάρακι, ἵν' ἢ περὶ τῷ φρουρίῳ δείσαντες
οἱ πρὸς ἡμᾶς μαχόμενοι καὶ βοηθεῖν προθυμούμενοι
νῶτά τε δείξωσι καὶ εὐκατέργαστοι γένωνται,
καθάπερ εἰκὸς ἐν ἀναχωρήσει ταχείᾳ καὶ εἰς μίαν
ὁδὸν ἅπαντες βιαζόμενοι, ἢ μένοντες αὐτόθι τὸν
3 χάρακα ἀποβάλωσιν. οὔτε γὰρ ἡ φυλάττουσα αὐτὸν δύναμις ἀξιόμαχός ἐστιν, ὡς εἰκάσειεν ἄν τις,
ἐπὶ τῷ ἐρυμνῷ τοῦ τόπου δοκοῦσα εἶναι πᾶν τὸ
ἀσφαλές· ἥ τε ἅμα σοι δύναμις ἀποχρῶσα γένοιτ'
ἄν, ἄνδρες ὀκτακόσιοι πολλῶν ἀθληταὶ πολέμων,
τεταραγμένους σκηνοφύλακας ἀπροσδόκητοι προσ-
4 πεσόντες τῷ τολμηρῷ ἑλεῖν." καὶ ὁ Σίκκιος
ἔφησεν· "' Ἀλλ' ἔγωγε ἅπαντα μὲν ἔτοιμος ὑπηρε-
τεῖν· τὸ μέντοι ἔργον οὐ ῥᾴδιον ὥσπερ σοι δοκεῖ.
ὑψηλή τε γὰρ ἡ πέτρα καὶ ἀπότομος ἐφ' ἧς ὁ
χάραξ, ὁδόν τε οὐδεμίαν ὁρῶ φέρουσαν ἐπ' αὐτὸν[3]
ἔξω τῆς μιᾶς ᾗ καταβήσονται οἱ πολέμιοι πρὸς
ἡμᾶς, φυλακήν τ' εἰκὸς ἀξιόμαχον εἶναι ἐν αὐτῇ·
κἂν ὀλίγη δὲ πάνυ καὶ φαύλη τις οὖσα τύχῃ, πρὸς
πολλῷ πλείονα ἢ τὴν σὺν ἐμοὶ δύναμιν ἀντέχειν οἵα
τε ἔσται, τό τε χωρίον αὐτὸ παρέξει τῇ φυλακῇ τοῦ
5 μὴ ἁλώσεσθαι τὸ ἀσφαλές. ἀλλὰ μάλιστα μὲν

---

[1] ἐκ before τῆς deleted by Sylburg.

the battle standards to be raised and led his army out
of the camp, posted the horse and foot according
to their companies, each in their proper places, and
then, summoning Siccius, said : " We, Siccius, are
going to engage the enemy here ; but as for you,
while we are still waiting and preparing on both sides
for the contest, do you march by yonder transverse
road to the top of the hill where the enemy's camp is
placed and give battle to the men inside, in order
that those who are engaged with us may either, fearing for their stronghold and eager to relieve it, show
their backs and thus be easily defeated, as likely
they will be when they are making a hasty retreat
and are all forcing their way into one road, or may,
by staying here, lose their camp. For not only is
the force guarding it not a match for you, in all
probability, believing as it does that its whole security depends on the natural strength of the position,
but the force with you, eight hundred men, veterans
of many wars, should be sufficient to capture by a bold
stroke mere tent-guards when thrown into confusion
by your unexpected attack." And Siccius replied :
" For my part, I am ready to obey in everything ; but
the task is not so easy as it seems to you. For the
cliff on which the camp is situated is lofty and steep,
and I see no road leading to it except the one by
which the enemy will come down against us, and it is
probable that there is an adequate guard placed over
it ; but even if it should chance to be a very small and
weak one, it will be able to hold out against a much
larger force than the one I have, and the place itself
will afford the guard security against being captured.

---

² προῆγεν R (?), προήγαγεν Kiessling : προσῆγεν B.
³ αὐτὸν Bb : αὐτοὺς ABa, αὐτὴν Kiessling.

ἀνάθου τὴν γνώμην· ἡ πεῖρα γὰρ ἐπισφαλής· εἰ δὲ
πάντως ἔγνωσταί σοι δύο τίθεσθαι μάχας ἐν ἑνὶ
καιρῷ, δύναμιν ἀξιόχρεων ἀνδρῶν ἐπιλέκτων τάξον
ἀκολουθεῖν μοι σὺν τοῖς πρεσβυτέροις. οὐ γὰρ
κλέψοντες τὸ χωρίον, ἀλλὰ βίᾳ καὶ φανερῶς ἐξελοῦντες[1] ἄνιμεν."

XLV. Ἔτι δ᾽ αὐτοῦ βουλομένου λέγειν τἀκό-
λουθα ὑπολαβὼν ὁ ὕπατος εἶπεν· " Οὐ πολλῶν δεῖ
λόγων, ἀλλ᾽ εἰ μὲν ὑπομένεις πράττειν τὰ προσταττ-
τόμενα, χώρει διὰ ταχέων καὶ μὴ παραστρατήγει,
εἰ δὲ ἀφίστασαι καὶ ἀποδιδράσκεις τὸν κίνδυνον,[2]
2 ἑτέροις εἰς τὸ ἔργον χρήσομαι. σὺ δὲ τὰς ἑκατὸν
εἴκοσι μάχας ἀγωνισάμενος καὶ τὰ τετταράκοντα
ἔτη στρατευσάμενος καὶ κατατετρωμένος ὅλον τὸ
σῶμα, ἐπειδὴ ἑκὼν ἦλθες, ἄπιθι μήτε ὁμιλήσας πολεμίοις μήτ᾽ ἰδὼν καὶ ἀντὶ τῶν ὅπλων ἀκόνα πάλιν
τοὺς λόγους οἷς ἀφθόνοις χρήσῃ κατὰ τῶν πατρι-
3 κίων.[3] ποῦ νῦν ἐκεῖνά σου τὰ πολλὰ ἀριστεῖα, οἱ[4]
στρεπτοὶ καὶ τὰ ψέλλια καὶ τὰ δόρατα καὶ τὰ
φάλαρα καὶ οἱ τῶν ὑπάτων στέφανοι καὶ τὰ ἐκ
τῶν μονομαχιῶν λάφυρα καὶ πᾶσα ἡ[5] ἄλλη βαρύτης ἦν τότ᾽ ἠνεσχόμεθά σου λέγοντος; ἐν ἑνὶ γὰρ
δὴ τῷδε τῷ ἔργῳ βασανιζόμενος, ἔνθα κίνδυνος ἦν
ἀληθινός, ἐξητάσθης οἷος ἦσθα, ὡς ἀλαζὼν[6] καὶ δό-
4 ξῃ τὸ ἀνδρεῖον ἐπιτηδεύων, οὐκ ἀληθείᾳ." καὶ ὁ
Σίκκιος δυσανασχετῶν ἐπὶ τοῖς ὀνείδεσιν· " Οἶδα,"
φησίν, " ὦ Ῥωμίλιε, ὅτι δυεῖν πρόκειταί σοι
θάτερον, ἢ ζῶντά με[7] διεργάσασθαι καὶ τὸ μηδὲν

---

[1] ἐξελοῦντες Bb : ἐξαιροῦντες A.   [2] τὸν κίνδυνον om. A.
[3] οἷς ἀφθόνοις χρήσῃ κατὰ τῶν πατρικίων Post, οἷς χρήσῃ κατὰ
τῶν πατρικίων R : οἷς χρήσῃ κατὰ τοῦ φθόνου τῶν πατρικίων AB,
Jacoby.

Do then, if possible, reconsider your purpose, for the attempt is hazardous ; but if you are absolutely determined to fight two battles at the same time, then order a sufficient force of chosen men to follow me and the older men. For we are not going up to take the place by surprise, but by main force and openly."

XLV. Although Siccius wanted to go on and finish his explanation, the consul interrupted him and said : "There is no need of many words. But if you can bring yourself to obey my orders, go at once and do not play the general ; if, however, you decline and run away from the danger, I shall use other men for the task. As for you, who fought those hundred and twenty battles and served those forty years and whose body is covered with wounds, since you came voluntarily, depart without either encountering the enemy or seeing them ; and instead of your arms, sharpen once more your words which you will expend without stint against the patricians. Where now are those many prizes given you for valour, those collars, bracelets, spears, and decorations, those crowns from the consuls, those spoils gained in single combat, and all your other tiresome boasting which we had to endure hearing from you the other day ? For when you were tested in this single instance where the danger was real, you proved what sort of man you were—a braggart practising bravery in imagination, not in reality." Siccius, stung by these reproaches, answered : " I am aware, Romilius, that the choice lies before you either to destroy me while alive and make me

---

⁴ οἱ added by Reiske.   ⁵ ἡ B : om. R.
⁶ ὡς ἀλαζὼν B : om. R.
⁷ με Portus, Sylburg : om. O, Jacoby.

ἀποδοῦναι δόξαν αἰσχίστην ἐνεγκάμενον δειλίας,
ἢ κακῶς καὶ ἀδήλως κατακοπέντα ὑπὸ τῶν πολεμίων ἀποθανεῖν,[1] ἐπειδὴ κἀγώ τις ἔδοξα εἶναι
τῶν ἀξιούντων ἐλεύθερα φρονεῖν· οὐ γὰρ εἰς ἄδηλον,
5 ἀλλ᾽ εἰς ἐγνωσμένον ἀποστέλλεις με θάνατον· πλὴν
ὑπομενῶ καὶ τοῦτο τὸ ἔργον καὶ πειράσομαι φανεὶς
ψυχὴν οὐ κακὸς ἢ κρατῆσαι τοῦ χάρακος ἢ μὴ
τυχὼν τῆς ἐλπίδος εὐγενῶς ἀποθανεῖν. ὑμᾶς δέ,
ὦ συστρατιῶται, μάρτυρας ἀξιῶ γενέσθαι μοι πρὸς
τοὺς ἄλλους πολίτας, ἐὰν πύθησθε τὸν ἐμὸν μόρον,
ὅτι με ἀπώλεσεν ἡ ἀρετὴ καὶ ἡ πολλὴ τῶν λόγων
6 ἐλευθερία.'' ταῦτα πρὸς τὸν ὕπατον ἀποκρινάμε-
νος καὶ δακρύσας τούς τε συνήθεις ἅπαντας ἀσπα-
σάμενος ᾤχετο τοὺς ὀκτακοσίους ἄνδρας ἄγων
κατηφεῖς καὶ δεδακρυμένους ὡς τὴν ἐπὶ θανάτῳ
πορευομένους· καὶ ἡ ἄλλη δὲ πᾶσα στρατιὰ δι᾽
οἴκτου τὸ πρᾶγμα ἔλαβεν ὡς οὐκέτι ὀψομένη τοὺς
ἄνδρας.

XLVI. Ὁ δὲ Σίκκιος ἑτέραν ἀποστραφείς, οὐχ
ἣν ὁ Ῥωμίλιος ὑπελάμβανε, παρὰ τὴν λαγόνα τοῦ
ὄρους ἦγεν. ἔπειτα, ἦν γάρ τις δρυμὸς ὕλην βα-
θεῖαν ἔχων, εἰς τοῦτον ἄγων τοὺς ἄνδρας ἵσταταί
τε[2] καί φησιν· ''Ὑπὸ μὲν τοῦ ἡγεμόνος ἀπεστάλ-
μεθα, ὥσπερ ὁρᾶτε, ἀπολούμενοι. ἐδόκει γὰρ ἡμᾶς
τὴν πλαγίαν χωρήσειν ὁδόν, ἣν ἀναβαίνοντας ἀμή-
χανον ἦν μὴ οὐ φανεροὺς τοῖς πολεμίοις γενέσθαι.
ἐγὼ δ᾽ ὑμᾶς ἄξω κατ᾽[3] ἄδηλον τοῖς ἐχθροῖς ὁδὸν

---

[1] ἀποθανεῖν ⟨ἐὰν⟩ Capps, to avoid an awkward change in
subject for the infinitive ἀποθανεῖν. Kiessling proposed to
read πρόκειταί μοι θ., ἢ ζῶντα διειργάσθαι καὶ εἰς τὸ μηδὲν
ἀποδοθῆναι, ἢ . . . ἀποθανεῖν. Post would read π. μοι θ., ἢ
ζῶντα ἐμαυτὸν διεργάσασθαι καὶ τὸ μὴ δέον ἀποδοῦναι.
[2] τε A : om. R. [3] κατ᾽ Reiske : καὶ O.

a mere nobody bearing the most shameful reputation for cowardice, or that I shall die [1] a miserable and obscure death, hacked to pieces by the enemy, because I too seemed to be one of those who insist on showing the spirit of free men. For you are sending me, not to a doubtful, but to a predetermined death. Yet I will undertake even this task and endeavour, showing myself no coward, either to capture the camp or, failing in that, gallantly to die. And I ask you, fellow soldiers, if you hear of my death, to bear witness for me to the rest of the citizens that I fell a sacrifice to my valour and to my great frankness of speech." Having thus answered the consul, with tears in his eyes, and embraced all his intimate friends, he set out at the head of his eight hundred men, all dejected and weeping, believing that they were taking the road to death. And all the rest of the army were moved to compassion at the sight, expecting to see these men no more.

XLVI. Siccius, however, turned off by a different road, not the one which Romilius had in mind, and marched along the flank of the hill. Then—for there was a thicket with a heavy growth of trees in it—he led his men into it, halted there and said : " We have been sent by the commander, as you see, to perish. For he expected us to take the transverse road, which we could not possibly have ascended without coming into full view of the enemy. But I will lead you by a way that is out of the enemy's sight and I have

---

[1] Or, following the suggestion of Capps, " or to let me die." According to Kiessling we should have : " the choice lies before me either to be destroyed and reduced to a mere nobody . . . or to die "; according to Post : " the choice lies before me either to destroy myself and pay the debt I do not owe . . . or to die."

καὶ πολλὰς ἐλπίδας ἔχω τρίβων ἐπιλήψεσθαί τινων
αἳ κατὰ κορυφῆς[1] ἄξουσιν ἡμᾶς ἐπὶ τὸν χάρακα·
2 καὶ ἐλπίδας χρηστὰς ἔχετε." ταῦτ' εἰπὼν ἦγε διὰ
τοῦ δρυμοῦ, καὶ πολὺν ἤδη διεληλυθὼς τόπον εὑ-
ρίσκει κατὰ δαίμονα ἄνδρα ἐξ ἀγροῦ ποθὲν ἀπιόντα,[2]
ὃν τοῖς νεωτάτοις συλλαβεῖν κελεύσας ἡγεμόνα
ποιεῖται τῆς ὁδοῦ. κἀκεῖνος αὐτοὺς ἄγων περὶ[3] τὸ
ὄρος σὺν πολλῷ χρόνῳ καθίστησιν ἐπὶ τὸν παρα-
κείμενον τῷ χάρακι λόφον, ὅθεν ἦν ταχεῖα καὶ
3 εὐεπίφορος ἐπ' αὐτὸν ὁδός. ἐν ᾧ δὲ ταῦτ' ἐγίνετο
χρόνῳ, συνῄεσαν αἵ τε τῶν Ῥωμαίων καὶ αἱ τῶν
Αἰκανῶν δυνάμεις ὁμόσε καὶ καταστᾶσαι ἐμάχοντο,
πλήθει τ' ἀγχώμαλοι οὖσαι καὶ ὁπλισμοῖς καὶ προθυμίαν παρεχόμεναι[4] τὴν αὐτήν· καὶ διέμειναν ἐπὶ
πολὺν χρόνον ἰσόρροποι, τοτὲ μὲν ἐπιβαίνοντες
ἀλλήλοις, τοτὲ δ' ὑποχωροῦντες, ἱππεῖς τε ἱππεῦσι
καὶ πεζοὶ πεζοῖς, καὶ ἔπεσον ἐξ ἑκατέρων ἄνδρες
4 ἐπιφανεῖς. ἔπειτα κρίσιν λαμβάνει ὁ πόλεμος ἐπι-
τελῆ. ὁ γὰρ Σίκκιος καὶ οἱ σὺν αὐτῷ, ἐπειδὴ
πλησίον ἐγένοντο τῆς παρεμβολῆς τῶν Αἰκανῶν,
ἀφύλακτον εὑρόντες ἐκεῖνο[5] τὸ μέρος τοῦ χάρακος
(ἐπὶ γὰρ θάτερα τὰ πρὸς τοὺς μαχομένους ἐστραμ-
μένα μέρη πᾶσα ἡ φυλάττουσα αὐτὸν δύναμις
ἐτράπετο κατὰ θέαν τοῦ ἀγῶνος), ἐπεισπεσόντες
κατὰ πολλὴν εὐπέτειαν κατὰ κορυφῆς γίνονται τῶν
5 φυλάκων. ἔπειτ' ἀλαλάξαντες ἔθεον ἐπ' αὐτούς· οἱ
δ' ὑπὸ τοῦ παρ' ἐλπίδα δεινοῦ ἐκταραχθέντες καὶ
οὐ τοσούτους εἶναι δόξαντες, ἀλλὰ τὸν ἕτερον ἥκειν
ὕπατον ἄγοντα τὴν σὺν αὐτῷ δύναμιν, ἐρρίπτουν
ἔξω τοῦ χάρακος ἑαυτούς, οὐδὲ τὰ ὅπλα οἱ πολλοὶ

---

[1] Reiske : κορυφὴν O.
[2] ἀπιόντα O : ἐπιόντα Grasberger.   [3] ἐπὶ A.

great hopes of gaining some paths that will bring us over the summit to their camp. So I bid you have the best of hopes." Having said this, he led the way through the thicket, and after going a good distance, by good fortune came upon a man who was on his way home from a farm somewhere ; and ordering him to be seized by the youngest men of his company, he took him for his guide. This man, leading them round the hill, brought them after a long time to the height adjacent to the camp, from which there was a short and easy descent to their goal. While this was happening, the forces of the Romans and of the Aequians engaged and fought steadfastly, since they were equally matched both in numbers and in armament and displayed the same ardour. For a long time they continued to be evenly balanced as they now attacked one another and now withdrew, horse against horse and foot against foot ; and prominent men fell on both sides. Then the battle took a definite turn. For Siccius and his men, when they came near the camp of the Aequians, found that part of it unguarded, since the entire force appointed to guard it had gone to the other side that faced the field of battle, in order to witness the conflict ; and bursting into the camp with great ease, they found themselves immediately overhead in relation to the guards. Then, uttering their war-cry, they attacked them on the run. The garrison, confounded by this unexpected danger and not imagining that their assailants were so few in number, but supposing that the other consul had arrived with his army, hurled themselves out of the camp, most of them not even

---

⁴ παρεχόμεναι R : παρεχόμενοι AB.
⁵ ἐκεῖνο B : om. R.

φυλάξαντες. οἱ δὲ περὶ τὸν Σίκκιον τοὺς κατα-
λαμβανομένους αὐτῶν φονεύοντες καὶ τοῦ χάρακος
6 κρατήσαντες ἐχώρουν ἐπὶ τοὺς ἐν τῷ πεδίῳ. οἱ
δὲ Αἰκανοὶ τοῦ χάρακος τὴν ἅλωσιν ἀπό τε τῆς
φυγῆς καὶ τῆς κραυγῆς τῶν σφετέρων αἰσθόμενοι
καὶ μετ' οὐ πολὺ κατὰ νώτου σφίσι τοὺς πολεμίους
ἐπιόντας ὁρῶντες, οὐκέτι γενναῖον οὐδὲν ἀπεδείξαντο, ἀλλὰ διασπάσαντες τὰς τάξεις ἔσωζον ἑαυτοὺς ἄλλοι κατ' ἄλλας ὁδούς· ἔνθα ὁ πλεῖστος
αὐτῶν ἐγίνετο[1] φόνος. οὐ γὰρ ἀνίεσαν οἱ Ῥωμαῖοι
μέχρι νυκτὸς διώκοντές τε καὶ κτείνοντες τοὺς[2]
7 ἁλισκομένους. ὁ δὲ πλείστους τ' αὐτῶν διαφθείρας
καὶ λαμπρότατα ἔργα ἀποδειξάμενος Σίκκιος ἦν,
ὅς, ἐπειδὴ τέλος ἑώρα τὰ τῶν πολεμίων ἔχοντα
σκότους ὄντος ἤδη, τὴν σπεῖραν ἄγων ἐπὶ τὸν
κρατηθέντα ὑπὸ σφῶν χάρακα ἀνέστρεφε μεγάλης
8 χαρᾶς καὶ πολλοῦ μεστὸς ὢν αὐχήματος. οἵ τε περὶ
αὐτὸν ἀθῷοι καὶ ἀβλαβεῖς πάντες, οὐ μόνον οὐδὲν
παθόντες ὧν προσεδόκησαν, ἀλλὰ καὶ δόξαν ἐπι-
φανεστάτην ἐξενεγκάμενοι, πατέρα καὶ σωτῆρα καὶ
θεὸν καὶ πάντα τὰ τιμιώτατα ὀνομάζοντες ἀπλή-
στως εἶχον ἀσπασμῶν τε τοῦ ἀνδρὸς καὶ τῶν
ἄλλων φιλοφρονήσεων.[3] ἐν δὲ τούτῳ καὶ ἡ ἄλλη
τῶν Ῥωμαίων φάλαγξ ἅμα τοῖς ὑπάτοις ἀπὸ[4]
τῆς διώξεως ἀνέστρεφεν ἐπὶ τὸν ἑαυτῆς χάρακα.

XLVII. Μέσαι τ' ἤδη νύκτες ἦσαν, καὶ ὁ Σίκκιος
μνησικακῶν τοῖς ὑπάτοις τῆς ἐπὶ τὸν θάνατον ἀπο-
στολῆς εἰς νοῦν βάλλεται τὴν δόξαν ἀφελέσθαι τοῦ
κατορθώματος. κοινωσάμενος δὲ τοῖς ἀμφ' αὐτὸν

---

[1] ἐγίνετο B : ἐγένετο A.   [2] τοὺς added by Sylburg.
[3] φιλοφρονήσεων Cobet : φιλοφρονήσεων ἡδονάς O; καὶ τῆς ἐκ
τῶν ἄλλων φιλοφρονήσεων ἡδονῆς Reiske.

holding on to their arms. Siccius and his men slew
all of them they overtook, and after possessing themselves of their camp, marched against those who were
in the plain. The Aequians, perceiving from the
flight and outcries of their men that their camp had
been taken, and then, not long afterwards, seeing the
enemy falling upon their rear, no longer displayed any
valour, but broke their ranks and endeavoured to save
themselves, some by one way and some by another.
And here they met with their greatest loss of life ;
for the Romans did not give over the pursuit till night,
killing all whom they captured. The man who slew
the largest number of them and performed the most
brilliant deeds was Siccius, who, when he saw that
the enemy's resistance was at an end, it being now
dark, returned with his cohort to the camp which they
had taken, filled with great joy and much exultation.
All his men, safe and uninjured, having not only
suffered none of the calamities they had expected,
but also won the greatest glory, called him their
father, their preserver, their god, and every other
honourable appellation, and could not sate themselves
with embracing him and showing every other mark
of affection. In the meantime the rest of the Roman
army with the consuls was returning from the pursuit
to their camp.

XLVII. It was now midnight when Siccius, full of
resentment against the consuls for having sent him
to his death, resolved to take from them the glory of
the victory ; and having communicated his intention

---

[4] ἀπὸ Steph., ἐκ Kayser : om. AB.

ἣν εἶχε διάνοιαν, ἐπειδὴ πᾶσιν ὀρθῶς[1] ἐφαίνετο, καὶ
οὐθεὶς ἦν ὃς οὐκ ἐθαύμαζε τῆς τε φρονήσεως καὶ
τῆς τόλμης τὸν ἄνδρα, λαβὼν τὰ ὅπλα καὶ τοὺς
ἄλλους κελεύσας ἀναλαβεῖν, πρῶτον μὲν[2] ἀνθρώπους ὅσους ἐν τῷ χάρακι κατέλαβε τῶν Αἰκανῶν
καὶ ἵππους καὶ τἆλλα ὑποζύγια κατέκοψεν· ἔπειτα
ὑφῆψε τὰς σκηνὰς ὅπλων τε καὶ σίτου καὶ ἐσθῆτος
καὶ τῶν εἰς τὸν πόλεμον ἐπιτηδείων γεμούσας τῶν
τε ἄλλων χρημάτων ὧν ἐκ τῆς Τυσκλανῶν λείας
2 ἐπήγοντο πολλῶν πάνυ ὄντων. ὡς δὲ ἅπαντα ὑπὸ
τοῦ πυρὸς ἠφάνιστο, περὶ τὸν ὄρθρον ἀπῄει φέρων
οὐθὲν ὅτι μὴ τὰ ὅπλα, καὶ διανύσας σπουδῇ τὴν
ὁδὸν εἰς Ῥώμην παρῆν. ὡς δ' ὤφθησαν ἄνθρωποι
καθωπλισμένοι παιανίζοντές τε καὶ σπουδῇ χωροῦντες αἵματι πολλῷ πεφυρμένοι, δρόμος ἐγίνετο
καὶ πολλὴ προθυμία τῶν βουλομένων ἰδεῖν τ' αὐτοὺς
3 καὶ τὰ πραχθέντα ἀκοῦσαι. οἱ δὲ μέχρις ἀγορᾶς
ἐλθόντες ἐδήλωσαν τοῖς δημάρχοις τὰ γενόμενα,
κἀκεῖνοι συναγαγόντες ἐκκλησίαν[3] ἐκέλευον αὐτοὺς
πρὸς ἅπαντας λέγειν. ὄχλου δὲ πολλοῦ συναχθέντος
παρελθὼν ὁ Σίκκιος τήν τε νίκην αὐτοῖς ἐδήλωσε
καὶ τὸν τρόπον τοῦ ἀγῶνος ἐνεφάνισε, καὶ ὅτι παρὰ
τὴν ἰδίαν ἀρετὴν καὶ τῶν σὺν αὐτῷ πρεσβυτέρων
ἀνδρῶν ὀκτακοσίων, οὓς ἀποθανουμένους ἀπέστειλαν οἱ ὕπατοι, ὅ τε χάραξ ὁ τῶν Αἰκανῶν ἐλήφθη
καὶ ἡ δύναμις ἡ[4] παραταξαμένη τοῖς ὑπάτοις ἠναγ-
4 κάσθη φυγεῖν· ἠξίου τε αὐτοὺς μηδενὶ τῆς νίκης
ἑτέρῳ τὴν χάριν εἰδέναι καὶ τελευτῶν ἔτι προσέθηκεν ἐκεῖνον τὸν λόγον, ὅτι " τὰς ψυχὰς καὶ τὰ
ὅπλα σῴζοντες ἥκομεν, ἄλλο δὲ οὐδὲν τῶν κε-
κρατημένων οὔτε μεῖζον οὔτ' ἔλαττον ἐξενεγκάμε-

to his companions and received their approval, every
one of them admiring the sagacity and daring of the
man, he took his arms and ordering the rest to do the
same, he first slaughtered all the Aequians he found in
the camp, as well as the horses and beasts of burden;
then he set fire to the tents, which were full of arms,
corn, apparel, warlike stores and all the other articles,
very many in number, which they were carrying off as
part of the Tusculan booty. After everything had
been consumed by the flames, he left the camp about
break of day, carrying with him nothing but his arms,
and after a hurried march came to Rome. As soon
as armed men were seen singing paeans of victory and
marching in haste, all covered with blood, the people
flocked to them, earnestly desiring both to see them
and to hear their exploits. When they had come as
far as the Forum, they gave an account to the tribunes
of what had passed ; and those magistrates, calling
an assembly, ordered them to tell their story to all.
When a large crowd had gathered, Siccius came forward and not only announced to them the victory, but
also described the nature of the battle, showing that
by his own valour and that of the eight hundred
veterans with him, whom the consuls had sent to be
slain, the camp of the Aequians had been taken and
the army arrayed against the consuls had been put to
flight. He asked them to give thanks for the victory
to no one else, and ended by adding these words :
" We have come with our lives and our arms safe, but
have brought with us nothing else, great or small, of

---

[1] ὀρθῶς om. B.   Retaining ὀρθῶς, Reiske added βεβουλεῦσθαι after ἐφαίνετο, Kayser ἔχειν before ἐφαίνετο.
[2] μὲν om. AB.   [3] ἐκκλησίαν R : εἰς ἐκκλησίαν B.
[4] ἡ Steph. : om. AB.

5 νοι." ὁ δὲ δῆμος ἀκούσας τὸν λόγον εἰς οἶκτόν τε
καὶ δάκρυα προὔπεσεν ὁρῶν μὲν τὰς ἡλικίας τῶν
ἀνδρῶν, ἐνθυμούμενος δὲ τὰς ἀρετάς, ἀγανακτῶν
δὲ καὶ νεμεσῶν τοῖς ἐπιβαλομένοις τοιούτων ἀνδρῶν ἐρημῶσαι τὴν πόλιν. ἐγεγόνει δέ, ὃ προὔλαβεν
ὁ Σίκκιος, μῖσος εἰς τοὺς ὑπάτους ἐξ ἁπάντων τῶν
6 πολιτῶν. οὐδὲ γὰρ ἡ βουλὴ τὸ πρᾶγμα μετρίως
ἤνεγκεν, ἣ οὔτ' ἐψηφίσατο αὐτοῖς πομπὴν θριάμβων
οὔτε ἄλλο τι τῶν ἐπὶ καλοῖς ἀγῶσι γινομένων. τὸν
μέντοι Σίκκιον ὁ δῆμος, ἐπειδὴ καθῆκεν ὁ τῶν
ἀρχαιρεσίων καιρός, δήμαρχον ἀπέδειξεν, ἧς κύριος
ἦν τιμῆς ἀποδιδούς. καὶ τὰ μὲν ἐπιφανέστατα τῶν
τότε πραχθέντων τοιάδ' ἦν.

XLVIII. Ἐν δὲ τῷ μετὰ τούτους τοὺς ὑπάτους[1]
ἔτει Σπόριος Ταρπήιος καὶ Αὖλος Τερμήνιος παραλαμβάνουσι τὴν ἀρχήν· οἳ τά τ' ἄλλα θεραπεύοντες
τὸν δῆμον διετέλεσαν καὶ τὸ τῶν δημάρχων[2] δόγμα
προεβούλευσαν, ἐπειδὴ πλέον μὲν οὐδὲν ἑώρων τοῖς
πατρικίοις γινόμενον ἐκ τοῦ κωλύειν, ἀλλὰ καὶ
φθόνον καὶ μῖσος καὶ βλάβας δὲ ἰδίας καὶ συμφορὰς
2 τοῖς προθυμότατα ὑπὲρ αὐτῶν ἀγωνιζομένοις. μάλιστα δ' αὐτοὺς εἰς δέος ἤγαγεν ἡ τῶν ὑπατευσάντων τὸν παρελθόντα ἐνιαυτὸν συμφορὰ νεωστὶ
γενομένη δεινὰ μὲν ὑπὸ τοῦ δήμου παθόντων, οὐδεμίαν δὲ παρὰ τῆς βουλῆς εὑρομένων βοήθειαν.
Σίκκιος μὲν γὰρ ὁ τὸν Αἰκανῶν στρατὸν αὐτῷ
χάρακι ἀράμενος δήμαρχος τότ' ἀποδειχθείς, ὥσπερ
ἔφην, τῇ πρώτῃ τῆς ἀρχῆς ἡμέρᾳ θύσας εἰσιτήρια[3]

---

[1] τοὺς ὑπάτους om. A.
[2] τὸ τῶν δημάρχων Lapus (in his translation) : τὸ περὶ
τῶν δ. O, Jacoby, τὸ παρὰ τῶν δ. Niebuhr, τὸ περὶ τῶν ἀρχῶν
Sylburg.   [3] εἰσιτήρια Reiske : σωτήρια O.

the things we captured." The populace, upon hearing this, burst into compassion and tears, as they
observed the age of the men and recalled their deeds
of valour ; and they were filled with resentment and
indignation against those who had attempted to
deprive the commonwealth of such men. For his
report, as Siccius foresaw, had drawn upon the consuls
the hatred of all the citizens. Indeed, not even the
senate took the matter lightly ; for it voted them
neither a triumph nor any of the other honours usually
bestowed for glorious engagements. As for Siccius,
however, when the time for the elections came, the
populace made him tribune, granting him the honour
of which they had the disposal. These were the
most important of the events at that time.

XLVIII. These consuls [1] were succeeded the following year by Spurius Tarpeius and Aulus Ter-
minius, who constantly courted the populace in all
matters and in particular secured the preliminary
decree of the senate for the measure of the tribunes ;
for they saw that the patricians reaped no advantage
from their opposition, but, on the contrary, that the
most zealous champions of their cause drew upon
themselves envy and hatred, as well as private losses
and calamities. But they were chiefly alarmed by
the recent misfortune of the consuls of the preceding
year, who had been severely treated by the populace
and had been unable to get any help from the senate.
For Siccius, who had destroyed the army of the
Aequians, camp and all, and had now been made a
tribune, as I stated, on the very first day of his magis-

---

[1] For chaps. 48-52 cf. Livy iii. 31, 5-8. The name of the
second consul should probably be Aternius (the MSS. of
Livy give Aeternius).

κατὰ νόμον, πρὶν ὁτιοῦν ἄλλο διαπράξασθαι τῶν
κοινῶν, προεῖπεν ἐν ἐκκλησίᾳ Τίτον Ῥωμίλιον
ἥκειν ἀπολογησόμενον ἀδικήματος δημοσίου δίκην
ἐπὶ δικαστῇ τῷ δήμῳ, τὸν χρόνον ἀποδείξας τοῦ
3 ἀγῶνος. Λεύκιος δὲ τότ' ἀγορανομῶν, δήμαρχος
δὲ τῷ παρελθόντι ἔτει γεγονώς, τὸν ἕτερον τῶν
περυσινῶν ὑπάτων Γάιον Οὐετούριον εἰς ὁμοίαν
δίκην προσεκαλέσατο.¹ πολλῆς δὲ γενομένης ἐν τῷ
μεταξὺ τοῦ ἀγῶνος χρόνῳ σπουδῆς τε καὶ παρακλήσεως ἀμφοτέρων οἱ μὲν ὑπόδικοι πολλὰς ἐλπίδας
εἶχον ἐπὶ τῇ βουλῇ καὶ τὸ κινδύνευμα ἐν ἐλαφρῷ
ἐποιοῦντο, ὑπισχνουμένων αὐτοῖς πρεσβυτέρων τε
4 καὶ νέων οὐκ ἐάσειν τὸν ἀγῶνα ἐπιτελεσθῆναι. οἱ
δὲ δήμαρχοι πάντα ἐκ πολλοῦ φυλαττόμενοι καὶ
οὔτε δεήσεις οὔτε ἀπειλὰς οὔτε κίνδυνον οὐδένα
ὑπολογιζόμενοι, ἐπειδὴ καθῆκεν ὁ τοῦ ἀγῶνος
καιρός,² ἐκάλουν τὸν δῆμον· ἦν δὲ παλαίτερον ἔτι
συνερρυηκὼς ἐκ τῶν ἀγρῶν ὁ χερνήτης καὶ αὐτ-
ουργὸς ὄχλος, καὶ προσνεμηθεὶς τῷ κατὰ πόλιν
τήν τε ἀγορὰν ἐνέπλησε καὶ τοὺς φέροντας εἰς
αὐτὴν στενωπούς.

XLIX. Πρώτη μὲν οὖν εἰσῆλθεν ἡ κατὰ Ῥωμιλίου δίκη. καὶ παρελθὼν ὁ Σίκκιος τά τε ἄλλα
κατηγόρει τοῦ ἀνδρὸς ὅσα ὑπατεύων βίᾳ εἰς τοὺς
δημάρχους ἔδοξε διαπράξασθαι, καὶ τελευτῶν τὴν
ἐπιβουλὴν διεξῄει τὴν ἐφ' ἑαυτῷ τε καὶ τῇ σπείρᾳ
γενομένην ὑπὸ τοῦ στρατηγοῦ· καὶ παρείχετο αὐτῶν μάρτυρας τοὺς ἐπιφανεστάτους τῶν συστρατευ-
σαμένων, οὐ δημοτικοὺς μόνους,³ ἀλλὰ καὶ⁴ πατρι-

---

¹ Reiske : προεκαλέσατο O.   ² καιρὸς A : χρόνος B.
³ μόνους (or μόνον) added by Cary.
⁴ καὶ AB : om. R (?).

tracy, after offering the usual inaugural sacrifices and
before transacting any other public business, had in
a meeting of the assembly cited Titus Romilius to
appear before the tribunal of the populace to make
his defence against a charge of injuring the state ;
and he had set a day for his trial. And Lucius,[1] who
was then aedile and had been tribune the year before,
had summoned Gaius Veturius, the other consul of
the preceding year, to a similar trial. During the
interval before the trial much partisan zeal and encouragement were shown to both of the accused, and
they accordingly placed great hopes in the senate
and made light of the danger, as both the older and
younger senators promised them that they would not
allow the trial to be carried out. But the tribunes,
who had long been providing against all contingen-
cies and paid no heed to either entreaties, threats or
any danger, when the time for the trial came, called
a meeting of the popular assembly. Even before
this the crowd of day-labourers and husbandmen
had flocked in from the country and, being added
to the city throng, filled not only the Forum, but
all the streets that led to it.

XLIX. The first trial to be held was that of Romilius. Siccius, coming forward, charged him with all
the acts of violence he was reputed to have committed
against the tribunes while he was consul, and then at
the end related the plot which the general had formed
against him and his cohort. He produced as witnesses to support his charges the most prominent
men who had served with him in the campaign,
not plebeians alone,[2] but patricians as well. Among

---

[1] Probably the man called L. Alienus by Livy (iii. 31, 5).

[2] See crit. note ; the Icilii (§ 4) were plebeians.

κίους· ἐν οἷς ἦν νεανίας οὐκ ἀφανὴς οὔτε κατὰ γένους
ἀξίωσιν οὔτε κατὰ τὴν ἰδίαν ἀρετὴν καὶ τὰ πολέμια
πάνυ ἀγαθός· Σπόριος Οὐεργίνιος ἦν ὄνομα αὐτῷ.
2 οὗτος ἔφη Μάρκον Ἰκίλλιον, ἑνὸς τῶν ἐκ τῆς
Σικκίου σπείρας υἱόν, ἡλικιώτην αὐτοῦ καὶ φίλον
ἀπολυθῆναι τῆς ἐξόδου βουληθείς, ὡς ἐπὶ θάνατον
ἐξιόντα μετὰ τοῦ πατρός, Αὖλον Οὐεργίνιον τὸν
ἑαυτοῦ θεῖον, πρεσβευτὴν τότε συστρατευόμενον,
παρακαλέσας ἐλθεῖν ἐπὶ τοὺς ὑπάτους, ἀξιῶν σφίσι
3 ταύτην δοθῆναι τὴν χάριν· ἀντιλεγόντων δὲ τῶν
ὑπάτων, ἑαυτῷ μὲν ἐπελθεῖν δάκρυα τὴν συμφορὰν
τοῦ¹ ἑταίρου προανακλαιομένῳ, τὸν δὲ νεανίαν,
ὑπὲρ οὗ τὰς δεήσεις ἐποιεῖτο, πεπυσμένον ταῦτα
ἐλθεῖν καὶ λόγον αἰτησάμενον εἰπεῖν ὅτι τοῖς μὲν
δεομένοις πολλὴν οἶδε χάριν, αὐτὸς δ' οὐκ ἂν ἀγα-
πήσειεν² τυχὼν χάριτος ἥτις αὐτὸν ἀφελεῖται τὸ
πρὸς τὸ γένος εὐσεβές, οὐδ' ἂν ἀπολειφθείη τοῦ
πατρός, τοσῷδε μᾶλλον ὅσῳ γ' ἀποθανούμενος
ἔρχεται,³ καὶ πάντες τοῦτο ἴσασιν· ἀλλὰ συνεξιὼν
ἐπαμυνεῖ τε,⁴ ὅσα δύναται, καὶ τῆς αὐτῆς ἐκείνῳ⁵
4 κοινωνὸς ἔσται τύχης. ταῦτα τοῦ μειρακίου μαρτυρήσαντος οὐδεὶς ἦν ὃς οὐκ ἔπασχέ τι πρὸς τὴν
τύχην τῶν ἀνθρώπων. ὡς δὲ καὶ αὐτοὶ κληθέντες
ἐπὶ τὴν μαρτυρίαν παρῆλθον ὅ τε πατὴρ Ἰκίλλιος
καὶ τὸ μειράκιον καὶ τὸ καθ' ἑαυτοὺς⁶ ἔλεξαν,
οὐκέτι κατέχειν τὰ δάκρυα οἱ πλείους ἐδύναντο
5 τῶν δημοτικῶν. ἀπολογηθέντος δὲ τοῦ Ῥωμιλίου
καὶ διελθόντος λόγον οὔτε θεραπευτικὸν οὔτε ἀρ-

---

¹ τοῦ AB : τὴν R, τὴν τοῦ Kruger, Jacoby.
² Sylburg : ἀγαπήσειν AB.
³ Cobet : οἴχεται O.
⁴ ἐπαμυνεῖ τε Cobet : ἐπαμυνεῖται O.

330

them there was a youth distinguished both for the
rank of his family and for his own merit, and a most
valiant soldier. His name was Spurius Verginius.
This youth related that, desiring to get Marcus
Icilius, the son of one of the men in the cohort of
Siccius, a youth of his own age and his friend, released from that expedition, since he believed that
he with his father would be going out to his death,
he had summoned Aulus Verginius, his uncle, who
was a legate on that campaign, and with him had
gone to the consuls asking that this favour be granted
to them. And when the consuls refused, he said that
he himself had wept and lamented in advance the
misfortune of his friend, but that the young man for
whom he had interceded, being informed of this, went
to the consuls, and asking leave to speak, said that,
while he was very grateful to those who were inter-
ceding for him, he would not be content to accept a
favour that would deprive him of the opportunity of
showing his filial devotion, and that he would not
desert his father, particularly when the other was
going to his death, as everyone knew, but that he
would go out with him, defend him to the utmost of
his power and share the same fortune with him.
After the young man had given this testimony, there
was not a single person who did not feel some emotion
at the fate of those men. And when the Icilii themselves, father and son, were called as witnesses and
gave an account of their experience, most of the
plebeians could no longer refrain from tears. Then,
when Romilius made his defence and delivered a
speech that was neither deferential nor suited to

---

⁵ αὐτῆς ἐκείνῳ Reiske : αὐτῶν ἐκείνων O.
⁶ αὐτούς B.

μόττοντα τοῖς καιροῖς, ἀλλ' ὑψηλὸν καὶ ἐπὶ τῷ
ἀνυπευθύνῳ τῆς ἀρχῆς μέγα φρονοῦντα, διπλασίως
ἐπερρώσθησαν[1] εἰς τὴν κατ' αὐτοῦ ὀργὴν οἱ πολλοί.[2] καὶ γενόμενοι τῶν ψήφων κύριοι κατέγνωσαν
ἀδικεῖν οὕτω σαφῶς[3] ὥστε πάσαις ταῖς ψήφοις
τῶν φυλῶν ἁλῶναι τὸν ἄνδρα. ἦν δὲ τὸ τίμημα τῆς
6 δίκης ἀργυρικόν, ἀσσάρια μυρία. καὶ τοῦτο οὐκ
ἄνευ προνοίας τινὸς ὁ Σίκκιος ποιῆσαί μοι δοκεῖ,
ἀλλ' ἵνα τοῖς τε πατρικίοις ἐλάττων ἡ περὶ τοῦ
ἀνδρὸς σπουδὴ γένηται, καὶ μηδὲν ἐξαμάρτωσι περὶ
τὴν ψηφοφορίαν, ἐνθυμηθέντες ὅτι εἰς ἀργύριον
ζημιώσεται ὁ ἁλοὺς καὶ εἰς οὐδὲν ἕτερον, καὶ τοῖς
δημοτικοῖς ἡ πρὸς τὴν τιμωρίαν ὁρμὴ προθυμοτέρα
μήτε ψυχῆς ἄνδρα ὑπατικὸν μήτε πατρίδος ἀπο-
στεροῦσιν. Ῥωμιλίου δὲ καταδικασθέντος οὐ πολ-
λαῖς ὕστερον ἡμέραις καὶ Οὐετούριος ἑάλω· τίμημα
δὲ καὶ ἐκείνῳ ἐπεγέγραπτο ἀργυρικόν, ἡμιόλιον
θατέρου.

L. Ταῦτα δὴ λογιζομένοις τοῖς ἐν ἀρχῇ ὑπάτοις
πολὺ παρέστη δέος καὶ τοῦ μὴ ταὐτὰ παθεῖν ὑπὸ
τοῦ δήμου μετὰ τὴν ὑπατείαν πρόνοια, ὥστ' οὐκέτι
ἀποκρυπτόμενοι τὰς γνώμας, ἀλλὰ φανερῶς τὰ τοῦ
δήμου πολιτευόμενοι διετέλουν. πρῶτον μὲν οὖν
ἐπὶ τῆς λοχίτιδος ἐκκλησίας νόμον ἐκύρωσαν ἵνα
ταῖς ἀρχαῖς ἐξῇ πάσαις τοὺς ἀκοσμοῦντας ἢ παρα-
νομοῦντας εἰς τὴν ἑαυτῶν ἐξουσίαν ζημιοῦν. τέως
γὰρ οὐχ ἅπασιν ἐξῆν, ἀλλὰ τοῖς ὑπάτοις μόνοις.[4]

[1] ἔτι before ἐπερρώσθησαν deleted by Cobet.
[2] πολλοί Kiessling : πολῖται O, Jacoby.
[3] οὕτω σαφῶς Capps : οὕτως O, Jacoby.
[4] μόνοις om. AB.

332

the occasion, but haughty and boastful of the irresponsible power of his magistracy, the majority[1]
were doubly confirmed in their resentment against
him. And upon being permitted to give their votes,
they found him so clearly guilty that he was condemned by the votes of all the tribes. The punishment in his case was a fine, amounting to 10,000 *asses*.
Siccius, now, did not do this,[2] it seems to me, without
some purpose, but to the end that the patricians, on
the one hand, might be less zealous in Romilius'
behalf and might commit no irregularities in connexion with the voting when they reflected that the
condemned man would be punished with nothing
more than a fine, and that the plebeians, on their side,
might be the more eager for punishment when they
were not going to deprive an ex-consul of either his
life or his country. A few days after the condemnation of Romilius, Veturius was likewise condemned ;
his punishment was also set down in the indictment
as a fine, one-half as much again as the other.

L. As they thought about these trials the consuls
then in office were in no little fear, and they took good
care to avoid suffering the same fate at the hands of
the populace after the expiration of their consulship ;
hence they no longer concealed their purposes but
openly directed all their measures in the interest of
the populace. First, then, they got a law ratified by
the centuriate assembly permitting all the magistrates to fine any persons who were guilty of disrespectful conduct or illegal attempts against their
authority. For until then none but the consuls pos-

---

[1] This is Kiessling's emendation: the MSS. read " citizens."

[2] *i.e.* set down the penalty he did in the indictment.

2 τὸ μέντοι τίμημα οὐκ ἐπὶ τοῖς[1] ζημιοῦσιν, ὁπόσον
εἶναι δεῖ, κατέλιπον, ἀλλ' αὐτοὶ τὴν ἀξίαν ὥρισαν,
μέγιστον ἀποδείξαντες ὅρον ζημίας δύο βοῦς[2] καὶ
τριάκοντα πρόβατα. καὶ οὗτος ὁ νόμος ἄχρι πολ-
3 λοῦ διέμεινεν ὑπὸ Ῥωμαίων φυλαττόμενος. ἔπειτα
περὶ τῶν νόμων οὓς ἐσπούδαζον οἱ δήμαρχοι κοινοὺς ἐπὶ πᾶσι Ῥωμαίοις γράφειν[3] καὶ εἰς ἅπαντα
χρόνον φυλαχθησομένους διάγνωσιν ἀπέδωκαν τῇ
βουλῇ. ἐλέχθησαν μὲν οὖν πολλοί τε καὶ ὑπὸ τῶν
κρατίστων ἀνδρῶν εἰς ἀμφότερα καὶ τὸ συγχωρεῖν
καὶ τὸ κωλύειν φέροντες λόγοι, ἐνίκα δ' ἡ τὰ δημο-
τικώτερα πρὸ τῶν ὀλιγαρχικῶν εἰσάγουσα Τίτου
Ῥωμιλίου γνώμη, παρὰ τὴν ἁπάντων δόξαν τῶν
4 τε πατρικίων καὶ τῶν δημοτικῶν γενομένη. οἱ μὲν
γὰρ ὑπελάμβανον πάντα τὰ ἐναντία τοῖς δημοτικοῖς
φρονήσειν τε καὶ λέξειν τὸν ἄνδρα νεωστὶ τὴν ἐν
τῷ δήμῳ δίκην ἑαλωκότα· ὁ δ' ἀναστὰς ἐπειδὴ
προσῆκεν αὐτῷ[4] γνώμην ἐρωτηθέντι κατὰ τὴν ἑαυτοῦ τάξιν ἀποκρίνασθαι (ἦν δὲ ἐν τοῖς διὰ μέσου
κατά τε ἀξίωσιν καὶ ἡλικίαν) ἔλεξεν·

LI. '' Ἃ μὲν ὑπὸ τοῦ δήμου πέπονθα, ὦ βουλή,
καὶ ὅτι οὐδὲν ἀδικῶν, ἀλλὰ τῆς πρὸς ὑμᾶς εὐνοίας
ἕνεκα,[5] φορτικὸς ἂν εἴην[6] ἐν εἰδόσιν[7] ἀκριβῶς λέ-
γων· μνήμην δὲ αὐτῶν ποιοῦμαι τοῦ ἀναγκαίου
ἕνεκεν,[8] ἵν' εἰδῆτε ὅτι οὐ κολακείᾳ τοῦ δημοτικοῦ
ἐπιτρέψας ἐχθροῦ μοι ὄντος, ἀλλ' ἀπὸ τοῦ βελτίσ-

---

[1] ἐπὶ τοῖς Kiessling, ἐπ' αὐτοῖς τοῖς Reiske : ἐπ' αὐτοῖς AB.
[2] Jacoby : βόας O.
[3] γράφειν AB : γραφῆναι R.
[4] Sylburg : ἑαυτῷ O.   [5] ἕνεκα B : χάριν A.
[6] εἴην B : εἴην ἔγωγε R(?).
[7] εἰδόσιν Hudson : εἰδόσιν ὑμῖν O.
[8] ἕνεκεν Bb : ἕνεκα R.

sessed this power. They did not leave the amount of the fine, however, to the discretion of those who should impose it, but limited the sum themselves, making the maximum fine two oxen and thirty sheep. This law long continued in force among the Romans. In the next place, they referred to the consideration of the senate the laws which the tribunes pressed to have drawn up, that should bind all the Romans alike and be observed forever. Many speeches were made on both sides by the best men, some tending to persuade the senate to grant the request and some to oppose it. But the opinion that prevailed was that of Titus Romilius, which supported the interest of the populace against that of the oligarchy, contrary to the expectation of everybody, both patricians and plebeians. For they supposed that a man who had recently been condemned by the populace would both think and say everything that was opposed to the plebeians. But he, when it was the proper time for him to speak, that is, when he was called upon to deliver his opinion in his turn—he was of the middle rank in point of both dignity and age—rose up and said :

LI. " I should be wearisome to you, senators, if I related what I have suffered at the hands of the populace and showed that it is not because of any wrongdoing on my part but because of my attachment to you, when you yourselves know the facts so well. I am forced, however, to mention these matters in order that you may know that in what I am going to say I am not condescending to flattery of the populace, which is hostile to me, but stating from the best of motives what is to the advantage of the common-

τοῦ τὰ συμφέροντα ἐρῶ. θαυμάσῃ δὲ μηθεὶς εἰ
πρότερόν τε πολλάκις καὶ ἡνίκα ὕπατος ἦν τῆς
ἑτέρας[1] προαιρέσεως γενόμενος νῦν ἐξαίφνης μετα-
βέβλημαι· μηδὲ ὑπολάβητε δυεῖν θάτερον ἢ τότε
βεβουλεῦσθαί με κακῶς ἢ νῦν ἀνατίθεσθαι τὰ δό-
2 ξαντα οὐκ ὀρθῶς. ἐγὼ γάρ, ὦ βουλή, ὅσον μὲν
χρόνον τὰ ὑμέτερα ἰσχυρὰ ἡγούμην, ὥσπερ ἐχρῆν
ἀριστοκρατίαν αὔξων περιεφρόνουν τὸ δημοτικόν,
ἐπεὶ δὲ τοῖς ἐμαυτοῦ σωφρονισθεὶς κακοῖς μετὰ
μεγάλων μισθῶν ἔμαθον ὅτι ἔλαττον ὑμῶν ἐστι τοῦ
βουλομένου τὸ δυνάμενον, καὶ πολλοὺς ἤδη τὸν
ὑπὲρ ὑμῶν ἀγῶνα αἰρομένους[2] περιείδετε ἀναρπασ-
θέντας ὑπὸ τοῦ δήμου τοῖς ἀναγκαίοις εἴξαντες,
3 οὐκέθ' ὅμοια ἔγνωκα. ἐβουλόμην δ' ἂν μάλιστα
μὲν[3] μήτ' ἐμαυτῷ συμβῆναι μήτε τῷ συνάρχοντί
μου ταῦτα ἐφ' οἷς ἅπαντες ἡμῖν[4] συμπαθεῖτε.
ἐπειδὴ δὲ τὰ μὲν καθ' ἡμᾶς τέλος ἔχει, τὰ δὲ λοιπὰ
ἔξεστιν ἐπανορθώσασθαι καὶ τοῦ μὴ παθεῖν ταῦτά[5]
ἑτέρους προϊδέσθαι, καὶ κοινῇ καὶ καθ' ἕνα ἕκαστον
ἰδίᾳ τὰ παρόντα εὖ τίθεσθαι παρακαλῶ. κράτιστα
γὰρ οἰκεῖται πόλις ἡ πρὸς τὰ πράγματα μεθαρμοτ-
τομένη, καὶ συμβούλων ἄριστος ὁ μὴ πρὸς τὴν ἰδίαν
ἔχθραν ἢ χάριν, ἀλλὰ πρὸς τὸ κοινῇ συμφέρον ἀπο-
δεικνύμενος γνώμην· βουλεύονταί τ' ἄριστα περὶ
τῶν μελλόντων οἱ παραδείγματα ποιούμενοι τὰ
4 γεγονότα τῶν ἐσομένων. ὑμῖν δ', ὦ βουλή, ὁσάκις
ἐνέστη τις ἀμφισβήτησις καὶ φιλονεικία πρὸς τὸν
δῆμον, ἀεί τι μειονεκτεῖν ἐξεγένετο, τὸ μὲν ἀκούειν[6]

---

[1] ἀπὸ τοῦ βελτίστου . . . τῆς ἑτέρας om. A.
[2] αἰρομένους Jacoby, ἀραμένους Sylburg : αἰρουμένους O.
[3] μὲν added by Cobet.
[4] ἡμῖν B : ὑμεῖς A.   [5] ταὐτὰ R : ταῦτα AB.

wealth.   Let no one wonder, if I, who was of a different opinion both earlier upon many occasions and
when I was consul, have now suddenly changed ; and
do not imagine either that my sentiments were then
ill grounded or that I am now altering them without
good reason.   For as long as I thought your party
strong, senators, I exalted the aristocracy, as was my
duty, and despised the plebeians ; but having been
chastened by my own misfortunes and having learned
at great cost that your power is less than your will
and that, yielding to necessity, you have already permitted many who undertook the struggle in your
behalf to be snatched away to destruction by the
populace, I no longer entertain the same sentiments.
I could have wished that, if possible, those misfortunes
for which you all show your sympathy with us had not
happened either to myself or to my colleague ; but
since our misadventure is over and you have it in your
power to correct what lies in the future and to see to
it that others do not suffer the same misfortunes, I
urge you, both all in common and each one by himself, to make good use of the present situation.   For
that state is best governed which adapts itself to
circumstances, and that man is the best counsellor
who expresses his opinion without regard to personal
enmity or favour but with a view to the public advantage ; and those persons deliberate best concerning the future who take past events as examples of
those that are to come.   As for you, senators, it has
happened that whenever a dispute or contention has
arisen with the populace you have always come off
at a disadvantage, sometimes having evil spoken of

---

[6] τὸ μὲν ἀκούειν (the three words later erased) B : τὰ μὲν
ἀκούειν A.

κακῶς,[1] τὸ δ'[2] εἰς ἀνδρῶν ἐπιφανῶν θανάτους τε
καὶ ὕβρεις καὶ ἐκβολὰς ζημιωθῆναι. καίτοι τί
γένοιτ' ἂν ἀτύχημα πόλει μεῖζον ἢ τοὺς κρατίστους τῶν ἀνδρῶν περικόπτεσθαι καὶ ταῦτα οὐ σὺν
δίκῃ; ὧν[3] ὑμῖν φείδεσθαι παραινῶ καὶ μήτε τοὺς
νῦν ἄρχοντας προβαλόντας[4] εἰς κίνδυνον πρόδηλον
ἔπειτα ἐγκαταλιπόντας[5] ἐν τοῖς δεινοῖς μετανοεῖν
μήτε τῶν ἄλλων τινὰ οὗ τι καὶ μικρὸν ὄφελος τῷ
5 κοινῷ. κεφάλαιον δ' ἐστὶν ὧν ὑμῖν παραινῶ,
πρέσβεις ἑλέσθαι τοὺς μὲν εἰς τὰς Ἑλληνίδας
πόλεις τὰς ἐν Ἰταλίᾳ, τοὺς δ' εἰς Ἀθήνας, οἵτινες
αἰτησάμενοι παρὰ τῶν Ἑλλήνων τοὺς κρατίστους
νόμους καὶ μάλιστα τοῖς ἡμετέροις ἁρμόττοντας
βίοις οἴσουσι δεῦρο. ἀφικομένων δ' αὐτῶν τοὺς
τότε ὑπάτους προθεῖναι τῇ βουλῇ σκοπεῖν τίνας
ἑλέσθαι δεήσει νομοθέτας καὶ ἥντινα ἕξοντας ἀρχὴν
καὶ χρόνον ὅσον καὶ τἆλλα, ὅπως ἂν αὐτῇ φαίνηται
συνοίσειν, στασιάζειν δὲ μηκέτι πρὸς τὸ δημοτικὸν
μηδ' ἄλλας ἐπ' ἄλλαις ἀναιρεῖσθαι συμφοράς, ἄλλως
τε καὶ περὶ νόμων φιλονεικοῦντας οἳ κἂν εἰ μηθὲν
ἄλλο τήν γέ τοι δόξαν τῆς ἀξιώσεως ἔχουσιν εὐπρεπῆ.''

LII. Τοιαῦτα εἰπόντος τοῦ Ῥωμιλίου οἵ τε ὕπατοι συνελαμβάνοντο τῆς γνώμης ἀμφότεροι πολλὰ
καὶ ἐκ παρασκευῆς συγκείμενα διεξιόντες, καὶ τῶν
ἄλλων βουλευτῶν συχνοί, καὶ ἐγένοντο πλείους οἱ
2 ταύτῃ προστιθέμενοι τῇ γνώμῃ. μέλλοντος δὲ
γράφεσθαι τοῦ προβουλεύματος ἀναστὰς ὁ δήμαρχος Σίκκιος ὁ τῷ Ῥωμιλίῳ προθεὶς[6] τὴν δίκην

---

[1] κακῶς added by Jacoby.
[2] τὸ δ' Jacoby : τὰ δὲ A, καὶ B.
[3] σὺν δίκῃ ; ὧν Reiske : συνδικῶν O.

338

you and sometimes being punished by the death, the abuse and the banishment of illustrious men. And yet what greater misfortune could happen to a state than to have its best men lopped off, and that undeservedly ? I advise you to spare these men and not to have to repent of first exposing to manifest danger and then deserting in the moment of peril either the present magistrates or anyone else who is of the slightest value to the commonwealth. The substance of my advice is that you choose ambassadors and send some of them to the Greek cities in Italy and others to Athens, to ask the Greeks for their best laws and such as are most suited to our ways of life, and then to bring these laws here. And when they return, that the consuls then in office shall propose for the consideration of the senate what men to choose as lawgivers, what magistracy they shall hold and for how long a time, and to determine everything else in such a manner as they shall think expedient ; and that you contend no longer with the plebeians nor add calamities to your calamities, particularly by quarrelling over laws which, if nothing else, have at least a respectable reputation for dignity."

LII. After Romilius had spoken to this effect, both consuls supported his opinion in long and carefully prepared speeches, and so did many other senators ; and those who espoused this opinion were in the majority. When the preliminary decree was about to be drawn up, the tribune Siccius, who had brought Romilius to trial, rising up, made a long

---

⁴ προβαλόντας Bb : προβάλλοντας ABa.
⁵ ἐγκαταλιπόντας Bb : ἐγκαταλείποντας ABa.
⁶ προθεὶς R : προσθεὶς AB, Jacoby.

πολὺν ὑπὲρ τοῦ ἀνδρὸς διῆλθε λόγον ἐπαινῶν τὴν
μεταβολὴν τῆς γνώμης καὶ τὸ μὴ τὰ ἴδια ἔχθη
κρείττονα ἡγεῖσθαι[1] τῶν κοινῇ χρησίμων, ἀλλ᾽
ἀπ᾽ ὀρθῆς γνώμης τὰ συμφέροντα ἀποδείξασθαι[2]·
3 "᾽Ανθ᾽ ὧν," ἔφη, "ταύτην αὐτῷ ἀποδίδωμι τιμὴν
καὶ χάριν· ἀφίημι τῶν ἐκτισμάτων ἐπὶ τῇ δίκῃ καὶ
εἰς τὸ λοιπὸν διαλλάττομαι· νικᾷ γὰρ ἡμᾶς χρηστὸς
ὤν." τὸ δ᾽ αὐτὸ καὶ οἱ ἄλλοι δήμαρχοι παριόντες
ὡμολόγουν. οὐ μὴν ὅ γε 'Ρωμίλιος ὑπέμεινε ταύτην λαβεῖν τὴν χάριν, ἀλλ᾽ ἐπαινέσας τοὺς δημάρχους τῆς προθυμίας ἀποδώσειν ἔφη τὴν καταδίκην.
ἱερὰν γὰρ ἤδη τῶν θεῶν εἶναι, καὶ οὔτε δίκαια οὔτε
ὅσια ποιεῖν ἂν[3] ἀποστερῶν τοὺς θεοὺς ἃ δίδωσιν
4 αὐτοῖς ὁ νόμος· καὶ ἐποίησεν οὕτως. γραφέντος δὲ
τοῦ προβουλεύματος καὶ μετὰ ταῦτ᾽ ἐπικυρώσαντος τοῦ δήμου πρέσβεις ἀπεδείχθησαν οἱ τοὺς παρὰ
τῶν 'Ελλήνων νόμους ληψόμενοι, Σπόριος Ποστόμιος καὶ Σερούιος[4] Σολπίκιος καὶ Αὖλος Μάλλιος·
οἷς τριήρεις τε παρεσκευάσθησαν ἐκ τοῦ δημοσίου καὶ ἄλλος κόσμος εἰς ἐπίδειξιν τῆς ἡγεμονίας
ἀποχρῶν. καὶ τὸ ἔτος ἐτελεύτα.

LIII. 'Επὶ δὲ τῆς ὀγδοηκοστῆς καὶ δευτέρας
ὀλυμπιάδος, ἣν ἐνίκα στάδιον Λύκος Θεσσαλὸς ἀπὸ
Λαρίσης,[5] ἄρχοντος 'Αθήνησι Χαιρεφάνους, ἐτῶν
τριακοσίων ἐκπεπληρωμένων ἀπὸ τοῦ 'Ρώμης συν-
οικισμοῦ, Ποπλίου 'Ορατίου καὶ Σέξτου Κοϊντι-
λίου διαδεδεγμένων[6] τὴν ὕπατον ἀρχήν, λοιμικὴ

---

[1] Sylburg : γίνεσθαι O, Jacoby.
[2] ἀποδείξασθαι A : ὑποδείξασθαι B, ἐπιδείξασθαι R.
[3] ποιεῖν ἂν Hertlein, ἂν ποιεῖν Cobet : ποιεῖν O, Jacoby.
[4] Sylburg : σερούιλιος AB.
[5] λαρίσης Ba : λαρίσσης ABb.
[6] διαδεδεγμένων R : δεδεγμένων Bb.

speech in his behalf, praising him for changing his
opinion and for not preferring his private grudges to
the public good, but delivering with sincerity the
advice that was advantageous. " In consideration of
which," he said, " I offer him this honour and this
favour : I remit the fine imposed on him at the trial
and reconcile myself with him for the future. For he
has overcome us by his probity." The rest of the tribunes came forward and made the same agreement.
Romilius, however, would not consent to accept this
favour, but having thanked the tribunes for their
goodwill, he said he would pay the fine, because it
was already consecrated to the gods and he should be
doing something unjust and unholy if he deprived the
gods of what the law gives them. And he acted
accordingly. The preliminary decree having been
drawn up and afterwards confirmed by the populace,
the ambassadors who were to get the laws from the
Greeks were chosen, namely, Spurius Postumius,
Servius Sulpicius and Aulus Manlius ; and they were
furnished with triremes at the public expense and
with such other appointments as were sufficient to
display the dignity of the Roman empire. And thus
the year ended.

LIII. In the eighty-second Olympiad [1] (the one at
which Lycus of Larissa in Thessaly won the foot-race),
Chaerephanes being archon at Athens, when three
hundred years were completed since the founding of
Rome, and Publius Horatius and Sextus Quintilius
had succeeded to the consulship, Rome was afflicted

---

[1] *Cf.* Livy iii. 32, 1-4. The year was 451. Livy gives the name
of the first consul as P. Curiatius (Curatius in most MSS.).

νόσος εἰς τὴν Ῥώμην κατέσκηψε μεγίστη τῶν ἐκ
τοῦ προτέρου[1] χρόνου μνημονευομένων· ὑφ᾽ ἧς οἱ
μὲν θεράποντες ὀλίγου ἐδέησαν πάντες[2] ἀπολέσθαι,
τῶν δ᾽ ἄλλων πολιτῶν ἀμφὶ τοὺς ἡμίσεις μάλιστα
διεφθάρησαν, οὔτε τῶν ἰατρῶν ἀρκούντων ἔτι[3] βοηθεῖν τοῖς καμάτοις οὔτε οἰκείων ἢ φίλων τἀναγκαῖα
2 ὑπηρετούντων. οἱ γὰρ ἐπικουρεῖν ταῖς ἑτέρων βουλόμενοι συμφοραῖς ἁπτόμενοί τε καματηρῶν σωμάτων καὶ συνδιαιτώμενοι τὰς αὐτὰς ἐκείνοις νόσους
μετελάμβανον, ὥστε πολλὰς οἰκίας ἐξερημωθῆναι
δι᾽ ἀπορίαν τῶν ἐπιμελησομένων. ἦν τε οὐκ ἐλάχιστον τῶν κακῶν τῇ πόλει καὶ τοῦ μὴ ταχέως
λωφῆσαι τὴν νόσον αἴτιον τὸ περὶ τὰς ἐκβολὰς τῶν
3 νεκρῶν γινόμενον. κατ᾽ ἀρχὰς μὲν γὰρ ὑπό τε αἰ-
σχύνης καὶ εὐπορίας[4] τῶν πρὸς τὰς ταφὰς ἐπιτηδείων ἔκαιόν τε καὶ γῇ παρεδίδοσαν τοὺς νεκρούς,
τελευτῶντες δὲ οἱ μὲν ἀπ᾽ ὀλιγωρίας τοῦ καλοῦ,
οἱ δὲ τἀπιτήδεια οὐκ ἔχοντες πολλοὺς μὲν ἐν
τοῖς ὑπονόμοις[5] τῶν στενωπῶν φέροντες ἐρρίπτουν
τῶν ἀπογενομένων,[6] πολλῷ δ᾽ ἔτι πλείους εἰς τὸν
ποταμὸν ἐνέβαλλον· ἀφ᾽ ὧν τὰ μέγιστα ἐκακοῦντο.
4 ἐκκυμαινομένων γὰρ[7] πρὸς τὰς ἀκτὰς καὶ τὰς
ἠϊόνας τῶν σωμάτων βαρεῖα καὶ δυσώδης προσ-
πίπτουσα καὶ τοῖς ἔτι ἐρρωμένοις ἡ τοῦ πνεύματος
ἀποφορὰ ταχείας ἔφερε τοῖς σώμασι τὰς τροπάς,
πίνεσθαί τε οὐκέτι χρηστὸν ἦν τὸ ἐκ τοῦ ποταμοῦ κομισθὲν ὕδωρ, τὰ μὲν ἀτοπίᾳ τῆς ὀσμῆς, τὰ
δὲ τῷ πονηρὰς τὰς ἀναδόσεις ποιεῖν τῆς τροφῆς.

---

[1] προτέρου R : πρότερον B.   [2] Jacoby : ἅπαντες O.
[3] ἔτι B : εἰς τὸ R.   [4] Sylburg : ἀπορίας O.
[5] εἰς τοὺς ὑπονόμους Portus, who also placed τῶν ἀπογινομένων after πολλοὺς μέν.

with a pestilence more severe than any of those recorded from past time. Almost all the slaves were carried off by it and about one half of the citizens, as neither the physicians were able any longer to alleviate their sufferings nor did their servants and friends supply them with the necessaries. For those who were willing to relieve the calamities of others, by touching the bodies of the diseased and continuing with them, contracted the same diseases, with the result that many entire households perished for want of people to attend the sick. Not the least of the evils the city suffered, and the reason why the pestilence did not quickly abate, was the way in which they cast out the dead bodies. For though at first, both from a sense of shame and because of the plenty they had of everything necessary for burials, they burned the bodies and committed them to the earth, at the last, either through a disregard of decency or from a lack of the necessary equipment, they threw many of the dead into the sewers under the streets and cast far more of them into the river ; and from these they received the most harm. For when the bodies were cast up by the waves upon the banks and beaches, a grievous and terrible stench, carried by the wind, smote those also who were still in health and produced a quick change in their bodies; and the water brought from the river was no longer fit to drink, partly because of its vile odour and partly by causing

---

[6] Kiessling : ἀπογινομένων O.

[7] ἐκκυμαινομένων γὰρ placed here by Cobet : after ἠϊόνας in the MSS. Jacoby retained the traditional order of words, punctuating after ἠϊόνας. Post, likewise keeping the order unchanged, would punctuate after ἐκκυμαινομένων, and read ἀπὸ γὰρ τῶν σωμάτων.

5 καὶ οὐ μόνον ἐν τῇ πόλει τὰ δεινὰ ἦν, ἀλλὰ καὶ ἐπὶ
τῶν ἀγρῶν· καὶ οὐχ ἥκιστα ὁ γεωργὸς ἐπόνησεν
ὄχλος ἀναπιμπλάμενος, καὶ προβάτων καὶ τῶν
ἄλλων τετραπόδων ἅμα διαιτωμένων, τῆς νόσου.
ὅσον μὲν οὖν χρόνον τοῖς πολλοῖς ἐλπίδος τι ὑπῆν
ὡς τοῦ θεοῦ σφίσιν ἐπικουρήσοντος, ἅπαντες ἐπί
τε θυσίας καὶ καθαρμοὺς ἐτράποντο· καὶ πολλὰ
ἐνεωτερίσθη Ῥωμαίοις οὐκ ὄντα ἐν ἔθει περὶ τὰς
6 τιμὰς τῶν θεῶν ἐπιτηδεύματα οὐκ εὐπρεπῆ. ἐπεὶ
δὲ ἐπέγνωσαν οὐδεμίαν αὐτῶν ἐπιστροφὴν ἐκ τοῦ
δαιμονίου γινομένην οὐδ' ἔλεον, καὶ τῆς περὶ τὰ
θεῖα λειτουργίας ἀπέστησαν. ἐν ταύτῃ τῇ συμφορᾷ
τῶν τε ὑπάτων ἅτερος ἀποθνήσκει, Σέξτος Κοϊν-
τίλιος,[1] καὶ ὁ μετὰ τοῦτον ἀποδειχθεὶς ὕπατος
Σπόριος Φούριος, καὶ τῶν δημάρχων τέτταρες, τῶν
7 τε βουλευτῶν πολλοὶ καὶ ἀγαθοί. ἐπεβάλοντο μὲν
οὖν ἐν τῇ νόσῳ τῆς πόλεως οὔσης στρατὸν ἐξάγειν
ἐπ' αὐτοὺς Αἰκανοὶ καὶ διεπρεσβεύοντο πρὸς τἆλλα
ἔθνη ὅσα Ῥωμαίοις πολέμια ἦν παρακαλοῦντες ἐπὶ
τὸν πόλεμον. οὐ μὴν ἔφθασάν γε προαγαγεῖν τὴν
δύναμιν ἐκ τῶν πόλεων. ἔτι γὰρ αὐτῶν παρασκευα-
ζομένων ἡ αὐτὴ νόσος κατέσκηψεν εἰς τὰς πόλεις.
8 διῆλθε δ' οὐ μόνον τὴν Αἰκανῶν, ἀλλὰ καὶ τὴν
Οὐολούσκων καὶ τὴν Σαβίνων γῆν, καὶ σφόδρα
ἐκάκωσε τοὺς ἀνθρώπους. ἐκ δὲ τούτου συνέβη
καὶ τὴν χώραν ἀγεώργητον ἀφεθεῖσαν λιμὸν ἐπὶ τῷ
λοιμῷ συνάψαι. ἐπὶ μὲν δὴ τούτων τῶν ὑπάτων
οὐδὲν ἐπράχθη Ῥωμαίοις διὰ τὰς νόσους οὔτε
πολεμικὸν οὔτε πολιτικὸν εἰς ἱστορίας ἀφήγησιν
ἐλθεῖν ἄξιον.

LIV. Εἰς δὲ τοὐπιὸν ἔτος ὕπατοι μὲν ἀπεδείχ-

---

[1] Sylburg : κόιντος A, κοίντιος B.

indigestion. These calamities occurred not only in
the city, but in the country as well; in particular,
the husbandmen were infected with the contagion,
since they were constantly with their sheep and the
other animals. As long as most people had any
hopes that Heaven would assist them, they all had
recourse to sacrifices and expiations; and many
innovations were then made by the Romans and unseemly practices not customary with them were
introduced into the worship of the gods. But when
they found that the gods showed no regard or compassion for them, they abandoned even the observ-
ance of religious rites. During this calamity Sextus
Quintilius, one of the consuls, died; also Spurius
Furius, who had been appointed to succeed him, and
likewise four of the tribunes and many worthy senators. While the city was afflicted by the pestilence,
the Aequians undertook to lead out an army against
the Romans; and they sent envoys to all the other
nations that were hostile to the Romans, urging them
to make war. But they did not have time to lead
their forces out of their cities; for while they were
still making their preparations, the same pestilence
fell upon their cities. It spread not only over the
country of the Aequians, but also over those of the
Volscians and the Sabines, and grievously afflicted
the inhabitants. In consequence, the land was left
uncultivated and famine was added to the plague.
Under these consuls, then, by reason of the pestilence nothing was done by the Romans, either in war
or at home, worthy of being recorded in history.

LIV. For the following year [1] Lucius Menenius

---

[1] For chaps. 54-56 cf. Livy iii. 32, 5-33, 6.

DIONYSIUS OF HALICARNASSUS

θησαν Λεύκιος Μενήνιος καὶ Πόπλιος Σήστιος[1]· ἡ
δὲ νόσος εἰς τέλος ἐλώφησε. καὶ μετὰ τοῦτο
θυσίαι τε χαριστήριοι θεοῖς ἐπετελοῦντο δημοσίᾳ
καὶ ἀγῶνες ἐπιφανεῖς λαμπραῖς πάνυ χορηγούμενοι
δαπάναις, ἐν εὐπαθείαις τε καὶ θαλίαις ἡ πόλις ἦν
ὥσπερ εἰκός· καὶ πᾶς ὁ χειμέριος χρόνος ἀμφὶ
2 ταῦτα ἐδαπανήθη. ἀρχομένου δ' ἔαρος σῖτός τε
πολὺς καὶ[2] ἐκ πολλῶν ἤχθη[3] χωρίων, ὁ μὲν πλείων
δημοσίᾳ συνωνηθείς, ὁ δέ τις καὶ ὑπ' ἰδιωτῶν
ἐμπόρων κομιζόμενος. ἔκαμνε γὰρ οὐχ ἥκιστα ἐν[4]
τῇ σπάνει τῆς τροφῆς ὁ λαὸς χέρσου τῆς γῆς
ἀφειμένης διὰ τὰς νόσους καὶ τὸν ὄλεθρον τῶν
γεωργῶν.

3   Ἐν δὲ τῷ αὐτῷ καιρῷ παρεγένοντο ἀπό τ' Ἀθη-
νῶν καὶ τῶν ἐν Ἰταλοῖς Ἑλληνίδων πόλεων οἱ
πρέσβεις φέροντες τοὺς νόμους. καὶ μετὰ τοῦτο
προσῆσαν οἱ δήμαρχοι τοῖς ὑπάτοις ἀξιοῦντες
ἀποδεῖξαι κατὰ τὸ ψήφισμα τῆς βουλῆς τοὺς νομοθέτας. οἱ δ' οὐκ ἔχοντες ὅτῳ ἂν αὐτοὺς ἀπ-
αλλάξειαν τρόπῳ προσκαθημένους καὶ λιπαροῦντας,
ἀχθόμενοι τῷ πράγματι καὶ οὐκ ἀξιοῦντες ἐπὶ τῆς
αὐτῶν ἀρχῆς[5] καταλῦσαι τὴν ἀριστοκρατίαν, πρόφασιν εὐπρεπῆ προὐβάλοντο, λέγοντες ἐν χερσὶν
εἶναι τὸν τῶν ἀρχαιρεσίων καιρόν, καὶ δέον[6] αὐτοὺς
4 τοὺς[7] ὑπάτους πρῶτον ἀποδεῖξαι, ποιήσειν[8] τοῦτ'
οὐκ εἰς μακράν, ἀποδειχθέντων δὲ τῶν ὑπάτων,
μετ' ἐκείνων ἀνοίσειν[9] τῷ συνεδρίῳ τὴν περὶ τῶν
νομοθετῶν διάγνωσιν. συγχωρούντων δὲ τῶν δημάρχων προθέντες ἀρχαιρέσια πολλῷ τάχιον ἢ τοῖς

---

[1] σήστιος Bb : σίκκιος A.   [2] καὶ B : om. R.
[3] κατήχθη Kiessling.   [4] ἐπὶ Kiessling.
[5] ἐπὶ τῆς αὐτῶν ἀρχῆς B : om. R.

and Publius Sestius were chosen consuls ; and the
pestilence finally ceased. After that public sacrifices
of thanksgiving were performed to the gods and
magnificent games celebrated at great expense ; and
the people were engaged in rejoicings and festivals,
as may be imagined. Indeed the whole winter season
was thus spent. In the beginning of spring a large
quantity of corn was brought in from many places ;
most of it was purchased with the public money,
but some was imported by private merchants. For
not least of the people's hardships was the dearth
of provisions, the land having lain uncultivated by
reason of the pestilence and the death of the husbandmen.

At the same time the ambassadors arrived from
Athens and the Greek cities in Italy, bringing with
them the laws. Thereupon the tribunes went to the
consuls and asked them to appoint the lawgivers
pursuant to the senate's decree. The consuls did not
know how to get rid of their solicitations and impor-
tunities, but as they disliked the business and were
unwilling for the aristocracy to be overthrown during
their consulship, they resorted to a specious excuse,
saying that the time for the election of magistrates
was at hand and, as it was their duty first to name
the new consuls, they would do so soon, and when
these were appointed, they would in conjunction
with them refer the matter of the lawgivers to the
senate for its consideration. When the tribunes
consented to this, they appointed the election much

---

[6] δεῖν Kiessling.   [7] τοὺς A : om. R.
[8] ποιήσειν Cary, ποιήσειν δὲ Reiske, ποιῆσαι δὲ Jacoby :
ποιήσεται δὲ A, ποιῆσαι τε B.
[9] ἔλεγον before ἀνοίσειν deleted by Vassis.

προτέροις ἔθος ἦν ὑπάτους ἀπέδειξαν Ἄππιον
Κλαύδιον καὶ Τίτον Γενύκιον,[1] καὶ μετὰ τοῦτο
πᾶσαν ἀποθέμενοι τὴν περὶ τῶν κοινῶν φροντίδα,
ὡς ἑτέρους ἤδη δέον ὑπὲρ αὐτῶν σκοπεῖν, οὐδὲν
ἔτι τοῖς δημάρχοις προσεῖχον, ἀλλὰ διακλέψαι τὸν
5 λοιπὸν χρόνον τῆς ὑπατείας διενοοῦντο. ἔτυχε δὲ
τὸν ἕτερον αὐτῶν Μενήνιον ἀρρωστία τις κατα-
λαβοῦσα χρόνιος. ἤδη δέ τινες ἔφασαν ὑπὸ λύπης
καὶ ἀθυμίας ἐμπεσοῦσαν[2] τῷ ἀνδρὶ τηκεδόνα δυσ-
απάλλακτον ἐργάσασθαι νόσον. ταύτην δὲ προσ-
λαβὼν τὴν πρόφασιν ὁ Σήστιος ὡς οὐδὲν οἷός τ'
ὢν[3] πράττειν μόνος ἀπεωθεῖτο τὰς τῶν δημάρχων
δεήσεις καὶ πρὸς τοὺς νέους ἄρχοντας ἠξίου τρέπε-
6 σθαι. οἱ δ' οὐκ ἔχοντες ὅ τι πράττωσιν[4] ἕτερον,
ἐπὶ τοὺς περὶ τὸν Ἄππιον οὔπω τὴν ἐξουσίαν
παρειληφότας ἠναγκάζοντο καταφεύγειν, τὰ μὲν ἐν
ταῖς ἐκκλησίαις δεόμενοι, τὰ δὲ κατὰ μόνας συντυγχάνοντες[5]· καὶ τέλος ἐξειργάσαντο τοὺς ἄνδρας
μεγάλας ὑποτείνοντες ἐλπίδας αὐτοῖς, εἰ τὰ τοῦ
δήμου πράγματα ἕλοιντο, τιμῆς καὶ δυναστείας.
7 εἰσῆλθε γάρ τις τὸν Ἄππιον ἐπιθυμία ξένην ἀρχὴν
περιβαλέσθαι καὶ νόμους καταστήσασθαι τῇ πατρίδι,
ὁμονοίας τε καὶ εἰρήνης καὶ τοῦ μίαν ἅπαντας
ἡγεῖσθαι τὴν πόλιν ἄρξαι τοῖς συμπολιτευομένοις.
οὐ μέντοι καὶ διέμεινέ γε χρηστὸς ἀρχῇ κοσμηθεὶς
μεγάλῃ, ἀλλ' ἐξέπεσε τελευτῶν εἰς φιλαρχίαν
ἀπαραχώρητον ὑπὸ μεγέθους ἐξουσίας διαφθαρεὶς

---

[1] Λεύκιον after Τίτον Γενύκιον deleted by Lapus.
[2] Sylburg : ἐμπεσούσης O, Jacoby.
[3] Reiske : ἦν O, Jacoby.
[4] Krüger, Cobet : πράττουσιν O.
[5] συντυγχάνοντες ΑΒ : ἐντυγχάνοντες R.

earlier than had been the custom with past elections, and nominated Appius Claudius and Titus
Genucius for consuls ; then, laying aside all thought
for the public business, as if it were now the concern of
others, they no longer paid any heed to the tribunes,
but determined to pass the remaining time of their
consulship in evasion of their duty. It chanced that
one of them, Menenius, was seized with a chronic
illness ; indeed, some said that a wasting disease,
which had come upon him because of grief and de-
spondency, had made his malady hard to be cured.
Sestius, availing himself of this additional excuse and
pretending that he could do nothing alone, kept
rejecting the pleas of the tribunes and advising them
to apply to the new consuls. Thus the tribunes, since
there was nothing else they could do, were forced to
have recourse to Appius and his colleague, who had
not yet entered upon their magistracy, and would
now plead with them in the meetings of the assembly
and now in private conferences. And at last they
overcame these men by holding out to them great
hopes of honour and power if they would espouse the
cause of the populace. For Appius was seized with
a desire to be invested with an alien magistracy,
to establish laws for the fatherland and to set an
example to his fellow citizens of harmony and peace
and the recognition by them all of the unity of the
commonwealth. Nevertheless, when he had been
honoured with this great magistracy, he did not
preserve his probity but, corrupted by the great-
ness of his authority, succumbed to an irresistible
passion for holding office and came very near to

καὶ ὀλίγου ἐδέησεν ἐπὶ τυραννίδα ἐλάσαι. περὶ ὧν κατὰ τὸν οἰκεῖον διαλέξομαι καιρόν.

LV. Τότε δ᾽ οὖν ἀπὸ τοῦ κρατίστου ταῦτα βουλευσάμενος καὶ τὸν συνάρχοντα πείσας, ἐπειδὴ πολλάκις αὐτὸν ἐπὶ τὴν ἐκκλησίαν ἐκάλεσαν οἱ δήμαρχοι, παρελθὼν πολλοὺς καὶ φιλανθρώπους διεξῆλθε λόγους· κεφάλαια δ᾽ αὐτοῦ τῆς δημηγορίας τοιάδε ἦν, ὅτι τὸ μὲν ἀποδειχθῆναι τοὺς νομοθέτας[1] καὶ παύσασθαι στασιάζοντας τοὺς πολίτας ὑπὲρ τῶν ἴσων αὐτῷ τε καὶ τῷ συνάρχοντι παντὸς[2] μάλιστα δοκεῖ, καὶ ἀποφαίνονται γνώμην φανεράν· τοῦ δ᾽ ἀποδεῖξαι τοὺς νομοθέτας αὐτοὶ μὲν οὐδεμίαν ἔχουσιν ἐξουσίαν οὔπω παρειληφότες τὴν ἀρχήν, τοῖς δὲ περὶ Μενήνιον ὑπάτοις οὐχ ὅπως ἐναντιώσονται πράσσουσι τὰ δόξαντα τῇ βουλῇ, ἀλλὰ καὶ
2 συνεργήσουσι καὶ πολλὴν εἴσονται χάριν. ἐὰν δ᾽ ἀναδύωνται σκῆψιν προβαλλόμενοι τὴν νέαν[3] ἀρχήν, ὡς οὐκ ἐξὸν αὐτοῖς ἑτέρους ἄρχοντας ὑπατικὴν ἐξουσίαν παραληψομένους ἀποδεικνύειν νέων[4] ἤδη κεκυρωμένων ὑπάτων, οὐδὲν ἐμποδὼν αὐτοῖς τὸ καθ᾽ ἑαυτοὺς ἔσεσθαι. ἑκόντες γὰρ ἀποστήσεσθαι τῆς ὑπατείας[5] τοῖς ἀνθ᾽ αὑτῶν αἱρεθησομένοις, ἐὰν
3 καὶ τῇ βουλῇ ταῦτα δοκῇ. ἐπαινοῦντος δὲ τοῦ δήμου[6] τὴν προθυμίαν τῶν ἀνδρῶν καὶ πάντων κατὰ πλῆθος ἐπὶ τὸ συνέδριον ὡσαμένων, ἀναγκασθεὶς ὁ Σήστιος τὴν βουλὴν συναγαγεῖν μόνος, ἐπειδὴ ὁ Μενήνιος ἀδύνατος ἦν παρεῖναι διὰ τὴν νόσον, προὔθηκεν ὑπὲρ τῶν νόμων λέγειν. ἐλέχθη-

---

[1] Sylburg : νόμους O, Jacoby.
[2] παντὸς om. B. [3] νέαν B : om. R.
[4] νέων Kiessling : ἡμῶν O, Jacoby, om. Kayser.
[5] τῆς ὑπατείας B : om. R.

running into tyranny ; all which I shall relate at the proper time.

LV. At any rate, at the time in question he took this resolution with the best of motives and prevailed upon his colleague to do the same ; and since the tribunes repeatedly invited him to appear before the assembly, he came forward and spoke many words of goodwill. The substance of his speech was as follows: That both he and his colleague held it to be a matter of the first importance that the lawgivers should be appointed and that the citizens should cease quarrelling over equal rights ; and they were declaring their opinion openly. But for the appointing of the lawgivers they themselves had no authority, since they had not yet entered upon their magistracy ; however, not only would they not oppose Menenius and his colleague in carrying out the decree of the senate, but they would actually assist them and be very grateful to them. If the others, however, should decline to carry out the decree, using the new magistracy as an excuse, claiming that it was not lawful for them, now that new consuls had been confirmed, to create other magistrates who would receive consular power, they said that so far as they themselves were concerned there would be nothing to prevent the present consuls from acting. For they would willingly resign the consulship to such magistrates as should be appointed in their stead, provided the senate too should approve of it. The populace praising them for their goodwill and rushing in a body to the senate-house, Sestius was forced to assemble the senate alone, Menenius being unable to attend by reason of his illness, and proposed to them the consideration of the laws.

---

⁶ δήμου R : δήμου καὶ B, Jacoby.

σαν μὲν οὖν καὶ τότε πολλοὶ ὑπ' ἀμφοτέρων λόγοι,
τῶν τε παραινούντων κατὰ νόμους πολιτεύεσθαι καὶ
τῶν ἀξιούντων τοὺς πατρίους φυλάττειν ἐθισμούς.
4 ἐνίκα δὲ ἡ τῶν εἰς νέωτα μελλόντων ὑπατεύειν
γνώμη, ἣν Ἄππιος Κλαύδιος πρῶτος ἐρωτηθεὶς
ἀπεφήνατο, ἄνδρας αἱρεθῆναι δέκα τοὺς ἐπιφανεστάτους ἐκ τῆς βουλῆς· τούτους δ' ἄρχειν εἰς
ἐνιαυτὸν ἀφ' ἧς ἂν ἀποδειχθῶσιν ἡμέρας, ἐξουσίαν
ἔχοντας ὑπὲρ ἁπάντων τῶν κατὰ τὴν πόλιν ἣν εἶχον
οἵ τε ὕπατοι καὶ ἔτι πρότερον[1] οἱ βασιλεῖς, τάς τ'
ἄλλας ἀρχὰς πάσας καταλελύσθαι ἕως[2] ἂν οἱ δέκα
5 μετέχωσι[3] τῆς ἀρχῆς· τούτους δὲ τοὺς ἄνδρας ἔκ τε
τῶν πατρίων ἐθῶν καὶ ἐκ τῶν Ἑλληνικῶν νόμων
οὓς ἐκόμισαν οἱ πρέσβεις ἐκλεξαμένους τὰ κράτιστα καὶ τῇ Ῥωμαίων πόλει πρόσφορα νομοθετήσασθαι[4]· τὰ δὲ γραφέντα ὑπὸ τῶν δέκα ἀνδρῶν, ἐὰν
ᾖ τε βουλὴ δοκιμάσῃ καὶ ὁ δῆμος ἐπιψηφίσῃ, κύρια
εἰς τὸν ἅπαντα εἶναι χρόνον, καὶ τὰς ἀρχὰς ὅσαι
ἂν ὕστερον ἀποδειχθῶσι κατὰ τούτους[5] τοὺς νόμους τά τε ἰδιωτικὰ συμβόλαια διαιρεῖν καὶ τὰ
δημόσια ἐπιτροπεύειν.

LVI. Τοῦτο τὸ δόγμα λαβόντες οἱ δήμαρχοι
προῆλθον εἰς τὴν ἐκκλησίαν καὶ ἀναγνόντες ἐν τῷ
δήμῳ πολλοὺς ἐπαίνους τῆς βουλῆς καὶ τοῦ προ-
θέντος[6] τὴν γνώμην Ἀππίου διεξῆλθον. ἐπεὶ δὲ
κατέλαβεν ὁ τῶν ἀρχαιρεσίων καιρός, ἐκκλησίαν
συναγαγόντες οἱ δήμαρχοι τούς τ' ἀποδειχθέντας
ὑπάτους ἥκειν ἠξίουν ἐμπεδώσοντας τῷ δήμῳ τὰς

---

[1] Sylburg : πρῶτον O.
[2] ἕως R : τέως Ba (?), Jacoby.
[3] μετέχωσι Cary : τύχωσι O, Jacoby.
[4] νομοθετήσασθαι B : νομοθετήσεσθαι R, Jacoby.

Many speeches were made on this occasion also both by those who contended that the commonwealth ought to be governed by laws and by those who advised adhering to the customs of their ancestors. The motion that carried was made by the men who were to serve as consuls for the next year ; it was delivered by Appius Claudius, who was first called upon, and was as follows : That ten persons be chosen, the most distinguished members of the senate, and that these govern for a year from the day of their appointment, possessing the same authority over all the affairs of the commonwealth as the consuls and, before them, the kings had enjoyed ; that all the other magistracies be abrogated for as long a time as the decemvirs held office ; that these men select both from the Roman usages and from the Greek laws brought back by the ambassadors the best institutions and such as were suitable to the Roman commonwealth, and form them into a body of laws ; that the laws drawn up by the decemvirs, if approved by the senate and confirmed by the people, should be valid for all time, and that all future magistrates should determine private contracts and administer the affairs of the public according to these laws.

LVI. The tribunes, having received this decree, went to the assembly and after reading it before the populace, bestowed much praise upon the senate and upon Appius, who had proposed it. And when the time came for the election of magistrates, the tribunes called an assembly and asked the consuls-elect to come and fulfil their promises to the popu-

---

⁵ τούτους added by Kiessling.
⁶ Kiessling : θέντος O.

ὑποσχέσεις, κἀκεῖνοι παρελθόντες ἐξωμόσαντο τὰς
2 ὑπατείας. τούτους ὁ δῆμος ἐπαινῶν τε καὶ θαυ-
μάζων διετέλει, καὶ ἐπειδὴ τοὺς νομοθέτας ψηφο-
φορεῖν ἔδει, πρώτους εἵλετο τῶν ἄλλων· καὶ
ἀπεδείχθησαν ἐν ἀρχαιρεσίαις ὑπὸ τῆς λοχίτιδος
ἐκκλησίας Ἄππιος μὲν Κλαύδιος καὶ Τίτος Γενύκιος,[1] οὓς ἔδει τοὐπιὸν[2] ἄρχειν ἔτος, Πόπλιος δὲ
Σήστιος ὁ τὸν ἐνιαυτὸν ἐκεῖνον ὑπατεύων, τρεῖς δὲ[3]
οἱ κομίσαντες παρὰ τῶν Ἑλλήνων τοὺς νόμους,
Σπόριος[4] Ποστόμιος καὶ Σερούιος[5] Σολπίκιος καὶ
Αὖλος Μάλλιος, εἷς δὲ τῶν ὑπατευσάντων τὸν
παρελθόντα ἐνιαυτόν, Τίτος Ῥωμίλιος, ὁ τὴν ἐν
τῷ δήμῳ δίκην Σικκίου κατηγορήσαντος ἁλούς,
ἐπειδὴ γνώμης ἐδόκει ἄρξαι δημοτικῆς· ἐκ δὲ τῶν
ἄλλων βουλευτῶν Γάιος Ἰούλιος καὶ Τίτος Οὐετούριος καὶ Πόπλιος Ὁράτιος, ἅπαντες ὑπατι-
κοί· αἱ δὲ τῶν δημάρχων τε καὶ ἀγορανόμων καὶ
ταμιῶν καὶ εἴ τινες ἦσαν ἄλλαι πάτριοι Ῥωμαίοις
ἀρχαὶ κατελύθησαν.

LVII. Τῷ δ᾽ ἑξῆς ἔτει παραλαβόντες οἱ νομοθέται τὰ πράγματα πολιτείας κόσμον τοιόνδε τινὰ
καθίστανται· εἷς μὲν αὐτῶν τάς τε ῥάβδους καὶ τὰ
λοιπὰ παράσημα τῆς ὑπατικῆς εἶχεν ἐξουσίας, ὃς
βουλήν τε συνεκάλει καὶ δόγματα ἐπεκύρου καὶ
τἆλλα ἔπραττεν ὅσα ἡγεμόνι προσῆκεν· οἱ δ᾽ ἄλλοι
συστέλλοντες ἐπὶ τὸ δημοτικώτερον τὸ τῆς ἐξουσίας ἐπίφθονον ὀλίγῳ τινὶ διήλλαττον ὀφθῆναι τῶν
πολλῶν· εἶτ᾽ αὖθις ἕτερος αὐτῶν ἐπὶ τὴν ἐξουσίαν

---

[1] Sylburg : τίτος λεύκιος γενύκιος AB.
[2] εἰς τοὐπιὸν Cobet, Jacoby.
[3] δὲ Kiessling : τε O.
[4] Σπόριος Sylburg : πόπλιος AB.

lace; and they, appearing, resigned their magistracy.
The populace kept praising and admiring them, and
when they were to vote for lawgivers, made them
their first choice. Those chosen at the election by
the centuriate assembly were Appius Claudius and
Titus Genucius, who were to have been consuls for
the following year; Publius Sestius, consul of that
year; the three who had brought the laws from the
Greeks, Spurius Postumius, Servius Sulpicius and
Aulus Manlius; one of the consuls of the preceding
year, Titus Romilius, the man who had been condemned when tried before the populace on a charge
brought by Siccius and was now chosen because he
was thought to have offered a motion favourable to
the populace [1]; and, from among the other senators,
Gaius Julius, Titus Veturius and Publius Horatius, all
ex-consuls. At the same time the offices of the
tribunes, aediles, quaestors and any other traditional
Roman magistrates were abrogated.

LVII. The next year [2] the lawgivers took over the
administration of affairs and established a form of
government of the following general description. One
of them had the rods and the other insignia of the
consular power, assembled the senate, certified its
decrees, and performed all the other functions belonging to the head of the state; while the others,
by way of reducing the invidious character of their
office to the more democratic level, differed in appearance but little from the mass of citizens. Then another of them in turn was vested with this authority,

[1] Cf. chaps. 50 f.
[2] For chaps. 57 f. cf. Livy iii. 33, 7–34, 11.

---

[5] Sylburg : σερουίλιος AB.

καθίστατο, καὶ τοῦτ' ἐκ περινομῆς[1] ἐγίνετο παραλλὰξ ἐπ' ἐνιαυτόν,[2] ἑκάστου[3] τὴν ἡγεμονίαν παραλαμβάνοντος εἰς συγκείμενόν τινα ἡμερῶν ἀριθμόν.
2 ἅπαντες δ' ἐξ ἑωθινοῦ καθεζόμενοι διῆτων τὰ ἰδιωτικὰ[4] συμβόλαια καὶ τὰ δημόσια, ὁπόσα πρός τε ὑπηκόους καὶ συμμάχους καὶ τοὺς ἐνδοιαστῶς ἀκρωμένους τῆς πόλεως ἐγκλήματα τυγχάνοι γινόμενα, μετὰ πάσης ἀνασκοποῦντες ἕκαστα ἐπι-
3 εικείας τε καὶ δικαιοσύνης. ἐδόκει δὲ ἄριστα τὸν ἐνιαυτὸν ἐκεῖνον ἡ Ῥωμαίων πόλις ὑπὸ τῆς δεκαδαρχίας[5] ἐπιτροπευθῆναι. μάλιστα δ' αὐτῶν ἐπηνεῖτο ἡ τοῦ δημοτικοῦ πρόνοια καὶ πρὸς ἅπαν τὸ βίαιον ὑπὲρ τῶν ἀσθενεστέρων ἀντίταξις· ἐλέχθη τε ὑπὸ πολλῶν[6] ὡς οὐδὲν ἔτι δεήσοι δήμου προστατῶν οὐδὲ τῶν ἄλλων ἀρχείων τῇ πόλει μιᾶς διοικούσης ἅπαντα ἡγεμονίας σώφρονος, ἧς ἀρχηγὸς Ἄππιος
4 εἶναι ἐδόκει. καὶ τὸν ὑπὲρ ὅλης τῆς δεκαδαρχίας ἔπαινον ἐκεῖνος ἐφέρετο παρὰ τοῦ δήμου. οὐ γὰρ μόνον ἃ μετὰ τῶν ἄλλων ἔπραττεν ἀπὸ τοῦ κρατίστου[7] χρηστότητος ἔφερεν αὐτῷ δόκησιν, ἀλλὰ πολὺ μᾶλλον ἃ κατ' ἰδίαν ἐπιτηδεύων διετέλει, κατά τ' ἀσπασμοὺς καὶ προσαγορεύσεις φιλανθρώπους καὶ τὰς ἄλλας τῶν πενήτων φιλοφρονήσεις.
5 Οὗτοι οἱ δέκα ἄνδρες συγγράψαντες νόμους ἔκ τε τῶν Ἑλληνικῶν νόμων καὶ τῶν παρὰ σφίσιν αὐτοῖς ἀγράφων ἐθισμῶν προὔθηκαν ἐν δέκα δέλτοις τῷ βουλομένῳ σκοπεῖν, δεχόμενοι πᾶσαν ἐπανόρθωσιν

---

[1] περινομῆς O : περιτροπῆς Cobet, Jacoby.
[2] Jacoby : ἐνιαυτοῦ A, αὐτοῦ B.
[3] ἑκάστου added by Reiske.
[4] ἰδιωτικὰ B : δημοτικὰ R. [5] Kiessling : δεκαρχίας O.
[6] ὑπὸ πολλῶν B : ὑπ' αὐτῶν καὶ ὑπὸ πολλῶν A.
[7] ἀπὸ τοῦ κρατίστου B : om. R.

and thus it went on in rotation for a year, each one in succession receiving the command for a certain number of days as agreed upon. But all of them sat from early morning arbitrating cases involving private and public contracts in which complaints might arise between citizens and the subjects and allies of the Romans and peoples of doubtful allegiance to Rome, examining each case with complete fairness and justice. That year the Roman commonwealth seemed to be exceedingly well governed by the decemvirs. Above all they were commended for their care of the plebeians and for opposing, in defence of the weaker parties, every kind of violence; and it was said by many that the commonwealth would have no further need of champions of the populace or any of the other magistracies so long as a single wise leadership was directing all the affairs of the state. Of this régime Appius was looked upon as the head, and all the praise that belonged to the whole decemvirate was given by the populace to him. For he gained a reputation for probity not only by those things which he did in concert with his colleagues from the best motives, but much more by the manner in which he conducted himself personally, as in the matter of greetings, friendly conversation and other kindly courtesies toward the poor.

These decemvirs, having formed a body of laws both from those of the Greeks and from their own unwritten usages, set them forth on ten tables to be examined by any who wished, welcoming every amendment suggested by private persons and en-

ἰδιωτῶν καὶ πρὸς τὴν κοινὴν εὐαρέστησιν ἀπευθύ-
νοντες τὰ γραφέντα. καὶ μέχρι πολλοῦ διετέλεσαν
ἐν κοινῷ μετὰ τῶν ἀρίστων ἀνδρῶν συνεδρεύοντες
καὶ τὴν ἀκριβεστάτην ποιούμενοι τῆς νομοθεσίας
6 ἐξέτασιν. ἐπειδὴ δ' ἀποχρώντως ἐφαίνετο αὐτοῖς
τὰ γραφέντα ἔχειν, πρῶτον μὲν τὴν βουλὴν συναγαγόντες οὐθενὸς ἔτι μεμφομένου τοῖς νόμοις
προβούλευμα περὶ αὐτῶν ἐκύρωσαν. ἔπειτα τὸν
δῆμον καλέσαντες[1] εἰς τὴν λοχῖτιν ἐκκλησίαν
ἱερομνημόνων τε καὶ οἰωνιστῶν καὶ τῶν ἄλλων
ἱερέων παρόντων καὶ τὰ θεῖα ὡς νόμος ἐξηγησα-
7 μένων ἀνέδωκαν τοῖς λόχοις τὰς ψήφους. ἐπικυρώσαντος δὲ καὶ τοῦ δήμου τοὺς νόμους, στήλαις
χαλκαῖς ἐγχαράξαντες αὐτοὺς ἐφεξῆς ἔθεσαν ἐν
ἀγορᾷ τὸν ἐπιφανέστατον ἐκλεξάμενοι τόπον. καὶ
ἐπειδὴ βραχὺς ὁ τῆς ἀρχῆς αὐτοῖς χρόνος ὁ
λειπόμενος ἦν, συναγαγόντες τοὺς βουλευτὰς προὔ-
θεσαν ὑπὲρ ἀρχαιρεσίων οἷα χρὴ γενέσθαι σκοπεῖν.

LVIII. Πολλῶν δὲ λεχθέντων ἐνίκησεν ἡ γνώμη
τῶν παραινούντων δεκαδαρχίαν αὖθις ἀποδεῖξαι τῶν
κοινῶν κυρίαν. ἀτελὴς τε[2] γὰρ ἡ νομοθεσία ἐφαίνετο, ὡς ἂν ἐξ ὀλίγου συντεθεῖσα χρόνου, καὶ ἐπὶ
τοῖς ἤδη κεκυρωμένοις, ἵνα ἑκόντες τε καὶ ἄκοντες
ἐν αὐτοῖς μένοιεν, ἐδόκει δή[3] τινος ἀρχῆς αὐτοκρά-
τορος δεῖν. τὸ δὲ μάλιστα πεῖσαν αὐτοὺς προελέ-
σθαι τὴν δεκαδαρχίαν ἦν τῶν δημάρχων κατάλυσις,
2 ὃ παντὸς μάλιστα ἐβούλοντο. ταῦτα μὲν ἐν κοινῷ
σκοπουμένοις αὐτοῖς ἐδόκει, ἰδίᾳ δὲ οἱ πρωτεύοντες
τοῦ συνεδρίου γνώμην ἐποιοῦντο μεταπορεύεσθαι

[1] Kiessling : ἐκάλεσαν O.
[2] τε B : om. R.
[3] Reiske : δέ O.

deavouring to correct them in such a manner as to give general satisfaction. For a long time they continued to consult in public with the best men and to make the strictest scrutiny of their code of laws. When they were satisfied with what was written, they first convened the senate and, no fresh objection being made to the laws, they got a preliminary decree passed concerning them. Then, having summoned the people to the centuriate assembly, the pontiffs, the augurs and the other priests being present and having directed the performance of the religious rites according to custom, they gave the centuries their ballots. And when the people too had ratified the laws, they caused them to be engraved on bronze pillars and set them up in order in the Forum, choosing the most conspicuous place. Then, as the remaining time of their magistracy was short, they assembled the senators and proposed for their consideration what kind of magistrates should be chosen at the next election.

LVIII. After a long debate the opinion of those prevailed who favoured choosing a decemvirate again to be the supreme power in the state. For not only was their code of laws manifestly incomplete, in view of the short time in which it had been compiled, but in the case of the laws already ratified some magistracy absolute in power seemed necessary in order that willingly or unwillingly people might abide by them. But the chief motive that induced the senate to give the preference to the decemvirate was the suppression of the tribunician power, which they desired above everything. This was the result of their public deliberations ; but in private the leading men of the senate resolved to canvass for this magis-

τὴν ἀρχήν, δεδιότες μὴ ταραχώδεις τινὲς ἄνθρωποι
τηλικαύτης ἐξουσίας λαβόμενοι κακόν τι μέγα
ἐργάσωνται. ἀγαπητῶς δὲ τοῦ δήμου τὰ δόξαντα
τῇ βουλῇ δεξαμένου καὶ μετὰ πλείστης προθυμίας
ἐπιψηφίσαντος αὐτοὶ μὲν οἱ δέκα ἄνδρες προεῖπον
τὸν τῶν ἀρχαιρεσίων καιρόν, μετῇεσαν δὲ τὴν ἀρχὴν
οἱ ἐντιμότατοί τε καὶ πρεσβύτατοι τῶν πατρικίων.
3 ἔνθα δὴ πολὺς ὑπὸ πάντων ἐπαινούμενος ἦν ὁ τῆς
τότε δεκαδαρχίας ἡγεμὼν Ἄππιος, καὶ πᾶς ὁ δη-
μοτικὸς ὄχλος ἐκεῖνον ἐπὶ τῆς ἀρχῆς ἠξίου κατέχειν ὡς οὐκ ἄλλου τινὸς ἄμεινον ἡγησομένου. ὁ
δ' ἀναίνεσθαι μὲν προσεποιεῖτο κατ' ἀρχὰς καὶ ἀπολύειν αὐτὸν[1] ἠξίου λειτουργίας καὶ[2] ὀχληρᾶς καὶ
ἐπιφθόνου. τελευτῶν δ' ὡς ἐλιπάρουν αὐτὸν ἅπαντες αὐτός τε ὑπέμενε μετιέναι τὴν ἀρχὴν καὶ τῶν
συμπαραγγελλόντων τοὺς ἀρίστους αἰτιασάμενος
οὐχ ἡδέως πρὸς ἑαυτὸν ἔχειν διὰ τὸν φθόνον, τοῖς
4 ἑαυτοῦ φίλοις συνηγωνίζετο φανερῶς. ἀποδείκνυ-
ταί τε πάλιν ἐν ἀρχαιρεσίαις λοχίτισι νομοθέτης
τὸ δεύτερον· σὺν δ' αὐτῷ Κόιντος μὲν Φάβιος
ὁ καλούμενος Οὐιβολανὸς ὁ τρὶς ὑπατεύσας, ἀνὴρ
ἀνεπίληπτος εἰς τόδε χρόνου γενόμενος περὶ πᾶσαν
ἀρετήν· ἐκ δὲ τῶν ἄλλων πατρικίων, οὓς ἐκεῖνος
ἠσπάζετο, Μάρκος Κορνήλιος καὶ[3] Μάρκος Σέρ-
γιος[4] καὶ Λεύκιος Μηνύκιος καὶ Τίτος Ἀντώνιος
καὶ Μάνιος Ῥαβολήιος,[5] ἄνδρες οὐ πάνυ ἐπι-
φανεῖς· ἐκ δὲ τῶν δημοτικῶν Κόιντος Ποιτέλ-
λιος καὶ Καίσων Δουέλλιος καὶ Σπόριος Ὄππιος[6].
προσελήφθησαν γὰρ καὶ οὗτοι πρὸς τοῦ Ἀππίου

---

[1] αὐτὸν B : om. R.   [2] καὶ B : om. R.
[3] Μάρκος Κορνήλιος καὶ Sylburg : om. AB.
[4] Sylburg : σερουίλιος AB.

tracy, fearing that certain turbulent spirits, if they gained such power, might cause some great mischief. The popular assembly having gladly received the resolution of the senate and confirmed it with the greatest enthusiasm, the decemvirs themselves appointed the time for the election ; and those among the patricians who were most distinguished for both their dignity and age stood candidates for the magistracy. Upon this occasion Appius, who was the chief of that decemvirate, received great praise from everybody and the whole crowd of plebeians desired to continue him in the magistracy, believing that no one else would govern better. He at first pretended to refuse it and asked them to excuse him from a service that was both troublesome and invidious ; but at last, when they all pressed him, he not only consented to seek the office himself, but also, accusing the best of the rival candidates of being ill disposed toward him through envy, openly espoused the candidacy of his friends. Thus he was again chosen in the centuriate assembly as a lawgiver, for the second time, and with him Quintus Fabius, surnamed Vibulanus, who had been thrice consul, a man adorned with every virtue and without reproach up to that time. From among the other patricians those favoured by Appius and chosen were Marcus Cornelius, Marcus Sergius, Lucius Minucius, Titus Antonius and Manius Rabuleius, men of no great distinction ; and from among the plebeians,[1] Quintus Poetelius, Caeso Duilius and Spurius Oppius. For these also were taken in by

[1] According to Livy (iv. 3, 17) the decemvirs were all patricians.

---

[5] Sylburg : ῥαβόλιος O.   [6] Sylburg : ἄππιος ABb.

κολακείας ἕνεκα τῶν δημοτικῶν, διδάσκοντος ὅτι
δίκαιόν ἐστι μιᾶς ἀρχῆς κατὰ πάντων ἀποδεικνυ-
5 μένης εἶναί τι καὶ τοῦ δήμου μέρος ἐν αὐτῇ. εὐδο-
κιμῶν δ' ἐφ' ἅπασι τούτοις καὶ δοκῶν κράτιστος
εἶναι βασιλέων τε καὶ τῶν κατ' ἐνιαυτὸν ἡγησα-
μένων τῆς πόλεως παραλαμβάνει πάλιν τὴν ἀρχὴν εἰς τὸν ἐπιόντα ἐνιαυτόν. ταῦτα κατ' ἐκείνην
ἐπράχθη τὴν δεκαδαρχίαν ὑπὸ[1] Ῥωμαίων, ἄλλο δ'
οὐθὲν ὅ τι καὶ λόγου ἄξιον.

LIX. Ἐν δὲ τῷ κατόπιν ἔτει παραλαβόντες τὴν
ὑπατικὴν ἐξουσίαν οἱ σὺν Ἀππίῳ Κλαυδίῳ δέκα
ἄνδρες εἰδοῖς μαΐαις (ἦγον δὲ τοὺς μῆνας κατὰ
σελήνην, καὶ συνέπιπτεν εἰς τὰς εἰδοὺς ἡ παν-
2 σέληνος), πρῶτα μὲν ὅρκια τεμόντες ἀπόρρητα τῷ
πλήθει συνθήκας σφίσιν αὐτοῖς ἔθεντο περὶ μηδενὸς
ἀλλήλοις ἐναντιοῦσθαι, ὅ τι δ' ἂν εἷς ἐξ αὐτῶν
δικαιώσῃ, τοῦθ' ἅπαντες ἡγεῖσθαι κύριον, τήν τ'
ἀρχὴν καθέξειν διὰ βίου καὶ μηδένα παρήσειν ἕτερον
ἐπὶ τὰ πράγματα, ἰσότιμοί τε ἅπαντες ἔσεσθαι καὶ
τὴν αὐτὴν ἕξειν δυναστείαν, βουλῆς μὲν ἢ δήμου
ψηφίσμασι σπανίως καὶ εἰς αὐτὰ τἀναγκαῖα χρώμενοι, τὰ δὲ πλεῖστα ἐπὶ τῆς ἑαυτῶν ἐξουσίας
3 ποιοῦντες. ἐνστάσης δὲ τῆς ἡμέρας ἐν ᾗ παραλαβεῖν αὐτοὺς ἔδει τὴν ἀρχήν, τοῖς θεοῖς προ-
θύσαντες ἃ νόμος (ἱερὰν δὲ ταύτην ἄγουσι Ῥωμαῖοι
τὴν ἡμέραν καὶ παντὸς μάλιστα ὀττεύονται μήτ'
ἀκοῦσαι μηδὲν ἀηδὲς ἐν αὐτῇ μήτ' ἰδεῖν) ἕωθεν
εὐθὺς ἐξῄεσαν οἱ δέκα τὰ παράσημα τῆς βασιλικῆς

1 ὑπὸ B : om. R.

---

1 For chaps. 59 f. cf. Livy iii. 35-38, 2.

Appius in order to flatter the plebeians; he pointed out that, as only one magistracy was appointed to govern all the citizens, it was just that the populace also should be represented in it. Thus Appius, who was in great repute for all these actions and was looked upon as superior to both their kings and the annual magistrates who had governed the state, assumed the magistracy again for the following year. These were the things done by the Romans during that decemvirate, and there was nothing else worth relating.

LIX. The following year [1] Appius Claudius and the other decemvirs, having received the consular power on the ides of May (for the Romans reckoned their months by the course of the moon, and the full moon fell on the ides), first of all took a solemn oath, without the knowledge of the populace, and made a compact among themselves not to oppose one another in anything, but that whatever was approved by any one of them should be ratified by all the others; and they agreed that they would hold their magistracy for life and admit no other person into the government, that they would all enjoy the same honours and possess the same power, and that they would rarely make use of the votes of the senate or populace and then only in absolutely necessary cases, but would do almost everything on their own authority. When the day came on which they were to enter upon their magistracy, after they had offered the usual initial sacrifices to the gods (for the Romans look upon this day as holy and particularly make it a point of religion neither to hear nor to see anything disagreeable during its course), the decemvirs set out early in the morning, each one accompanied by

4 ἐξουσίας ἅπαντες ἐπαγόμενοι. ὁ δὲ δῆμος, ὡς
ἔμαθεν αὐτοὺς οὐκέτι φυλάττοντας τὸ δημοτικὸν
ἐκεῖνο καὶ μέτριον σχῆμα τῆς ἡγεμονίας οὐδὲ δι-
αμειβομένους τὰ παράσημα τῆς βασιλικῆς ἀρχῆς
ὡς πρότερον, εἰς πολλὴν ἦλθε δυσθυμίαν καὶ κατ-
5 ήφειαν. ἐφόβουν θ᾽ οἱ προσηρτημένοι ταῖς δέσμαις
τῶν ῥάβδων πελέκεις, οὓς ἔφερον οἱ προηγούμενοι
τῶν ἀνδρῶν ἑκάστου δώδεκα ὄντες ἀναστέλλοντες
ἐκ τῶν στενωπῶν πληγαῖς τὸν ὄχλον, ὃ καὶ ἐπὶ
τῶν βασιλέων ἐγένετο πρότερον. κατελύθη γὰρ
εὐθὺς τὸ ἔθος τοῦτο μετὰ τὴν ἐκβολὴν τῶν μονάρ-
χων ὑπ᾽ ἀνδρὸς δημοτικοῦ Ποπλίου Οὐαλερίου τὴν
ἐκείνων ἐξουσίαν μεταλαβόντος, ᾧ πάντες οἱ μετ᾽
ἐκεῖνον ὕπατοι καλοῦ πράγματος δόξαντι ἄρξαι τὰ
ὅμοια πράττοντες οὐκέτι ταῖς δέσμαις τῶν ῥάβδων
προσῆρτων τοὺς πελέκεις ὅτι μὴ κατὰ τὰς στρατείας καὶ τὰς ἄλλας ἐξόδους τὰς ἐκ τῆς πόλεως.
6 πόλεμον δ᾽ ἐξάγοντες ὑπερόριον ἢ τῶν ὑπηκόων
πράγματα ἐπισκεπτόμενοι,[1] τότε καὶ τοὺς πελέκεις
ταῖς ῥάβδοις προσελάμβανον, ἵνα τὸ τῆς ὄψεως
φοβερόν, ὡς κατ᾽ ἐχθρῶν ἢ δούλων γινόμενον,
ἥκιστα φαίνηται τοῖς πολίταις ἐπαχθές.

LX. Τοῦτο δὴ θεασαμένοις ἅπασιν, ὃ τῆς βασιλικῆς ἐξουσίας σημεῖον ἐνομίζετο εἶναι, πολὺ παρ-
ειστήκει δέος, ὥσπερ ἔφην, ἀπολωλεκέναι νομίζουσι
τὴν ἐλευθερίαν καὶ δέκα βασιλεῖς ἑλομένοις ἀνθ᾽
ἑνός. τοῦτον δὲ τὸν τρόπον καταπληξάμενοι τοὺς
ὄχλους οἱ δέκα ἄνδρες καὶ γνόντες ὅτι δεῖ φόβῳ τὸ
λοιπὸν αὐτῶν[2] ἄρχειν, ἑταιρίαν ἕκαστοι συνῆγον
ἐπιλεγόμενοι τοὺς θρασυτάτους τῶν νέων καὶ σφί-
2 σιν αὐτοῖς ἐπιτηδειοτάτους. τὸ μὲν οὖν ἐκ τῶν

---

[1] ἐπισκεπτόμενοι R : ἐπισκεψόμενοι B, Jacoby.

the insignia of royalty. When the people saw that they no longer preserved the same democratic and modest form of leadership or passed on the insignia of royalty from one to another, as before, they fell into great despair and dejection. They were terrified by the axes attached to the bundles of rods which were borne by the lictors, twelve of whom preceded each of the decemvirs and with blows forced the throng back from the streets, as had been the practice formerly under the kings. This custom, however, had been abolished, immediately after the expulsion of the kings, by Publius Valerius, a friend of the populace, who succeeded to their power, and all the consuls after him, following the good example he was felt to have set, no longer attached the axes to the bundles of rods except when they went out of the city either upon military expeditions or upon other occasions; but when they set out on a foreign war or inspected the affairs of their subjects, they then added the axes to the rods. This was in order that the terrifying sight, as one employed against their enemies or slaves, might give as little offence as possible to the citizens.

LX. When, therefore, they all saw this token, which was considered to be a mark of the kingly power, they were in great fear, as I said, believing that they had lost their liberty and chosen ten kings instead of one. The decemvirs having by this means struck terror into the masses and made up their mind that they must rule them by fear thereafter, each of them formed a faction, choosing from among the youth those who were most daring and most attached to their persons. Now the fact that most

---

² αὐτῶν om. B.

ἀπόρων καὶ τῶν ταπεινῶν ταῖς τύχαις τοὺς πλείους
φανῆναι τυραννικῆς κόλακας ἐξουσίας, τοῦ κοινοῦ
συμφέροντος ἀλλαξαμένους τὰς αὑτῶν ὠφελείας,
οὔτε παράδοξον οὔτ᾽ ἀνέλπιστον ἦν· τὸ δὲ καὶ ἐκ
τῶν πατρικίων εὑρεθῆναι συχνοὺς ἔχοντάς τι καὶ
ἐπὶ πλούτῳ καὶ ἐπ᾽ εὐγενείᾳ μέγα φρονεῖν τοὺς ὑπομένοντας συγκαταλύειν τοῖς δεκαδάρχοις[1] τὴν τῆς
πατρίδος ἐλευθερίαν, τοῦτο θαυμαστὸν ἅπασιν εἶναι
ἐδόκει. οἱ δὲ[2] πάσαις κολακεύοντες ἡδοναῖς, ὁπόσαι
πεφύκασιν ἀνθρώπων κρατεῖν, κατὰ πολλὴν ἄδειαν
ἦρχον τῆς πόλεως, βουλὴν μὲν ἢ δῆμον ἐν οὐδεμιᾷ
μερίδι τιθέμενοι, πάντων δὲ αὐτοὶ νομοθέται τε καὶ
δικασταὶ γινόμενοι, καὶ[3] πολλοὺς μὲν ἀποκτιννύντες
τῶν πολιτῶν, πολλοὺς δ᾽ ἀφαιρούμενοι τὰς οὐσίας
3 ἀδίκως. ἵνα δ᾽ αὐτοῖς εὐπρεπῶς τὰ γινόμενα ἔχῃ,
παράνομα καὶ δεινὰ ὄντα, ὡς δὴ σὺν τῷ δικαίῳ
πραττόμενα, δικαστήρια ἐφ᾽ ἑκάστῳ χρήματι ἀπ-
εδίδοσαν· ἦσαν δὲ οἵ τε κατήγοροι ὑπ᾽ αὐτῶν ἐκείνων ἐκ τῶν συγκατασκευαζόντων τὴν τυραννίδα
ὑποπεμπόμενοι, καὶ τὰ[4] δικαστήρια ἐκ τῶν ἑταί-
ρων ἀποδεικνύμενα, οἳ διημείβοντο ἀλλήλοις κατα-
4 χαριζόμενοι τὰς δίκας. πολλὰ δὲ τῶν ἐγκλημάτων
καὶ οὐ τὰ ἐλαχίστου ἄξια ἐφ᾽ ἑαυτῶν οἱ δέκα
ἔκρινον, ὥστ᾽ ἠναγκάζοντο οἱ μειονεκτοῦντες τῷ
δικαίῳ προσνέμειν ἑαυτοὺς ταῖς ἑταιρίαις, ἐπειδὴ τὸ
ἀσφαλὲς οὐκ ἐνῆν ἄλλως αὐτοῖς ἔχειν, καὶ ἐγένετο
σὺν χρόνῳ πλεῖον τοῦ ὑγιαίνοντος ἐν τῇ πόλει τὸ
διεφθαρμένον καὶ νοσοῦν. οὐδὲ γὰρ ἠξίουν ἔτι
μένειν ἐντὸς τείχους οἷς τὰ πραττόμενα ὑπὸ τῶν

---

[1] δεκαδάρχοις B : δεκάρχοις R.
[2] οἱ δὲ Jacoby : οἱ ABb, ὁ Ba.
[3] καὶ deleted by Reiske.

men of no means and low condition showed themselves flatterers of a tyrannical power and preferred
their private advantages to the public good, was
neither extraordinary nor surprising ; but that there
were found many even of the patricians who, though
they had some reason, on the basis of either wealth
or birth, to feel great pride, nevertheless consented
to join with the decemvirs in destroying the liberty
of their country, that seemed an amazing thing to
everybody. But the decemvirs, by humouring people
with all the pleasures that are calculated to subdue
mankind, governed the commonwealth with great
ease, holding the senate and people in no account, but
becoming themselves both the lawgivers and the
judges in all matters, putting many of the citizens
to death and stripping others of their estates un-
justly. In order, however, that their acts, illegal
and cruel as they were, might have a specious appearance and seem to be carried out in accordance
with justice, they appointed courts to try every
matter ; but the accusers, chosen from among the
instruments of their tyranny, were suborned by the
decemvirs themselves and the courts filled with men
of their factions, who gratified one another by turns
in rendering their decisions. Many complaints, and
those not the ones of least importance, the decemvirs decided by themselves. Hence the litigants
who had less right on their side were under the
necessity of attaching themselves to the factions,
since they could not otherwise be sure of success ;
and in time the corrupted and infected element in the
city became more numerous than the sound element.
For those to whom the doings of the decemvirs

---

[4] τὰ added by Kiessling.

δεκαδάρχων ἀνιαρὰ ἦν, ἀλλ' ἀνεχώρουν εἰς τοὺς
ἀγροὺς τὸν τῶν ἀρχαιρεσίων σκοποῦντες χρόνον ὡς
ἀποθησομένων τῶν δέκα ἀνδρῶν τὰς δυναστείας,
ὅταν τὸν ἐνιαύσιον ἐκτελέσωσι χρόνον, καὶ ἀπο-
5 δειξόντων ἑτέρας ἀρχάς. οἱ δὲ περὶ τὸν Ἄππιον
τοὺς λοιποὺς συγγράψαντες νόμους ἐν δέλτοις δυσὶ καὶ ταύτας ταῖς πρότερον ἐξενεχθείσαις προσ-
έθηκαν· ἐν αἷς καὶ ὅδε ὁ[1] νόμος ἦν,[2] μὴ ἐξεῖναι
τοῖς πατρικίοις πρὸς τοὺς δημοτικοὺς ἐπιγαμίας
συνάψαι—δι' οὐδέν, ὡς ἐμοὶ δοκεῖν, ἕτερον ἢ τὸ μὴ
συνελθεῖν εἰς ὁμόνοιαν τὰ ἔθνη γάμων ἐπαλλαγαῖς
6 καὶ οἰκειοτήτων κοινωνίαις συγκερασθέντα. ὡς
δὲ καὶ ὁ τῶν ἀρχαιρεσίων ἐπέστη χρόνος, πολλὰ
χαίρειν φράσαντες τοῖς τε πατρίοις ἐθισμοῖς καὶ
τοῖς νεωστὶ γραφεῖσι νόμοις, οὔτε βουλῆς ψήφισμα
ποιήσαντες οὔτε δήμου διέμειναν ἐπὶ τῆς αὐτῆς
ἀρχῆς.

---

[1] ὁ Bb : om. R. [2] ἦν om. A.

were obnoxious would not consent even to remain
any longer within the city's walls, but retired to the
country while awaiting the time for the election of
magistrates, in the expectation that the decemvirs
would resign their power after completing their
year's term and would appoint other magistrates.
As for Appius and his colleagues, they caused the remaining laws to be inscribed on two tables and added
them to those they had published before. Among
these new laws was this one, that it should not be
lawful for the patricians to contract marriages with
the plebeians—a law made for no other reason, in
my opinion, than to prevent the two orders from
coming together in harmony when once blended
together by intermarriages and ties of affinity.
And when the time for the election of magistrates
was at hand, the decemvirs bade a hearty farewell
to both the ancestral customs and the newly-written
laws, and without asking for a vote of either senate
or people, continued in the same magistracy.

INDEX

INDEX

INDEX

Printed in Great Britain by R. & R. Clark, Limited, *Edinburgh*

THE LOEB CLASSICAL LIBRARY

VOLUMES ALREADY PUBLISHED

LATIN AUTHORS

AMMIANUS MARCELLINUS. **J. C. Rolfe.** 3 Vols.
(Vols. I. and II. *2nd Imp. revised.*)

APULEIUS. THE GOLDEN ASS (METAMOR-
PHOSES). W. Adlington (1566). Revised by S. Gaselee. (*7th Imp.*)

ST. AUGUSTINE, CONFESSIONS OF. W. Watt
(1631). 2 Vols. (Vol. I. *6th Imp.*, Vol. II. *5th Imp.*)

ST. AUGUSTINE, SELECT LETTERS. J. H. Baxter.

AUSONIUS. H. G. Evelyn White. 2 Vols.

BEDE. J. E. King. 2 Vols.

BOETHIUS: TRACTS AND DE CONSOLATIONE
PHILOSOPHIAE. Rev. H. F. Stewart and E. K.
Rand. (*4th Imp.*)

CAESAR: CIVIL WARS. A. G. Peskett. (*4th Imp.*)

CAESAR: GALLIC WAR. H. J. Edwards. (*9th Imp.*)

CATO AND VARRO: DE RE RUSTICA. H. B. Ash and
W. D. Hooper. (*2nd Imp.*)

CATULLUS. F. W. Cornish; TIBULLUS. J. B.
Postgate; AND PERVIGILIUM VENERIS. J. W.
Mackail. (*11th Imp.*)

CELSUS: DE MEDICINA. W. G. Spencer. 3 Vols.
(Vol. I. *2nd Imp. revised.*)

CICERO: BRUTUS AND ORATOR. G. L. Hendrickson
and H. M. Hubbell. (*2nd Imp.*)

1

CICERO: DE FATO; PARADOXA STOICORUM; DE PARTITIONE ORATORIA. H. Rackham. (With De Oratore, Vol. II.)

CICERO: DE FINIBUS. H. Rackham. (*3rd Imp. revised.*)

CICERO: DE NATURA DEORUM and ACADEMICA. H. Rackham.

CICERO: DE OFFICIIS. Walter Miller. (*4th Imp.*)

CICERO: DE ORATORE. E. W. Sutton and H. Rackham. 2 Vols. (*2nd Imp.*)

CICERO: DE REPUBLICA and DE LEGIBUS. Clinton W. Keyes. (*2nd Imp.*)

CICERO: DE SENECTUTE, DE AMICITIA, DE DIVINATIONE. W. A. Falconer. (*5th Imp.*)

CICERO: IN CATILINAM, PRO MURENA, PRO SULLA, PRO FLACCO. Louis E. Lord. (*2nd Imp. revised.*)

CICERO: LETTERS TO ATTICUS. E. O. Winstedt. 3 Vols. (Vol. I. *6th Imp.*, Vols. II. and III. *3rd Imp.*)

CICERO: LETTERS TO HIS FRIENDS. W. Glynn Williams. 3 Vols. (Vols. I. and II. *2nd Imp.*)

CICERO: PHILIPPICS. W. C. A. Ker. (*2nd Imp.*)

CICERO: PRO ARCHIA, POST REDITUM, DE DOMO, DE HARUSPICUM RESPONSIS, PRO PLANCIO. N. H. Watts. (*2nd Imp.*)

CICERO: PRO CAECINA, PRO LEGE MANILIA, PRO CLUENTIO, PRO RABIRIO. H. Grose Hodge. (*2nd Imp.*)

CICERO: PRO MILONE, IN PISONEM, PRO SCAURO, PRO FONTEIO, PRO RABIRIO POSTUMO, PRO MARCELLO, PRO LIGARIO, PRO REGE DEIOTARO. N. H. Watts.

CICERO: PRO QUINCTIO, PRO ROSCIO AMERINO, PRO ROSCIO COMOEDO, CONTRA RULLUM. J. H. Freese. (*2nd Imp.*)

CICERO: TUSCULAN DISPUTATIONS. J. E. King. (*2nd Imp.*)

CICERO: VERRINE ORATIONS. L. H. G. Greenwood. 2 Vols. (Vol. I. *2nd Imp.*)

CLAUDIAN. M. Platnauer. 2 Vols.

COLUMELLA: DE RE RUSTICA. H. B. Ash. 2 Vols. Vol. I. Books I.-IV.

CURTIUS, Q.: HISTORY OF ALEXANDER. J. C. Rolfe. 2 Vols.

FLORUS. E. S. Forster; and CORNELIUS NEPOS. J. C. Rolfe. (*2nd Imp.*)

FRONTINUS: STRATAGEMS AND AQUEDUCTS. C. E. Bennett and M. B. McElwain.

FRONTO: CORRESPONDENCE. C. R. Haines. 2 Vols.

GELLIUS. J. C. Rolfe. 3 Vols. (Vols. I. and II. *2nd Imp.*)

HORACE: ODES AND EPODES. C. E. Bennett. (*13th Imp. revised.*)

HORACE: SATIRES, EPISTLES, ARS POETICA. H. R. Fairclough. (*8th Imp. revised.*)

JEROME: SELECT LETTERS. F. A. Wright.

JUVENAL AND PERSIUS. G. G. Ramsay. (*6th Imp.*)

LIVY. B. O. Foster, F. G. Moore, Evan T. Sage and A. C. Schlesinger. 13 Vols. Vols. I.-VII., IX.-XII. (Vol. I. *3rd Imp.*, Vols. II., III. and IX. *2nd Imp. revised.*)

LUCAN. J. D. Duff. (*2nd Imp.*)

LUCRETIUS. W. H. D. Rouse. (*6th Imp. revised.*)

MARTIAL. W. C. A. Ker. 2 Vols. (Vol. I. *5th Imp.*, Vol. II. *3rd Imp. revised.*)

MINOR LATIN POETS: from PUBLILIUS SYRUS to RUTILIUS NAMATIANUS, including GRATTIUS, CALPURNIUS SICULUS, NEMESIANUS, AVIANUS, with "Aetna," "Phoenix" and other poems. J. Wight Duff and Arnold M. Duff. (*2nd Imp.*)

OVID: THE ART OF LOVE AND OTHER POEMS. J. H. Mozley. (*3rd Imp.*)

OVID: FASTI. Sir James G. Frazer.

OVID: HEROIDES AND AMORES. Grant Showerman. (*4th Imp.*)

OVID: METAMORPHOSES. F. J. Miller. 2 Vols. (Vol. I. *9th Imp.*, Vol. II. *7th Imp.*)

OVID: TRISTIA AND EX PONTO. A. L. Wheeler. (*2nd Imp.*)

PETRONIUS. M. Heseltine; SENECA: APOCOLO-CYNTOSIS. W. H. D. Rouse. (*7th Imp. revised.*)

PLAUTUS. Paul Nixon. 5 Vols. (Vols. I. and II. *4th Imp.*, Vol. III. *3rd Imp.*)

PLINY: LETTERS. Melmoth's Translation revised by W. M. L. Hutchinson. 2 Vols. (Vol. I. *5th Imp.*, Vol. II. *4th Imp.*)

PLINY: NATURAL HISTORY. H. Rackham and W.H.S. Jones. 10 Vols. Vols. I.-IV. (Vols. I.-III. *2nd Imp.*)

PROPERTIUS. H. E. Butler. (*5th Imp.*)

QUINTILIAN. H. E. Butler. 4 Vols. (*2nd Imp.*)

REMAINS OF OLD LATIN. E. H. Warmington. 4 Vols. Vol. I. (Ennius and Caecilius). Vol. II. (Livius, Naevius, Pacuvius, Accius). Vol. III. (Lucilius, Laws of the XII Tables). Vol. IV. (Archaic Inscriptions).

SALLUST. J. C. Rolfe. (*3rd Imp. revised.*)

SCRIPTORES HISTORIAE AUGUSTAE. D. Magie. 3 Vols. (Vol. I. *2nd Imp. revised.*)

SENECA: APOCOLOCYNTOSIS. *Cf.* PETRONIUS.

SENECA: EPISTULAE MORALES. R. M. Gummere 3 Vols. (Vol. I. *3rd Imp.*, Vols. II. and III. *2nd Imp. revised.*)

SENECA: MORAL ESSAYS. J. W. Basore 3 Vols. (Vol. II. *3rd Imp. revised.*)

SENECA: TRAGEDIES. F. J. Miller. 2 Vols. (Vol. I. *3rd Imp.*, Vol. II. *2nd Imp. revised.*)

SIDONIUS: POEMS AND LETTERS. W. B. Anderson. 2 Vols. Vol. I.

SILIUS ITALICUS. J. D. Duff. 2 Vols. (Vol. II. *2nd Imp.*)

STATIUS. J. H. Mozley. 2 Vols.

SUETONIUS. J. C. Rolfe. 2 Vols. (Vol. I. *6th Imp.*, Vol. II. *5th Imp.*)

TACITUS: DIALOGUS. Sir Wm. Peterson; and AGRICOLA AND GERMANIA. Maurice Hutton. (*6th Imp.*)

TACITUS: HISTORIES AND ANNALS. C. H. Moore and J. Jackson. 4 Vols. (Vols. I. and II. *2nd Imp.*)

TERENCE. John Sargeaunt. 2 Vols. (Vol. I. *6th Imp.*, Vol. II. *5th Imp.*)

TERTULLIAN: APOLOGIA AND DE SPECTACULIS. T. R. Glover; MINUCIUS FELIX. G. H. Rendall.

VALERIUS FLACCUS. J. H. Mozley. (*2nd Imp. revised.*)

VARRO: DE LINGUA LATINA. R. G. Kent. 2 Vols. (*2nd Imp.*)

VELLEIUS PATERCULUS AND RES GESTAE DIVI AUGUSTI. F. W. Shipley.

VIRGIL. H. R. Fairclough. 2 Vols. (Vol. I. *16th Imp.*, Vol. II. *13th Imp. revised.*)

VITRUVIUS: DE ARCHITECTURA. F. Granger. 2 Vols. (Vol. I. *2nd Imp.*)

ACHILLES TATIUS. S. Gaselee. (*2nd Imp.*)

AENEAS TACTICUS, ASCLEPIODOTUS AND ONASANDER. The Illinois Greek Club.

AESCHINES. C. D. Adams. (*2nd Imp.*)

AESCHYLUS. H. Weir Smyth. 2 Vols. (Vol. I. *5th Imp.*, Vol. II. *4th Imp.*)

APOLLODORUS. Sir James G. Frazer. 2 Vols. (*2nd Imp.*)

APOLLONIUS RHODIUS. R. C. Seaton. (*4th Imp.*)

THE APOSTOLIC FATHERS. Kirsopp Lake. 2 Vols. (Vol. I. *6th Imp.*, Vol. II. *5th Imp.*)

APPIAN'S ROMAN HISTORY. Horace White. 4 Vols. (Vol. I. *3rd Imp.*, Vols. II., III. and IV. *2nd Imp.*)

ARATUS. *Cf.* CALLIMACHUS.

ARISTOPHANES. Benjamin Bickley Rogers. 3 Vols. (*4th Imp.*) Verse trans.

ARISTOTLE: ART OF RHETORIC. J. H. Freese. (*3rd Imp.*)

ARISTOTLE: ATHENIAN CONSTITUTION, EUDEMIAN ETHICS, VIRTUES AND VICES. H. Rackham. (*2nd Imp.*)

ARISTOTLE: GENERATION OF ANIMALS. A. L. Peck. (*2nd Imp.*)

ARISTOTLE: METAPHYSICS. H. Tredennick. 2 Vols. (*3rd Imp.*)

ARISTOTLE: MINOR WORKS. W. S. Hett. ON COLOURS, ON THINGS HEARD, PHYSIOGNOMICS, ON PLANTS, ON MARVELLOUS THINGS HEARD, MECHANICAL PROBLEMS, ON INDIVISIBLE LINES, SITUATIONS AND NAMES OF WINDS, ON MELISSUS, XENOPHANES, AND GORGIAS.

ARISTOTLE: NICOMACHEAN ETHICS. H. Rackham. (*5th Imp. revised.*)

ARISTOTLE: OECONOMICA AND MAGNA MORALIA. G. C. Armstrong. (With Metaphysics, Vol. II.) (*3rd Imp.*)

ARISTOTLE: ON THE HEAVENS. W. K. C. Guthrie. (*2nd Imp.*)

ARISTOTLE: ON THE SOUL, PARVA NATURALIA, ON BREATH. W. S. Hett. (*2nd Imp. revised.*)

ARISTOTLE: ORGANON. H. P. Cooke and H. Tredennick. 3 Vols. Vol. I. (Vol I. *2nd Imp.*)

ARISTOTLE: PARTS OF ANIMALS. A. L. Peck; MOTION AND PROGRESSION OF ANIMALS. E. S. Forster. (*2nd Imp.*)

ARISTOTLE: PHYSICS. Rev. P. Wicksteed and F. M. Cornford. 2 Vols. (*2nd Imp.*)

ARISTOTLE: POETICS and LONGINUS. W. Hamilton Fyfe; DEMETRIUS ON STYLE. W. Rhys Roberts. (*4th Imp. revised.*)

ARISTOTLE: POLITICS. H. Rackham. (*2nd Imp.*)

ARISTOTLE: PROBLEMS. W. S. Hett. 2 Vols. (Vol. I. *2nd Imp. revised.*)

ARISTOTLE: RHETORICA AD ALEXANDRUM. H. Rackham. (With Problems, Vol. II.)

ARRIAN: HISTORY OF ALEXANDER and INDICA. Rev. E. Iliffe Robson. 2 Vols. (Vol. I. *2nd Imp.*)

ATHENAEUS: DEIPNOSOPHISTAE. C. B. Gulick. 7 Vols. (Vol. V. *2nd Imp.*)

ST. BASIL: LETTERS. R. J. Deferrari. 4 Vols.

CALLIMACHUS and LYCOPHRON. A. W. Mair; ARATUS. G. R. Mair.

CLEMENT OF ALEXANDRIA. Rev. G. W. Butterworth. (*2nd Imp.*)

COLLUTHUS. *Cf.* OPPIAN.

DEMOSTHENES: DE CORONA and DE FALSA LEGATIONE. C. A. Vince and J. H. Vince. (*2nd Imp. revised.*)

DEMOSTHENES: MEIDIAS, ANDROTION, ARISTOCRATES, TIMOCRATES, ARISTOGEITON. J. H. Vince.

DEMOSTHENES: OLYNTHIACS, PHILIPPICS and MINOR ORATIONS: I.-XVII. and XX. J. H. Vince.

DEMOSTHENES: PRIVATE ORATIONS and IN NEAERAM. A. T. Murray. 3 Vols. (Vol. I. *2nd Imp.*)

DIO CASSIUS: ROMAN HISTORY. E. Cary. 9 Vols. (Vols. I. and II. *2nd Imp.*)

DIO CHRYSOSTOM. 5 Vols. Vols. I. and II. J. W. Cohoon. Vol. III. J. W. Cohoon and H. Lamar Crosby. Vol. IV. H. Lamar Crosby.

THE LOEB CLASSICAL LIBRARY

DIODORUS SICULUS. 12 Vols. Vols. I.-IV. C. H.
Oldfather. Vol. IX. Russe M. Geer. (Vol. I. *2nd Imp.*)

DIOGENES LAERTIUS. R. D. Hicks. 2 Vols. (Vol.
I. *3rd Imp.*, Vol. II. *2nd Imp.*)

DIONYSIUS OF HALICARNASSUS: ROMAN ANTI-
QUITIES. Spelman's translation revised by E. Cary.
7 Vols. Vols. I.-VI. (Vol. I. *2nd Imp.*)

EPICTETUS. W. A. Oldfather. 2 Vols. (Vol. I. *2nd
Imp.*)

EURIPIDES. A. S. Way. 4 Vols. (Vols. I., II. and
IV. *6th Imp.*, Vol. III. *5th Imp.*) Verse trans.

EUSEBIUS: ECCLESIASTICAL HISTORY. Kirsopp
Lake and J. E. L. Oulton. 2 Vols. (Vol. I. *2nd Imp.*,
Vol. II. *3rd Imp.*)

GALEN: ON THE NATURAL FACULTIES. A. J.
Brock. (*3rd Imp.*)

THE GREEK ANTHOLOGY. W. R. Paton. 5 Vols.
(Vols. I. and II. *4th Imp.*, Vols. III. and IV *2nd Imp.*)

THE GREEK BUCOLIC POETS (THEOCRITUS,
BION, MOSCHUS). J. M. Edmonds. (*6th Imp.
revised.*)

GREEK ELEGY AND IAMBUS with the ANACRE-
ONTEA. J. M. Edmonds. 2 Vols. (Vol. I. *2nd
Imp.*)

GREEK MATHEMATICAL WORKS. Ivor Thomas.
2 Vols.

HERODES. *Cf.* THEOPHRASTUS: CHARACTERS.

HERODOTUS. A. D. Godley. 4 Vols. (Vol. I. *4th Imp.*,
Vols. II., III. and IV. *3rd Imp.*)

HESIOD and THE HOMERIC HYMNS. H. G. Evelyn
White. (*6th Imp. revised and enlarged.*)

HIPPOCRATES and the FRAGMENTS OF HERA-
CLEITUS. W. H. S. Jones and E. T. Withington. 4 Vols.
Vols. I., II. and IV. *2nd Imp.*, Vol. III. *3rd. Imp.*)

HOMER: ILIAD. A. T. Murray. 2 Vols. (*6th Imp.*)

HOMER: ODYSSEY. A. T. Murray. 2 Vols. (*7th Imp.*)

ISAEUS. E. S. Forster. (*2nd Imp.*)

ISOCRATES. George Norlin and LaRue Van Hook.
3 Vols.

ST. JOHN DAMASCENE: BARLAAM AND IOA-
SAPH. Rev. G. R. Woodward and Harold Mattingly.
(*2nd Imp. revised.*)

THE LOEB CLASSICAL LIBRARY

JOSEPHUS. H. St. J. Thackeray and Ralph Marcus.
9 Vols. Vols. I.-VII. (Vol. V. *2nd Imp.*)

JULIAN. Wilmer Cave Wright. 3 Vols. (Vols. I. and II.
2nd Imp.)

LONGUS: DAPHNIS AND CHLOE. Thornley's Translation revised by J. M. Edmonds; AND PARTHENIUS.
S. Gaselee. (*3rd Imp.*)

LUCIAN. A. M. Harmon. 8 Vols. Vols. I.-V. (Vols.
I. and II. *3rd Imp.*)

LYCOPHRON. *Cf.* CALLIMACHUS.

LYRA GRAECA. J. M. Edmonds. 3 Vols. (Vol. I.
3rd Imp., Vol. II. *2nd Ed. revised and enlarged*, Vol. III.
3rd Imp. revised.)

LYSIAS. W. R. M. Lamb. (*2nd Imp.*)

MANETHO. W. G. Waddell. PTOLEMY: TETRA-
BIBLOS. F. E. Robbins. (*2nd Imp.*)

MARCUS AURELIUS. C. R. Haines. (*3rd Imp. revised.*)

MENANDER. F. G. Allinson. (*2nd Imp. revised.*)

MINOR ATTIC ORATORS. 2 Vols. Vol. I. ANTI-
PHON, ANDOCIDES. K. J. Maidment.

NONNOS: DIONYSIACA. W. H. D. Rouse. 3 Vols.
(Vo'. III. *2nd Imp.*)

OPPIAN, COLLUTHUS, TRYPHIODORUS. A. W. Mair.

PAPYRI. NON-LITERARY SELECTIONS. A. S.
Hunt and C. C. Edgar. 2 Vols. (Vol. I. *2nd Imp.*)
LITERARY SELECTIONS. Vol. I. (Poetry). D. L.
Page. (*2nd Imp.*)

PARTHENIUS. *Cf.* DAPHNIS AND CHLOE.

PAUSANIAS: DESCRIPTION OF GREECE. W. H. S.
Jones. 5 Vols. and Companion Vol. arranged by R. E.
Wycherle/ (Vols. I. and III. *2nd Imp.*)

PHILO. 11 Vols. Vols. I.-V. F. H. Colson and Rev.
G. H. Whitaker; Vols. VI.-IX. F. H. Colson. (Vol. IV.
2nd Imp. revised.)

PHILOSTRATUS: THE LIFE OF APOLLONIUS OF
TYANA. F. C. Conybeare. 2 Vols. (Vol. I. *3rd Imp.*,
Vol. II. *2nd Imp.*)

PHILOSTRATUS: IMAGINES; CALLISTRATUS:
DESCRIPTIONS. A. Fairbanks

PHILOSTRATUS AND EUNAPIUS: LIVES OF THE
SOPHISTS. Wilmer Cave Wright. (*2nd Imp.*)

PINDAR. Sir J. E. Sandys. (*7th Imp. revised.*)

PLATO: CHARMIDES, ALCIBIADES, HIPPARCHUS,

8

THE LOVERS, THEAGES, MINOS **and** EPINOMIS. W. R. M. Lamb.

PLATO: CRATYLUS, PARMENIDES, GREATER HIPPIAS, LESSER HIPPIAS. H. N. Fowler. (*3rd Imp.*)

PLATO: EUTHYPHRO, APOLOGY, CRITO, PHAEDO, PHAEDRUS. H. N. Fowler. (*9th Imp.*)

PLATO: LACHES, PROTAGORAS, MENO, EUTHYDEMUS. W. R. M. Lamb. (*2nd Imp. revised.*)

PLATO: LAWS. Rev. R. G. Bury. 2 Vols. (*2nd Imp.*)

PLATO: LYSIS, SYMPOSIUM, GORGIAS. W. R. M. Lamb. (*4th Imp. revised.*)

PLATO: REPUBLIC. Paul Shorey. 2 Vols. (Vol. I. *4th Imp.*, Vol. II. *3rd Imp.*)

PLATO: STATESMAN, PHILEBUS. H. N. Fowler; ION. W. R. M. Lamb. (*3rd Imp.*)

PLATO: THEAETETUS **and** SOPHIST. H. N. Fowler. (*3rd Imp.*)

PLATO: TIMAEUS, CRITIAS, CLITOPHO, MENEXENUS, EPISTULAE. Rev. R. G. Bury. (*2nd Imp.*)

PLUTARCH: MORALIA. 14 Vols. Vols. I.-V. F. C. Babbitt; Vol. VI. W. C. Helmbold; Vol. X. H. N. Fowler.

PLUTARCH: THE PARALLEL LIVES. B. Perrin. 11 Vols. (Vols. I., II., III., VI., VII. and XI. *2nd Imp.*)

POLYBIUS. W. R. Paton. 6 Vols.

PROCOPIUS: HISTORY OF THE WARS. H. B. Dewing. 7 Vols. (Vol. I. *2nd Imp.*)

PTOLEMY: TETRABIBLOS. *Cf.* MANETHO.

QUINTUS SMYRNAEUS. A. S. Way. Verse trans. (*2nd Imp.*)

SEXTUS EMPIRICUS. Rev. R. G. Bury. 4 Vols. Vols. I.-III. (Vol. I. *2nd Imp.*)

SOPHOCLES. F. Storr. 2 Vols. (Vol. I. *8th Imp.*, Vol. II. *5th Imp.*) Verse trans.

STRABO: GEOGRAPHY. Horace L. Jones. 8 Vols. (Vols. I., V. and VIII. *2nd Imp.*)

THEOPHRASTUS: CHARACTERS. J. M. Edmonds; HERODES, etc. A. D. Knox. (*2nd Imp.*)

THEOPHRASTUS: ENQUIRY INTO PLANTS. Sir Arthur Hort. 2 Vols.

THE LOEB CLASSICAL LIBRARY

THUCYDIDES. C. F. Smith. 4 Vols. (Vol. I. 3rd Imp.,
Vols. II., III. and IV. 2nd Imp. revised.)
TRYPHIODORUS. Cf. OPPIAN.
XENOPHON: CYROPAEDIA. Walter Miller. 2 Vols.
(Vol. I. 2nd Imp., Vol. II. 3rd Imp.)
XENOPHON: HELLENICA, ANABASIS, APOLOGY,
AND SYMPOSIUM. C. L. Brownson and O. J. Todd.
3 Vols. (3rd Imp.)
XENOPHON: MEMORABILIA AND OECONOMICUS.
E. C. Marchant. (2nd Imp.)
XENOPHON: SCRIPTA MINORA. E. C. Marchant.
(2nd Imp.)

VOLUMES IN PREPARATION

GREEK AUTHORS

ALCIPHRON. A. R. Benner and F. H. Fobes.
ARISTOTLE: DE MUNDO, etc.
ARISTOTLE: HISTORY OF ANIMALS. A. L. Peck.
ARISTOTLE: METEOROLOGICA. H. D. P. Lee.
DEMOSTHENES: EPISTLES, etc. N. W. and N. J.
DeWitt.
PLOTINUS.

LATIN AUTHORS

S. AUGUSTINE: CITY OF GOD.
[CICERO:] AD HERENNIUM. H. Caplan.
CICERO: DE INVENTIONE. H. M. Hubbell.
CICERO: PRO SESTIO, IN VATINIUM, PRO
CAELIO, DE PROVINCIIS CONSULARIBUS, PRO
BALBO. J. H. Freese and R. Gardner.
PHAEDRUS AND OTHER FABULISTS. B. E. Perry.
PRUDENTIUS. H. J. Thomson.

DESCRIPTIVE PROSPECTUS ON APPLICATION

CAMBRIDGE, MASS.   LONDON
HARVARD UNIV. PRESS   WILLIAM HEINEMANN LTD
Cloth $2.50   Cloth 10s.